Dollarization

Dollarization

edited by Eduardo Levy Yeyati and Federico Sturzenegger

The MIT Press
Cambridge, Massachusetts
London, England

This book was set in Palatino on 3B2 by Asco Typesetters, Hong Kong, and was printed and bound in the United States of America.

Library of Congress Cataloging-in-Publication Data

Dollarization / edited by Eduardo Levy Yeyati and Federico Sturzenegger.
    p.   cm.
  Includes bibliographical references and index.
  ISBN 0-262-12250-2 (alk. paper)
  1. Money. 2. Dollar, American. 3. Foreign exchange. 4. Currency question.
5. International finance. I. Levy Yeyati, Eduardo. II. Sturzenegger, Federico.
HG221 .D55   2003
332.4′54—dc21   2002069586

Contents

Preface

The Russian default in 1998, and the subsequent squeeze in lending to emerging economies, inflicted a significant blow to the growth process in many of these countries. Since then, and in light of the persistent instability in international financial markets, emerging economies have started to explore new alternatives for reducing exposure to capital flow volatility. While many chose to float their formerly pegged exchange rates, others, following the success of the euro, began to consider seriously the possibility of giving up their domestic currencies in favor of using, as legal tender, a hard currency, such as the U.S. dollar or the euro.

In the case of Argentina, during the 1990s and prior to the demise of the fixed exchange rate regime, the Central Bank looked for alternative ways to enhance the credibility of the currency board, in the hope that this would isolate Argentina from the general pattern of capital flows. Following the Brazilian devaluation of January 1999, the Argentine authorities advocated more openly the view that Argentina should move on to a de jure dollarization. To that aim, the Treasury and the Central Bank of Argentina maintained high-level contacts with their counterparts in the United States to explore the possibility of a monetary treaty under which Argentina would become part of the dollar zone. The reaction of the U.S. authorities was receptive from an intellectual point of view but extremely skeptical about the political viability of the proposal. In addition, the U.S. authorities were concerned about the implicit responsibilities they might be taking by signing such a treaty, particularly as a potential lender of last resort of the Argentine financial sector. Furthermore, the proposal received a lukewarm reception in Argentina itself.

These responses convinced the monetary authorities that more had to be learned about dollarization before moving forward with a formal plan. This conclusion, combined with a renewed interest in the topic both in Europe and in the United States, prompted the Central Bank of Argentina and the Konrad Adenauer Foundation to cosponsor the preparation of a comprehensive study that presented and discussed the different issues related to dollarization within an unbiased and rigorous framework. This volume is the result of that study.

Our strategy was to ask renowned academics that had been previously working on the topic to write a piece on specific issues relevant to the dollarization debate in a rigorous yet accessible style. The resulting papers were presented in a closed seminar at Universidad Torcuato Di Tella, Buenos Aires, and were thoroughly revised based on extensive comments by a group of international discussants gathered for the occasion. The result offers, we believe, a broad coverage of all the aspects involved in the dollarization debate, where the adjective *broad* applies both to the perspective of the different pieces (for example, empirical vs. theoretical) as well as to the underlying personal stance of the authors regarding the convenience of dollarization.

The first chapter of the book provides a synthesis of the issues discussed more at length in the remaining chapters, as well as an introduction to the dollarization debate's existing literature. In chapter 2, Roberto Chang and Andrés Velasco present a stylized theoretical model that illustrates the trade-offs involved in the choice of the dollarization alternative vis-à-vis other exchange rate arrangements. In particular, they discuss the implications in terms of the loss of seignorage revenues, the implementation of optimal monetary policy, and the central bank's capacity to function as lender of last resort to the domestic banking sector. In chapter 3, Pablo Andrés Neumeyer and Juan Pablo Nicolini explore the impact of dollarization on the government's budget constraints, as a function of the banking sector balance sheets and the currency denomination of the government's liabilities. The implications of de jure dollarization on the ability of the central bank to operate as lender of last resort is addressed by Christian Broda and Eduardo Levy Yeyati in chapter 4. They also examine alternative insurance mechanisms suggested in the literature to argue that dollarization entails a costly limitation that cannot be fully eliminated by the existence of substitutes. However, they conclude, these limitations are already in place in countries with widespread de facto dollarization. In chapter

5, Ugo Panizza, Ernesto Stein, and Ernesto Talvi assess the costs and benefits of dollarization from an empirical perspective, highlighting the main characteristics that determine the trade-off between dollarization and alternative regimes. One of the most pervasive arguments in favor of de jure dollarization has been the idea that the elimination of currency risk would lead to a decline in sovereign risk and the cost of capital for the dollarizing country. To test this hypothesis, Andrew Powell and Federico Sturzenegger address the link between sovereign risk and currency risk in chapter 6. They find that the relation between the two types of risk depends crucially on the characteristics of the financial sector of the economy, especially regarding the currency of denomination of (private and public) liabilities. A more operational perspective is taken by William Gruben, Mark Wynne, and Carlos Zarazaga in chapter 7 to discuss implementation issues. Should contracts be changed? How can seignorage be salvaged? What are the steps leading up to successful dollarization? The chapter provides a step-by-step guide on how to go from the decision to dollarize to the practical execution of a dollarization plan. Finally, in chapter 8, Jeffry Frieden discusses the political economy of dollarization, assessing the political feasibility of a dollarization plan by characterizing potential winners and losers among the influential groups within a country.

In putting together this book, we received support and aid from many fronts. We are particularly indebted to the Fundación Gobierno y Sociedad of Argentina for its encouragement and logistic assistance. Hildegard Ahumada, Fernando Aportela, Sergio Berenstein, Miguel Angel Broda, Alfredo Canavese, Tito Cordella, Ilan Goldfajn, Miguel Kiguel, Pedro Pou, Klaus Schmidt-Hebbel, and three anonymous referees contributed either by providing useful insights to the authors of the chapters or by offering suggestions that improved the overall quality of the volume. Finally, we benefited from the editing expertise of Elizabeth Murry from MIT Press, who guided us through the finishing touches.

We hope that this book, the result of two intense years of discussion and learning, will help enrich and disseminate the dollarization debate in future years, thus contributing to better and more informed policy decisions on the subject.

Eduardo Levy Yeyati and Federico Sturzenegger
Buenos Aires, January 2002

1 Dollarization: A Primer

Eduardo Levy Yeyati and Federico Sturzenegger

1.1 Introduction

Recent turmoil in financial markets has revealed the inherent vulnerability of intermediate exchange rate regimes and conventional pegs to sudden aggregate shocks in a context of rapidly growing global financial integration. As a result, an increasing number of economists and policymakers have endorsed the idea that financially open economies are best served by more flexible regimes. Alternatively, many analysts have recently argued in favor of the relative merits of extreme exchange rate regimes, or "hard pegs," that exhibit a stronger commitment to a fixed parity (as in the case of currency boards) or directly relinquish control over their own currency (as in the case of currency unions and dollarized economies), as opposed to intermediate arrangements and conventional, or "soft," pegs. At any rate, there seems to be a growing consensus that arrangements anywhere between floating regimes and hard pegs are not sustainable in the long run.

To some extent, this so-called bipolar view appears to be supported by the evidence, as witnessed by the collapse of "soft" pegs in Southeast Asia and Latin America, on the one hand, and the swift move to monetary integration in Europe in the aftermath of the European Monetary System (EMS) crisis of 1992 and the recent adoption of the U.S. dollar as legal tender in Ecuador and El Salvador, on the other.[1] In addition, assuming a broader perspective, the fact reported by the International Monetary Fund, IMF (1997) that the number of flexible exchange rate arrangements increased from eleven to fifty-two over the period 1976–1996 should be contrasted with the list of Eastern European economies waiting to join the European Monetary Union (EMU), and some Latin American and

African countries seriously considering a unilateral dollarization strategy.

Although strong fixes, such as currency boards, are typically cited as examples of a fixed exchange rate regime with sufficient credibility to weather the storms of current international financial markets, the runs on the Argentinean peso in 1995 and 2001, and on the Hong Kong dollar in 1997 showed that even a currency board may be insufficient to ensure credibility. As a result, a discussion has gained momentum on the potential beneficial effects of moving forward toward full (de jure) dollarization, understood here as the adoption of a (presumably stronger) foreign currency as sole legal tender.[2] The recent adoption of the U.S. dollar in Ecuador is a significant example in which the credibility factor was crucial, and where renouncing the national currency was seen as the only way to commit to more reasonable macroeconomic policies. On the other hand, the case of El Salvador illustrates that the regime switch may arise as a consequence of a long debate on its benefits and pitfalls (including trade gains unrelated to credibility concerns), as opposed to a last resort option due to a terminal crisis.

The present debate has been triggered by "credibility" issues, but dollarization has received support from other quarters as well. On the one hand, there is growing evidence that the use of a common currency may induce a substantive increase in trade, which in turn may fuel economic growth; on the other, the role of foreign-currency-denominated liabilities in the financial sector and of the associated currency imbalance has also hinted at the potential for big gains from the full elimination of currency risk. Yet the debate is far from settled. For example, the successful move to full floating regimes in Mexico, Chile, and (more debatably) Brazil has contributed arguments to those in favor of a more flexible arrangement that may eventually work as a shock absorber in the event of external shocks.

The purpose of this chapter (as well as that of the book in general) is not to settle this complex debate that, as many of the papers in this volume note, hinges on country-specific characteristics and, as such, can only be resolved, if ever, once sufficient dollarization experiences are in place to conduct a thorough comparison. Rather, we intend here to provide an impartial survey of the main issues associated with dollarization and their most relevant empirical and analytical underpinnings, to contribute a framework for the more specific and detailed discussions undertaken in the following chapters. When judging the benefits and disadvantages of a full dollarization strategy, we will try to distill a cohesive view whenever possible, emphasizing the historical determinants of the debate and the importance of the initial macroeconomic conditions in each particular country.

The plan of this chapter is as follows: In section 1.2, we try to provide a historical perspective for the current dollarization debate, tracing back its origins to recent developments in domestic and international financial markets that have influenced the traditional fix versus flex debate. In section 1.3, we introduce the main arguments for and against dollarized economies, drawing from chapters 2 to 6 in this volume, as well as from the existing literature. In section 1.4, we discuss the main issues involved in the transition toward full dollarization and its political-economy aspects, addressed in chapters 7 and 8. Finally, section 1.5 lays down a preliminary balance of the debate.

1.2   History: Where Are We Coming From?

The idea of full dollarization as a regime choice is relatively recent. Whereas there are a few cases of dollarized economies in the world, until 1999 all of these experiments had been the result of specific political and historical factors, and in most cases had been put in place even before a local currency was created. Simple inspection of the upper panel of table 1.1 reveals that in a way, Panama, the most salient dollarization example until very recently, has been something of an outlier, with a size, both measured in terms of population and GDP, that largely exceeded those of other members in the group.[3] The fact that all of these long-standing dollarization cases have been adopted more because of historical and political reasons than due to an evaluation of the pros and cons of alternative arrangements or the short-run cost involved in the transition to the new regime (aspects at the center of the current debate) detracts from their value as comparator cases.

The two more recent full dollarization processes may prove more influential and more illustrative of what a transition to full dollarization may involve. It was only in 2000 and 2001, respectively, that Ecuador and El Salvador joined the group of fully dollarized economies. Their experiences, and particularly the way they arrived at the

Table 1.1
Dollarized economies

Country	Population	Political status	Currency used	Year adopted
Andorra	63,000	Independent	French franc and Spanish peseta	1278
Channel Islands	140,000	British dependencies	Pound sterling	1797
Cocos Islands	600	Australian external territory	Australian dollar	1955
Cyprus, Northern	180,000	de facto independent	Turkish lira	1974
Greenland	56,000	Danish self-governing region	Danish krone	Before 1800
Guam	150,000	U.S. territory	U.S. dollar	1898
Kiribati	80,000	Independent	Australian dollar	1943
Liechstenstein	31,000	Independent	Swiss franc	1921
Marshall Islands	60,000	Independent	U.S. dollar	1944
Micronesia	120,000	Independent	U.S. dollar	1944
Monaco	30,000	Independent	Euro (French franc since 1865)	1999
Nauru	8,000	Independent	Australian dollar	1914
Niue	2,000	New Zealand self-governing territory	New Zealand dollar	1901
Norfolk Island	2,000	Australian external territory	Australian dollar	Before 1900
Northern Mariana Islands	48,000	U.S. commonwealth	U.S. dollar	1944
Palau	18,000	Independent	U.S. dollar	1944
Panama	2.5 mil.	Independent	1 balboa = U.S.$1; uses dollar notes	1904
Pitcairn Island	56	British dependency	New Zealand and U.S. dollars	1800s
Puerto Rico	3.5 mil.	U.S. commonwealth	U.S. dollar	1899
Saint Helena	6,000	British colony	Pound sterling	1834
Samoa, American	60,000	U.S. territory	U.S. dollar	1899
San Marino	24,000	Independent	Euro (Italian lira since 1897)	1999
Tokelau	1,600	New Zealand territory	New Zealand dollar	1926
Turks and Caicos Islands	14,000	British colony	U.S. dollar	1973
Tuvalu	10,000	Independent	Australian dollar	1892
Vatican City	1,000	Independent	Euro (Italian lira since 1929)	1999
Virgin Islands, British	17,000	British dependency	U.S. dollar	1973
Virgin Islands, U.S.	100,000	U.S. territory	U.S. dollar	1917

Table 1.1
(continued)

Country	Population	Political status	Currency used	Year adopted
Ecuador	12.9 mil.	Independent	U.S. dollar	2000
El Salvador	6.1 mil.	Independent	U.S. dollar	2001
Austria	8.1 mil.	Independent	Euro	1999
Belgium	10.2 mil.	Independent	Euro	1999
Finland	5.2 mil.	Independent	Euro	1999
France	58.8 mil.	Independent	Euro	1999
Germany	82.0 mil.	Independent	Euro	1999
Ireland	3.7 mil.	Independent	Euro	1999
Italy	57.6 mil.	Independent	Euro	1999
Luxembourg	0.43 mil.	Independent	Euro	1999
Netherlands	15.7 mil.	Independent	Euro	1999
Portugal	10.0 mil.	Independent	Euro	1999
Spain	39.4 mil.	Independent	Euro	1999

Source: Goldfajn and Olivares (2000).

decision, differed significantly. Ecuador, on the one hand, resorted to dollarization as a way to cope with a widespread political and financial crisis rooted in massive loss of credibility in its political and monetary institutions. El Salvador, on the other, decided to adopt the U.S. dollar as legal tender, after years of an unofficial peg, as a result of an internal debate, and in a context of stable macroeconomic fundamentals. Unfortunately, although there is preliminary evidence that both arrangements have delivered partial results, the cases are too recent to be useful for any meaningful empirical analysis. However, they can be used to illuminate some of the institutional and political factors involved in the transition.

The caveats mentioned in the previous paragraphs apply also to the euro area launched in 1999, which might be considered as a variety of a full-commitment regime similar to full dollarization inasmuch as we are willing to regard it as a (disguised) adoption of the deutsche mark by the participant countries. Several additional differences distinguish the euro experiment from other dollarization projects, though. First, the euro area groups developed countries that differ in their very nature from developing small open economies with which the dollarization debate is usually associated. In this regard, the convergence process of developing Eastern European countries currently in the EMU accession list offers richer case studies.

Second, and perhaps more to the point, all countries within EMU preserve their influence (albeit limited) over monetary policy as they are proportionally represented at the Board of the European Central Bank. Although this is true also for other existing currency unions,[4] the euro is allowed to float against other major reference currencies, so that in the end the rigidity of the new arrangement is only restricted to the loss of flexibility in cross exchange rates within the group.[5]

In sum, at least at this point, the debate on full dollarization suffers from a lack of relevant experiments to test most of its economic implications empirically. In line with this, the origins and nature of the current debate have not been influenced much by existing examples of dollarized economies that are either barely representative or too recent to be appraised. One can gain a better historical perspective of the issues at stake by tracing the evolution from the traditional fix versus float debate to the current dollarization debate in light of some important factors that have informed the view economists have of the economic connotations of different regimes. We turn next to this subject.

1.2.1 The Traditional Fix versus Flex Debate

If we think of the regime choice set as a ladder that climbs from full flexibility toward increasing exchange rate rigidity, we can regard the particular case of full dollarization as a step further upward from a conventional fixed exchange rate regime. It is not surprising, then, that most analyses of the dollarization option rely, at least partially, on considerations that have permeated the traditional (and longer standing) fix versus flex debate, which can be traced back to the pioneering work of Mundell and Fleming in the 1960s, refined by Dornbusch in the 1970s.[6]

One of the main implications of the Mundell-Fleming-Dornbusch model is that in a context of flexible exchange rates, unanticipated permanent shifts in money demand may have an impact on the real economy due to the presence of (temporarily) sticky prices.[7] In particular, according to the model, an increase in the demand for money should result, given money supply, in a temporary contraction with a period of higher interest rates, lower output, and higher unemployment as prices take their time to fall and adjust to the now higher demand for real balances. Indeed, higher nominal interest rates are expected to induce an exchange rate appreciation, both because the interest rate differential make domestic-currency-denominated assets more attractive and because the expected deflation implies a lower exchange rate in the long run, depressing the current exchange rate even further.[8]

By contrast, a fixed exchange rate regime fully eliminates any real effect as the monetary authorities accommodate any increase in the demand for money through nonsterilized interventions. However, any money supply shock is reflected automatically in a change in international reserves, placing a limit on the capacity of monetary authorities to conduct countercyclical monetary policy.

A different conclusion is obtained from the model for the case of real shocks.[9] In this case, although a flexible regime can accommodate the shock through a change in the nominal exchange rate that restores the long-run full employment equilibrium, a fix requires an adjustment in domestic nominal prices that in the presence of sticky prices would entail a period of depressed domestic demand and high unemployment.

Hence, this point affirms the familiar argument that in order to minimize output fluctuations, fixed (flexible) exchange rates are preferred if nominal (real) shocks are the main source of disturbance in the economy.[10] As a result, one should expect that the choice of exchange rate regime depends to certain extent on the importance of real relative to monetary shocks. Indeed, lack of insulation against real shocks is still the main argument against fixed (and, in particular, fully dollarized) regimes. Moreover, as real shocks become increasingly important due to growing trade flows and capital market integration (alternatively, as monetary shocks or inflation concerns become less of a priority), one should expect to see a trend toward more flexible regimes around the globe.

Optimal Currency Areas

The role of the nominal exchange rate as an instrument to isolate the economy against real shocks is at the center of the optimal currency area (OCA) approach to monetary integration. The traditional OCA theory, developed in the 1960s by Mundell (1961), McKinnon (1963), and Kenen (1969), identifies a number of factors that determine the benefits and costs of a currency union. The benefits are generally associated with the reduction in transaction costs between member countries as a result of the use of a common currency, a reduction proportional to the degree of economic integration (i.e., trade flows) within the union (McKinnon). The costs, in turn, are the result of the loss of the nominal exchange rate as an adjustment mechanism against real macroeconomic shocks that alter the equilibrium real exchange rate vis-à-vis the rest of the union. These costs will be relatively less important the higher the degree of factor (labor and capital) mobility within the region (Mundell), and the higher the symmetry of shocks between member countries (Kenen).

Although one would expect that a currency union that eliminates any restriction to labor mobility should stimulate labor integration, other barriers such as culture or language may prove surprisingly resilient, as witness the case of the euro zone. Moreover, in the particular case of unilateral dollarization, the regime switch does not imply any relaxation of the legal impediments to labor migration already in place. Naturally, the fact that most possible dollarization marriages entail adopting the currency of a country with a much higher per capita income makes labor integration even less likely.

Regarding the symmetry of shocks argument, the union can float against other currencies, so that shocks elsewhere in the world will entail some sort of disequilibrium only to the extent that its effect differs across member countries.[11] Then, we could add that the costs would be related not only to the correlation of real shocks among participating countries but also to the symmetry of the response to external shocks within the region. At any rate, the argument appears to suggest that similar countries are more likely to constitute an optimal currency area.

However, a counterargument can easily be made if either labor or capital is mobile: countries with asymmetric shocks (or asymmetric shock responses) enjoy a larger scope for diversification, inasmuch as the proper instruments are in place. More precisely, if shocks are asymmetric, adverse shocks in one region would generally be accompanied by positive shocks in another, so that they compensate each other as factors move to the temporarily more productive region. Even in the absence of factor mobility, a scheme of fiscal transfers between member countries can yield the same result. Accordingly, the role the symmetry argument should play while testing the OCA condition should be qualified.

How important are OCA considerations in today's discussion of dollarization? A casual inspection of the recent literature on the subject will reveal that the "modern approach" to dollarization has given priority to credibility issues over the trade gains–shock insulation trade-off implicit in the traditional OCA approach. Two main reasons appear to have induced this change in focus. First, most OCA tests of existing currency unions have yielded mixed results as to the *ex ante* convenience of the union, suggesting the presence of other (both political and historical) factors behind them. For example, some analysts tend to see the convergence process toward EMU as a scheme by which European countries borrowed monetary policy credibility by implicitly pegging their currencies to the deutsche mark, and ultimately by modeling the European Central Bank after the Bundesbank.[12] In contrast, the African franc zone may have owed more to a common colonial past than to previous extended trade links among the members.

Second, many countries that are currently considering adopting a major foreign currency as legal tender are moved primarily by the need to reduce their vulnerability to financial shocks, rather than by the promise of a boost in trade. However, the experiences of various free trade areas (FTAs) such as the European Common Market (ECM) or North American Free Trade Agreement (NAFTA) have shown that substantial trade gains can be achieved without a common currency or even a peg against the regional reference currency. Thus, in the context of highly sophisticated financial markets, the incremental gains to be derived from unifying the currency may not to be that important after all.[13]

If this is so, then the evaluation of whether to relinquish the domestic currency in favor of a foreign common currency involves weighting the costs of losing the exchange rate instrument against whatever credibility can be derived from the new (presumably stronger) currency. However, once the decision to dollarize is made, OCA considerations still play an important role at the time of choosing the right reference currencies, underscoring the conventional view of the euro as the natural choice for Eastern European economies, and the U.S. dollar as the obvious candidate for most Latin American economies.

Capital Account Liberalization

The relative size of real shocks is not the only way the trend toward global integration has informed the fix versus flex debate. A key ingredient of the textbook Mundell-Fleming-Dornbusch framework is the assumption of perfect capital mobility that implies international interest rate arbitrage across countries in the form of the uncovered interest parity. In particular, this assumption implies that deviations of the domestic currency interest rate from the exogenously given international interest rate should only reflect expected changes in the domestic price of foreign currency (the exchange rate). From this, it follows that monetary policies cannot be aimed both at maintaining stable exchange rates and smoothing cyclical output fluctuations due to real shocks, in what is usually referred to as the "impossible trinity."[14]

This key assumption, however, has not been always binding in the past (and, in many cases, it is still not in the present). Financial innovation, and the dramatic decline in transaction costs induced by it, fueled a gradual trend toward more open capital accounts that start only in the early 1970s in industrial countries and spread in the following decades to what are typically denoted as emerging-market economies. This trend, in turn, made the restrictions implicit in the impossible trinity argument more stringent, pushing the choice between independent monetary policy and exchange rate stability back to the forefront.

In particular, the reluctance of many developing countries to undergo the fiscally necessary adjustment during contractionary periods combined with the widespread use of exchange rate anchors to fight price instability made the countries increasingly vulnerable to speculative attacks on the currency, which resulted in higher output volatility and only temporary success in reducing inflation. Moreover, the development of secondary markets for debt of emerging economies led many of these countries to rely on foreign (usually short-run) capital to ignite their economies and postpone the necessary fiscal adjustment, making exchange-rate-based stabilizations (and conventional pegs in general) even more vulnerable to sudden shifts in market sentiment and self-fulfilling crises. In a twist to the previous argument, it has been argued that in countries that have suffered a significant loss in competitiveness and higher unemployment rates due to the presence of inertial inflation or the strength of the peg currency, high political costs make an exchange rate defense less likely and make the regime more vulnerable to a successful attack.[15]

Whatever the model or mix of models that one judges more representative of recent currency crises, it is apparent that the surge in the dollarization debate in recent years has been largely induced by considerations related to the increased vulnerability (and, in turn, falling credibility) exhibited by conventional fixed exchange rate regimes. In turn, vulnerability aspects are intimately related to the degree of de facto dollarization that pervades most developing economies. To this we turn next.

De Facto Dollarization
Globally grouped as de facto dollarization, high degrees of currency substitution and financial dollarization represent an important (and often understated) factor underscoring the recent debate on dollarization.[16] These practices already impose some of the constraints usually associated with de jure dollarization. Also, because of their implications for inflation and banking sector fragility, they limit the scope of exchange rate fluctuations that monetary authorities can afford to tolerate. In other words, it could be argued that de facto dollarized economies reduce both the costs of a transition to de jure dollarization and the exchange rate flexibility lost in the process.

Most of the earlier literature on de facto dollarization is concerned with currency substitution, reflected in the emphasis on the expected returns of holding different currencies (as opposed to the expected returns of interest-bearing assets denominated in those currencies). As a result, the discussion typically centers on the dynamics of money demand (and the link between dollarization and the inflation *level*) and the implications for monetary policy. The focus on currency substitution also seems to underlie the presumption, usually subscribed to by this literature, that dollarization should recede with price stability.[17]

This presumption has been repeatedly at odds with the empirical evidence. Although de facto dollarization appears to have been fueled by recurrent high inflation episodes, it remained a common feature of developing economies around the globe after inflation levels were brought down during the 1990s, even in countries such as Argentina, Bolivia, and Peru, where several years of stable macroeconomic policies should have gradually improved confidence.[18]

As noted by many observers, however, much of the empirical literature on which the argument is based is plagued by a definitional problem, as interest-bearing deposits, which generally account for the bulk of measured dollarization, are used to estimate money demand equations. Moreover, the papers that specifically address the issue of dollarization as a portfolio choice problem generally do not fully recognize the nature of financial dollarization, namely, the fact that deposit dollarization generally has loan dollarization as its mirror image, which is crucial to determine both the extent and the implications of dollarization.[19]

An exception is Ize and Levy Yeyati (2000) where, using a portfolio choice model and considering both sides of the banks' balance sheets (deposits and loans), they find that financial dollarization depends on the volatility of *real* returns on assets denominated in each currency, in turn a function of the volatility of real exchange rates changes relative to that of inflation. This approach leads to four important implications. First, countries that allow foreign currency deposits in the domestic-banking sector will naturally generate some degree of financial dollarization.[20] Second, policies that target (at least partially) a stable real exchange rate to preserve competitiveness should not be expected to reduce financial dollarization. Third, economies with high pass-through coefficients (either due to widespread dollar pricing as a result of previous high inflation spells or because of their very open nature) will exhibit higher dollarization ratios irrespective of their current inflation levels.[21] Fourth, from a more general standpoint, there is no reason why changes in inflation (and in *nominal* interest rates) should affect the choice of portfolio denomination, inasmuch as these changes are incorporated in nominal interest rates to leave *real* interest rates unchanged.[22] This implication, derived in Thomas (1985), and reinstated in Calvo and Vegh (1997), is key to distinguishing financial dollarization from a currency substitution phenomenon. The fact that most of the recent debate regarding dollarization has revolved around financial dollarization issues shows just how relevant this distinction is.

As mentioned earlier, there are many reasons why the degree of de facto dollarization should be considered as an important determinant of the choice of regime and, in particular, of the decision to proceed to de jure dollarization. De facto dollarized economies with an inflation target cannot afford to allow wide exchange rate fluctuations because of their detrimental impact on inflation performance. As Chang and Velasco (2000) point out, "any scheme to control the rate of inflation at a short horizon must control, to some extent, the nominal exchange rate" (p. 74). In view of the previous discussion, we could complement this statement by noting that the extent to which inflation-targeting countries can let the nominal exchange rate fluctuate depends negatively on the degree of exchange rate pass-through, itself a function of de facto dollarization.[23]

But the inflation response is not the only concern that prevents de facto dollarized economies from adopting fully floating exchange rates. The inherent currency mismatch introduced by widespread financial dollarization makes the financial sector (and the economy as a whole) highly vulnerable to exchange rate fluctuations. Notably, the fact that banks are usually precluded by regulations to hold open foreign currency positions does not eliminate the problem, inasmuch as dollar loans simply transfer the currency risk to non-dollar-earning borrowers, at the cost of greater, exchange-rate-related, credit risk to the bank. Thus, the degree of loan dollarization determines the financial system's exposure to systemic credit risk in the event of large devaluations and, more in general, the willingness of the monetary authorities to use the exchange rate to accommodate real or external shocks.[24]

Interestingly, the authorities' reluctance to let the exchange rate fluctuate may in itself induce more financial dollarization, as foreign currency borrowers anticipate a stable exchange rate and lower currency risk. One may argue that frequent currency crises proved this anticipation to be incorrect, but the same logic by which the government may find it optimal to avoid a sudden appreciation indicates that in the case of a currency collapse, dollar borrowers are likely to be (at least partially) bailed out.[25]

An additional factor underlying the authorities' preference for a stable exchange rate is that the vast majority of countries hold a substantial stock of foreign-denominated sovereign external debt. This pattern is typically attributed to the country's inability to borrow in its own currency, presumably due to the currency's weakness,[26] although one could alternatively argue that the outcome is the result of a deliberate decision not to incur the cost of a currency risk premium that is judged to be excessive by most governments.

Calvo and Guidotti (1990) argue that the government faces a time inconsistency problem at the time of choosing the denomination of its debt, because once the home currency debt is issued, it is optimal for the government to partially repudiate its obligations by devaluing. Investors anticipate this and require a higher interest rate so that expected returns are comparable to international levels. Devaluation (and a higher than optimal inflation rate) occur in equilibrium.

The case of fixed exchange rate regimes is an interesting illustration of this problem. Because the sole purpose of borrowing in the domestic currency is to hedge against the possibility of a depreciation, the issuance of home currency debt can only be interpreted as signaling the government's belief in the possibility of a future change in the parity, which in itself defeats the goal of gaining confidence in the regime. Alternatively, a government committed to a fixed parity should have no reason to pay the currency premium if it is convinced of its capacity to maintain the peg. Thus, the dollarization of external liabilities could be interpreted as a consequence rather than as a cause of a fixed exchange rate regime.[27]

Finally, as is argued in more detail in chapter 5, the existence of a large proportion of dollar assets in the banking sector as a result of financial dollarization naturally reduces the central bank's capacity to provide lender of last resort assistance in the event of systemic liquidity crunches without substantially increasing its stock of liquid international reserves.[28]

In sum, although de jure dollarization entails very specific costs (i.e., the loss of the exchange rate as an adjustment mechanism, and the loss of the lender of last resort function of the central bank), the magnitude of these costs may be relatively minor in de facto dollarized economies. It is not surprising, then, that the dollarization debate has developed greater momentum in these economies, as the persistence of the dollarization phenomenon and the extent of its implications became increasingly apparent. Indeed, in extreme cases, de jure dollarization can be viewed as reaping important credibility benefits (e.g., from the outright elimination of currency risk) without the imposition of sizable additional costs.

1.2.2   The Bipolar View

Advocates of the bipolar view argue that conventional fixes may fall short from achieving the desired credibility gains and that if exchange rate stability is the first priority, the stronger commitment that characterizes hard pegs may be in order.[29] Accordingly, they tend to group regimes into three broad categories, namely, "hard pegs," fully floating regimes, and a number of intermediate managed floats and conventional fixes they generically label "soft pegs." Underlying this classification is the view that countries, particularly those with open capital markets, have been moving, either voluntarily or forced by market pressures, toward the extremes, a view partially supported by the data.

Thus, although most recent currency crises in Asia and Latin America resulted in the floating of the exchange rate, an increasing number of countries have moved (or are in the process to do so) toward de jure dollarization or currency unions.[30]

It should be noted that the apparent movement away from intermediate regimes is far from conclusive. For reasons mentioned in the previous section, many of the new floaters exhibit flexible exchange rates merely formally, allowing short-run exchange rate fluctuations only within certain limits.[31] Similarly, many conventional pegs that ended in currency crises simply reflected past monetary policies that were rendered inconsistent by a growing integration of domestic and international capital markets.

However, this mismatch between claims and actual practices notwithstanding, it remains true that as capital markets are liberalized, the choice of the de jure regime has increasingly favored the extremes, thereby avoiding a commitment to a fixed parity that may make the economy vulnerable to speculative attacks and financial contagion. Figures 1.1a–1.1b offer some support for this hypothesis. The figure replicates the analysis of regime distribution over time in Fischer (2001), with some minor modifications. First, within the "intermediate" group, we distinguish conventional (soft) pegs from other intermediate arrangements. Second, we use a standard IMF-based de jure regime classification, as well as Levy Yeyati and Sturzenegger's (2000) de facto classification.[32] As can be seen, results in both cases are broadly comparable and go in the same direction: Emerging economies that in the 1990s have gradually opened to international capital markets have exhibited a growing preference for either floating regimes or hard pegs, whereas less financially integrated developing countries have displayed no clear trend in any direction.

Advocates of hard pegs claim they have the advantage of reaping the low inflation benefits that historically motivated conventional pegs, while avoiding their usual pitfalls, namely, greater output volatility and slower growth, typically associated with frequent and costly speculative attacks.[33] In addition, recent work on currency unions has found that a common currency area significantly increases trade among members, which, if we are willing to accept international trade as one of the drivers of output growth, points at an additional benefit.[34]

However, in a recent piece, Levy Yeyati and Sturzenegger (2001b) partially contradict these claims by showing that although hard pegs do contribute to a substantial reduction in inflation, their growth

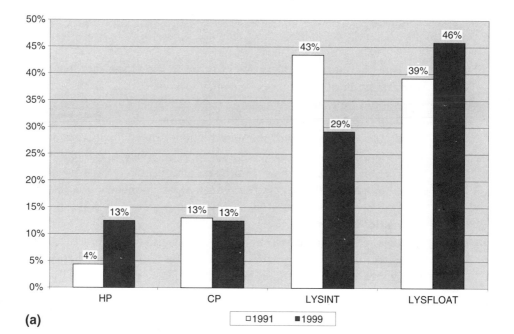

(a)

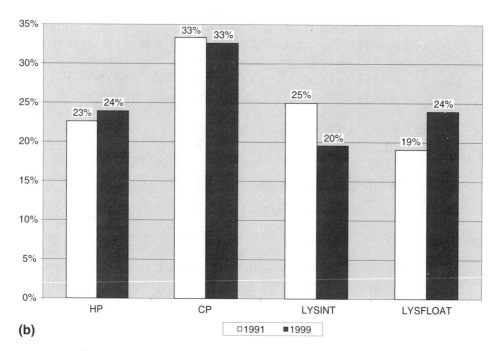

(b)

Figure 1.1
(a) Emerging markets (Levy Yeyati and Sturzenegger (2002), LYS classification). Emerging-economies listed in EMBI Globol or Morgan Stanley Capital International Emerging Markets Indexes. (b) All other non-industrial countries (LYS classification).

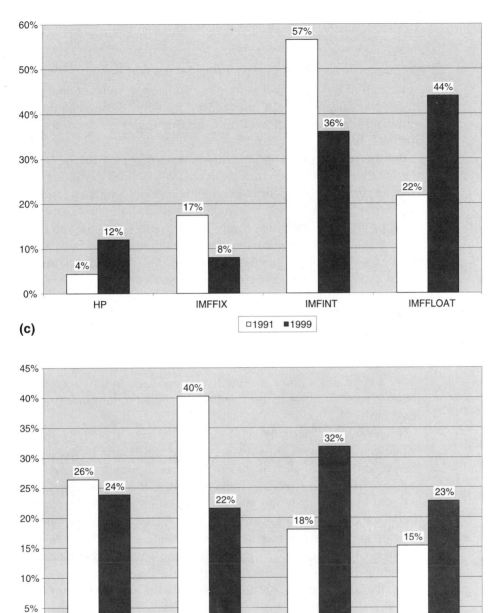

(c)

(d)

Figure 1.1
(c) Emerging markets (IMF classification). Emerging-economies listed in EMBI Globol or Morgan Stanley Capital International Emerging Markets Indexes. (d) All other non-industrial countries (IMF classification).

performance lags behind that of more flexible regimes. Thus, it appears that hard pegs deliver better results than conventional pegs in general and exhibit an outstanding inflation record but do not eliminate the inflation-growth trade-off that underscores the fix versus float dilemma.

But the relevant question remains: Do hard pegs actually deliver the credibility gains they are expected to provide? Naturally, the chances that a government holds the line against an attack (and the probability that the attack is actually launched in the first place) depend positively on the cost (both political and economic) of abandoning a peg. In this regard, the implementation of a hard peg raises the stakes involved in a currency collapse, by placing legal, and in many cases economic, barriers to a reversal to a float. Thus, the stronger commitment to a peg is naturally interpreted by the markets as implicit insurance against exchange rate risk, fueling financial dollarization and foreign-currency-denominated cross-border flows.[35] These events, in turn, increase the overall currency imbalance of the economy, adding to the country's vulnerability in the event a large devaluation eventually materializes and, by increasing the exit costs, adding to the credibility of the commitment to the fixed parity.

However, this (partially self-inflicted) extreme sensitivity to devaluations may cut both ways because by substantially worsening the postcollapse scenario, it makes the economy more vulnerable to sudden changes in market sentiment; hence, the strong correlation between currency risk and country risk exhibited by many highly dollarized countries. The example of the Argentinean currency board is a case in point. After successfully forestalling an attack in 1995 as a spillover of the Tequila Crisis and exhibiting a remarkable monetary discipline during the Asian crisis period, the Argentinean peg could not gather the needed credibility to insulate the economy against the Brazilian devaluation. This lack of credibility certainly played a role in the protracted recession that has followed since, and in the demise of convertibility.[36]

At any rate, it is interesting to note in passing that currency boards, a hard peg variety that enjoyed a short-lived period of fame in the aftermath of the Mexican crisis, have lately been regarded with increasing disbelief, following a speculative attack on the Hong Kong dollar and its collapse in Argentina.[37] Then, it is not obvious that a hard peg that falls short of full dollarization is sufficient to dispel doubts about the sustainability of the regime, as opposed to being simply another "intermediate" peg bound to be tested recurrently by the market. Under this even more radical version of the bipolar view, the exchange rate regime menu would be narrowed down to only two sustainable alternatives: floating arrangements or full dollarization (in any of the varieties discussed in the following text).

1.3   Implications: What Do We Talk about When We Talk about Dollarization?

Having briefly surveyed the main driving forces behind the current dollarization debate, we turn in this section to the main subject of this volume, namely, the advantages and disadvantages of dollarization in its different varieties, and their relevant determinants.

As Chang and Velasco state in the introduction to chapter 2, the importance of an analytical framework within which to weight the costs and benefits of dollarization cannot be overemphasized. If not for anything else, the already mentioned scarcity of relevant empirical experiments on the subject forces us to use a fair amount of speculation to assess the practical importance of the different considerations involved in the debate.

To help in this process, they introduce each of these main issues in the context of an analytical model of a small open economy whose government faces the decision of whether or not to dollarize. From a theoretical point of view, they show the trade-off between a suboptimal response to external shocks due to the exchange rate rigidity (an issue that relates to OCA theory), and the gain from mitigating the inflation bias that results from the time-inconsistency problem associated with monetary policy. This same inflation bias determines the credibility gains typically attributed to credible fixed exchange rates (and, in particular, dollarization). As expected, they conclude that the net social welfare effect of dollarization is an empirical matter that will depend, among other things, negatively on the variability of the exogenous shocks buffeting the economy, on the one hand, and the credibility problems faced by the authorities at the time the decision is made, on the other.

Theory is again useful to take a different look at one of the negative aspects of dollarization, namely, the loss of seignorage revenue. As stressed in chapter 2, for seignorage losses to be counted as social (as opposed to fiscal) losses, one should assume as nonexistent policy credibility problems that result in an inflation bias; otherwise, we would be regarding as an economic gain the proceeds of an excessive (and welfare-reducing) inflation tax. Finally, turning to the lender of last resort function of the central bank, the authors emphasize that its loss may increase the probability of financial crises, much in the same way that the lack of deposit insurance is viewed as increasing the probability of bank runs.[38]

Although the analytical preamble helps us elucidate the main trade-offs involved from a general perspective, the lack of unambiguous answers highlights the importance of specific characteristics of the countries facing the decision and the precise way dollarization would be put in place. Clearly distinguishing the initial conditions that may increase the convenience of dollarizing for particular countries is perhaps the main challenge of this volume, the outcome that will contribute to qualifying arguments that are typically framed in too general terms. In this section, we try to present the findings of the volume on these issues in a succinct way. However, before getting into the cost-benefit analysis of dollarization, it will help us to define up front the different monetary arrangements we will broadly group as "dollarized" regimes and to point out the main distinction between them.

1.3.1 Varieties

Going back to our "ladder" analogy of exchange rate regimes, one can conceive the varieties of full dollarization as different steps that reach increasing levels of monetary policy integration (or decreasing levels of policy independence). Thus, unilateral dollarization, the scheme that first comes to mind in discussions about dollarization, entails the decision by an individual country to adopt a foreign currency as sole legal tender, a priori without any requirement to coordinate policies with the issuer of the foreign currency.

A further degree of integration is implicit in a monetary treaty that negotiates the provision by the foreign country's central bank of some of the services formerly offered by the domestic central bank, most notably, seignorage income and liquidity insurance (lender of last resort function). In this regard, both recently dollarized countries such as Ecuador and El Salvador, and former dollarization candidates such as Argentina, tested, so far unsuccessfully, the possibility of reaching an agreement by which the United States would reimburse part of the seignorage revenue to these countries, or use it as collateral for future liquidity assistance to domestic financial institutions. Thus, such treaty would modify to some extent the U.S. monetary policy, which no longer is indifferent to the countries' decision to dollarize.[39]

Another, deeper degree of policy coordination is involved in a monetary union. Whatever the common currency of choice, the main difference between a currency union and standard dollarization lies in the existence of a common central bank in which all members are represented. Despite the fact that in practice large countries tend to influence the central bank policy more strongly, the broad membership representation smooths out the potential misalignments that may arise if the anchor country were to run monetary policy based only on domestic considerations, in the event of asymmetric shocks within the region. Moreover, a currency union implicitly introduces a common lender of last resort, through which weaker countries benefit from the larger clout of stronger economies.

Note also that the case of a small country with little influence on the union's decision, although quite closer to the case of unilateral dollarization in terms of policy coordination, still benefits from the presence of the common central bank as guarantor, a factor that may induce a rapid convergence to the region's cost of capital, something not likely to be seen in unilateral dollarized countries. The same is true even if the central bank of the anchor country remains as the central bank of the union, the likely situation in the event that a Latin American monetary union ever comes into place.

Although we typically tend to think of dollarization as an arrangement of the standard unilateral type, most of the advantages and disadvantages of the standard type extend to the other two varieties. This allows us to analyze the pros and cons of dollarization, abstracting from specific varieties and qualifying the discussion whenever a distinction between each of them is warranted. Chapters 2 to 5 are largely devoted to this kind of analysis. In the remaining part of this section, we present a brief summary of their main conclusions.

1.3.2   The Pros

The economic literature identifies three main advantages of dollarization, understood as the adoption of a *strong* foreign currency as sole legal tender. First, it reduces transaction costs among countries using the same currency, along the lines stressed by the OCA theory. Second, it enhances (both monetary and fiscal) policy credibility, resulting in lower inflation rates, lower real exchange rate volatility, and, possibly, a deepening of the financial system. Third, it reduces sovereign risk by eliminating currency risk and the occurrence of costly speculative attacks. Chapter 5 reviews each of the advantages in light of the experience of Central American countries, a group that benefits from the presence of the most interesting long-lived example of a dollarized economy and the fact that most of its members are relatively homogenous. Chapter 6, concentrates in detail on the third expected effect, by examining the impact of exogenous changes in currency risk on country risk and looking into its potential determinants. Finally, some important aspects of the measurement of currency risk are highlighted in chapter 3. Here, we draw on these works to summarize the main findings.

Reduced Transaction Costs
As mentioned in the previous section, the traditional OCA theory implicitly assumes that there are gains to be obtained from currency unification beyond and above those achievable through a free trade agreement with no commitment to a fixed parity. In the literature we find at least two ways the impact of currency unification can be inferred from the data. First, there is a large body of research on the effect of exchange rate volatility on trade that in most cases finds the effect to be significantly negative. In chapter 5, Panizza, Stein, and Talvi estimate the effect of exchange rate volatility on trade for a large sample of developing countries and for Central American countries, and find in both cases a significant and negative effect. They conclude that the trade gains from dollarization are potentially large.

Second, there are transaction costs associated with the need to operate with multiple currencies, which the European Community (EC) Commission estimates for the European Union to be between 0.25 and 0.5 percent of GDP per year. We should expect these costs to increase with the higher bid-ask spreads prevalent in less-developed economies.

Rose (2000) estimates the combined gains from reduced exchange rate volatility and transaction costs by comparing the bilateral trade flows between countries that share the same currency with trade flows that are obtained from a standard gravity model, finding substantive incremental effects.[40] Along the same lines, Panizza, Stein, and Talvi conclude that given these gains are larger the stronger the trade links are within the common currency area, for the case of Central American countries analyzed in chapter 5 a common currency may induce important trade gains.

Enhanced Credibility

Fixed exchange rate regimes advocates traditionally highlighted two important dimensions (monetary and fiscal) in which a commitment to a fixed parity can provide a country with important credibility benefits. First, by forcing a passive monetary policy, the commitment eliminates the inflation bias à la Barro-Gordon by which a government may be tempted to inflate the economy through unanticipated money injections. Second, by eradicating inflationary financing of the deficit, the commitment imposes stronger financial constraint on the government, which in turn has no option but to keep its budget in check. This tie-up-one's-hands approach, however, is not without risks, because if the self-imposed limitation does not necessarily lead to further discipline, the regime could become rapidly unsustainable. The argument can be partially extended to the case of dollarization, which in this context can be seen as a peg without any control over monetary policy.

In principle, dollarization would imply that monetary policy in general, and inflation rates in particular, would tend to converge toward the currency issuer's inflation rate, adjusted by differentials in productivity changes. Unsurprisingly, if hard pegs fare unambiguously better than their more flexible counterparts in any dimension, it is in their inflation record. Casual evidence and several econometric studies have found that, on average, dollarized regimes have systematically displayed lower inflation levels. Unfortunately, with the exception of Ecuador, the latest additions to the dollarized troupe, El Salvador and, arguably, EMU countries, entered the new regime after achieving a substantial degree of price stability, so that the impact effect of the regime switch is difficult to ascertain.[41] However, the preliminary performance of Ecuador, and the fact that the implementation of sustainable conventional pegs has been accompanied by a substantial decline in inflation, supports the view of dollarization as providing important benefits on the inflation front.[42]

The record on fiscal discipline is more ambiguous. In a recent study Fatás and Rose (2001) have found that currency unions are associated with a smaller government size (which can be measured, as the ratio of expenditures and tax revenues over GDP), whereas both currency unions and unilaterally dollarized economies exhibit narrower fiscal deficits. However, as in Rose (2000), most observations of unilaterally dollarized economies in the sample correspond to subnational entities that may not be representative of a standard small open economy. An alternative, more casual look, at the issue is provided by table 1.2. There, we use observations included in Levy Yeyati and Sturzenegger (2001a) to compare countries that belong to a currency union, both against the rest of the sample, and against de facto fixes.[43] As a reference, we also include the figures for Panama, the only unilaterally dollarized IMF-reporting country as of the end of 1999. As can be seen, while the first group exhibits smaller governments (measured either as government expenditure, tax revenues, or fiscal deficit), Panama does not differ significantly from either currency unions or other conventional pegs.[44] We interpret the results, which are broadly in line with Fatás and Rose's, as providing (weak) support to the claim that dollarization may elicit fiscal discipline.

Reduced Country Risk
A crucial issue related to credibility gains is the extent to which, by dollarizing, a country can improve its international creditworthiness. A high cost of capital, both external and internal, is possibly one of the most important factors hampering the development of nonindustrial countries. This is particularly so for emerging economies that have undergone important institutional reforms and have achieved a level of political stability in many cases comparable to those of more advanced countries.

In chapter 6, Powell and Sturzenegger stress that although the gains from trade would depend on the degree of openness and may in principle be achieved by other means, the impact of a sizable decline in the cost of capital may have substantial direct consequences for the country's wealth.

The arguments in favor of a fall in country risk are to some extent at odds with the experience of Panama, where sovereign risk has not only been systematically above that in the United States but also has responded to external negative shocks much in the same way as other nondollarized economies. This contrasts with the evidence of a rapid country risk convergence of industrial European economies on their way to EMU. In both cases, however, other more fundamental factors may be in play, including the fiscal record (mixed in the Panamanian case and substantially improved in Europe during the Maastricht period) and the distinction between unilateral dollarization and a currency union with the presence of a common lender of last resort.[45] Thus, while a decline in sovereign risk is likely to benefit Eastern European countries if they join EMU, the same is not so obvious for Latin American countries unilaterally adopting the U.S. dollar.

At any rate, the question of whether borrowing costs will increase or decrease is key to evaluating the convenience of dollarization. Powell and Sturzenegger list a number of reasons why we should expect these costs to move up or down with dollarization. Among the reasons they give for increased costs, they include the loss of the inflationary tax as a financing mechanism, the impact of the loss of seignorage on the government budget constraints, the loss of the diversification margin in a context of imperfect substitutability,[46] and the impact of the greater output volatility associated with dollarization. Among reasons for decreased costs, they mention the impact of the elimination of devaluation risk on default risk through balance sheet effects in currency-imbalanced economies,[47] the reduction in the cost of interest rate defenses against speculative attacks,[48] the increased efficiency in financial intermediation arising from the use of a common reference currency, enhanced monetary and fiscal policy credibility, and the perceived seniority of external (foreign-currency-denominated) over internal (home-currency-denominated) debt.[49]

Whatever the relative size of other intervening factors, their main results confirm the importance of balance sheet effects, as country risk in financially dollarized countries (where these effects are bound to be more substantial) tend to fall significantly on news that increases the probability of dollarization. The opposite effect is detected in Chile and Colombia, where the virtual absence of domestic financial dollarization combines with very low levels of external, foreign-currency-denominated debt.[50]

Their findings highlight that most emerging economies do not borrow internationally in their own currency, presumably because of the domestic currency's weakness. As the argument goes, the financial fragility that results from this unavoidable currency

Table 1.2
Hard pegs and fiscal policy

	Currency unions (CU)			Non-CU (NCU)			Fix de facto (without CU)			Test (CU = NCU) p-value		Test (CU = Fix) p-value	
	Obs.[1]	Mean	Median	Obs.	Mean	Median	Obs.	Mean	Median	Means	Medians[2]	Means	Medians[2]
Total expenditure	168	26.2	26.9	1639	28.1	25.7	460	31.7	30.7	0.08	0.37	0.00	0.00
Current revenue	171	21.9	23.1	1642	23.5	21.6	462	26.8	26.3	0.06	0.30	0.00	0.00
Overall budget surplus	166	−2.5	−1.6	1630	−4.2	−3.3	449	−4.5	−3.4	0.00	0.00	0.00	0.00
Tax revenue	171	18.0	20.3	1650	19.4	17.3	463	21.6	18.3	0.07	0.65	0.00	0.00
Governmental consumption	406	16.4	15.6	2023	15.6	14.3	608	17.7	16.3	0.05	0.00	0.00	0.03

	Panama			Test (Panama = CU) p-value		Test (Panama = Fix) p-value	
	Obs.	Mean	Median	Mean	Medians[2]	Mean	Medians[2]
Total expenditure	25	28.6	28.9	0.22	0.25	0.37	0.61
Current revenue	25	25.1	25.4	0.09	0.27	0.64	0.95
Overall budget surplus	25	−3.5	−4.0	0.24	0.08	0.55	0.95
Tax revenue	25	18.6	18.4	0.98	0.36	0.23	0.84
Governmental consumption	19	17.9	17.6	0.45	0.04	0.84	0.22

Source: World Bank (2000).

Note: The currency unions observed are Antigua and Barbuda, Benin, Burkina Faso, Cameroon, Central African Republic, Congo, Côte d'Ivoire, Chad, Dominica, Equatorial Guinea, Gabon, Grenada, Guinea-Bissau, Mali, Niger, Saint Kitts and Nevis, Saint Lucia, Saint Vincent and the Grenadines, Senegal, and Togo. Variables are defined as follows:

Total expenditure: Includes current and capital (development) expenditures and excludes lending minus repayments.

Current revenue: Includes all revenue from taxes and current nontax revenues (other than grants), such as fines, fees, recoveries, and income from property or sales. Data are for the central government only.

Overall budget surplus: Includes current and capital revenue, and official grants received, less total expenditure and lending minus repayments.

Tax revenue: Comprises compulsory, unrequited, nonrepayable receipts for public purposes collected by central governments. It includes interest collected on tax arrears and penalties collected on nonpayment or late payments of taxes and is shown net of refunds and other corrective transactions.

Government consumption: Consists of current spending for purchases of goods and services (including wages and salaries). It also includes most expenditures on national defense and security but excludes government military expenditures that are part of government capital formation.

All variables are expressed as a percentage of GDP and apply to the central government only.

[1] Number of observations.

[2] Wilcoxon/Mann-Whitney test.

imbalance can only be eliminated by adopting as sole legal tender the foreign currency in which the external debt is denominated. The argument, as always, should be qualified because external debt is often denominated in more than one reference currency, so the indexation to the foreign currency that full dollarization implies eliminates currency risk only partially.

However, if foreign currency borrowing is an important source of country risk, why not develop the domestic currency debt market? Indeed, there is not systematic evidence that the lack of domestic-currency-denominated debt is due to the inability to borrow in the home currency, as opposed to a deliberate decision not to incur the cost of a currency risk premium judged to be excessive by most governments, particularly if they are commited to a fixed parity.

In the same vein, fully floating regimes, by dollarizing their debt, change their incentive structure to make an opportunistic devaluation less likely. As Neumeyer and Nicolini stress in chapter 3, the chances that a government repudiates its debt by a surprise devaluation is negatively related to the degree of financial dollarization. Interestingly, by dollarizing their debt, governments gain a credibility they cannot later exploit by issuing debt in their own currency. Thus, the discipline obtained by this self-imposed restrictions brings with it an increase in vulnerability to events beyond the control of local governments.

1.3.3 The Cons

Three main disadvantages are often attributed to a dollarized economy. First, the standard fix-flex argument concerning the loss of the exchange rate instrument to buffer the economy against real or external shocks (alternatively, the loss of monetary independence) applies identically in this case. Second, the elimination of the local currency entails a fiscal cost arising from the loss of seignorage revenues. Third, the use of a foreign currency for financial intermediation eliminates the capacity of the domestic central bank to finance its LLR activities by printing the domestic currency. Here, we summarize the discussion of the first point, included in chapter 5, and the analysis of the issue of the LLR and different alternatives to the standard central bank liquidity assistance presented in chapter 4. In the final part of the section, we briefly address the issue of seignorage: its measurement and its potential magnitude.

The Loss of the Exchange Rate Instrument

One of the standard arguments against fixed exchange rate regimes in general, and full dollarization in particular, stresses that a flexible exchange rate is better equipped to isolate the real economy from external and real shocks. Indeed, there is evidence that fixed regimes are associated with higher output volatility.[51] Moreover, because the price rigidity underscoring the lack of adjustment in fixed regimes tends to be higher when it comes to reducing prices, the succession of quantity adjustments during recessions and price adjustment during expansions may result in a smaller growth rate in the long run.[52]

However, some analysts have argued that the shocks faced by individual countries are not totally exogenous to the exchange regime. Thus, Calvo (1999b) argues in favor of full dollarization by stressing that the poor performance of conventional pegs is not independent of the fact that they are inherently more vulnerable to speculative attacks based on rumors or financial contagion, an outcome the elimination of the national currency automatically rules out.

The analysis in chapter 5 fails to find a significantly different response to real (terms of trade) shocks under different regimes, partially contradicting the results in Broda (2000). However, one should note that Broda also finds that for highly dollarized economies (as is the Central American countries examined in the chapter 5), the difference in output response ceases to depend on the exchange rate arrangement.

An issue related to the loss of exchange rate flexibility is that in the context of a small open economy, full dollarization eliminates the scope for (countercyclical) monetary policy. Standard arguments against adopting a fixed exchange rate emphasize that a floating regime has the ability to protect the country from external interest rate fluctuations and to use monetary policy as an aggregate demand management tool, under the presumption that domestic interest rates are (more) independent in this case. This provides an alternative way to test the isolation properties of flexible exchange rates and the costs of fixing them.

The existing evidence on this point is rather mixed. Previous analysis of the effect of external interest rate fluctuations (measured either as foreign borrowing costs or as changes in U.S. interest rates) on domestic rates under different exchange regimes provides no evidence that flexible regimes are successful in isolating domestic monetary variables from external ones.[53] These conclusions are confirmed by the tests provided in chapter 5. In particular, the authors find that domestic interest rates in Latin American countries seem more sensitive to external financing costs (dollar rates on sovereign bonds) and to worldwide shocks affecting emerging markets as a whole (measured as change in the J. P. Morgan Emerging Markets Bond Index Plus, abbreviated as EMBI+) under more flexible regimes. Indeed, interest rates in Panama appear not to be significantly influenced by external rates, suggesting an important credibility aspect underlying the link between external and domestic interest rates.

In addition, the authors look at the evolution of interest rates over the cycle and find no systematic countercyclicality in flexible regimes.[54] It is interesting at this point to emphasize that for many reasons, monetary policy procyclicality seems to be the norm rather than the exception among developing countries, contrary to what we observe in industrial economies. This pattern is, undoubtedly, partially explained by credibility factors that result in the closure of international markets at the time these countries face domestic financial constraints. The failure of international capital markets to "insure" developing economies against cyclical fluctuations detracts from the usefulness of monetary policy as a short-term adjustment mechanism, rendering it less valuable.

In short, although the loss of the exchange rate regime flexibility appears to be associated, in general, with higher output volatility, the benefits of a flexible exchange rate seem to be limited in the context of de facto dollarized economies. Moreover, the dependence of monetary policy on external events under flexible regimes is, at best, similar to that prevalent under pegs. Indeed, the resilience of domestic rates in Panama indicates that full dollarization, by tying domestic rates to U.S. rates, may have provided a better isolation device against temporary changes in market sentiment toward emerging economies, a benefit that appears to more than offset the loss of independent monetary policy.

The Loss of the Lender of Last Resort

Among the main costs attributed to full dollarization is the loss of the domestic central bank's capacity to play its lender of last resort (LLR) function, namely, its ability to provide additional liquidity to the banking sector in the event of a transitory shortage. Trivially, although central banks can issue the domestic currency at no cost, an excess demand of the foreign currency in the market can only be met by the existence of a (costly) stock of liquid foreign-currency-denominated reserves.

Many observers have pointed out the existence of alternative mechanisms to provide liquidity insurance. In fact, there are at least two ways the LLR can be preserved in a context of full dollarization. First, it is easy to conceive (though more difficult to implement) a scheme by which the international financial community (e.g., a consortium of international banks) charges an insurance fee in exchange for a commitment to provide a credit line to a domestic agency (e.g., the domestic central bank) in charge of liquidity management in the banking sector, or to individual banks separately, much in the same way as a standard insurance contract works.

Second, it is still possible that the domestic agency collects the contributions directly from the domestic banking sector and insures them up to the certain amount that in the aggregate will be limited by the total accumulated insurance fund. This arrangement, which resembles the usual deposit insurance scheme, can be alternatively implemented through direct funding by the domestic treasury. In both cases, the option is no different from what highly dollarized economies tend to do in practice: avail themselves of a large inventory of international reserves.

As argued in detail in chapter 4, feasible as both alternatives may be, they still imply important incremental costs, particularly if they are engineered to isolate the banking sector from systemic shocks.[55] The external insurance strategy involves the payment of an insurance fee that is likely to increase more than proportionally with the coverage of the policy, as the insurer's diversification margin narrows. The Argentinean contingent credit line represents the closer example of such scheme.[56] Although the fee was relatively minor compared with the inventory cost of holding reserves, the insurer benefits from the fact that the policy is activated only after the large existing liquid assets reserves are exhausted, and even then the coverage (and the associated risk for the insurer banks) is relatively limited.[57] One can only speculate about the feasibility and cost of a scheme based solely on this type of private insurance. In addition, the private insurance strategy leaves opens another (and so far unanswered) question related to moral hazard issues: what would prevent that as the probability of a crisis increased, participating banks hedged their exposure in the market, contributing to the crisis?

But this is not the only practical limitation of the strategy to outsource the LLR. As any insurance contract, this one suffers from two moral hazard problems. The first stems from the fact that the occurrence of a crisis is not independent of the government's actions. It follows that the privatization of the LLR could substantially reduce the government's incentives to monitor and reduce risk, arising both from its own imbalances and from leniency in the enforcement of a prudential framework. That is the main reason why the insurance contract is bound to require some kind of collateral. However, as noted in chapter 4, it is not at all clear to what extent the issuer of the contract will be willing or able to comply with the policy in case of a widespread crisis, particularly if this type of arrangement generalizes across countries that historically have exhibited a high correlation of external shocks. Thus, the chapter concludes, the private alternative should be considered only as part of a larger insurance package.[58]

Most of these previous shortcomings may be attenuated if the LLR function is assigned to an international agency such as the IMF (International Monetary Fund). Indeed, the IMF has already been performing this role, albeit reluctantly, during much of the 1990s. The benefits of this strategy are obvious. By encompassing countries around the world, such an agency could exploit its scope for diversification and reduce the liquidity stock needed to fulfill its role. Moreover, as a supranational agency, it can include conditionalities on the extension of the insurance, something that would be unthinkable for a private consortium of banks. However, its very supranational nature would make it vulnerable to political pressures that may worsen the moral hazard problems and create the perception of an implicit insurance that is independent of the country's compliance with the conditionality.[59] At any rate, it is to be expected that dollarized countries with reduced access to last resort liquidity will rely heavily on IMF assistance.[60]

The alternative of holding a large stock of liquid assets as a precautionary liquidity fund involves the usual inventory cost of maintaining a sizable stock of reserves in a context of high borrowing costs. More precisely, as the domestic cost of capital is typically higher than the return on liquid assets that constitute the major part of reserves, reserve holdings entail a cost proportional to the spread

between short-term safe foreign assets and longer and riskier domestic government paper. The cost largely reflects two types of premiums: a liquidity premium associated with the shorter maturity of
reserves needed for liquidity management in the domestic financial
sector, and a risk premium associated with a higher probability of
default.[61]

The cost of holding reserves for liquidity insurance purposes is
proportional to the probability distribution of shocks (which in turn
determines the needed stock of reserves for a given confidence level)
and to the external debt spread (which determines the optimal confidence level) that the government has to pay when it borrows to invest on low-yield, safe reserve assets. The optimal level of reserves
is not straightforward, though, as the volatility of liquidity shocks is
itself endogenous to the amount of reserves: the higher the amount,
the less likely a confidence crisis or a bank run will actually occur.

At any rate, the previous arguments highlight one important
(and often underemphasized) aspect of the debate: Central banks in
countries with extensive de facto financial dollarization suffer, albeit
to a lesser degree, from the same shortcoming, as liquidity shortages
in the banking sector forcefully take the form of an excess demand
for the foreign currency.[62] Thus, as before, the actual lender of last
resort cost specifically attributable to full dollarization is smaller the
higher the initial financial dollarization ratio.

One can in principle estimate the cost of losing the LLR function
of the central bank directly as the cost of holding the stock of excess
reserves that substitutes for it. If we are willing to accept that reserves are primarily used as an insurance against systemic shocks,
then a reasonable approximation to the optimal stock may be obtained as a stress test of the domestic central bank's aggregate portfolio, taking into account all contingent liabilities arising from the
expected assistance of the financial sector in the event of a systemic
crisis.

In this regard, the nature of the reserves decision is no different
from a standard inventory problem involving a trade-off between
the cost of holding reserves and the cost of facing immediate liquidity needs that, if anything, can be met in international markets at
a very large premium. In order to solve this problem, we need to
answer three questions: (1) How much liquidity will be mopped
out of the system during a crisis (for example, due to a run on deposits)? (2) What is the probability that such a crisis actually occurs

for a given reserve coverage?[63] (3) What is the cost of carrying the reserves?

It is interesting that as full dollarization trivially increases the degree of dollarization of financial assets, it raises the optimal stock of precautionary reserves.[64] However, as noted earlier, dollarization eliminates an important source of economic disturbance, namely, the possibility of a currency crisis that negatively affects the banking sector through the balance sheet channel; it reduces the probability of systemic liquidity shortages (for example, due to self-fulfilling prophecies) and the optimal stock of reserves for any given dollarization ratio. Thus, a highly dollarized country such as Argentina may indeed benefit from the latter effect, whereas a relatively non-dollarized country such as Brazil may be forced to increase its liquidity requirements.

In short, although there are several alternatives available to substitute for the LLR function of the central bank, none of them is costless or even complete. However, the incremental cost of the limitations imposed by dollarization is relatively minor for countries that already exhibit a substantial degree of de facto dollarization.

The Loss of Seignorage

How large is the loss of seignorage associated with dollarization? A correct estimation of seignorage losses needs to take into account two components: the need to purchase the initial stock of foreign currency to be used as currency, and the costs of purchasing later increases in the stock of currency. Alternatively, one can think of these costs as the lost income from international reserves used to exchange the monetary base for the foreign currency, and from future increases in the stock of reserves as a result of increases in the demand for money.

A quick calculation can be made based on two simplifying assumptions: (1) output and prices grow at constant rates g and π, where the latter is assumed to follow the inflation rate in the foreign country from which the new currency is borrowed; (2) the currency-to-(nominal) GDP ratio remains constant at the initial level, denoted by γ.[65] Under these assumptions, it follows that the total flow of seignorage is exactly equivalent to a perpetuity that pays an interest rate i on a stock of international reserves that grows at a rate $\rho = (1+\pi)(1+g) - 1$, the rate of growth of the demand for currency on which seignorage is collected. In turn, the present value of the perpetuity is given by

$$S = \sum_{t=0}^{\infty} i(\gamma \text{GDP}_0)[(1+\pi)(1+g)]^t/(1+i)^{t+1} = i(\gamma \text{GDP}_0)/(i-\rho)$$

where i is the government's opportunity cost. Because the real interest rate can be computed directly as $r = (1+i)/(1+\pi) - 1$, the equation immediately gives us the seignorage cost in terms of GDP for any expected real interest, inflation, and growth rates and for any expected monetization ratio. To illustrate the point, table 1.3 presents the estimated numbers under the assumption of a constant currency-to-GDP ratio of 4 percent, and a real interest rate, r, of 4 percent, for different growth and inflation assumptions. As an example, for a growth rate of 3 percent and an inflation rate of 2 percent we obtain a sizable value of the seignorage costs of close to 23.8 percent of GDP.[66]

From this exercise we can conclude that seignorage costs are by no means trivial when correctly computed.[67] Indeed, the value of future increases in the demand for money represents the larger part of total seignorage costs.[68] Thus, the final number depends heavily on the expected rates of growth and inflation, as well as on the evolution of the currency-to-GDP ratio, which is so far assumed constant, for simplicity.

The degree of monetization is higher in developed than in developing countries, which suggests that for the latter, the rate of growth of the demand for money may be higher in the short run than in the steady state if levels eventually converge to those of more developed economies. This entails an additional seignorage cost, in the form of

Table 1.3
Loss of seignorage revenues (in percent of GDP)

Growth rate (%)	Inflation rate %			
	1	2	3	4
0	5.0	6.0	6.9	7.8
1	6.7	7.9	9.2	10.5
2	10.0	11.9	13.8	15.7
3	20.0	23.8	27.7	31.4

Note: Real interest rate, $r = 4\%$; currency-to-GDP ratio, $\gamma = 4\%$.

higher flow costs in the transition period. However, one can present an argument in the opposite direction, by pointing at the presence of a declining trend in the demand for real balances in developed economies (due primarily to financial innovation) that would require a downward adjustment in our estimation of seignorage costs.

1.4   Applications: How Do We Get There?

Besides the cost-benefit analysis already discussed, the dollarization decision entails a number of important questions related to the institutional arrangements to be implemented and, in particular, to the smoothness of the transition process to the new environment. These considerations, in turn, involve not only technical questions regarding, for example, the "correct" entering exchange rate or the treatment of contracts during the path to dollarization but also the political economy of the process that underscores the search for political support, a necessary condition for a successful dollarization plan. In this section we discuss the most salient points in these two groups of issues, which are tackled in full detail in the last two chapters of the volume.

1.4.1   Institutional Arrangements

Chapter 7 presents a thorough analysis of the main institutional aspects of the transition to full dollarization, broadly dividing the discussion along the lines of whether the goal is unilateral dollarization or a monetary union.[69]

A number of important technical points are posed by the analysis. First and foremost, there is the question of the exchange rate at which the economy should enter the new arrangement, that is, the rate at which the domestic currency should be exchanged with the foreign currency at the beginning of the process. Here, there are at least two alternatives. The easier way is simply to compute the exchange rate that makes current international reserves equal to the sum of the money base and the outstanding stock of domestic currency interest rate-bearing securities issued by the central bank. However, although there will always be a rate that will make foreign currency assets equal to domestic currency liabilities of the central bank, the exchange rate may be excessively high if international reserves are relatively scarce, and a substantial devaluation may be in order.[70] Alternatively, the exchange rate may be allowed to float during a short period of time in order for the market to achieve its equilibrium in anticipation of the dollarization exchange rate. In either case, one would expect domestic prices to adjust upward in time. A potential problem could arise if a large stock of international reserves calls for an appreciation of the currency, which in the context of downward price inflexibility could have adverse effects on the real economy. However, it is easy to conceive of a scheme in which the central bank (or the treasury) keeps part of existing reserves, for example, as a fund to substitute for the loss of the lender of last resort or to buy back sovereign debt.

As in the case of trade and capital account liberalization, the debate on dollarization has also delved into the issue of sequencing. The proponents of a gradual process toward dollarization argue that a number of complementary institutional and economic reforms are in order to guarantee the sustainability of the new arrangement, including fiscal adjustment to offset the loss of seignorage and inflation tax revenues, labor market reform to allow for a more flexible adjustment to external shocks, and financial reform and a strengthening of the banking sector to cope with the loss of the LLR.[71] In contrast, the proponents of a rapid move toward dollarization have emphasized that all necessary preconditions are likely to be put in place once the limitations imposed by the new regime become apparent. In any case, they argue, waiting for the reforms to happen is the best way to postpone forever.[72]

An interesting issue related to the transition to dollarization is the rate at which existing domestic currency contracts are converted to the new regime. The problem is illustrated well by the example of a domestic currency bank deposit. Should the deposit be converted at the exchange rate attendant at the time of its issuance, or at the rate at which the money base was purchased? In the former case, the holder of the deposit will be granted a benefit from the change in regime that will be equal to the local-foreign currency interest rate spread. In the former case, however, the bank will benefit inasmuch as the spread already incorporated expectations of a regime change, based on information available at the time the deposit was made. Gruben, Wynne, and Zarazaga conclude that under the rational expectations hypothesis, the second of the two cases applies, from which it follows that contracts should be converted at the rate established under the dollarization plan. However, if we accept that expectations are formed in an adaptative way, this alternative would imply a transfer of wealth from domestic currency creditors to domestic currency debtors. Moreover, as is mentioned in note 20 of chapter 7, this may in turn induce a negative balance sheet effect if firms indebted in the local currency find it difficult to meet the (now higher) debt service burden. The concomitant adverse effect on the financial sector should not be underestimated. To attenuate these types of disturbance, the authorities should allow a long enough transition period in which existing contracts expire or are voluntarily renegotiated.[73]

Another technical aspect in implementing dollarization is the possibility of a seignorage-sharing scheme. The recent proposal of the Joint Economic Committee of the U.S. Senate hinted at the possibility of sharing an unspecified fraction of the seignorage accruing to the United States from the unilateral dollarization of foreign countries, based on the money base at the time the dollarization process is started. Alternatively, Barro (1999) proposes replacing the flow of seignorage payments by an up-front disbursement that may help prevent the sharp devaluation needed when the stock of international reserves is small relative to the money base. The moral hazard associated with an advance of seignorage revenues (a crucial shortcoming of the Barro proposal) may in principle be mitigated by issuing a long-term foreign-currency-denominated bond to collateralize the advance that for all practical purposes, would be equivalent to a loan from the issuer of the foreign currency. However, the increase in sovereign debt implied by the last alternative may detract from the beneficial effect of dollarization on country risk. At any rate, none of these alternatives has received any serious political support in the United States.

Many of the issues discussed here are still present in a monetary union, although in a different fashion. Thus, seignorage is not lost in this case, but members have to come up with a sharing scheme.[74] Similarly, although there is a scope for a domestic LLR, it is not obvious whether this function should lie within the common central bank, with the national reserves banks, or with some other decentralized agency. The same moral hazard concerns that justify the reluctance of the U.S. Federal Reserve to provide LLR services to unilaterally dollarized countries underline the decision of EMU to separate the LLR function from the European Central Bank (ECB) (however, this has not dispelled concerns about the perception of an implicit insurance by the ECB, concerns additionally fueled by the lack of a transparent LLR procedure) and apply to the location of the supervisory function.

But perhaps the most salient distinction between the two varieties of dollarization is the greater bearing on monetary policy decisions that member countries have in a monetary union, which, in turn, requires a longer and more restrictive convergence process prior to the launch of the union. This is only logical if we think of a union as a long-term partnership by which members assume joint responsibility over a range of issues. More precisely, although the United States has no bearing on the policies undertaken in Ecuador or on their impact on its population, monetary authorities within a union should aim at the welfare of the whole constituency of member countries. Accordingly, to prevent some particular country from free riding on other members' good behavior, the union needs prospective members to be in a comparably good standing.[75] Examples of this free-riding problem are not difficult to find. Countries may be tempted to incur excessive fiscal expenses financed by debt that is (at least implicitly) backed by the rest of the union. Similarly, national supervisory bodies may relax banks' prudential supervision in the belief that the national banking sector is implicitly insured by the common central bank.

Thus, a monetary union limit some of the adverse consequences of unilateral dollarization (mainly, the loss of the LLR and seignorage revenues) but introduces moral hazard issues that can only be (at least partially) resolved through a much longer transition period and, in particular, through more stringent qualifying requirements, especially from the countries from which monetary policy credibility is to be gained.[76] A monetary union also presumes the willingness of such a country to open its decision process to newcomers, something that may still be a long shot for many developing economies.

1.4.2   Political Economy

The success of a dollarization plan will depend to a large extent on the popular support it can gather. Chapter 7 suggests the need to hold a referendum on the plan to ensure the backing of a broad majority. However, just as important is the political support from different interest groups in the economy, this support probably a condition for a referendum to be held in the first place. This is the subject of chapter 8, where Frieden addresses the impact of dollarization on different influential sectors in the economy, as well as the relevance of the country's economic structure, macroconditions, and electoral institutions on the likelihood that the needed consensus about the dollarization plan is actually created.

The chapter asks which sectors are more likely to benefit or suffer from a move to full dollarization, and it stresses the importance of the relative political influence of "winners" and "losers" in the creation of political consensus. Among the former, we can identify sectors involved in cross-border operations (multinationals, financial institutions, and international trade intermediaries), where the use of a common currency and the elimination of exchange risk are bound to have a large positive effect. We could add to this group exporters who benefit from the deepening of trade links within the common currency area. Among the latter, we find import-competing producers, for whom the lack of exchange rate adjustments would entail a greater volatility of demand. Thus, the "identikit" of a prospective dollarizer should show a fairly open economy with an internationally oriented private sector, as opposed to a closed economy with a powerful domestic, market-based, import-competing sector.

Several additional factors are singled out in chapter 8: the presence of a strong government capable of leading the regime shift, macroconditions that increase the dollarization benefits (for example, persistently high inflation as in Ecuador), institutional stability that guarantees the credibility of the commitment embedded in the dollarization process (as in El Salvador), and even political ties with the issuer of the candidate foreign currency.

Indeed, it could be argued that EMU involved not only economic considerations such as those discussed in the previous section but also (and perhaps mainly) a "prerequisite to seat at the table for other important European decisions," as Frieden puts it. Similarly, a plan for a Pan-American free trade area may deepen political links among the intervening countries, increase the cost of competitive devaluations (and reduce the value of a floating exchange rate), and fuel the interest in a common currency and (particularly in the United States) in arrangements that go beyond unilateral dollarization.[77]

In the end, a serious evaluation of the viability of dollarization should not be blind to many of its consequences that escape the economic sphere. The political and strategic dimensions discussed in chapter 8 complement the cost-benefit analysis of section 1.3. Ultimately, what makes dollarization a feasible alternative is not only its welfare implications but also the way in which this implications affects in particular those in charge of making the decisions.

1.5   Preliminary Balance: The Importance of Initial Conditions

An outside observer will be immediately struck by the sharply contrasting views offered in the current dollarization debate, which can only be explained by a combination of fragmentary and rather unrepresentative real experiments and an important ideological component. However, the preceding survey of the issues involved goes a long way to motivate the apparent lack of consensus, as it flags the complexity of issues at stake and the relevance of individual countries' initial conditions at the time of choosing whether or not to dollarize.

Taking the side of hard peg advocates, one could argue that de facto dollarized economies under a flexible regime do not actually float, due to concerns that extreme fluctuations would lead to financial fragility (balance sheets effects) or high inflation (pass-through effects). In addition, conventional pegs are subject to frequent confidence crises, many of them triggered without any significant change in fundamentals, which through the two effects just mentioned may affect the financing costs and, ultimately, the solvency of the country. Similarly, as we have stressed, central banks in financially dollarized economies are likely to face serious limitations to their capacity to perform as LLRs without resorting to a large and costly stock of international reserves, and they are equally limited in their capacity to conduct independent monetary policy. However, although there is some evidence of the presence of "fear of floating" in many developing countries,[78] and of the practice of holding a sizable stock of international reserves in financially dollarized economies, the data are by no means conclusive enough to suggest that flexible regimes completely sacrifice the benefits of exchange rate adjustments.

Also of note is that existing hard pegs have proved highly successful in increasing monetary discipline and lowering inflation, but the evidence of their impact on government size and fiscal performance is rather weak. Finally, extreme fixes appear to have exhibited slower growth and higher output volatility, confirming the existence of real effects of giving up the exchange rate as an adjustment mechanism. Moreover, even hard peg advocates recognize the need for wage and price flexibility in order to minimize the burden of real shock adjustments, but there is no systematic evidence that existing hard pegs have been successful on these fronts.

In the end, the main conclusions that can be drawn from this debate point to the importance of very specific initial conditions. On the one hand, benefits from de jure dollarization are likely to outweigh costs in countries that have high financial dollarization, that seek to adopt important trade links with other users of the foreign currency, that have pervasive credibility problems that result in high country risk, and that experience persistent high inflation or frequent currency collapses whenever they attempt to use an exchange rate anchor. On the other hand, countries with limited financial dollarization, diversified trade links, or stable flexible monetary regimes and high creditworthiness are likely to profit the least from the adoption of a dollarized regime. The evolution of ongoing experiences will ultimately be the final test of these preliminary conclusions.

Notes

1. Other Latin American countries, including Guatemala and Nicaragua, are seriously considering following the El Salvadoran example.

2. In the text that follows, the terms *full dollarization* and *de jure dollarization* are used interchangeably. Similarly, as is customary in the literature, the term *dollarization* is applied here to the use of any foreign currency, with the understanding that in many cases the U.S. dollar is not the foreign currency of choice.

3. Indeed, Panama differs also in that many of these other included cases can hardly be compared with a standard independent economy. However, Panama shared with most of them its large degree of openness and its concentration in the production of services.

4. Existing currency unions include the Eastern Caribbean Monetary Union and the two unions that comprise the African franc zone.

5. For example, the degree of exchange rate flexibility of currency unions in the Caribbean or the franc zone is further restricted by pegging the common currency against the U.S. dollar and the French franc, respectively, which in practice implies the subordination of the union's monetary policy.

6. See Fleming (1962), Mundell (1963, 1964), and Dornbusch (1976). See also De Grauwe (1994) for a recent survey.

7. Changes in money demand may be due, for example, to financial innovation affecting money velocity or the money multiplier.

8. The result that current exchange rates react more than proportionally to monetary shocks is Dornbusch's well-known overshooting effect. The impact of an unanticipated increase in money supply has exactly the opposite effect.

9. Real shocks could include changes in external demand for the domestic product (e.g., as a result of a devaluation of trading partners' exchange rate) or exogenously induced changes in the cost of capital (e.g., due to an increase in the country's risk premium).

10. In the cases of either fixed or flexible exchange rates given that prices tend to be more rigid to downward adjustment, the adjustment period is likely to be particularly long and taxing in the event of an adverse shock, the more so the less flexible domestic prices are.

11. Note that different countries in principle require different adjustments in the nominal exchange rate in the event of a external shock.

12. In addition, the Maastricht Treaty has been seen as a commitment mechanism that helped participant governments curb fiscal deficits and reduce inflation.

13. The work done by Frankel and Rose (2000) and Rose (2000) on the trade effects of a currency union deserve a special mention. In their work, they find countries sharing the same currency to trade among each other significantly more than countries that do not, even after controlling for the existence of an FTA. It should be mentioned, however, that their sample includes dependencies, territories, colonies, and overseas departments, leaving open the question of whether the common currency effect is not reflecting very specific historical, political, and cultural ties that might not be captured by the control variables used in their test (language, common colonial past, etc.). Moreover, a recent paper by Persson (2001) find that the result virtually disappears once he corrects for "treatment effects."

14. The three pillars of the trinity being capital mobility, an independent monetary policy, and a fixed exchange rate.

15. These three arguments have been associated, respectively, with the so-called first-, second-, and third-generation models of currency crises. Note that the third argument implies that the credibility of a peg may actually decline over time, as opposed to the view of a gradual credibility buildup. The case of Argentina's protracted recession since 1998 is a good example.

16. Here, *currency substitution* refers to the use of a foreign currency as a means of payment or unit of account, whereas *financial dollarization*, following Ize and Levy Yeyati (2000), denotes the holding by residents of foreign-currency-denominated assets and liabilites.

17. The dollarization literature is too extensive to be summarized here. Recent surveys can be found in Calvo and Vegh (1992, 1997), Giovannini and Turtleboom (1994), and Savastano (1996).

18. Explanations of dollarization persistence (referred to in the literature as *hysteresis*) typically hinge on lack of credibility (e.g., the presence of large inflationary memory, as in Savastano 1996) or network externalities (e.g., the costs of switching the currency of denomination of everyday transactions, as in Guidotti and Rodriguez 1992). Both arguments, again, are consistent with a view of dollarization as a currency substitution phenomenon.

19. See, for example, Thomas (1985) and Sahay and Vegh (1997).

20. Reasons that have prompted monetary authorities to introduce (and even facilitate) foreign currency deposits in the domestic-banking sector include the need to limit

capital flight and to protect banks from runs induced by changes in the currency composition of local portfolios during inflationary episodes.

21. This statement follows from the fact that for given inflation and nominal exchange rate volatilities, the higher the pass-through, the lower the real exchange rate volatility in the economy. As noted by the authors, the argument implies that currency substitution (e.g., in the form of exchange rate indexation) may induce financial dollarization, although the converse is not necessarily true.

22. In particular, successful exchange-rate-based stabilizations should not be expected to reduce financial dollarization, as long as they do not alter the relation between inflation and real exchange rate volatility.

23. Trivially, currency substitution in the form of dollar pricing (i.e., the use of the dollar as a unit of account) increases the exchange rate pass-through, impairing the ability of the monetary authority to limit price variations in the presence of exchange rate fluctuations.

24. This argument is proposed by Calvo (1999a, 2000a) and others to account for the common practice among many emerging economies of avoiding substantial exchange rate volatility by intervening actively in foreign exchange markets, a phenomenon Calvo and Reinhart (2000) label "fear of floating."

25. Indeed, this implicit guarantee has been validated in many recent crises (Mexico in 1994 and Brazil in 1998 are two examples). See Burnside, Eichenbaum, and Rebelo (1999) for an analytical model of this implicit guarantee.

26. See Hausmann (1999).

27. The time-inconsistency argument, however, does not explain why some countries borrow in their own currency and some do not, a difference often attributed to credibility associated with the country's track record (as, e.g., in the "original sin" argument in Hausmann 1999).

28. Alternative sources of liquidity are discussed in more detail in the text that follows. Let us just note for the moment that all these alternatives are costly and that, at any rate, the problem is not specific to fully dollarized economies.

29. See, for example, Eichengreen (1994) and, more recently, Fischer (2001) and Summers (2000). Needless to say, this view is consistent with a preference for floating regimes when monetary policy objectives take the lead.

30. "Hard peg" candidates include countries such as Guatemala and Nicaragua that are currently considering following the steps of El Salvador, European countries in the accession list for EMU, and seven African countries (Cape Verde, Gambia, Ghana, Guinea, Liberia, Nigeria, and Sierra Leone) that plan to launch a monetary union by 2003 as a first step to join the West African Economic and Monetary Union (WAEMU) and form a broader common currency area.

31. In this sense, the IMF's de jure classification does not capture the actual behavior of the regimes and may lead to a misrepresentation of current trends. For an analysis on the recent evolution of exchange regimes based on a de facto regime classification, see Levy Yeyati and Sturzenegger (2002).

32. Fischer (2001) uses a specification of exchange rate categories from the IMF's *Annual Report 2000* (141–143), based on the IMF staff's assessment of de facto regimes.

Interestingly, however, the bipolar pattern appears to be more visible when the de jure criterion is used.

33. See the piece on currency boards by Ghosh, Gulde, and Wolf (1998) for empirical results in this direction and Fischer (2001) for an argument concerning hard pegs in general.

34. See note 14.

35. This increased de facto dollarization may be actively fostered by the local authorities in an attempt to express their commitment. For example, the choice of a one-to-one parity in the case of Argentina was quite possibly aimed at putting dollar and peso intermediation on equal grounds. Chapter 4 discusses an additional channel through which financial dollarization can be endogenously deepened in the context of a bimonetary economy.

36. It could be argued, however, that skepticism about Argentina has been (at least partially) triggered by concerns about the country's ability to serve its external debt rooted in persistent fiscal deficits. To what extent full dollarization, as opposed to a currency board, would have been an attenuating factor in this particular instance is difficult to assess.

37. See figure 6.1 (in chapter 6).

38. Section 5 of chapter 2 introduces the discussion on the impact of dollarization on country risk, resumed in more detail in chapters 3 and 6.

39. Even at this degree of disaggregation, we can find cases not fully represented by any of these categories. Take, for example, the countries within the rand zone (Botswana, Lesotho, Namibia, and Swaziland) that use the South African rand as legal tender and even perceive seignorage revenues from the South African Central Bank, while at the same time preserve their own central bank and their own currency, albeit with a 100 percent reserves backup requirement much as in the case of a currency board.

40. These results have to be treated with caution, however. On this, see note 16.

41. One could argue that price stability is a precondition to dollarization, as opposed to a consequence of the regime.

42. See, for example, Ghosh et al. (1997), Ghosh, Gulde, and Wolf (1998), and Levy Yeyati and Sturzenegger (2001a), for a large set of industrial and nonindustrial countries, and Domac and Martinez (2000) for transition economies.

43. The currency union sample includes Antigua and Barbuda, Benin, Burkina Faso, Cameroon, the Central African Republic, Congo, Côte d'Ivoire, Chad, Dominica, Equatorial Guinea, Gabon, Grenada, Guinea-Bissau, Mali, Niger, Saint Kitts and Nevis, Saint Lucia, Saint Vincent and the Grenadines, Senegal, and Togo.

44. One should note that the results concerning unilaterally dollarized economies suffer from a small-sample problem. In our sample these economies are represented by Panama (arguably not a good example of fiscal restraint), and Fatás and Rose only find data for thirty-two observations.

45. Although in theory the European Central Bank (ECB) is not assigned LLR functions, the lack of a clear LLR arrangement in EMU certainly contributes to this perception.

46. Under this argument, agents willing to diversify their currency exposure would be willing to pay a premium on local-currency-denominated debt.

47. Indeed, as they note, even in a currency-balanced economy, imbalances are to be expected at the microlevel.

48. Note that even unsuccessful attacks impose a considerable (albeit temporary) real cost to the economy.

49. This last point relates to the option to depreciate the domestic currency, reducing the burden of home currency debt and thus the probability of a generalized default. Chapter 3 discusses the conditions under which this option is likely to be exercised. While there is no systematic evidence of a differential treatment of external and internal debt, one could speculate that the sensitivity of country risk to financial shocks decreases as the share of domestic currency debt that can be partially diluted through devaluation increases. Here, again, the initial financial dollarization ratio plays a crucial role.

50. Interestingly, for the case of nonfinancially dollarized Brazil, they find a positive, albeit much weaker, effect, possibly reflecting the dollarization of external debt.

51. See, among others, Ghosh et al. (1997), Broda (2000), and Levy Yeyati and Sturzenegger (2001b).

52. Levy Yeyati and Sturzenegger (2001a) suggest this explanation as one possible reason behind the slower growth rate they find for conventional and, to a lesser extent, "hard" pegs.

53. Frankel (1999), Hausmann et al. (1999), and Borensztein and Zettelmeyer (2000).

54. This confirms previous findings in Hausmann et al. (1999).

55. Idiosyncratic shocks to individual banks can usually be handled by the interbank market or directly by the central bank through the use of a limited amount of reserves. Systemic shocks, on the other hand, requires that individual banks or the central bank be able to borrow from abroad, at a time in which access to international markets is severely limited.

56. On this, see chapters 2 and 4.

57. Additional provisos of the scheme made disbursement less likely. This included a 20 percent margin call requirement, which means that in the event the value of the sovereign bonds used as collateral declined by more than 20 percent, it had to be met in cash.

58. The fact that most countries compensate for the limitations of the LLR by increasing their stock of reserves seems to suggest that private insurance may not be a readily available alternative in practice.

59. One could argue, however, that this implicit insurance is already present and will ultimately be unavoidable, and that an explicit commitment to insure countries under certain conditions may improve rather than worsen the moral hazard problem.

60. Panama, with its sequence of seventeen IMF Programs since 1973, is a case in point. On this, see Edwards (2001).

61. Note that even though in an efficient market increases in the risk premium should be perfectly offset by an *ex ante* lower expected cost of debt servicing, *ex post* a country

that honors its debt is "punished" by a higher debt spread that raises the opportunity cost of capital and the cost of holding low-yield reserve assets. In addition, the higher default risk and higher volatility of returns that characterize developing-country debt are penalized by risk-averse international investors.

62. Arguably, unlike in fully dollarized countries, central banks in financially dollarized economies still can print the domestic currency to assist the banking system, but at the cost of a sharp increase in the exchange rate and high inflation that will be proportional to the *ex ante* degree of financial dollarization. In turn, the associated devaluation may worsen the fragility of the banking sector due to balance sheet effects, adding to the cost of the bailout and detracting from the effectiveness of the LLR.

63. Note that although the crisis can be completely exogenous, it can also result from a self-fulfilling confidence crisis, which will be negatively related to the insurance coverage.

64. In the limit, a country with no foreign currency liabilities would only need reserves for exchange market interventions.

65. This is equivalent to assuming a unit income elasticity of the demand for real balances so that they grow at the same pace at the real domestic GDP.

66. Note that this figure already includes the costs of purchasing the current monetary base, which appears as the present discounted flow of income on the initial money supply. Fischer (1982) alternatively computes seignorage costs as an annual cash flow in terms of current nominal GDP, which, under the assumption of a constant currency-to-GDP ratio, would be equal to γ in the current period and $p\gamma$ in all subsequent periods. For the values of the example, this will represent a cost of 4 percent today and around 0.2 percent in all future years. See Levy Yeyati and Sturzenegger (2000) for a recent application of this approach to Latin American countries.

67. It should be noted, however, that although the loss involves a clear and non-negligible fiscal cost, its welfare effect has to be qualified in most cases to the extent that a potentially large part of it may originate in a suboptimal inflation tax, as Chang and Velasco stress in chapter 2.

68. They account for more than 80 percent of the total cost in the previous example. The number is obtained by subtracting the value of the current stock of 4 percent of GDP from the total of 23.8 percent.

69. The intermediate case, a monetary treaty, is addressed in conjunction with the first type of arrangement, unilateral dollarization.

70. This appears to have been the case in the recent dollarization process in Ecuador.

71. Note that the first two conditions are present, albeit to a lesser extent, in the decision to fix the exchange rate.

72. As Zarazaga argues, much in the way the discussion evolved in the liberalization debate, the issue of sequencing may prove to be of secondary importance, because the dollarization plan's final fate will ultimately depend on the quality and credibility of the policies in place rather than on the order in which these policies are implemented.

73. Voluntary renegotiation is certainly still an option once dollarization is in place, but massive and simultaneous renegotiations of contracts are not easy to achieve and may entail nontrivial economic costs.

74. In EMU, for example, seignorage is distributed among members according to a ratio calculated as the simple average of their population and GDP shares.

75. This convergence process involves, among other things, the harmonization of statistics, prudential norms, and tax practices. In addition, the launch of a common money market requires the linkage of national payment systems.

76. Underscoring the credibility problem is that fact that, if the union itself is to deliver credibility gains, it requires that the participating countries show a high degree of credibility. Thus, currency unions between countries that suffer long-standing credibility problems are unlikely to reap the credibility benefits. See Levy Yeyati and Sturzenegger (2000) for a discussion of this argument in the context of a common currency within Mercosur, whose member states are Argentina, Brazil, Paraguay, and Uruguay.

77. Whereas the credibility benefits from monetary integration should be clear for countries that need to build their credibility, the gains for the "anchor" country that provides the guarantee are less obvious. Many of the potential gains for Germany arising from EMU—exchange rate and capital flows stability, the building of institutions that could provide explicit bailout mechanisms—may be minor for the United States and its much smaller potential partners. A more realistic alternative advanced by Frieden (1998) suggests the role of "linkage" politics by which EMU may have helped Germany to gain European support for its foreign policy initiatives in Eastern Europe. At any rate, we should not underestimate the political aspects of a monetary unification process.

78. See Calvo and Reinhart (2000) and Levy Yeyati and Sturzenegger (2002).

References

Barro, Robert (1999). Let the Dollar Reign from Seattle to Santiago, *Wall Street Journal*, March 8, 1999.

Borensztein, Eduardo, and Jeronim Zettelmeyer (2000). Does the Exchange Rate Regime Make a Difference?, mimeo, IMF.

Broda, Christian (2000). Terms of Trade and Exchange Rate Regimes in Developing Countries, mimeo, Massachusetts Institute of Technology.

Burnside, Craig, Martin Eichenbaum, and Sergio Rebelo (1999). Hedging and Financial Fragility in Fixed Exchange Rate Regimes, NBER Working Paper, No. 7143.

Calvo, Guillermo (1999a). On Dollarization, mimeo, University of Maryland, College Park.

——— (1999b). Fixed versus Flexible Exchange Rates: Preliminaries of a Turn-of-Millennium Rematch, mimeo, University of Maryland.

——— (2000a). The Case for Hard Pegs in the Brave New World of Global Finance, mimeo, University of Maryland.

——— (2000b). Testimony on Dollarization, mimeo, University of Maryland.

Calvo, Guillermo, and Pablo Guidotti (1990). Credibility and Nominal Debt: Exploring the Role of Maturity in Managing Inflation. IMF Working paper, WP/89/73.

Calvo, Guillermo, and Carmen Reinhart (2000). Fear of Floating, NBER Working Paper, No. 7993.

Calvo, Guillermo, and Carlos Vegh (1992). Currency Substitution in Developing Countries: An Introduction. *Revista de Análisis Económico* 7, pp. 3–28.

――― (1997). From Currency Substitution to Dollarization and Beyond: Analytical and Policy Issues, in Guillermo Calvo, *Essays on Money, Inflation and Output*. Cambridge, MA: MIT Press.

Chang, Roberto, and Andrés Velasco (2000). Exchange Rate Policy for Developing Countries, American Economic Review 90, pp. 71–75.

De Grauwe, P. (1994). *The Economics of Monetary Integration*. Oxford: Oxford University Press.

Domac, Ilker, and M. Soledad Martinez Peria (2000). Banking Crises and Exchange Rate Regimes: Is There a Link? World Bank Policy Research Working Paper, No. 2489.

Dornbusch, Rudiger (1976). Expectations and Exchange Rate Dynamics, *Journal of Political Economy* 84, pp. 1161–1176.

Edwards, Sebastián (2001). Dollarization Myths and Realities, mimeo, University of California.

Eichengreen, Barry (1994). *International Monetary Arrangements for the 21st Century*. Washington, DC: The Brookings Institution.

Fatás, Antonio, and Andrew Rose (2001). Do Monetary Handcuffs Restrain Leviathan? Fiscal Policy in Extreme Exchange Rate Regimes, *IMF Staff Papers* 47, pp. 40–61.

Fischer, Stanley (1982). Seigniorage and the Case for a National Money, *Journal of Political Economy* 90 (April), pp. 295-313.

――― (2001). Exchange Rate Regimes: Is the Bipolar View Correct? *Journal of Economic Perspectives* 15, pp. 3–24.

Fleming, Marcus (1962). Domestic Financial Policies under Fixed and under Floating Exchange Rates, IMF Staff Papers 9, pp. 369–379.

Frankel, Jellrey (1999). No Single Currency Regime is Right for All Countries or at All Times, NBER Working Paper, No. 7338.

Frankel, Jeffrey, and Andrew Rose (2000). Estimating the Effect of Currency Unions on Trade and Output, NBER Working Paper, No. 7857.

Frieden, Jeffry (1998). The Political Economy of European Exchange Rates: An Empirical Assessment. Mimeo. Harvard University.

Ghosh, A., A. M. Gulde, J. Ostry, and H. Wolf (1997). Does the Nominal Exchange Rate Regime Matter? NBER Working Paper, No. 5874.

Ghosh, A., Anne-Marie Gulde, and Holger C. Wolf (1998). Currency Boards: The Ultimate Fix? International Monetary Fund Working Paper, No. 98/8.

Giovannini, Alberto, and Bart Turtleboom (1994). Currency Substitution, in Frederick van der Ploeg, ed. *Handbook of International Macroeconomics*. Cambridge, MA: Blackwell Publishers, pp. 39–436.

Goldfajn, Ilan, and Gino Olivares (2000). Full Dollarization: the Case of Panama, mimeo, The World Bank.

Guidotti, Pablo, and Carlos Rodriguez (1992). Dollarization in Latin America: Gresham's Law in Reverse? IMF Staff Papers, Washington: International Monetary Fund, Vol. 39, pp. 518–544.

Hausmann, Ricardo (1999). Should There Be Five Currencies or One Hundred and Five? *Foreign Policy*, Fall.

Hausmann, Ricardo, Carmen Pagés-Serra, Michael Gavin, Michael Stein, and H. Ernesto (1999). Financial Turmoil and Choice of Exchange Rate Regime, Research Department, Inter-American Development Bank Working Paper, No. 400, January 1999.

Ize, Alain, and Eduardo Levy-Yeyati (2002). Financial Dollarization, forthcoming, *Journal of International Economics*.

Kenen, P. (1969). The Theory of Optimal Currency Areas: An Eclectic View, in R. Mundell and Swoboda, eds. *Monetary Problems of the International Economy*.

Levy Yeyati, Eduardo, and Federico Sturzenegger (2000). Is EMU a Blueprint for Mercosur? *Cuadernos de Economía* 37, Vol. 110, pp. 63–99.

——— (2001a). Exchange Rate Regimes and Economic Performance, IMF Staff Papers, Vol. 47, pp. 62–98.

——— (2001b). To Float or to Trail: Evidence on the Impact of Exchange Rate Regimes, CIF Working Paper, No. 01/2001, Universidad Torcuato Di Tella, Buenos Aires, available at ⟨www.utdt.edu/~ely⟩.

——— (2002). Classifying Exchange Rate Regimes: Deeds vs. Words. Mimeo. Universidad Torcuato Di Tella, Buenos Aires, available at ⟨www.utdt.edu/~fsturzen⟩.

McKinnon, Ronald (1963). Optimal Currency Areas, *American Economic Review* 53, pp. 717–725.

Mundell, Robert (1961). A Theory of Optimum Currency Areas, *American Economic Review* 51, pp. 657–665.

——— (1963). Capital Mobility and Stabilization Policy under Fixed and Flexible Exchange Rates, *Canadian Journal of Economics and Political Science* 29, pp. 475–485.

——— (1964). A Reply: Capital Mobility and Size, *Canadian Journal of Economics and Political Science* 30, pp. 421–431.

Persson, Torsten (2001). Currency unions and trade: How large is the treatment effect? *Economic Policy* 33, 433–448.

Rose, Andrew (2000). One Money, One Market? The Effects of Common Currencies on International Trade, *Economic Policy* 15, No. 30.

Sahay, Ratna, and Carlos Vegh (1997). Dollarization in Transition Economies: Evidence and Policy Implications, in Paul Mizen and Eric J. Pentecost, ed., *The Macroeconomics of International Currencies, Theory, Policy and Evidence*. Brookfield, VT: Edward Elgar, 1996.

Savastano, Miguel A. (1996). Dollarization in Latin America: Recent Evidence and Some Policy Issues, IMF Working Paper, 96/4, Washington: International Monetary Fund, January 1996.

Summers, Lawrence (2000). International Financial Crises: Causes, Prevention and Cures, *American Economic Review, Papers and Proceedings*, Vol. 90, No. 2.

Thomas, L. R. (1985). Portfolio Theory and Currency Substitution, *Journal of Money, Credit, and Banking* 17, pp. 347–357.

World Bank (2000). World Development Indicators.

2   Dollarization: Analytical Issues

Roberto Chang and Andrés Velasco

2.1   Introduction

Dollarization would involve benefits as well as costs for a developing country. The identification of those costs and benefits, as well as the measurement of their relative importance, is the subject of a currently heated debate. To place the arguments in perspective and aid in the discussion, this chapter presents and summarizes main analytical considerations related to dollarization.

The usefulness of theory in evaluating dollarization cannot be overemphasized. There are very few observed cases of dollarization, and hence history provides little guidance on its consequences. One must then resort to theoretical analysis for conjectures about how dollarization may work. Unfortunately, received theory has some important gaps, some of which will become apparent in the text that follows. However, there are also several points of agreement; we shall emphasize those, as well as some observations that have been relatively ignored in the current debate.

Our discussion is organized around a very simple model of a small open economy with a government that must decide whether to dollarize. We start by discussing the implications of dollarization for macroeconomic policy; much of the current debate has been concerned with precisely this issue. In our framework we show that as emphasized in the literature, dollarization would prevent the implementation of an optimal policy. This is because the exchange rate would no longer serve as an adjustment tool and, in this respect, dollarization resembles an irrevocably fixed exchange rate system. However, dollarization implies a further loss, namely, that the stock of domestic base money would have to be retired from circulation and exchanged for dollars. In other words, the so-called (stock) seignorage would accrue to the U.S. Federal Reserve. The welfare costs of dollarization, relative to the optimal policy, are due to both the fixity of exchange rates and the loss of seignorage. The magnitude of the costs are shown to depend on the variability of the exogenous shocks hitting the economy, a finding reminiscent of Mundell's (1961) *optimal currency area* approach.

The costs just identified are only relevant if the government, in fact, implements an optimal policy. But this may not be the case, in particular if the government is not able to commit, at the beginning of time, to date-state contingent policies. In that case, analysis of policy determination, and hence the cost of dollarization, must take into account the possibility of *time inconsistency* or *lack of credibility* and how dollarization may help ameliorate those problems.

We discuss the possibility that dollarization may act as a commitment device and thus reduce the distortion associated with policy incredibility. It follows from the discussion, however, that whether dollarization is desirable under such circumstances is, at the end, an empirical matter. Dollarization buys credibility at the expense of a suboptimal response to shocks, and may or may not be worth it.

We also emphasize that when there is a policy credibility problem, the interpretation of the seignorage lost with dollarization is delicate. In particular, the measured dollar loss of seignorage may be associated with an increase in social welfare. The implication is that computed seignorage losses can only be unambiguously interpreted as "real losses" to the economy if policy credibility problems are assumed away, a point that seemes to have been missed in the debate. A similar caveat applies, although perhaps not as starkly, to the Mundellian criteria.

The possibility of financial panics and exchange rate crises has provided a strong impetus to calls for dollarization. Hence we discuss the role of dollarization in generating or preventing crises within our simple model. We show that dollarization would prevent the domestic central bank from acting as an LLR (*lender of last resort*), which, as in Chang and Velasco (2000b, 2000c), may exacerbate financial fragility and the possibility of crises. However, we also argue that there are solutions to that problem, such as Argentina's policy of contracting contingent lines of credit with foreign banks, that may be inexpensive.

In addition to analyzing the LLR issue, we tackle the contention that dollarization can be hoped to reduce the severity of the shocks hitting the economy or reduce the cost of foreign credit. We argue that both contentions are unwarranted and, in fact, we describe examples in which exactly the opposite would be true. In particular, if dollarization indeed increased the possibility of crises relative to a domestic currency regime, rational expectations imply that country risk would increase, reflecting a compensation to foreign creditors for defaults during crises.

Finally, we identify some putative consequences of dollarization that, at least so far, resist an analytical treatment. An example is the contention that dollarization would reduce market incompleteness.

The rest of this chapter is organized as follows. Section 2.2 presents the economic environment. Section 2.3 discusses optimal macroeconomic policy and the effect dollarization would have on it. The effects of dollarization on the credibility of government policy are analyzed in section 2.4. Section 2.5 discusses how dollarization affects the availability of a lender of last resort. Section 2.6 considers a number of issues not included in our formal discussion. Section 2.7 concludes the chapter.

2.2   The Economic Environment

In this section we describe the model that will serve as the focal point of our discussion. We should emphasize that in the following text we impose a number of exceedingly strong and seemingly ad hoc assumptions. However, this is only for expositional purposes and because we hope that, in this way, our basic points will be most transparent. Indeed, most of the assumptions can be substantially relaxed, and hence our results can be extended to much more realistic setups.

Consider a small *home* economy that is part of a much larger world and lasts for only two periods, indexed by $t = 1, 2$.[1] In each period there is a single, perishable consumption good, which is fully traded and has a fixed price, normalized to one, in terms of a world currency (the *dollar*).

The home economy is inhabited by a large number of identical individuals and a government. The representative agent is endowed with some amount $e > 0$ of the consumption good in period 1. In period 2 he has no endowment of goods, but he can produce l units of consumption by working l hours, where $0 \leq l \leq 1$.

The representative individual enjoys consumption and dislikes labor effort. In addition, he is assumed to derive utility from holding the currency that circulates in the home economy. *Which* currency circulates at home is a government decision. Under a *dollarization* plan, that currency is the dollar. However, the government may also impose the use of a domestic currency, called the *peso*, which can be costlessly created and destroyed by a domestic central bank.

For simplicity, we assume that home residents can only save by holding currency. Hence the preferences of the representative agent are given by

$$u(c_1) + v(m_1) + E[c_2 + v(m_2) - H(l)] \qquad (2.1)$$

where $E[.]$ is the expectation operator; u, v, and H are continuously differentiable, strictly increasing, and strictly concave functions; c_t denotes consumption in period t; and m_t is the real value of currency holdings at the end of period t. Note that under dollarization, m_t denotes a holding of dollars, whereas in a domestic currency regime $m_t = M_t/P_t$, where M_t denotes the holding of pesos and P_t is the peso price of consumption. In the latter case, and because the Law of One Price holds, P_t must also equal the *exchange rate*, the price of dollars in terms of pesos.

The presence of the expectation operator $E[.]$ in utility function (2.1) allows for the inclusion of uncertainty in the model. To be concrete, we shall assume that one of S possible states is realized in period 2. The realization of one of these states determines a number of macroeconomic variables, two of which are of concern to the representative agent: the rate of a tax on labor income and, in a peso regime, the exchange rate.

All of these assumptions imply that under dollarization, the budget constraints of the representative agent can be written as

$$c_1 + m_1 \leq e \qquad (2.2)$$

$$m_{2s} + c_{2s} \leq (1 - \tau_s)l_s + m_1, \quad s = 1, 2, \ldots, S \qquad (2.3)$$

where τ denotes the tax rate in labor income and, in constraint 2.3 and the rest of this chapter, a subscript s refers to a value that is contingent on the realization of state s.

In contrast, the budget constraints in a regime of domestic currency are given by

$$P_1 c_1 + M_1 \leq P_1 e \qquad (2.4)$$

$$M_{2s} + P_{2s}c_{2s} \leq (1 - \tau_s)P_{2s}c_{2s} + M_1, \quad \text{for all } s \qquad (2.5)$$

However, note that after dividing both sides by P_1, inequality 2.4 reduces to inequality 2.2. Also, constraint 2.5 can be rewritten as

$$m_{2s} + c_{2s} \leq (1 - \tau_s)l_s + m_1(1 - \pi_s) \tag{2.6}$$

which is the same as constraint 2.3, except for the presence of the term $(1 - \pi_s) = P_1/P_{2s}$. The term $\pi_s = (P_{2s} - P_1)/P_{2s}$ reflects the "inflation tax" in state s and is obviously absent in constraint 2.3, because the dollar price of consumption is assumed to be constant.

Now we turn to the specification of government finance. The home government inherits a debt of d dollars to foreigners, which, for the time being, is assumed to be due for repayment at the end of period 2. At that time, the government will have some additional and exogenous need of g_s units of consumption, which is contingent on the state of nature; this is the only source of exogenous uncertainty that we consider.

In order to finance its expenditures, the government has two potential sources of revenue: the proceeds from the labor tax and, in a peso regime, the revenue from creating pesos, or seignorage. In the latter case, we assume that the seignorage collected in period 1 can be saved in the world market at a zero interest rate. More precisely, if in a peso regime the government issues M_1^* pesos in period 1, it then collects $M_1^*/P_1 = m_1^*$ units of consumption, worth m_1^* dollars, that can be effectively stored until period 2.

In equilibrium, the supply of pesos M_t^* must equal the demand M_t. It follows that in a peso regime, the government's budget constraint in period 2 can be written as

$$P_{2s}(g_s + d) \leq \tau_s P_{2s}l_s + (M_{2s} - M_1) + P_{2s}m_1$$

or, after dividing by P_{2s} and rearranging,

$$g_s + d \leq \tau_s l_s + m_{2s} + \pi_s m_1 \tag{2.7}$$

The interpretation is obvious: the final government revenue requirements, given by the LHS (left-hand-side), must be met by labor taxes $(\tau_s l_s)$ or by seignorage. Seignorage is, in turn, the sum of a *flow* inflation tax $(\pi_s m_1)$ plus a *stock* component, m_{2s}, as emphasized in Fischer (1982).

Under dollarization, in contrast, there is no peso creation, and the government flow constraint is simply

$$g_s + d \leq \tau_s l_s \tag{2.8}$$

In other words, dollarization implies that the government loses seignorage as a source of real revenue. But the significance of the seignorage loss cannot be evaluated independently of the determination of government policy. This is because the seignorage lost, $m_{2s} + \pi_s m_1$, depends on policy, both through the rate of the inflation tax and through the effect of policy on peso demand. This is a straightforward but important observation to which we shall return.

This completes the description of the economic environment. Of the model's assumptions, the way we have described the difference between a dollarized regime and a peso regime deserves special comment. Imposing that the government can choose between one or the other is crude but seems to be reasonable, given historical experience. But we have gone beyond that by imposing that dollars and pesos enter in exactly the same way in the representative agent's utility function, v. Our justification is that one typically thinks of v as capturing the extent of the ignorance regarding transactions costs, payments arrangements, and the like, which are reduced with the use of a fiat currency. Naturally, one may conjecture that if the relevant fiat currency changes, v may itself change. However, existing monetary theory provides essentially no guidance on how v would change with dollarization. And, in the dollarization debate some have indeed argued that dollars would provide for a "better" currency than existing national currencies, whereas others have argued exactly the opposite.[2] We prefer to be agnostic here. Given the absence of better microfoundations, it is probably best to impose an assumption that does not bias the desirability of dollarization in one way or another.

2.3   Dollarization and Optimal Policies

As already emphasized, the outcomes of the model, and how they are affected by dollarization, depend on government policy and how it is chosen. Even if, as we shall assume, the government is benevolent and chooses policy to maximize the welfare of its representative citizen, the model yields different outcomes according to when and how strongly the government can commit to its decisions. In this section, we assume that the government commits perfectly to the policies it chooses at the beginning of time. In this ideal and unrealistic situation, dollarization implies a number of costs, to which we now turn.

Consider first the situation with a national currency. Given perfect commitment, the government's problem is to choose a policy and an associated macroeconomic allocation in order to maximize the domestic agent's expected welfare, subject to the constraints imposed by competitive equilibrium. The latter include not only the government budget constraint but also the optimality conditions for the representative agent, which are summarized by the first order conditions:[3]

$$u'(e - m_1) = v'(m_1) + E[(1 - \pi)] \tag{2.9}$$

$$H'(l_s) = 1 - \tau_s \tag{2.10}$$

$$v'(m_{2s}) = 1 \tag{2.11}$$

Formally, then, the government's problem (sometimes called the *Ramsey problem*, or *rule*) is to choose a policy, that is, a contingent set of labor tax rates τ_s and inflation tax rates π_s, and an aggregate allocation summarized by m_1, m_{2s}, and l_s, in order to maximize the utility function 2.1 subject to constraints 2.7 and 2.9–2.11.

Assuming an interior solution, optimal policy must satisfy the following version of the Ramsey rule:

$$\frac{1 - H'(l_s)}{1 - H'(l_s) - l_s H''(l_s)}$$

$$= \frac{1 - [v'(m_1) - u'(e - m_1)]}{1 - [v'(m_1) - u'(e - m_1)] + m_1[u''(e - m_1) + v''(m_1)]} \tag{2.12}$$

for $s = 1, \ldots, S$.

The Ramsey rule has an intuitive interpretation. Each numerator is the distortionary effect of a tax. If, for example, the labor tax rate were zero in state s, labor supply would satisfy $H'(l_s) = 1$. Hence the difference $1 - H'(l_s)$ is a measure of the distortion caused by τ_s. In turn, each denominator can be shown to be proportional to the revenue raised by a marginal increase in the respective tax rate. So the Ramsey rule equalizes the marginal distortion of each tax, relative to revenue raised.

There are a number of important implications for our discussion. As long as the government has no access to a lump sum tax, optimal policy requires recourse to the inflation tax to at least some degree. This is a very general conclusion known at least since Phelps (1973) and implies that, in our model, it is in general optimal for the exchange rate to change in a forecastable way over time.

In fact, in the context of the present model, there is a much stronger implication. Because equation 2.12 must apply to *all* states, and the RHS (right-hand-side) is not state contingent, then l_s cannot be state contingent and, by equation 2.10, τ_{2s} cannot either. Hence, the revenue from labor taxation must be independent of the state of nature and, consequently, any unexpected shock to the government revenue needs is best financed via a devaluation. This result, developed in a much more general model by Calvo and Guidotti (1993), is a consequence of the fact that only *anticipated* devaluation has distortionary effects: equation 2.9 implies that only expected inflation affects peso demand decisions. But *ex post*, that is, once m_1 is determined, unanticipated inflation acts as a lump sum tax. Hence, as long as possible, any unanticipated government need should be met by surprise inflation.

As inflation and devaluation coincide in this simple model, the implication for the exchange rate regime is clear. An optimal policy calls for exchange rates highly sensitive to exogenous shocks to the environment, in this case shocks to g. Naturally, this means that curbing the needed flexibility would imply a welfare loss.

One set of restrictions is given by a regime of *fixed* exchange rates. Suppose that the government solves the same problem as before but is commited to keeping the exchange rate fixed between periods. That restriction obviously requires that $P_1 = P_{2s}$, or that $\pi_s = 0$, for all s. The resulting government's problem is the same as the Ramsey problem except for this additional constraint, and social welfare must fall in general. The loss would reflect the elimination of both anticipated inflation, as predicted by Phelps (1973), and unanticipated inflation, as implied by Calvo and Guidotti (1993).

Under fixed exchange rates, there is no *flow* seignorage: the term $\pi_s m_1$ in the government budget constraint 2.7 is zero. However, because $m_2 > 0$ and the government creates pesos at no cost, the government still collects the stock seignorage revenue given by m_2 in constraint 2.7. This is because, even if there is no inflation, the government creates pesos worth m_1 dollars in the first period and $(m_2 - m_1)$ dollars in the second period.

The effects of a switch to dollarization are now easy to trace. In this model, dollarization has two important effects. The first is that inflation must be zero as in the rest of the world: hence there is no flow seignorage. The implications of this effect are exactly the same as imposing fixed exchange rates. The second effect is that the government no longer collects the stock seignorage: the budget constraint of the government is given by equation 2.8, which excludes m_2.

The government policy problem under dollarization is straightforward to tackle directly, but it is easy and illuminating to analyze it in a slightly different way. Note that the real demand for money in the last period, under either a peso regime or a dollarized regime, is given by equation 2.11, and hence m_{2s} must equal some noncontingent quantity $\hat{m}_2$, for all s. Thus, rewrite the budget constraint in the dollarized regime as

$$g_s + d + \hat{m}_2 = \hat{g}_s + d = \hat{m}_2 + \tau_s l_s$$

where $\hat{g}_s = g_s + \hat{m}_2$. Then a moment's thought reveals that the government's problem is the same as in a peso regime with fixed exchange rates, except that the government revenue needs are increased from g_s to $\hat{g}_s$, that is, by the amount of stock seignorage.

Hence, under perfect government commitment, dollarization implies a further welfare loss relative to a peso regime with fixed exchange rates. Such a cost is due to the loss of stock seignorage.

Given our analysis, it is straightforward to calculate the dollar value of the seignorage that would be colected in a peso regime, either under the optimal policy or fixed exchange rates. Because seignorage is zero with dollarization, such a quantity would be a measure of the dollar cost of dollarization in terms of lost seignorage. But it may be more meaningful to derive an expression for the seignorage cost in terms of *welfare*.

Starting from a dollarized economy, suppose that the government were able to print and market a quantity of pesos equal to a unit worth of consumption. As we have discussed, this is equivalent, in welfare terms, to a decrease of one unit in g_s in all states, whose effect on expected utility is

$$E\left[\frac{1 - H'(l_2^*)}{1 - H'(l_2^*) - l_2^* H''(l_2^*)}\right]$$

where l_2^* denotes the (state contingent) labor effort required to finance government expenditures under dollarization (that is, for each s, l_2^* solves constraints 2.8 and 2.10). In words, the (marginal) welfare cost associated with the stock seignorage lost under dollarization is equal to the expected distortionary effect of the required labor taxes. The implication is that the measured loss of seignorage due to dollarization indeed reflects a welfare cost for the domestic economy.

More generally, it is clear that dollarization imposes a cost to the domestic economy. The extent of these costs depends on the parameters of the model. In particular, it should be obvious that the cost increases with the variability of the government revenue needs. In this sense, our analysis is reminiscent of the *optimal currency area arguments* first proposed by Mundell (1961). Mundell focused on the costs of irrevocably fixing the exchange rate between two countries when nominal rigidities are present. He pointed out that such costs would be larger the less correlated were the economic shocks hitting the two economies. This is, loosely speaking, because exchange rate changes are more valuable as adjustment tools if the fundamentals of the two different countries are less synchronized.

Although our analysis yields a similar conclusion, it departs from Mundell's in several ways. Mundell emphasized the role of nominal rigidities in the analysis, whereas here we have emphasized public finance aspects. The two perspectives are clearly complementary. Also, Mundell focused on the distinction between flexible and fixed exchange rates without discussing the choice of currencies. Our analysis highlights that there is a clear difference between fixed exchange rates and dollarization: stock seignorage is lost in the latter but not in the former.

We derived the results of this section under the maintained assumption that the government has perfect commitment power. If such an assumption is dropped, our results need to be severely qualified, as we shall now see.

2.4   Dollarization and Policy Credibility

The assumption that the government commits once and for all to a policy choice is obviously unrealistic. In practice, governments make policy choices over time, although they may promise that they will take some particular actions in the future. The sequential nature of policymaking then leads to the possibility that the government's promises may not be believed. This may be the case because when the time comes the government's incentives may have changed so as to make it profitable to renege. This problem was first recognized by Kydland and Prescott (1977) and Calvo (1978), and has been since the subject of a huge literature on time inconsistency, credibility, and commitment.

To illustrate the time inconsistency problem with our model, return to the case of a peso regime with flexible exchange rates and assume that the government can change policy in period 2, just after g_s has been realized. At that point, c_1 has already been consumed, and m_1 is given by previous decisions. Hence, the government's problem is effectively to choose the labor tax rate τ_s and a devaluation rate in order to maximize

$$c_{2s} + v(m_{2s}) - H(l_s)$$

subject to its budget constraint 2.7 and the consumer's optimality conditions 2.10 and 2.11. Crucially, equation 2.9 is irrelevant at this point, although it determined the choice m_1 in the *previous* period.

For simplicity, assume that τ_s must belong to the unit interval. The analysis is easy once it is noted that because m_1 is given by history, the inflation tax involves no further distortion. On the other hand, the labor tax is associated with deadweight losses. It follows that the inflation tax should be used as much as possible; the government's choice will be either

$$\tau_s = 0 \quad \text{and} \quad \pi_s m_1 = g_s + d - \hat{m}_2 \qquad (2.13)$$

or

$$\pi_s = 1 \quad \text{and} \quad g_s + d - m_1 - \hat{m}_2 = \tau_s l_s \qquad (2.14)$$

where l_s is determined by equation 2.10 and $\hat{m}_2$ by equation 2.11.

Clearly, this solution departs from the Ramsey rule. This is clear if condition 2.13 holds, that is, if the revenue from the inflation tax is enough by itself to cover the government needs in state s. In that case, labor taxes will be zero if the government can reoptimize in period 2, but the Ramsey rule and, therefore, the optimal policy under commitment stipulate that labor taxes be positive in all states. Obviously, the departure from the optimal policy is even greater if equation 2.14 holds, as the inflation rate is infinite. This is interpretable as a total repudiation of the pesos issued in period 1.

Assuming rational expectations, the representative agent will understand that in the absence of government commitment, the inflation tax in period 2 will be given by conditions 2.13–2.14 no matter what the government announces in the first period. And, accordingly, this will affect period 1 money demand, as given by equation 2.9. Clearly, m_1 will be smaller than under commitment, because inflationary revenues must be larger. But then π_s must be even larger than if m_1 had been chosen on the basis of expectations that the optimal policy would be followed. The outcome will be given by the simultaneous solution of the money demand equation 2.9 and the government's optimality conditions 2.13–2.14. This, of course, tends to lead to a particularly bad outcome. The worst outcome happens if condition 2.14 holds for all s. Then, money demand in period 1 satisfies $u'(e - m_1) = v'(m_1)$. If this implies a small m_1, the revenue from the labor tax must be relatively large. The public's anticipation of hyperinflation then may reduce money demand to such an extent that not only does the hyperinflation happens, but also distortionary labor taxation must increase relative to the commitment case.

Note that the government would like to make the public believe that it will implement the Ramsey policy. However, the absence of commitment implies that any announcement to that effect will be incredible. In this sense, the time inconsistency problem is one possible way to model a government with a "credibility problem."

This perspective may also help understand institutions and rules that one observes in practice: they may be designed to alleviate a government's credibility problem or, in our context, act as commitment devices. The general idea is that although the government may not be able to commit to complicated date and state contingent Ramsey policies, it may commit to simpler rules such as zero inflation or pegged exchange rates.

To illustrate, suppose the government can commit to a fixed exchange rate or, in our context, to a fixed price level. Such a commitment means that $\pi_s = 0$, for all s. Then, the money demand equation 2.9, with $\pi = 0$, determines m_1. In addition, even if the government is able to reoptimize in period 2, the labor tax rate in period s is determined by constraint 2.7, with $\pi_s = 0$, and equations 2.10 and 2.11. But these are the exact conditions that determine the outcome of the commitment case with fixed exchange rates. In other words, if the government can indeed make an irrevocable commitment to fixing the exchange rate, the credibility problem ceases to be relevant.

However, as we saw in the preceding subsection, fixing the exchange rate involves a welfare loss relative to the Ramsey policy. So, in the absence of commitment, expected welfare under fixed exchange rates may or may not improve. There is a trade-off between credibility and flexibility, and the better choice depends on model parameters.

When available, the option to dollarize the economy may be valuable if even a limited commitment to fixed exchange rates is impossible. This may be the case, for instance, if the government in period 1 is able to promise not to devalue, but only if it stays in power. If there is a positive probability that the government will be replaced in period 2, and even if the new government is itself benevolent, a credibility problem remains. In contrast, by dollarizing the economy, the period-1 government in effect would change the taxation technology so as to take away the inflation tax from any successor.

Clearly, if the economy is dollarized, the credibility problem goes away, and the outcome is the same as that of a dollarized economy under commitment. This means that dollarization involves its own costs. In particular, stock seignorage is lost; this means that dollarization may or may not be preferable to keeping a national currency, even if the latter option involves living with a policy credibility problem.

Our analysis thus yields several implications that are relevant for the current debate on dollarization. The first is that as we have just established, even if a government suffers from poor credibility, and even if dollarization would improve credibility, it is not necessarily the case that dollarization is desirable. Whether dollarization is preferable to flexible rates in such a situation has to be demonstrated empirically.

A second noteworthy implication concerns the interpretation of the seignorage that would be lost with dollarization. In a peso regime, and in the absence of commitment, one would observe that the government is collecting a nonzero seignorage revenue. That revenue, which is straightforward to calculate, would be lost with dollarization. However, this would not mean that the loss of seignorage, however big, is costly for the economy. Indeed, it would be quite possible for expected welfare to *improve* with dollarization, in which case the elimination of seignorage would be *good* for the economy.

The lesson is that the numerous calculations of the seignorage that would be lost with dollarization are meaningful only in conjunction with some explicit or implicit assumption about the policymaking process and, in particular, of the credibility problem that may be affecting policy. Only in the absence of such credibility problems one can assert unambiguously that the loss of seignorage would, in fact, be a loss. If there is a credibility problem, the interpretation is much more problematic and, as we have argued, the loss of seignorage may in fact be beneficial in welfare terms. This point seems to have been missed by even advocates of dollarization, which in general concede that the loss of seignorage should be counted as one price to pay. At the same time, this observation has a bearing on the debate about how much seignorage should be "rebated" by the U.S. Federal Reserve to a dollarizing country. For, if eliminating seignorage is already good for that country's residents, why should the U.S. taxpayers give them back the value of seignorage in addition?

A similar observation applies to optimal currency area arguments. Under commitment, an increase in the variability of exogenous shocks unambiguously raises the value of flexibility and increases the welfare loss associated with dollarization. However, this is not necessarily the case in the absence of commitment: because the equilibrium policy in a peso regime is suboptimal, there is no presumption that increased uncertainty will raise its value relative to that of dollarization. Hence, the calculation of Mundellian criteria to evaluate the welfare cost of dollarization requires a further justification unless one assumes away policy credibility problems.[4]

We close this subsection with three remarks. First, once the economy is dollarized, there would remain a strong incentive for the government to reintroduce a national currency. Consider again the possibility that the original government is replaced by a new one in period 2. Even if the first government had dollarized the economy, the new government would benefit from reintroducing the peso and collect the stock seignorage, $\hat{m}_2$. Although a more sophisticated analysis of a possible "dedollarization" would require a model with more periods, it should be noted that it is an open problem in the absence of policy commitments and that there is a temptation to go back that can be measured by the stock of domestic base money (Fischer 1982).

Second, and more generally, the credibility case for dollarization takes it for granted that dollarization is available as a commitment device. But the validity of such an assumption is not obvious, so it is desirable to ask how dollarization may come to enjoy such a special status.

Third, it must be noted that there may be other solutions to the policy credibility problem that do not involve fixed exchange rates, dollarization, and the like. Particularly, if the economy and its government are both long lived, the government's temptation to depart from Ramsey policies may be tempered by the adverse effect of the deviation on the public's expectations about future policies. This implies that the Ramsey outcome may be self-sustaining as an equilibrium, even if the government must choose its actions sequentially (Barro and Gordon 1983).

2.5   Dollarization and the Lender of Last Resort

The recent crises in emerging markets have underscored a crucial question: What is the role of exchange rate policy in the generation or prevention of those crises? Arguably, it is this issue that has provided the main impetus for dollarization proposals in developing countries. And, paradoxically, consideration of the same question has led to calls for the exact opposite: flexible exchange rates.

The debate has been influenced by some prominent aspects of observed crises. In them, the financial system, and particularly domestic banks, played a key role. Exchange rate pegs often collapsed as the central bank was attempting to bail out the domestic financial system in the midst of a panic.[5] The panic was possible, in turn, because the countries that went into crises were in a state of *international illiquidity:* their short-term potential liabilities, measured in international currency, clearly exceeded the value of the assets they could have access to on short notice.[6]

In this context, it has been argued that dollarization would make crises more likely by preventing the domestic central bank from acting as a domestic *lender of last resort* (LLR). Loosely speaking, an LLR is an institution that stands ready to provide credit to banks in the event that they experience a sudden demand for liquidity, as when bank runs occur. Such an institution is crucial in a system of banks with fractional reserves, in order to reassure bank depositors and short-term creditors that their claims on the banks will always be honored if they attempt to liquidate them. This may help prevent confidence crises and associated bank runs.

In most countries, the role of the LLR has traditionally been played by central banks. This role is natural because the central bank can create credit quickly and at a negligible cost simply by issuing domestic currency. But the ability to print currency would disappear under dollarization, and hence the central bank would no longer be able to serve as the LLR.

Bringing full justice to this issue would require a proper modeling of financial institutions, as in Chang and Velasco (2000b). However, a relatively minor amendment of our model here hopefully suffices to give a flavor of the argument, as well as help evaluating its significance.

So far the debt, d, of the government has played a negligible role, and in fact we have treated it just as another revenue requirement due at the end of period 2. Let us suppose now that the debt, d, is of short maturity, in the sense that it is due for repayment at the *beginning* of period 2, after g_s is realized but before markets open.

To be concrete, assume that d is owed by the home government to a continuum of identical foreigners. If the continuum is assumed to have measure one, the representative creditor is owed d dollars at the beginning of period 2. The problem is that at that time, the government may not have d dollars to repay its obligations that are due. The only way the government may cope with early requests for repayments is by printing pesos.

Let us suppose that each foreigner decides, simultaneously, whether or not to demand repayment of his or her share. If the foreigner does not demand repayment, that share is rolled over until the end of the period with no interest. But if repayment is demanded, the individual is entitled to early repayment from the government.

Finally, we assume that early withdrawals are costly for the government: the government's revenue needs at the end of the period increase with early repayments. In particular, if all creditors demand early repayment, the revenue needs change from g_s to $g_s + \chi$, for some $\chi > 0$.

We are ready to analyze the outcomes of alternative exchange rate regimes. For simplicity, suppose that the government has perfect commitment power, and consider *fixed* exchange rates. In particular, for each state s, the government budget constraint 2.7 (with $\pi_s = 0$) holds; note that d still denotes the initial debt, but now it is interpreted as a *short-term* debt. This implies that if all creditors agree to roll over their debt holdings, it is individually optimal for each of them to do so. This is because if all of the debt is rolled over, the government will have enough resources to honor it in full. Hence, each creditor is guaranteed that his or her debt will be repaid if rolled over. In other words, it is an equilibrium outcome for the creditors not to *run*.

However, suppose that also

$$T + \hat{m}_2 < g_s + d + \chi \tag{2.15}$$

where T denotes the maximum revenue from labor taxes (that is, the maximum value of $\tau_s l_s$ subject to equation 2.10). Then, if all creditors panic and demand early repayment, there is no feasible combination of labor taxation and money creation that allows the government to both meet its revenue requirements and its debt obligations. Under plausible auxiliary assumptions,[7] there will be default on the foreign debt, which makes it optimal for the foreign creditors to demand early repayment. In other words, a panic is *also* an equilibrium.

The commitment to a fixed exchange rate is at least partly to blame for the possibility of runs. To see this, assume that, in addition,

$$g_s + d + \chi < T + \hat{m}_2 + m_1 \tag{2.16}$$

Then, *if* the commitment to a fixed rate is dropped, there is a government policy such that a run cannot take place in any equilibrium. Suppose that all foreign creditors demand early repayment. Then the government can offer to cancel its debt by paying $L = P_{2s}d$ pesos to each creditor, where P_{2s} is the exchange rate (and the price level) that is (rationally) anticipated to prevail at the end of period 2. If so, each lender would be happy to take the L pesos as repayment of his or her claim, in anticipation of being able to exchange them for d dollars before the end of the day. Alternatively, it can be assumed that the government prints L pesos to purchase consumption goods from home agents and then sells the consumption goods for the d dollars it needs.

It can be now checked that the condition 2.16 guarantees that there is a labor tax rate, a final supply of pesos, and a price P_{2s} such that the government will also be able to finance its final revenue requirement, $g_s + \chi$, with a combination of labor taxes and money issue. But then, there is no reason for foreigners to demand early repayment or, in other words, a run cannot happen in equilibrium.

Two remarks are in order. The first is that if the run condition 2.15 holds, preventing runs is not consistent with a fixed exchange rate: out of equilibrium, the inflation tax must be used. In that sense, exchange rate flexibility plays a useful role.

Second, the reader may find little resemblance between the scenario just described and the common meaning of "last resort lending." But this objection may be more apparent than real. When the government prints pesos to face early withdrawals, it is in effect creating credit to lend to itself. More vividly, suppose that the government is composed of a treasury, which is the initial debtor, collects the labor tax, and pays for government purchases, and of a central bank, which prints pesos and collects seignorage. Then the same results would obtain and, at the same time, with flexible exchange rates one can think of the pesos issued in a run as an emergency loan from the central bank to the treasury.

The shortcomings of fixed exchange rates are shared by dollarization. In fact, the situation is even worse. The condition for runs to be possible becomes

$$T < g_s + d + \chi \tag{2.17}$$

because dollarization implies that stock seignorage is not available to the home government. In fact, it is possible that for condition 2.15 to fail and condition 2.17 to hold; in such a case, crises are not possible in a peso regime, even one of fixed exchange rates, but they may occur with dollarization.

Advocates of dollarization admit that it would prevent the central bank from acting as a domestic LLR but that this may not be too difficult to deal with. One way to cope with the possibility of financial panics, which Argentina actually implemented, would be to secure foreign lines of short-term credit to be drawn upon in the event of a run. It should be clear that such a strategy would succeed in eliminating equilibrium runs in our model. Take the dollarized case, and assume that the home government had the right to borrow, at the beginning of period 2, at least $g_s + d + \chi - T$ from some foreign agent or institution, at a zero interest rate. Then it is obvious that there cannot be a run in equilibrium.

This argument suggests that the welfare impact of losing the central bank's ability to be the LLR can be measured by the cost of a contingent line of credit large enough to prevent runs. What "large enough" means is debatable. In light of our model, and recalling the meaning of international illiquidity, the size of the credit line should be at least as large as the gap between the potential short-run liabilities and assets of the financial system, which can be substantial. In particular, the Argentinean credit lines are unlikely to have met this criterion. However, the "commitment rate" at which the Argentinean lines were secured was small enough that the total cost of the strategy would have been relatively small even if the credit line had to increase severalfold.[8]

Note that as in many models that deliver multiple equilibria, we have not specified which equilibrium obtains when several exist. This is not too difficult to deal with, and in the literature it is often assumed that one of the equilibria is selected by some otherwise irrelevant random device, such as animal spirits or sunspots.[9] Such a selection mechanism would have the noteworthy implication that observationally it may seem that a change from a peso regime to dollarization exacerbates the role of exogenous uncertainty. This would be the case if the economy was immune to runs in the peso regime but subject to runs under dollarization. This is an important observation insofar as some have claimed that one of the advantages of dollarization is that it would reduce the severity of exogenous shocks. Our analysis implies exactly the opposite.

In the same scenario, the contractual interest rate on loans to the home country would be higher than the world interest rate in cases in which runs occured with nonzero probability. This risk premium would compensate foreign creditors for the probability of debt default. But the implication is that in this model, dollarization may well be associated with an *increase* in the *dollar* interest rate applicable to the home country. This is in contrast to claims that dollarization would reduce the cost of foreign credit.[10]

2.6   Some Arguments in Need of a Theory

There are a number of arguments related to the dollarization debate that, to date, have not been formalized with the tools of modern economic theory. Many of these arguments sound plausible, but their relative importance will remain unknown unless more progress is made in formulating them adequately.

The first contention is that dollarization would be beneficial by reducing transaction costs, such as the costs of calculating dollar equivalents of national currency quantities. In principle, one can hardly disagree with this claim. However, measuring its significance is much trickier. For one thing, the transaction costs relevant for the argument are likely to be very small. Also, including them in economic models has proven to be much harder than expected, and no satisfactory and tractable procedure has emerged. As a consequence, measures of the quantitative importance of transaction costs have played little role in the debate. Finally, the transaction costs in question are likely to be already negligible in a system of irrevocably fixed exchange rates, and hence the marginal savings that dollarization would bring along this dimension are arguably insignificant.

A second argument, this one voiced by some opponents of dollarization, is that currencies are national symbols, and hence their elimination would be costly in terms of national pride, identity, and the like. Such an argument is sometimes politically effective and, in spite of its being quickly dismissed by many economists, may have some validity. However, how to formalize it or assess its economic importance is competely unknown.

A third claim is that dollarization would reduce market incompleteness. For example, Hausmann (1999) states that "[dollarization] would expand the menu of financial options open to emerging-market governments and firms and, in so doing, would increase financial stability" (p. 75). Again, this is not an implausible claim but is one that cannot be analyzed in the context of standard models. This is because standard models take the degree of market completeness as a given. To our knowledge, there is no theory dealing with *how* dollarization would "expand the menu of financial options," let alone what implications such an expansion would have on allocations and welfare.

Finally, consider the claim that official dollarization is presumably beneficial because it would legalize the spontaneous dollarization that is already observed in several countries. At one level, our analysis can be amended in a straight-forward manner to deal with such an argument. One may suppose that before dollarization is imposed by policy, the home agent derives utility not only from holding pesos but also from holding dollars. This can be formalized by making v depend on some aggregate of the real value of pesos and dollars, a modeling device that has been employed in the literature on currency substitution. The resulting extension is likely to yield essentially the same lessons as the original model and, in that sense, the observation of currency substitution by itself does not provide independent support for dollarization.

We admit, though, that the fact that dollarization is already taking place in many countries may reflect the effect of some fundamentals about which we know little or nothing; such an effect is buried in the specification of the v function in our model. Given this possibility, it may be not implausible to conjecture that the way such fundamentals work may change, in a favorable way, if dollarization is made official. However, such a conjecture needs to be made explicit and cast in terms of modern economic theory if it is to become more than wishful thinking.

2.7 Final Remarks

We have conducted a fairly thorough, although surely not exhaustive, discussion of the theoretical issues associated with dollarization. Our analysis has been organized around a simple, single framework that can be extended in many directions. We emphasize that the study of a single framework is useful for at least two reasons: It gives readers an idea of how the different aspects of the dollarization debate are related to each other, and such a modeling strategy provides the foundation for a satisfactory quantitative comparison of the associated costs and benefits.

We have borrowed from previous literature, and we have also provided new observations, for and against dollarization. Among the former, we noted that calculations of seignorage loss should no longer be automatically taken as a con of dollarization. Among the latter, we emphasized that there is no presumption that dollarization should reduce interest rates.

Perhaps most important, we have identified some arguments that lack satisfactory theoretical foundations. Given the interest in dollarization, these arguments remain fertile ground for future research.

Notes

We are indebted to Eduardo Levy Yeyati, Will Roberds, and Federico Sturzenegger for useful comments and suggestions. Of course, we are solely responsible for any shortcomings.

1. This economy is a version of that in Persson and Tabellini (1990, chapter 6).

2. See, for instance, Hanke and Schuler (1999).

3. We shall assume that the individual's solution is always interior, which may be guaranteed by assumptions of the Inada type on utility.

4. Panizza, Stein, and Talvi (2000) attempt to evaluate and compare some of these considerations for a number of Central American economies.

5. That this association is systematic was convincingly shown by Kaminsky and Reinhart (1999).

6. See Chang and Velasco (2000c) for a more detailed discussion and analysis of the evidence.

7. In particular, suppose that at the end of the period the government must pay for its exogenous revenue needs before it can pay any creditors left. Then, under equation 2.15, if a run occurs, the government will not have enough money to pay any debt rolled over. This means that it is optimal for each individual creditor to demand early repayment, as the creditor would not collect anything if he or she agreed to roll over the claim.

8. Here is a very rough calculation of the cost of the Argentinean strategy. In 1996 the Argentinean private line of credit reached U.S.\$6.1 billion, at a cost of about U.S.\$18 million a year—about 0.3 percent. Assuming that this rate remains the same, the total cost of the strategy would depend on how large a credit line is "enough." At the end of 1999, Argentina's M2 (the sum of its monetary and quasimonetary banking system liabilities) was U.S.\$88.2 billion. Because it had U.S.\$26.5 in international reserves, the banking system's net liquid liabilities were arguably as large as U.S.\$88.2 − U.S.\$26.5 = U.S.\$51.7 billion. At 0.3 percent a year, a line of credit large enough to cover that amount in whole would cost somewhat more than U.S.\$150 million per year. Although this is not a negligible figure, it is only a small fraction of Argentina's GDP.

9. See Chang and Velasco (2000a) for a formalization of this idea in the financial panics context.

10. See Powell and Sturzenegger (2002) for an empirical assessment of such a claim.

References

Barro, R., and D. Gordon. 1983. "Rules, discretion and reputation in a model of monetary policy." *Journal of Political Economy* 12 (July): 101–121.

Calvo, G. 1978. "On the Time Consistency of Optimal Policy in a Monetary Economy." *Econometrica* 46 (November), 1411–1428.

Calvo, G., and P. Guidotti. 1993. "On the Flexibility of Monetary Policy: The Case of the Optimal Inflation Tax." *Review of Economic Studies* 60, 667–687.

Chang, R., and A. Velasco. 2000a. "Banks, Debt Maturity, and Financial Crises," *Journal of International Economics* 51, 169–194.

———. 2000b. "Financial Fragility and the Exchange Rate Regime." *Journal of Economic Theory* 92, 1–34.

———. 2000c. "Liquidity Crises in Emerging Markets: Theory and Policy." In *NBER Macroeconomics Annual 1999* (Ben Bernanke and Julio Rotemberg, eds.). Cambridge: The MIT Press.

Fischer, S. 1982. "Seigniorage and the Case for a National Money." *Journal of Political Economy* 90 (April), 295–313.

Hanke, S. H., and K. Schuler. 1999. "A Monetary Constitution for Argentina: Rules for Dollarization." *CATO Journal* 18 (Winter), 405–420.

Hausmann, R. 1999. "Should There Be Five Currencies or One Hundred and Five?" *Foreign Policy* 116, 65–79.

Kaminsky, G., and C. M. Reinhart. 1999. "The Twin Crises: the Causes of Banking and Balance of Payments Problems." *American Economic Review* 89 (3), 473–500.

Kydland, F. E., and E. C. Prescott. 1977. "Rules Rather than Discretion: The Inconsistency of Optimal Plans." *Journal of Political Economy* 85 (June), 473–492.

Mundell, R. 1961. "A Theory of Optimum Currency Areas." *American Economic Review* 51, 657–675.

Panizza, U., E. Stein, and E. Talvi. 2000. "Assessing Dollarization: An Application to Central American countries." Working Paper, Inter-American Development Bank (IDB).

Persson, T., and G. Tabellini. 1990. *Macroeconomic Policy, Credibility, and Politics*. Chur, Switzerland: Harwood Academic Publishers.

Phelps, E. 1973. "Inflation in the Theory of Public Finance." *Swedish Journal of Economics* 75, 67–82.

Powell, A., and F. Sturzenegger, 2002. "The Link Between Devaluation and Default Risk." This volume.

3 Using Balance Sheet Data to Identify Sovereign Default and Devaluation Risk

Pablo Andrés Neumeyer and Juan Pablo Nicolini

3.1 Introduction

The relationship between devaluation and default risk is a central issue in the discussion of the costs and benefits of dollarizing emerging economies. Correct measures of these two unobserved variables are essential for assessing the welfare implications of dollarization. This chapter studies the role of private sector balance sheets in measuring devaluation and default risk.

A leading argument in favor of dollarization rests on the causal link between devaluation risk and country default risk. According to this view, "firms and households in emerging economies have dollar-denominated debts, some of them acquired through domestic transactions like the purchase of a car or a refrigerator. Therefore, fluctuations in the exchange rate run the risk of creating serious financial stress" (Calvo 2000, p. 2.). As devaluations cause defaults, dollarization can substantially reduce default risk in emerging economies by taking away the government's ability to devalue. Assessing the empirical relevance of this argument requires the analyst to measure devaluation and sovereign risk.

In our interpretation of the argument, the chain through which devaluations lead to defaults has two crucial links: the liability dollarization problem (net dollar liabilities and net peso assets) and explicit or implicit government bailouts designed to avoid generalized bankruptcy. Consider this scenario: Assume that under certain unexplained circumstances (an exogenous fiscal shock?), a government must devalue while private sector balance sheets exhibit a liability dollarization problem. Under these conditions, following a devaluation the credit market will collapse. To avoid the supposedly costly generalized default, the government may have to make transfers to banks. If this transfers are sufficiently high, the government may have to default on its debt. If this is the way the world functions, then when the (exogenous in the scenario) expected devaluation goes up, the expected default will go up. A minimal empirical test that this theory should pass is a positive correlation between expected devaluation and default risk.

The standard approach to measuring sovereign default risk and devaluation risk rests on two no-arbitrage conditions restricting the return on peso-denominated (emerging) sovereign bonds and the return on dollar-denominated (emerging) sovereign bonds on one hand, and the return on dollar-denominated (emerging) sovereign bonds and the return on dollar-denominated, risk-free bonds on the other. The absence of risk-free, peso-denominated bonds creates an identification problem, as there are two arbitrage equations to measure three unobserved variables: sovereign default risk on peso bonds, sovereign default risk on dollar bonds, and devaluation risk.[1]

This chapter shows that the identification problem can be solved with information about government and private sector balance sheets and a simple off-the-shelf model of optimal default and devaluation. The model provides a theory on how a benevolent government jointly decides the three default alternatives it has available, namely, the devaluation rate, the default rate on peso-denominated bonds, and the default rate on dollar-denominated bonds. A key assumption of the model, motivated by the current debate on dollarization, is that government guarantees banks a minimum level of profits. This implies that if there is a currency mismatch in private sector balance sheets that would induce banks to go bankrupt in the event of a large devaluation, banks (depositors) will be bailed out by the government.

The model predicts that the choice between defaulting on domestic currency debt through an explicit default or through devaluation depends on the private sector's balance sheet positions. In general, government will prefer to default on its domestic currency debt by devaluing its currency rather than through an explicit default. The incentive to do so stems from the fact that a devaluation is more profitable because it amounts to a default on the government's domestic currency debt *plus* its monetary liabilities. In economies with a liability dollarization problem, where the private sector has net dollar liabilities (or net peso assets), governments may choose to explicitly default on domestic currency debt instead of devaluing.

This is because, in this case, the devaluation will trigger a bailout of the banking system. The optimal choice between devaluation and explicit default will depend on the trade-off between the fiscal gain of depreciating government monetary liabilities and the fiscal cost of bailing out the financial system. If the latter exceeds the former, the government will prefer to default on its domestic debt, rather than devaluing and triggering a bailout.

Using data on Argentine balance sheets for the period 1994–2000, we find that it is never optimal for the government to default on its domestic currency debt when we take currency denomination of balance sheets at face value. Using this identifying assumption, expected devaluations are measured by the difference between the return on domestic currency sovereign bonds and the risk-free dollar rate. If we assume that all nonsecured loans denominated in dollars are actually in pesos, this result is reversed: it is never optimal for a government to devalue, because a devaluation will trigger a financial crisis and, therefore, a bank-bailout that will offset the fiscal gain of devaluing.

3.2 The Identification Problem without an Optimizing Government

The standard approach to looking at the correlation between sovereign default risk and devaluation risk rests on the linearized no-arbitrage restrictions,

$$i_t - i_t^* = E\delta_{t+1} + E\varepsilon_{t+1} - E\delta_{t+1}^*,$$

$$i_t^* - r_t = E\delta_{t+1}^*,$$

(3.1)

where i and i^* are the interest rate on dollar- and peso-denominated sovereign debt, r is the risk-free dollar rate, δ^* and δ are the repudiation rates of dollar and peso-denominated sovereign debt, and ε is the devaluation rate. For simplicity, we assume that agents are risk neutral. The identification problem arises because these two equations and the interest rate data are insufficient to uncover the unobserved variables of interest: $E\delta_{t+1}$, $E\varepsilon_{t+1}$, and $E\delta_{t+1}^*$.

Alternative assumptions about the government's default policy have very different implications for the interpretation of the data. Consider first the case in which the government always defaults on domestic and foreign currency debt simultaneously: $\delta_t = \delta_t^*$, for all t. Under this assumption,

$$i_t - i_t^* = E\varepsilon_{t+1},$$

$$i_t^* - r_t = E\delta_{t+1}^*,$$

so the currency spread and the sovereign spread reveal the devaluation risk and the default risk on foreign currency sovereign bonds. Alternatively, consider the case in which the government never defaults explicitly on domestic currency sovereign debt, but it does so implicitly by devaluing. In this case, $\delta_t = 0$, for all t,

$$i_t - r_t = E\varepsilon_{t+1},$$

$$i_t^* - r_t = E\delta_{t+1}^*.$$

The covariance between $i_t - i_t^*$ and $i_t^* - r_t$ is

$$cov(i_t - i_t^*, i_t^* - r_t) = cov(E\delta_{t+1} + E\varepsilon_{t+1} - E\delta_{t+1}^*, E\delta_{t+1}^*)$$

$$= cov(E\varepsilon_{t+1}, E\delta_{t+1}^*) + [cov(E\delta_{t+1}, E\delta_{t+1}^*) - var(E\delta_{t+1}^*)].$$

In the first case with $\delta_t = \delta_t^*$, $cov(i_t - i_t^*, i_t^* - r_t) = 0$ implies that the case for dollarization is weak because in the data there is no relation between currency and sovereign default risk on foreign currency debt. In the second case, the same observation implies that $cov(E\varepsilon_{t+1}, E\delta_{t+1}^*) = var(E\delta_{t+1}^*) > 0$, so the case for dollarization is consistent with the data.

The next section addresses this identification problem by studying a simple dynamic Ramsey problem for a government that chooses devaluation rates and default rates, and guarantees a minimum profit to banks. The theory will tell us when the government is going to default on its domestic currency debt explicitly through repudiation or implicitly through devaluation.

3.3 Sovereign Default and Devaluation in a Ramsey Problem with Bank Bailouts

As we mentioned in the introduction, we want to study the choice of default rates a government would set if it chose, for reasons we do not explain, to default. To do this, we need a theory of government behavior. Following the approach of Lucas and Stokey (1983), we assume that the government is benevolent and maximizes social welfare. The main advantage of this choice is that these models have been widely analyzed in the literature; to the extent that our approach was to check the consistency of the scenario with off-the-shelf models, this seems a natural choice. In addition, we will not explain why the government chooses to bail out the private sector; we will just impose that it will in our model, to keep our analysis in line with the scenario, which takes the bailout as given. Finally, we allow the government to default only once. The natural way to do it in the context of the optimal policy literature, is to solve a Ramsey problem with commitment. This leaves the government the additional degree of freedom at the beginning, where its choices will be determined by the exogenously given initial private sector balance sheet. Thus, all the action is determined by initial balance sheet positions, which are exogenous, as they are in the scenario on which this chapter is based. Introducing dynamic considerations to allow for balance sheet positions to be determined in an equilibrium with default and modeling government's incentives to bail out banks are well beyond the scope of this chapter.

We study the decision problem faced by the government of a small open economy that, at time $t = 0$, must finance a given stream of government expenditures choosing a sequences of income tax rates, exchange rates, and default rates on debts it inherits from the past. We assume that there is a fixed exchange rate regime in which the government commits to exchange any amount of domestic and foreign currency at preannounced exchange rates. Another key assumption of our model is that the government guarantees a minimum level of profits to the banking system. It is assumed throughout the exercise that this government can commit perfectly to future policies.

3.3.1   Economic Environment and Definition of Equilibrium

At each date, the state of the economy is denoted by s_t, where $\pi(s_t)$ is its probability.

There are two goods produced with the linear technology,

$$y_{1t} = n_{1t},$$

$$y_{2t} = n_{2t},$$

where y_{it}, n_{it} denote output and labor for goods $i = 1, 2$. Good 1 is not traded internationally, and good 2 is. Purchasing power parity holds for the traded good.

Firms choose labor inputs to maximize

$$p_{1t}y_{1t} + e_t p_{2t}^* y_{2t} - w_t(n_{1t} + n_{2t}), \tag{3.2}$$

subject to $n_{1t}, n_{2t} \geq 0$. The variables e_t, w_t, p_{1t}, are the domestic currency prices of foreign currency, labor, and the nontraded good respectively. The variable p_{2t}^* is the foreign currency price of the traded good. This problem has an interior solution only if

$$p_{1t} = e_t p_{2t}^* = w_t, \quad \text{for all } t.$$

Other possibilities will not be considered.[2]

Household preferences over these two goods and work effort, n_t, are described by the utility function

$$\sum_{t=0}^{\infty} \beta^t E[u(c_{1t}) + u(c_{2t}) - \alpha n_t], \tag{3.3}$$

where $0 < \beta < 1$, $\alpha > 0$, and $u : R \to R$ is monotonically increasing, concave, and satisfies $\lim_{x \to 0} u'(x) = \infty$ and $\lim_{x \to \infty} u(x) = 0$.

Purchases of the nontradable good c_{1t} have to be paid with domestic cash, whereas those of c_{2t} can be paid with credit. The cash-in-advance constraint for good 1 is

$$p_{1t}c_{1t} \leq M_t, \quad \text{for all } t. \tag{3.4}$$

Household's budget constraints are given by

$$(B_t^H + M_t + D_t - L_t) + e_t(B_t^{H*} + D_t^* - L_t^*)$$

$$\leq M_{t-1} + (1 + i_{t-1}^b)(1 - \delta_t(s_t))B_{t-1}^H + (1 + i_{t-1})(D_{t-1} - L_{t-1})$$

$$+ e_t(1 + i_{t-1}^{b*})(1 - \delta_t^*(s_t))B_{t-1}^{H*} + (1 + i_{t-1}^*)(D_{t-1}^* - L_{t-1}^*)$$

$$\times \Pi_t + p_{1t}g + w_t(1 - \tau_t)n_t - p_{1t}c_{1t} - p_{2t}^* e_t c_{2t},$$

for all s_t and $t = 0, 1, 2, \ldots$, where B_t^H, B_t^{H*} are one-period bonds held by households from t to $t+1$ in domestic and foreign currency, respectively; M_t are end-of-period money balances; D_t, D_t^*, L_t, L_t^* are domestic- and foreign-currency-denominated end-of-period bank deposits and loans; g are government transfers; τ_t are income tax rates; and Π_t are bank profits. The inequalities $0 \leq \delta_0, \delta_0^* \leq 1$, represent default rates on domestic and foreign bonds at time 0.

In addition to the flow budget constraint above, households are restricted by a no-Ponzi-game condition.

Financial intermediaries costlessly receive deposits and lend money to the government and to the private sector. End-of-period balance sheets are described by

$$L_t + e_t L_t^* + B_t^b + e_t B_t^{b*} = D_t + e_t D_t^*, \quad \text{for } t = -1, 0, 1, \dots$$

and bank profits are described by

$$\Pi_t = (1 + i_{t-1}^b)(1 - \delta(s_t))B_{t-1}^b + (1 + i_{t-1})(L_{t-1} - D_{t-1})$$
$$+ e_t(1 + i_{t-1}^{b*})(1 - \delta^*(s_t))B_{t-1}^{b*} + (1 + i_{t-1})(L_{t-1}^* - D_{t-1}^*) + T_t,$$
$$\text{for } t = 0, 1, 2, \dots$$

The variable T_t is a transfer scheme that guarantees banks a minimum level of profits. In our case this level of profits is zero, but we can easily accommodate any constant. The transfer scheme is

$$T_t = \max\{-\Pi_t + T_t, 0\}.$$

A government insurance protects the banking system from aggregate shocks such as devaluations and sovereign defaults. The rule is meant to capture in a simple way the contingent debt nature of banks' negative profits for the government.

Perfect foresight and no-arbitrage conditions imply that bank profits and bailouts are zero, for all $t \geq 1$. Bank bailouts at $t = 0$ are

$$T_0(e_0, \delta_0, \delta_0^*) = \max\{(1 + i_{t-1}^b)(1 - \delta(s_t))B_{t-1}^b + (1 + i_{t-1})(L_{t-1} - D_{t-1})$$
$$+ e_t(1 + i_{t-1}^{b*})(1 - \delta^*(s_t))B_{t-1}^{b*} + (1 + i_{t-1})(L_{t-1}^* - D_{t-1}^*), 0\}.$$

Observe that defaults on government bonds may cause transfers to banks. Also, liability dollarization in the banking system makes the transfers that occur when banks have negative profits an increasing function of the exchange rate.

The government has to service its debt and pay for transfers to banks and households by levying income taxes, issuing money, and choosing repudiation rates on its liabilities. Let B_t^{g*}, B_t^g be government bond holdings. Government's budget constraints are

$$e_0 B_0^{g*} + B_0^g - M_0 = (1 + i_{-1})(1 - \delta_0)B_{-1}^g - M_{-1}$$
$$+ e_0(1 + i_{-1}^*)(1 - \delta_0^*)B_{-1}^{g*} + \tau_0 \omega_0 n_0 - p_{10} g_0 - T_0$$

in the first period, and

$$e_t B_t^{g*} + B_t^g - M_t = (1 + i_{t-1}) B_{t-1}^g - M_{t-1}$$
$$+ e_t(1 + i_{t-1}^*) B_{t-1}^{g*} + \tau_t \omega_t n_t - p_{1t} g$$

for $t = 1, 2, \ldots$. The no-Ponzi-game condition is

$$\lim_{t \to \infty} \beta^{t+1} \frac{e_{t+1} B_{t+1}^{g*} + B_{t+1}^g - M_{t+1}}{e_{t+1} p_{2,t+1}^*} \geq 0.$$

For simplicity, assume the foreign government follows the Friedman rule for monetary policy—that is,

$$i_t^* = 0, \quad \text{for } t = -1, 0, 1, \ldots$$

$$p_{2t}^* = \beta^t, \quad \text{for } t = 0, 1, \ldots$$

for $t = 0, 1, 2, \ldots$ To normalize, we also assume that $e_{-1} = 1$, $i_{-1} = 0$.

A consequence of this assumption is that an equilibrium exists only if exchange rates satisfy

$$e_{t+1} \geq e_t, \quad \text{for all } t. \tag{3.5}$$

Otherwise, interest on domestic bonds will be negative, creating an arbitrage opportunity.

Combining household's and government's flow budget constraints, the no-Ponzi-game condition, expressions for bank profits, and the Friedman rule assumption for foreign monetary policy, we obtain

$$\sum_{t=0}^{t} \beta^t \left[c_{1t} + c_{2t} + \left(1 - \frac{e_t}{e_{t+1}}\right) \frac{M_t}{p_{1t}} - (1 - \tau_t) n_t - g \right]$$

$$\leq \frac{M_{-1} + (1 - \delta_0)(B_{-1}^H + B_{-1}^B)}{e_0} + (1 - \delta_0^*)(B_{-1}^{H*} + B_{-1}^{B*})$$

$$+ \frac{T_0(e_0, \delta_0, \delta_0^*)}{e_0} \tag{3.6}$$

for households, and

$$\sum_{t=0}^{\infty} \beta^t \left[g - \left(1 - \frac{e_t}{e_{t+1}}\right) \frac{M_t}{p_{1t}} - \tau_t n_t \right]$$

$$\leq (1 - \delta_0) \frac{B_{-1}^g - M_{-1}}{e_0} + (1 - \delta_0^*) B_{-1}^{g*} - \frac{T_0(e_0, \delta_0, \delta_0^*)}{e_0} \tag{3.7}$$

for the government.

Adding the government's and the household's budget constraint, we obtain the country's budget constraint,

$$\sum_{t=0}^{\infty} \beta^t((c_{1t} - n_{1t}) + (c_{2t} - n_{2t})) \leq (1 - \delta_0)\frac{B_{-1}^H + B_{-1}^B + B_{-1}^g}{e_0}$$

$$+ (1 - \delta_0^*)(B_{-1}^{H*} + B_{-1}^{B*} + B_{-1}^{g*}). \qquad (3.8)$$

Market clearing for the non-internationally traded good, labor, and bonds requires

$$n_{1t} = c_{1t}, \quad \text{for all } t, \qquad (3.9a)$$

$$n_{1t} + n_{2t} = n_t, \quad \text{for all } t, \qquad (3.9b)$$

$$B_{-1}^H + B_{-1}^B + B_{-1}^g = 0, \quad \text{for all } t, \qquad (3.9c)$$

$$B_{-1}^{H*} + B_{-1}^{B*} + B_{-1}^{g*} + B_{-1}^{F*} = 0, \quad \text{for all } t. \qquad (3.9d)$$

We assume that all domestic currency bonds are held domestically. Thus when markets clear, the government budget constraint becomes

$$\sum_{t=0}^{\infty} \beta^t(c_{2t} - y_{2t}) \leq (1 - \delta_0^*)(B_{-1}^{H*} + B_{-1}^{B*} + B_{-1}^{g*}). \qquad (3.10)$$

This equation states that the present value of the country's trade deficits equal the country's initial nondefaulted net foreign assets.

Denote initial portfolios as

$$I_0 = \{M_{-1}, B_{-1}^H, B_{-1}^B, B_{-1}^G, D_{-1}, L_{-1}, B_{-1}^{*H}, B_{-1}^{*B}, B_{-1}^{*G}, D_{-1}^*, L_{-1}^*\}.$$

For given initial portfolios I_0, an allocation $\{c_{1t}, c_{2t}, n_{1t}, n_{2t}, M_t\}_{t=0}^{\infty}$ is a competitive equilibrium with bank bailouts, taxes and default if, and only if

1. consumers maximize utility 3.3 subject to the budget constraint 3.6 and cash-in-advance constraint 3.4,

2. government policies $\{\delta_0, \delta_0^*\}$ and $\{g, , \tau_t, e_t\}_{t=0}^{\infty}$ are consistent with the government's budget constraint 3.7 and the nonnegativity of domestic currency interest rates constraint 3.5,

3. firms solve function 3.2, and

4. the market clearing conditions 3.7a–3.7d are satisfied.

The first-order conditions of the household's problem for $t = 0$, $1, 2, \ldots$ are

$$\frac{u'(c_{1t})}{u'(c_{2t})} = \left(1 + \left(1 - \frac{e_t}{e_{t+1}}\right)\right),$$

$$\frac{\alpha}{u'(c_{2t})} = (1 - \tau_t) \tag{3.11}$$

and

$$M_t = p_{1t}c_{1t}, \tag{3.12a}$$

$$c_2 = (1 - \beta)a_0 + g$$
$$+ (1 - \beta) \sum_{t=0}^{t} \beta^t \left[(1 - \tau_t)n_t - c_{1t} - \left(1 - \frac{e_t}{e_{t+1}}\right)\frac{M_t}{e_t p_{2t}^*}\right], \tag{3.12b}$$

where

$$a_0 = \frac{M_{-1} + (1 - \delta_0)(B_{-1}^H + B_{-1}^B)}{e_0} + (1 - \delta_0^*)(B_{-1}^{H*} + B_{-1}^{B*}) + \frac{T(\delta_0, \delta_0^*, e_0)}{e_0}.$$

The household's optimality conditions, the nonnegativity of interest rates in constraint 3.5, and the budget constraint 3.6 yield the implementability conditions

$$u'(c_2)[(1 - \beta)a_0^H + g] + (1 - \beta) \sum_{t=0}^{t} \beta^t [\alpha n_t - u'(c_{1t})c_{1t} - u'(c_2)c_2] = 0$$

$$u'(c_{1t}) \geq u'(c_2). \tag{3.13}$$

Using the implementability condition we obtain a simpler definition of equilibrium. For initial portfolios I_0 given, an allocation $\{c_{1t}, c_{2t}, n_{1t}, n_{2t}\}_{t=0}^{\infty}$ is a competitive equilibrium with bank bailouts, taxes, and default if, and only if, it satisfies the conditions 3.6, 3.7, and 3.13.

3.4 Solution of the Ramsey Problem

The government's problem is to choose $\{e_0, \delta_0, \delta_0^*\}$ and $\{c_{1t}, c_{2t}, n_{1t}, n_{2t}, M_t\}_{t=0}^{\infty}$ in order to maximize utility 3.3 subject to conditions 3.6, 3.7, and 3.13, with initial portfolios I_0 given. Conditions 3.6, 3.7, and 3.13 insure that the chosen allocation is a competitive equilibrium.

The taxes and exchange rates that implement each allocation are given by condition 3.9.

We will focus on the case where all bonds at $t = -1$ are issued by the government and all private agents have initial positive bond holdings—that is,

$$B^H_{-1}, B^B_{-1}, -B^G_{-1}, B^{*H}_{-1}, B^{*B}_{-1}, B^{*F}_{-1}, -B^{*G}_{-1} > 0.$$

Note that consumption of the credit good must be constant over time, so the government can only choose the level of the tax but must keep it constant. On the other hand, the government can choose different values for consumption of the cash good over time by changing the devaluation rate constrained to satisfy the nonnegativity of nominal interest rates. Finally, the government also chooses the initial nominal exchange rates and default rates. The government chooses $\{c_{1t}, n_{1t}, n_{2t}\}^{\infty}_{t=0}$ and $\{c_2, e_0, \delta_0, \delta^*_0\}$ to maximize the Lagrangian

$$\mathscr{L} = \sum \beta^t [U(c_{1t}) + U(c_2) - \alpha(n_{1t} + n_{2t})]$$

$$- \lambda \left[u'(c_2)[(1 - \beta)a^H_0 + g] + (1 - \beta) \sum^t_{t=0} \beta^t [\alpha n_t - u'(c_{1t})c_{1t} - u'(c_2)c_2] \right]$$

$$- \sum \beta^t \gamma_t [c_{1t} - n_{1t}] - \omega \left[\sum \beta^t (c_{2t} - n_{2t}) - (1 - \delta^*_0)B^*_{-1} \right]$$

$$- \mu_0[0 - \delta_0] - \mu_1[\delta_0 - 1] - \mu^*_0[0 - \delta^*_0] - \mu^*_1[\delta^*_0 - 1].$$

We ignore the nonnegativity constraints on nominal interest rates and later verify that they will be satisfied.

First, we discuss the necessary conditions for an interior optimum with respect to consumption and labor. To simplify the discussion and focus on the optimal choices of default rates and devaluation rates, consider the case in which $U(c) = c^{1-\sigma}/(1 - \sigma)$. These first-order conditions can be combined to yield

$$U'(c_{1t}) = \frac{[1 + \lambda(1 - \beta)]}{[1 + \lambda(1 - \beta)(1 - \sigma)]} \tag{3.14}$$

and

$$U'(c_2) - \lambda U''(c_2)(1 - \beta)[(1 - \beta)a^H_0 + g] = \frac{[1 + \lambda(1 - \beta)]}{[1 + \lambda(1 - \beta)(1 - \sigma)]}. \tag{3.15}$$

First, note that condition 3.1 implies that the optimal nominal interest rate is constant over time, as is the case in the solution $c_{1t} = c_1$, for all t. Also, combining conditions 3.14 and 3.15 we obtain

$$U'(c_2) - \frac{\lambda U''(c_2)(1 - \beta)[(1 - \beta)a_0^H + g]}{[1 + \lambda(1 - \beta)(1 - \sigma)]} = U'(c_1).$$

Note also that the multiplier λ is positive, because it measures the marginal cost of increasing the transfers, g. Thus, $U'(c_2) < U'(c_1)$, which means that

$$\left(1 + \left(1 - \frac{e_t}{e_{t+1}}\right)\right) > 1, \quad \text{or} \quad 1 > \frac{e_t}{e_{t+1}}.$$

Thus, the optimal policy is characterized by a positive and constant devaluation rate.[3] These results are standard in the literature on dynamic Ramsey problems.

We now focus on the optimal choice of devaluation and default rates at time zero in an economy with bank bailouts.

Using the bank's balance sheets at $t = -1$, and assuming $i_{-1} = i_{-1}^* = 0$, $e_{-1} = 1$, bank bailouts can be written as

$$\frac{T(\delta_0, \delta_0^*, e_0)}{e_0} = \max\left\{\left(1 - \frac{1}{e_0}\right)(B_{-1}^B + L_{-1} - D_{-1}) + \delta_0 \frac{B_{-1}^B}{e_0} + \delta_0^* B_{-1}^{B*}, 0\right\}$$

$$= \max\left\{\left(1 - \frac{1}{e_0}\right)(D_{-1}^* - B_{-1}^{B*} - L_{-1}^*) + \delta_0 \frac{B_{-1}^B}{e_0} + \delta_0^* B_{-1}^{B*}, 0\right\}.$$

Changes in exchange rates and default on bonds held by banks may trigger bailouts. The relation between bailouts and exchange rates depends on the currency exposure of banks, as shown by the expression

$$\frac{\partial \frac{T(\delta_0, \delta_0^*, e_0)}{e_0}}{\partial e_0} = \frac{(1 - \delta_0)B_{-1}^B + L_{-1} - D_{-1}}{e_0^2}.$$

The size of bank bailouts is an increasing function of devaluations when banks have positive net assets denominated in domestic currency. If banks have net liabilities in domestic currency, devaluations contribute to *ex post* bank profits and reduce the size of bailouts. If there is no default on domestic currency bonds, the bank's domestic currency exposure is equal to $D_{-1}^* - B_{-1}^{B*} - L_{-1}^*$. Bailouts are an increasing function of the exchange rate when there is liability dollarization—$D^*_{-1} > B^{B*}_{-1} + L^*_{-1}$. When there is a currency mismatch in banks portfolios, we will say that there is liability dollarization when $(1 - \delta_0)B^B_{-1} + L_{-1} > D_{-1}$.

Depending on whether there is liability dollarization or not, bailouts are positive or negative depending on whether $e_0 \gtrless \bar{e}_0$:

If $(1 - \delta_0)B^B_{-1} + L_{-1} - D_{-1} > 0 : T(\delta_0, \delta^*_0, e_0) > 0 \Leftrightarrow e_0 > \bar{e}_0$,

If $(1 - \delta_0)B^B_{-1} + L_{-1} - D_{-1} < 0 : T(\delta_0, \delta^*_0, e_0) > 0 \Leftrightarrow e_0 < \bar{e}_0$,

where

$$\bar{e}_0 = \frac{(1 - \delta_0)B^B_{-1} + L_{-1} - D_{-1}}{(B^B_{-1} + L_{-1} - D_{-1}) + \delta^*_0 B^{B*}_{-1}}.$$

It will be useful to have expressions for private assets with and without bailouts. If there is no bailout, private assets are

$$a_0 = \frac{M_{-1} + (1 - \delta_0)(B^H_{-1} + B^B_{-1})}{e_0} + (1 - \delta^*_0)(B^{H*}_{-1} + B^{B*}_{-1}),$$

whereas in the case in which there is a bailout, they are

$$\bar{a}_0 = \frac{M_{-1} + (1 - \delta_0)B^H_{-1} + D_{-1} - L_{-1}}{e_0} + (1 - \delta^*_0)B^{H*}_{-1}$$

$$+ B^{B*}_{-1} + B^B_{-1} + L_{-1} - D_{-1}.$$

Consider now the first-order conditions of the Ramsey problem with respect to δ^*_0:

$$-\lambda U'(c_2)(1 - \beta) \frac{\partial a^H_0}{\partial \delta^*_0} - \omega B^*_{-1} = \mu^*_1 - \mu^*_0 \qquad (3.16)$$

and

$$\frac{\partial a^H_0}{\partial \delta^*_0} = -(B^{H*}_{-1} + B^{B*}_{-1}) \quad \text{with no bailout,}$$

$$\frac{\partial \bar{a}^H_0}{\partial \delta^*_0} = -B^{H*}_{-1} \quad \text{with bailout.}$$

Thus, under the assumption $B^{H*}_{-1}, B^{B*}_{-1} > 0$, in either case the derivative is negative. As we also assume that initially the country is a net debtor (i.e., $B^{F*}_{-1} > 0$), the left-hand side of condition 3.16 is positive, and because the multipliers ought to be nonnegative, then $\mu^*_1 > \mu^*_0 =$

0, which means that $\delta_0^* = 1$ is optimal. The intuition is very simple. Even though it is true that by defaulting on foreign-currency-denominated bonds the government can increase the contingent liabilities because banks can be holding some of those bonds, the net effect is positive, to the extent that households and foreigners hold positive amounts of foreign-currency-denominated debt.

Now, let us focus on the joint choices of e_0 and δ_0. Note that the derivative of the Lagrangian with respect to δ_0 is given by

$$-\lambda U'(c_2)(1 - \beta)\frac{\partial a_0^H}{\partial \delta_0} = \mu_1 - \mu_0,$$

where

$$\frac{\partial a_0^H}{\partial \delta_0} = -\frac{B_{-1}^H + B_{-1}^B}{e_0} \quad \text{with no bailout,}$$

$$\frac{\partial \bar{a}_0^H}{\partial \delta_0} = -\frac{B_{-1}^H}{e_0} \quad \text{with bailout.}$$

Under our assumptions on initial portfolios, as long as e_0 is bounded, in both cases $\mu_1 > \mu_0 = 0$ and it is optimal to set $\delta_0 = 1$. Note, however, that in the case in which e_0 is arbitrarily large, the value of δ_0 is inessential. As there is no benefit from defaulting, we will assume that government chooses $\delta_0 = 0$ when e_0 is arbitrarily large.

The first order condition with respect to e_0 is

$$-\lambda U'(c_2)(1 - \beta)\frac{\partial a_0^H}{\partial e_0},$$

where

$$\frac{\partial a_0^H}{\partial e_0} = -\frac{1}{e_0^2}[M_{-1} + (1 - \delta_0)(B_{-1}^H + B_{-1}^B)] \qquad \text{with no bailout,}$$

$$\frac{\partial \bar{a}_0^H}{\partial e_0} = -\frac{1}{e_0^2}[M_{-1} + D_{-1} + (1 - \delta_0)B_{-1}^H - L_{-1}] \quad \text{with bailout.}$$

The optimal choice of the initial exchange rate depends crucially on the interaction between private balance sheet positions and bailouts.

If $(1 - \delta_0)B_{-1}^B + L_{-1} < D_{-1}$, bailouts are a decreasing function of the exchange rate and become zero for $e_0 > \bar{e}_0$. In this case, for a large enough exchange rate there is no bailout, because banks are net debtors in domestic currency and for a large enough e_0 *ex post* bank profits will be nonnegative. As $M_{-1} + (1 - \delta_0)(B^H_{-1} + B^B_{-1}) > 0$, it is optimal to set e_0 as large as possible. The devaluation removes the incentives to set $\delta_0 = 1$, because it makes the real value of the domestic currency government debt equal to zero.

If there is liability dollarization in the banking system, $(1 - \delta_0)B^B_{-1} + L_{-1} > D_{-1}$, bailouts are an increasing function of the exchange rate and are positive for $e_0 > \bar{e}_0$. The optimal choice of e_0 in this case depends on whether $M_{-1} + (1 - \delta_0)B^H_{-1} \gtrless L_{-1} - D_{-1}$.

If $M_{-1} + (1 - \delta_0)B^H_{-1} > L_{-1} - D_{-1}$, it is optimal to increase the nominal exchange rate without bound. Note that this expression will be positive when the gains from devaluing, given by $M_{-1} + (1 - \delta_0)B^H_{-1}$, exceeds the bailout required to keep the banking sector from going bankrupt, given by the net domestic-currency-denominated assets in the banking sector, $L_{-1} - D_{-1}$. In this case, the net fiscal effect of a devaluation is positive. As we mentioned before, in this case there is no point in using the instrument δ_0, so we set $\delta_0 = 0$.

If $M_{-1} + (1 - \delta_0)B^H_{-1} < L_{-1} - D_{-1}$ and there is liability dollarization, the optimal exchange rate is $e_0 = \bar{e}_0$. For $e_0 < \bar{e}_0$ there is no bailout, so $\partial a^H_0 / \partial e_0 > 0$. For $e_0 > \bar{e}_0$ there is a bailout, and $\partial a^H_0 / \partial e_0 < 0$. The intuition for this result is that if there is no bailout, the government levies a lump-sum tax by devaluing. If there is a bailout, the net fiscal effect of a devaluation in this case is negative. Furthermore, because the optimal e_0 is finite, government will set $\delta_0 = 1$. As the government lowers e_0 (revalues), it improves bank profits, reducing transfers to banks. It will do so until the value of the transfers is zero. The gain from reducing bailouts exceeds the cost that arises from the increase in the real value of nondefaulted nominal government liabilities, M_{-1}. The value of $\bar{e}_0$ when $\delta_0 = \delta^*_0 = 1$ is lower than one $(\bar{e}_0 < 1)$.[4]

In summary, the government always defaults on foreign-currency-denominated liabilities. In addition, when a devaluation does not reduce the profits of domestic banks $(B^B_{-1} + L_{-1} < D_{-1})$, the government will devalue. When the devaluation does reduce the profits of banks a bailout follows a devaluation. In this case, as the previous discussion argues, the optimal decisions with respect to either devaluing or defaulting on peso-denominated bonds imply corner solutions. Thus, we can treat them as a binary decision problem.

If the government defaults on domestic bonds, the gains are given by B_{-1}^B; whereas if the government devalues, the gains are given by $B_{-1}^B + M_{-1} - L_{-1} + D_{-1}$. The decision to devalue will be optimal when $B_{-1}^B < B_{-1}^B + M_{-1} - L_{-1} + D_{-1}$, or $0 < M_{-1} - L_{-1} + D_{-1}$.

The following table summarizes all the possible cases for the optimal choice of e_0, δ_0, and δ_0^*:

	δ_0^*	δ_0	e_0
$B_{-1}^B + L_{-1} < D_{-1}$	1	0	∞
$B_{-1}^B + L_{-1} > D_{-1}$ and $M_{-1} > L_{-1} - D_{-1}$	1	0	∞
$B_{-1}^B + L_{-1} > D_{-1}$ and $M_{-1} < L_{-1} - D_{-1}$	1	1	$\bar{e}_0$

3.5 Application to Argentine Data: 1994–2001

To evaluate which scenario is relevant for the Argentine case, we use aggregated monthly data of government and private sector balance sheets covering the period 1994–2001.

3.5.1 The Data

The Argentine Central Bank (BCRA) has published its Consolidated Financial Statements on a monthly basis since 1994 in its statistical bulletin (the *Boletín Estadístico*). They are available and can be downloaded at the BCRA's website ⟨http://www.bcra.gov.ar⟩. Government debt data has been obtained from the Informe Económico and the Boletín Fiscal, both published by the Ministerio de Economía.

Most of the balance sheet variables appear in the BCRA publications. Others needed to be constructed. The monetary circulation outside the financial system account was chosen to represent the monetary base variable (M) because the theoretical model does not allow for banks to have a money demand. The bank's money demand was treated as if banks were holding government bonds. The loans variable (L) was computed as peso-denominated Credit to the Private Sector following the Central Bank's Boletín Estadístico. This account includes overdrafts, discounts, mortgage loans, pledge lending, personal loans, private securities, and accrued resources on loans. These last two concepts were included because they do not differ significantly from the definition of loans in the theoretical model, and because the Accrued Resources on Loans account includes interest funds that were not paid but were agreed on at the time of taking out the loan. This item accounted for almost 14.7 percent of the total in January 1994.

Deposits (D) are calculated as domestic currency Deposits Made by the Private Sector, including current accounts, savings accounts, and time deposits. Accrued Resources on Deposits were not included; because at less than 0.4 percent of total peso deposits, they make no difference.

Government bonds in banks' portfolios (B^B) were calculated as the sum of the Credit to the Public Sector account, in domestic currency and monetary circulation in financial institutions net of deposits made by the public sector. Credit to the public sector includes loans to the national, provincial, and municipal governments and to official entities, public securities, and the Use of Unified Funds account. The funds in the Accrued Resources on Loans account are included, because this item accounted for 22.3 percent of the total in January 1994. The Deposits Made by the Public sector account includes deposits of national, provincial, and municipal governments and the same type of deposits included in D. The Accrued Resources on Deposits account was not included, because it represented less than 0.17 percent of the total in January 1994. The variable B^B is negative in the first half of 1994 and then turns positive until December 1997 with two exceptions, in January and May 1997. From January 1998 to the present, B^B is negative at all times.

We constructed the series

$$R_1 = D_{-1} - B^B_{-1} - L_{-1}$$

and

$$R_2 = M_{-1} + D_{-1} - L_{-1}.$$

The model predicts that if $R_1 \geq 0$, $D_{-1} \geq B^B_{-1} + L_{-1}$, then it is optimal to devalue, and that if $R_1 < 0$, a bailout to the banks follows a devaluation. When $R_2 > 0$, the cost of the bailout is not too large, so a devaluation follows. If $R_2 < 0$, the bailout is larger than the gains from devaluing, which means that the government will never devalue.

The values for R_1 and R_2 when bank's currency positions are taken at face denomination are plotted in figure 3.1. The value for R_1 is negative until the end of 1997. This means that there is no liability dollarization and a devaluation is optimal. Starting in 1998,

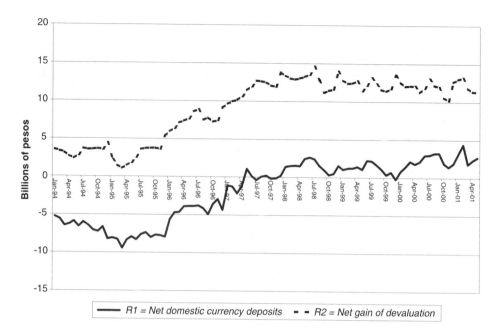

Figure 3.1
Balance sheet positions

R_1 becomes positive, which means that a bailout to the banks follows a devaluation. However, R_2 is positive, so the gains from devaluing outweigh the bailout; thus, a devaluation is still optimal.

If this calculation were the appropriate one, the identification assumption would be that the default rate on peso-denominated bonds is zero, so

$$i_t - r_t = E[\varepsilon_{t+1}]$$

$$i_t^* - r_t = E[\delta_{t+1}^*],$$

Figure 3.2 reports the interest rate differentials $i_t - r_t$, $i_t - i_t^*$, and $i_t^* - r_t$, as defined in the introduction. The standard interpretation is that $i_t - r_t$ is the total risk on an Argentinean bond, relative to a U.S. bond. This total risk is typically decomposed into a sovereign risk, $i_t^* - r_t$, and a devaluation risk, $i_t - i_t^*$. The identifying restriction of our theoretical model coupled with the calculations of figure 3.1 imply that $i_t - r_t$ represents devaluation risk, whereas $i_t - i_t^*$ represents the difference between the devaluation risk and the sovereign risk. In this case, the standard interpretation severely underestimates the expected devaluation rate.

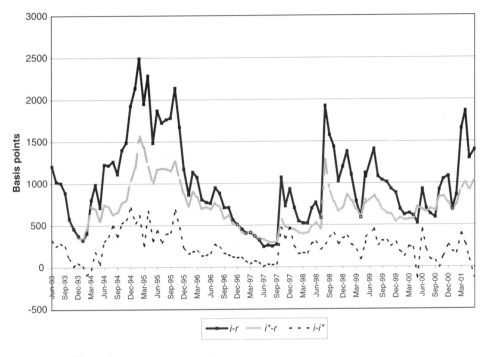

Figure 3.2
Interest rate differentials

A problem with the computations presented in figure 3.1 is that part of the assets of banks, although denominated in dollars, may represent liabilities of firms that would suffer substantially form a depreciation of the real exchange rate that could follow a nominal devaluation. As a first approximation to the problem, we did the calculations as if all dollar-denominated noncollateralized loans of the banking sector were in pesos. Figure 3.3 depicts the results of this exercise. As can be seen, the results change dramatically: R_1 becomes negative for the whole period, meaning that a bailout of the banks follows a devaluation. In addition, R_2 is also negative, meaning that the cost of the bailout is larger than the fiscal gain of the devaluation. Therefore, according to this interpretation, the government would never devalue.

If these calculations were right, the identifying assumption would be that the expected devaluation should be zero and that the expected default should be the same in both currencies. Thus, the correct formulas would be

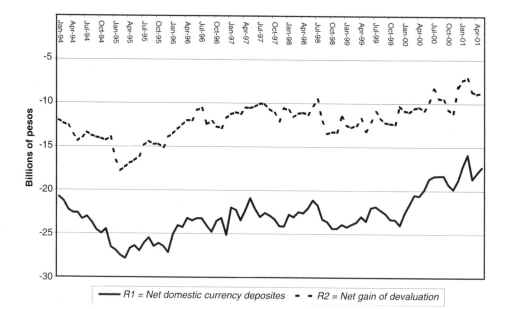

Figure 3.3
Adjusted balance sheet positions (all nonsecured loans of banks interpreted as peso loans)

$$i_t = i_t^*$$

$$i_t^* - E[\delta_{t+1}] = r_t,$$

Obviously, this identification hypothesis seems inconsistent with the data, because we observed $i_t > i_t^*$.

An interpretation that we would prefer, though, is that the incentives to default on peso-denominated assets via a devaluation or a direct default on bonds depends on the effective size of the bailout to the banking system and that it is hard to measure it *ex ante*. Thus, the decision the government would take relative to peso-denominated assets in the event of a default is seen by the market as a random variable. If this is indeed the case, then, expected default in peso-denominated bonds is positive, but less than expected default on dollar-denominated bonds. Then, $E[\varepsilon_{t+1}] > 0$, and $0 < E[\delta_{t+1}] < E[\delta_{t+1}^*]$, so

$$E[\varepsilon_{t+1}] = i_t - i_t^* + E[\delta_{t+1}^*] - E[\delta_{t+1}] > i_t^* - i_t$$

$$E[\delta_{t+1}^*] = i_t^* - r_t,$$

Under this interpretation, the devaluation risk, measured by $i_t^* - i_t$ in figure 3.2, underestimates the true devaluation risk but not as much as if $E[\delta_{t+1}] = 0$.

Finally, recall that in our analysis, when a devaluation is optimal, any value for $E[\delta_{t+1}]$ is a solution, so we set $E[\delta_{t+1}] = 0$. Note, however, that this decision is indeed important. In particular, had we chosen $E[\delta_{t+1}] = 1$, in the first case in which it was optimal to devalue, the real measure of the devaluation risk would have been $i_t^* - i_t$! So, our model above is consistent with the standard approach, but only as a knife edge, in the sense that any other value for the default rate is as good as that one.

These numerical exercises are clearly preliminary. The aim is to highlight the importance of the underlying identifying assumption typically made in the literature when decomposing interest rate differentials into different risk sources. Obtaining more precise estimates of the true default and devaluation risks, within the simple theoretical model sketched here, requires a much deeper numerical analysis. Moreover, considering alternative theoretical frameworks in order to incorporate other relevant features of emerging economies seems an obvious avenue for future research.

3.6   Concluding Remarks

A key issue in the discussion of the benefits of dollarization is the hypothesis that in economies where there is liability dollarization in the banking sector, a devaluation will cause a default on sovereign debt. If this alleged causal relationship actually exists, removing the technology to devalue will reduce sovereign risk with all the benefits that this entails. Testing whether this positive correlation between default risk and devaluation risk exists in the data is crucial when evaluating the benefits of dollarizing an economy. Uncovering this correlation in the data is difficult because expected defaults and expected devaluations are unobserved variables. The main problem in uncovering these default and expected devaluation rates is that the lack of peso-denominate bonds issued by, say, the U.S. Treasury introduces an identification problem: we only have two arbitrage conditions to unravel the expected devaluation rate and the default rates on peso- and dollar-denominated bonds issued by the Argentinean government.

In order to solve for this identification problem, we propose an off-the-shelf model of government behavior. We solve a simple dynamic model of a small open economy with fixed exchange rates where the government bails out banks with negative profits and chooses devaluation and default rates on domestic and foreign currency to interpret the data.

The model is very simple and as such has many limitations, discussed in more detail in this chapter. Its purpose is to highlight the identification problem and how government choices affect the interpretation of interest rate differentials. Some obvious weaknesses of the model are that we take initial balance sheet positions and the willingness of governments to bail out banks as given. In the identification exercise, we also ignore the possibility that for some reason not captured in the model, the government may have to default.[5] The model is also completely silent with respect to the virtues of dollarization. It predicts that in economies where liabilities are dollarized, governments will never chose to devalue. It suggests that the case for dollarization is strong when for some reason outside our model the government devalues, even though that is not the optimal policy.

An application to Argentina during the period 1994–2001 provides mixed results, depending on the interpretation of bank balance sheets. When these are taken at face value, the data suggest that in case of a default a devaluation is preferred to a default on peso-denominated bonds. However, when balance sheets are adjusted so that bank's nonsecured dollar-denominated loans are considered as if they were in pesos, the results change. In this scenario, a devaluation is never optimal, because it triggers a bank bailout that is costlier than the fiscal gains of the devaluation.

Our own interpretation is that given this mixed results, the decision to devalue or default, in case of crisis, must be seen as a random variable by the market. In this case, the standard way to measure devaluation risk underestimates the true risk. Under this interpretation, the literature that discusses the empirical relationship between default and devaluation risk may be misleading.

Notes

We thank Rodolfo Campos for valuable research assistance. We also wish to express thanks for comments from participants at the Universidad Torcuato Di Tella (UTDT)

Conference on Dollarization and at the Fifth Annual Meeting of the Latin American and Caribbean Economic Association (LACEA) in Rio de Janeiro, 2000.

1. An implicit assumption in the literature, that we mantan in the paper, is that the U.S. government never defaults. Thus, if the U.S. government were to issue peso-denominated bonds, we would have three interest rate differentials to identify the three unobserved risks.

2. This decision will not cause a loss of generality, because there are no equilibria with corner solutions.

3. In this economy, the Friedman rule fails to be optimal, because the value of the government liabilities depends on the value of consumption of the credit good at time one—note that this is the source of time inconsistency in Lucas and Stokey (1983). If this were a close economy, this effect would change the relative price between the cash and the credit good only at time zero, and the Friedman rule would be optimal from time one on. However, in this open economy model, the value of credit good consumption must be constant over time; thus, this effect distorts the relative price between cash and credit goods at every period.

4. The fiscal effects of this revaluation are likely to be small, so in the numerical exercise of the next subsection we will ignore this effect and assume that in this case the government does not change the nominal exchange rate.

5. Some plausible reasons are a run on banks coupled with a run on the central bank's reserves, or a fiscal shock coupled with a lack of access to the credit markets that forces the government to use the reserves to pay for that fiscal shock.

References

Calvo, Guillermo A. (2000): "Testimony on Dollarization," Joint Hearing of the Subcommittees on Economic Policy and International Trade and Finance of the United States Congress, Washington, DC, April 22.

Calvo, Guillermo A. (2000): "Testimony on Dollarization," Hearing of the Subcommittee on Domestic and Monetary Policy, Committee on Banking and Financial Services, Washington, DC, June 22.

Hausmann, Ricardo; Pagés-Serra, Carmen; Gavin, Michael; and Stein, Ernesto H. (1999): "Financial Turmoil and Choice of Exchange Rate Regime," Research Department, Inter-American Development Bank, Working Paper 400, January.

Robert E. Lucas, Jr., and Stokey, Nancy L. (1983): "Optimal Fiscal and Monetary Policy in an Economy without Capital," *Journal of Monetary Economics*, 12, 55–94.

4 Dollarization and the Lender of Last Resort

Christian Broda and Eduardo Levy Yeyati

4.1 Introduction

During the nineteenth century and the beginning of the twentieth century, banking panics were common in the financially developed world. Both the United States and England recurrently faced problems with their banking sectors. It was in this context that the theory of the lender of last resort (LLR) was forged. In particular, it was Walter Bagehot who, in his *Lombard Street*, first set the guidelines for how a central bank should behave in a crisis.[1] These guidelines are still influencing the conventional wisdom on the area and are the traditional benchmark against which LLR practice is measured. Indeed, there is substantial evidence suggesting that the actions of monetary authorities broadly following the Bagehot gospel have reduced the frequency and impact of episodes of financial distress. No financial crisis has occurred in the United States since 1933 and none in the United Kingdom since 1866.

With the deepening of financial markets in developing countries, banking crises have spread across the world. From a set of ninety episodes since the 1970s, Caprio and Klingebiel (1996) show that the length of the average bank crisis was 4.5 years at an average resolution cost of 13.6 percent of GDP. The potential significance of an LLR as a means of reducing the probability or severity of these events becomes clear from the large magnitudes of the crises involved.

The classical explanation for a bank run has been succinctly described by Anna Schwartz (1986): "A run is fuelled by fears that means of payment will be unobtainable at any price and, in a fractional reserve banking system, leads to a scramble for high powered money" (p. 11). A run on an individual bank, in turn, can generate a panic when it gets propagated throughout the whole banking sector.

Another, and, in the case of emerging economies, possibly more relevant cause of a banking crisis is a panic generated by a systemic shock potentially affecting the solvency of the entire sector—for example, triggered by fears of a devaluation in an economy with important dollar liabilities. Given the limited ability of liquid institutions within the private sector to provide perfect liquidity insurance (in the first case, due to moral hazard arising from imperfect information about the solvency of individual banks, in the second, to an aggregate liquidity crunch), an LLR could enhance welfare by averting a banking crisis through the timely provision of liquidity.[2]

It is the ability to print money as needed that places the central bank in a privileged position to offer such a facility.[3] Therefore, once this ability ceases to exist, limits to the LLR function appear. De jure dollarization fully eliminates this possibility and hence diminishes the central bank's ability to bail out the financial system. However, limitations to the LLR function are important also in the more common case of widespread de facto dollarization.[4] As intuition suggests, the incremental costs associated with the loss of the LLR when we move to de jure dollarization must be measured relative to those of the prevailing regime. These costs are inversely related to the degree of financial dollarization and the flexibility of the current regime.

Although the aforementioned issues are indeed common to countries with both de facto and de jure dollarization, there is one often overlooked aspect of the problem that depends crucially on whether financial intermediation is carried on in two (or more) currencies, or in a single currency, namely, the endogeneity of the level of dollarization to the presence of an LLR. As we will argue in this chapter, the existence of an LLR—or a deposit insurance scheme (DIS)—may induce unwarranted dollarization.

We illustrate the underlying intuition behind this problem by means of a simple model of bicurrency intermediation in which we have assumed, for simplicity, that changes in the exchange rate (more specifically, devaluations) are the only source of risk. Any degree of financial dollarization that exceeds the fraction of the real economy effectively dollarized implies the existence of a currency mismatch somewhere in the economy. In the event of a sudden devaluation, the erosion of the dollar value of peso-denominated assets impinges on the capacity to repay either dollar-indebted firms or currency-imbalanced banks. An LLR that provides limited insurance to the bank reduces the costs of (and creates incentives for) risk taking, which in the previous context entails increasing the dollar share of deposits. Therefore, banks will be willing to increase their level of dollarization as part of the currency risk is transferred to the provider of bank insurance. Moreover, dollar depositors are protected against exchange rate fluctuations whenever the devaluation does not precipitate a default, whereas they share the losses with peso depositors in the case of default. Thus, an LLR, by reducing the probability of default, increases the insurance value of the dollar deposits, reinforcing the incentive for banks to increase the level of dollarization.

Therefore, the combination of a bicurrency financial sector and a credible LLR endogenously drives up dollarization. However, because the key underlying factor is the fair play that dollar depositors are usually given in the event of a bank default, it is easy to conceive (although less so to implement) LLR rules that undo the problem (for example, by making the LLR assistance contingent on the degree of dollarization of individual banks). Alternatively, full dollarization or the prohibition of dollar deposits trivially eliminates the currency mismatch in the economy, thereby ruling out the source of distortion.

Some analysts have recently argued that the LLR function should not be thought of as inextricably linked to its ability to print base money, because in practice there are alternative ways of providing bank liquidity.[5] This discursive argument, however, is rather simplistic and leaves out important considerations. The option of a domestic insurance fund that accumulates reserves entails important fiscal costs. On the other hand, an international LLR—an IMF-like agency—is subject to traditional moral hazard problems. In addition, particularly in the case of a private LLR, complex double moral hazard issues are introduced. Thus, as we conclude in the final section of the paper, the outsourcing of the LLR should be considered only a partial solution to the loss of the LLR as a result of de jure dollarization.

The chapter has the following plan. Section 4.2 contains a brief review of the traditional LLR theory, an analytical illustration of the moral hazard issues typically associated with the LLR, and a selective survey of the ongoing debate regarding its application to dollarized economies. Section 4.3 builds on the simple model of section 4.2 to introduce financial intermediation in a bicurrency economy, and it examines the impact of bank insurance on dollarization. Section 4.4 resumes the discussion in section 4.2 and explores the different alternatives to a standard LLR in a dollarized economy, and their relative costs and advantages. Finally, section 4.5 concludes the chapter.

4.2   LLR in Theory and Practice

The traditional role of the lender of last resort is associated with Bagehot (1873). Bagehot's doctrine emphasizes the difficulty a bank will face if it must transmit credible information to the market during a crisis. His view is captured by his well-known maxim: "Lend freely to temporarily illiquid but nonetheless solvent banks at a penalty rate and on good collateral." Modern analysis of this theory (see Freixas and Rochet 1998) suggests that Bagehot's advice seems rather simple compared with its far more complex practical implementation.[6] In this section, we discuss different rationales for an LLR that have emerged in the literature and show, using a simple model, the complexities underlying the need for a bailout policy.

A classic rationale for an LLR comes from the fact that bank runs can materialize even if the banking system is solvent. Diamond and Dybvig (1983), show that self-fulfilling runs on deposits can be prevented with an LLR. Throughout the remainder of this chapter, we will refer to this theory as "DD." In their setup, banks allow depositors to smooth consumption by pooling resources and being able to profit from long-term investments. However, banks can only promise contracts that depend on other depositors' withdrawal behavior. In this context and with no unanticipated shocks, a "sunspot" run is possible. If an excessive number of depositors claim their money back at an early stage, they can trigger a general withdrawal. The very existence of an LLR providing an elastic supply of reserves can prevent these liquidity crises, because the run on deposits becomes unnecessary when short-term liquidity is available from the LLR and bankruptcy is avoided. The liquidity provision, however, can be performed by instruments other than the credit of the LLR. Traditionally, deposit insurance has served the same preventive role.

Information asymmetries can give rise to alternative justifications for the need of an LLR. In the benchmark case of a solvent banking sector subject to idiosyncratic shocks, Bhattacharya and Gale (1987) show that the interbank market can redistribute liquidity among banks and provide perfect insurance for these shocks. This is the consequence of a clearing condition in a market with no informational problems or regulatory constraints and hence no need for intervention. However, as soon as one acknowledges the existence of imperfect information about the solvency of the banks, the same liquidity shock can give rise to a market failure and thus a rationale for an LLR. Potential lenders unable to tell solvent from insolvent borrowers, and fearful of being hit by a liquidity shock themselves (contagion effects), would extend too little credit to distressed institutions, and possibly hold excessive low-yield liquid assets.[7]

This information-related market failure, not uncommon to other industries, takes particular importance in the case of banks owing to their high leverage ratios and vulnerability, and the linkages through which a bank's failure could precipitate failure on the part of its creditors. Indeed, even if a bank is insolvent but this is not known by the general public, it may be justifiable to intervene and avoid the spillover effects that its bankruptcy may have on the rest of the banking sector and hence on the payment system as a whole.[8] It is precisely this aspect that is usually invoked when the LLR is called into action. The timely provision of liquidity by the central bank can prevent costly interruption of investment projects as well as the bankruptcy of financial intermediaries that provide welfare-enhancing services.

A particular example of the role for an LLR in the event of a systemic shock is a banking crisis caused by unexpected capital outflows, as illustrated in Chang and Velasco (2001) and Goldfajn and Valdes (1996). In these papers, foreign depositors run à la DD against domestic banks, precipitating in the process a collapse of the exchange rate that feeds back negatively into bank solvency.[9] Causality can go the other way: the defense of the exchange rate under pressure requires a sharp increase in interest rates that exacerbates the problems of the banks due to the typical maturity mismatch between assets and liabilities.[10] In these circumstances, the LLR intervenes to relieve banks by providing liquidity to the banking system. This injection partially counteracts the interest rate hike and ultimately becomes a wealth transfer to the banks, the depositors, or both, that is to be borne by the fiscal authority (and through it, by the whole population). Hence, these circumstances raise the typical dilemma of whether to preserve the rights of the creditors, or face the disruptive effects of the crisis. Other shocks that can have similar consequences include a fall in bond prices when banks are subject to "market risk" or a sudden fall in the level of activity that can endanger the firms' capacity to repay loans and substantially increase the share of non-performing loans that are written off.

As will be further explored in section 4.4, the theory of LLR can be reinterpreted in a contract theory framework as a special case of bank insurance. Whereas insurance against diversifiable risk (idiosyncratic shocks) can be largely supplied by the interbank market, the presence of aggregate shocks (and the information problems associated with the difficulty of disentangling one from the other) places the central bank in a privileged position to provide this service without the need for carrying large stocks of liquid reserves, due to its ability to print money.

The evidence regarding the effects of the LLR on the banking sector are overwhelmingly positive. Lenders of last resort have helped avoid banking panics (see Miron 1986 and Freixas and Rochet 1998, for a quick survey) and have mitigated the risk of contagion (see, for example, Aharony and Swary 1983). Bordo (1990) compares the United States and the United Kingdom in a period where, although the business cycles were very similar, "the difference in the incidence of panics is striking—the U.S. had four, while Britain had none ... the key difference between the two countries was successful LLR action by the British authorities in defusing incipient crises" (p. 16).

As should be clear by now, the distinction between illiquidity and (temporary) insolvency required by Bagehot's gospel is hardly obvious, rendering its implementation far from mechanical.[11] The historical experience shows, however, that the central bank pays little attention to the solvency issue (and hence to Bagehotian principles) when immersed in a full-blown crisis that threatens to paralyze the financial sector or even when a large financial institution is at stake. An example of the latter was the lifeboat rescue of Baring Brothers in 1890 by a committee of other banks and the Bank of England. This event anticipated the "too big to fail" doctrine which is now common practice among central bankers.[12] A notable exception, as argued in Friedman and Schwartz (1963), was the inability of the Federal Reserve to react to the several banking panics during the period 1929–1933, once it was clear that the private provision of bank insurance became seriously impaired.[13]

Besides why and when a LLR should come into play, the issue of how the LLR function should be implemented also divides academics. The classical view, as represented by Bagehot, states that the conditions under which the lender of last resort would lend should be *clearly stated in advance*, with the view that the knowledge of the availability of LLR facilities in the event of a crisis would reduce the incentive to run on otherwise healthy institutions, just as the availability of deposit insurance should prevent runs in a DD setup. On the other hand, the *constructive ambiguity* approach that has become increasingly popular in recent years emphasizes the moral hazard created by the existence of the lender of last resort, and therefore seeks to leave potential borrowers in doubt as to whether they will be able to borrow if in trouble.[14]

The evidence of the effect of an LLR on the behavior of banks is difficult to measure. For example, in a recent study Gonzalez-Eiras (2000) looks at the announcement of a credit contingent line purchase by the Central Bank of Argentina on December 1996. He conjectures that since the most likely use of the funds is to enhance the central bank's ability to act as an LLR, this implicit insurance should lead banks to reduce their buffer stock of liquidity, reflected in their excess holdings of liquid assets. He further assumes that international branches should be less affected by this measure relative to domestic banks, as the former are implicitly insured against temporary liquidity shocks by the parent, or, at any rate, they enjoy greater access to international liquidity in the event of a systemic crisis in the country. He finds evidence that the demand for liquidity of domestic banks decreased significantly relative to that of international banks, something that in principle may be interpreted as a sign of moral hazard associated with the LLR.[15] We turn next to these issues.

4.2.1 Bank Insurance and Moral Hazard

Unlike DD setups, where risk is exogenous and moral hazard inexistent, or in Holmstrom and Tirole (1998), where banks privately choose their risk level after the aggregate liquidity shock occurs (thus making the risk decision independent of the existence of insurance) Cordella and Levy Yeyati (1999) examine the role of bank insurance and moral hazard. The authors show that in a repeated game where banks privately choose risk *before* being subject to an aggregate shock, bank insurance (e.g., a preannounced rescue package contingent on the occurrence of a negative aggregate shock), by raising the continuation value of the bank, may increase the incentives to behave prudently, more than offsetting the moral hazard problem raised by the very existence of insurance. Thus, the introduction of an observable exogenous shock can be used to provide a rationale for a liquidity window with no penalty rates and, in the limit, for a plain bailout. In this section, we use a simplified version of the setup presented in Cordella and Levy Yeyati (1999) to illustrate how the traditional LLR practice may be motivated solely by risk considerations, abstracting from any social cost of bank failures.

Assume that bank managers, acting in the interest of risk-neutral shareholders, collect funds from depositors and invest them in a portfolio with stochastic returns. Risk-neutral depositors can either invest in bank deposits or in a risk-free asset offering a (gross) rate of $r_f \geq 1$. Bank deposits are protected by a comprehensive deposit insurance scheme, so that depositors invest in the bank at any posted deposit rate $r \geq r_f$.[16] For simplicity, we assume that the aggregate supply of funds is fixed, and we normalize it to unity.

A moral hazard problem exists whenever banks can affect the risk-return profile of their portfolios in an unobservable way.[17] In particular, we assume that the gross rate of return $\tilde{R}$ of a portfolio X is distributed as follows:

$\tilde{R} = X$ with probability $p(X, \gamma)$,

$\tilde{R} = 0$ with probability $1 - p(X, \gamma)$,

where γ is an aggregate exogenous shock that can assume two values: γ_H or γ_L ($\gamma_H > \gamma_L$), with equal probability, so

$$\mu \equiv \frac{\gamma_L + \gamma_H}{2} < 1 \tag{4.1}$$

is the expected value of the shock.

In order to keep our analysis as simple as possible, we impose the following functional form for the probability of success:

$p(X, \gamma) = \gamma p(X),$

so expected returns can be written as

$$E[\tilde{R}] = \mu p(X) X. \tag{4.2}$$

Accordingly, the higher the realization of γ, the higher the probability of success for any given portfolio choice X. The interesting problem arises when a higher X is associated with a higher portfolio risk p (i.e., $\partial p/\partial X < 0$), introducing a trade-off between risk and re-turn and a potential incentive to engage in excessive risk.[18]

In each period $t \in [0, \infty)$, a bank chooses X_t and, if at the end of the period the investment goes sour ($\tilde{R}_t = 0$), the central bank decides whether to transfer deposit liabilities to the deposit insurance fund and withdraw the bank license, or to give money to the distressed bank to pay depositors and continue in business. The structure of the model is recursive; in the case that the charter is not withdrawn, the bank faces the same problem at the beginning of period $t + 1$.[19]

The bank's problem consists of maximizing the discounted flow of profits, V_t, valued at period t, which, exploiting the recursive nature of the problem and dropping the time subscripts, can be written as[20]

$$V = \max_X \frac{\Pi}{1 - \delta s(X, \gamma)}, \tag{4.3}$$

where $\delta < 1$ is a discount factor, $s(X, \gamma)$ is the bank's probability of survival in the current period, and Π is expected current profits. In the absence of bank insurance, $s(X, \gamma) = p(X, \gamma)$.

Naturally, the bank's portfolio decision affects both the current profits and the probability of either going bankrupt or continuing operations in the next period.

Because the deposit rate, r, is given, the problem of the bank re-duces to maximizing the discounted flow of profits, as described in equation 2.3, with respect to the risk-return profile of its investment (summarized by its nominal return, X). The first-order condition can then be expressed as

$$\frac{\partial V}{\partial X} = \frac{1}{1 - \delta s} \left(\frac{\partial \Pi}{\partial X} + \delta \frac{\partial s}{\partial X} V \right) = 0. \tag{4.4}$$

As expected, gains in current profits from increasing monitoring expenses ($\partial \Pi/\partial X > 0$) are offset by losses in terms of expected future rents ($\partial s/\partial X < 0$). Accordingly, the bank's choice of effort depends positively on these rents, represented by the franchise value V, and on the degree of conservatism of bank shareholders, represented by the discount factor δ, which measures the weight assigned to future income (alternatively, the inverse of the opportunity cost of bank equity).

Assume now that the central bank commits to bailing out troubled banks at no cost *only in the event of a negative aggregate shock*. Denoting with the subindex B the new values, the probability of survival increases to

$$s_B = p(X)\frac{\gamma_H}{2} + \frac{1}{2} > s,$$

where

$$\frac{\partial s_B}{\partial X} = p'(X)\frac{\gamma_H}{2} > p'(X)\mu = \frac{\partial s}{\partial X},$$

and the value of the bank and the first-order condition 4.4 modify to

$$V_B = \max_X \frac{\Pi}{1 - \delta s_B(X, \gamma)}, \tag{4.5}$$

$$\frac{\partial \Pi}{\partial X} + \delta \frac{\partial s_B}{\partial X} V_B = 0, \tag{4.6}$$

respectively. Thus, the announcement of a bailout affects the bank's problem in two mutually offsetting ways. First, it reduces the marginal improvement in the probability of success arising from an additional monitoring effort, as indicated by $\partial s_B / \partial X > \partial s / \partial X$. This moral-hazard-inducing effect of a bailout policy is due to the fact that in the new environment, survival only depends on effort in the event of a positive shock, because the central bank fully guarantees the bank's liabilities in bad times. On the other hand, by increasing the expected probability of survival, the central bank guarantee *enhances the value of the bank license* ($V_B > V$) and, in turn, the cost to bank shareholders of a potential default.

Using conditions 4.4 and 4.6, it can be easily shown that this "value effect" dominates the moral hazard component ($e_B > e$) if, and only if

$$\frac{\partial s_B}{\partial X} V_B > \frac{\partial s}{\partial X} V = \frac{\partial s}{\partial X} \frac{1 - \delta s_B}{1 - \delta s} V_B,$$

or, using $\mu = (\gamma_L + \gamma_H)/2$, and simplifying:

$$\gamma_L < \delta \mu.$$

Thus, when adverse shocks are sufficiently strong, an explicit bank insurance policy against systemic downturns has the unexpected effect of mitigating the moral hazard problem, resulting in banks that are more risk aware.[21] Note that the key policy ingredient is that the central bank distinguishes between good and bad states of nature, and only subsidizes banks in the latter. Therefore, it is easy to show that if the assistance is extended in all states of nature, the insurance policy indeed results in a higher level of risk. However, one can reasonably agree that systemic crises, either endogenously driven or due to exogenous shocks, are in general easily identified. In fact, most of the historical experience of the LLR is consistent with this model of insurance, though the explicit motivations advanced by the authorities tend to diverge.

4.2.2   Dollarization and the Limits to the LLR

It has often been argued that highly dollarized economies are vulnerable to self-fulfilling currency (and, in turn, banking) crises. A sudden devaluation can represent a serious cost for banks. The consequences are obvious if banks are allowed to hold open positions in foreign currency. However, even in the most usual situation in which banks' open positions are subject to prudential limits, dollar credits may become rapidly unrecoverable and force the bank into bankruptcy if the dollar-indebted firms earn their income in domestic currency. Depositors are aware of these problems and, if devaluation expectations increase, have a strong incentive to withdraw their deposits, which in turn results in an increase in the demand for the foreign currency, feeding back into devaluation expectations.[22]

Full dollarization trivially eliminates any currency mismatch throughout the entire economy, so devaluation expectations cannot cause (or aggravate) a banking crisis, thus reducing the need for an LLR, as argued in Berg and Borenzstein (2000). Along the same lines, Calvo (1999) sustains that full dollarization will likely result in interest rates that are both lower and less sensitive to contagion. Furthermore, de jure dollarization may reduce the probability of a bank run that originates for reasons unrelated to the occurrence of a currency crisis. For instance, a dominant role of large and solid foreign banks in the banking system (which presumably would be encouraged by dollarization, as the Panamanian experience shows) would also reduce the danger of a weakened LLR, both because those banks could indirectly bring support from foreign central banks through their parents and because depositors' confidence on the financial backing of those institutions would be significantly higher.[23]

Nonetheless, the limits dollarization imposes on the ability of a central bank to act as an LLR still point to a crucial caveat of de jure dollarization. These limits have to be measured against some benchmark regime, which in the absence of a better alternative could be associated with the regime ongoing at the time the decision to dollarize is being considered.[24] We will make no claim of optimality in this paper—too many relevant factors are left out in our analysis. Rather, we will concentrate on the *incremental* costs that dollarization brings about only in the form of limitations to the LLR function of the central bank.

It is intuitive to think of these costs as inversely related both to the degree of de facto financial dollarization and to the flexibility of the exchange rate regime. The discretion to print money unlimitedly is what places the central bank in a privileged position to guarantee all the domestic currency the financial sector claims. Although this intervention may come at the cost of inflation, it is conceivable that an injection of funds to keep afloat institutions in distress should have the effect of preventing a recession rather than fueling an escalation of prices. Thus, if the availability of liquid funds on request is what characterizes the LLR function of the central bank, a de jure dollarized economy is qualitatively similar to both a fully de facto dollarized economy and a pure currency board. It is similar to a dollarized economy because the central bank cannot guarantee dollar assets beyond its usable stock of liquid international reserves; and it is similar to a pure currency board because by definition money cannot be discretionally printed.

This oversimplified view highlights the importance of the initial conditions under which the dollarization decision is discussed, at least in its LLR-related aspects.[25] The reality is considerably more complex. First, under an "impure" currency board à la Williamson (1995), the central bank may preserve a certain degree of flexibility to affect the monetary stance, for example through the use of reserve requirements or the change in the composition of foreign assets. Thus, Argentina's currency board allows the central bank to meet up to a certain fraction of the required backup of base money with dollar-denominated public debt so that in the event of a liquidity crunch it can increase the amount of debt so computed to release dollar liquidity. Second, a reduction in the level of reserve requirements amounts to the same effect.[26] Whereas the former recourse can still be available under full dollarization (e.g., by imposing a liquid asset requirement much as the Argentinean case today), the second is definitely out of hand as soon as the central bank is disposed of.[27]

The de jure dollarization does not seem to represent a qualitative change from de facto dollarization from a dollar liquidity needs perspective, but there is at least one often overlooked aspect that may introduce an important distinction between the two. As long as there is a demand for local currency, the central bank can buy its way out of a crisis by printing money to purchase the dollars it needs to assist the banking sector. Alternatively, if we are willing to accept that dollar depositors are simply insuring themselves against exchange rate risk, then financial dollarization could largely be regarded as dollar indexation. In either case, dollar liquidity can be replaced by the central bank's capacity to issue domestic currency, a recourse that de jure dollarization completely eliminates.[28]

4.3 LLR and Endogenous Financial Dollarization

In this section we depart from the issues concerning the limitations that de jure dollarization would imply on the LLR function to address some questions not yet explored in the new literature of financial dollarization. In particular, we intend to provide a framework better suited to examine the interaction between de facto dollarization and the LLR function.

In a bimonetary (i.e., de facto dollarized) economy, the presence of an LLR works as an implicit insurance, both to the bank and to depositors, inducing further endogenous dollarization. The logic is straightforward. In the first case, an LLR entails a blanket bank insurance against exchange rate shocks, leading banks to undervalue currency risk and fostering financial dollarization. In the second, dollar deposits introduce a currency mismatch in the economy and are inherently more risky than peso deposits. Therefore, any (explicit or implicit) insurance that does not discriminate between currencies is more valuable for dollar depositors, making them more attractive and, again, stimulating dollarization.[29]

From this perspective the only consequence of financial dollarization is an increase in macroeconomic risk, so the presence of endogenous dollarization should be regarded as a handicap. In particular, the more financially dollarized the economy, the greater the incentive of the central bank to hold a substantive stock of reserves, either to defend the exchange rate if it comes under pressure, or to bail out troubled institutions in case a devaluation cannot be avoided. However, the previous argument suggests that de facto dollarization may be at least partially explained by the distortions associated with the presence of a strong LLR in a bimonetary economy. There is some ground to conclude, then, that a bimonetary economy with a strong LLR may tilt toward an equilibrium of high dollarization, massive reserves, and pervasive central bank intervention. Note that although the use of foreign currencies may be optimal to a certain extent, the final outcome may entail excessive dollarization and risk.

We use the model of section 2 and borrow from Broda and Levy Yeyati (2000) to illustrate these points. The only source of risk comes from uncertainty on the future exchange rate. The point is relevant to highlight the endogenous components of the dollarization phenomenon and the creation of devaluation-related risk.

4.3.1 Lender of Last Resort under Full Deposit Insurance

Consider a bank that faces the following recursive problem: given the market peso and dollar deposit rates, it has to decide the optimal currency composition of its liability portfolio (or funding strategy). We implicitly assume that the bank cannot commit to a posted interest rate, reflecting the fact that rates are customarily negotiated with each client on a personal basis. Note that we can easily frame the problem in terms of the model in section 2, as the risk-return profile of the bank's portfolio can be fully characterized by its currency composition. Expressing values in dollar terms, we can characterize the bank's decision again as

$$V = \max_{\lambda} \frac{\Pi}{1 - \delta s(X, \gamma)},$$ (4.7)

where

$$\Pi(\lambda) = \int_0^1 \max[0, e(R - (1 - \lambda)r_p) - \lambda r_d)]f(e)\,de,$$ (4.8)

λ is the share of dollar deposits, and $f(e)$ is the probability density function (p.d.f.) of the (dollar-peso) exchange rate at the end of the period, with support $[0, 1]$ and mean e^m. The current exchange rate is set to one for simplicity. We can think of e as driven by an exogenous shock, with low values (large depreciations) corresponding to bad states of nature. The variable R denotes (gross) returns on bank assets, assumed to be fixed in nominal (peso) terms. This assumption captures a common feature of economies with a bimonetary banking sector: the existence of a currency mismatch somewhere in the economy. For simplicity, in the model the mismatch appears in the bank's balance sheet.[30] Finally, also for simplicity, we assume that the distribution of end-of-period exchange rates is identical in each period (i.e., does not depend on history).

The similarity with the moral hazard problem of section 2 is apparent once we restate the profit function as

$$\Pi = \int_{e_c(\lambda)}^{1} [e(R - (1 - \lambda)r_p) - \lambda r_d]f(e)\,de = P(\lambda)[\bar{e}(\lambda)R - C(\lambda)] \tag{4.9}$$

with[31]

$$e_c(\lambda) \equiv \frac{\lambda r_d}{R - (1 - \lambda)r_p}; \quad P(\lambda) = \int_{e_c(\lambda)}^{1} f(e)\,de$$

$$\bar{e}(\lambda) = \frac{\int_{e_c(\lambda)}^{1} ef(e)\,de}{P(\lambda)}; \quad C(\lambda) = \bar{e}(\lambda)(1 - \lambda)r_p + \lambda r_d. \tag{4.10}$$

As before, depositors are assumed to be risk neutral and can either invest in fully insured dollar or peso deposits, or in an outside, risk-free asset with return r_f. Depositors do not observe the bank's dollarization share.[32] Equilibrium is defined as the triplet (λ^*, r_p, r_d), such that $\lambda^* = \lambda^e$, and the bank maximizes equation 4.7.

Under these assumptions, it can be shown that a central planner would choose $\lambda^C = 0$.[33] This logic is straightfoward: on the one hand, dollarization does not entail any gain in terms of investment returns; on the other, it generates a potential risk of default with the associated liquidation costs.

The individual bank, in contrast, maximizes the discounted flow of profits, taking into account the probability $P(\lambda)$ of surviving the current period:

$$V = \max_{\lambda} \frac{\Pi(\lambda)}{1 - \delta P(\lambda)}. \tag{4.11}$$

In this case, the peso-dollar spread depends on the expected devaluation e^m, namely, $r_p/r_d = 1/e^m$. Differentiating with respect to the dollarization ratio, we obtain the following first-order condition:[34]

$$\frac{\partial V_D}{\partial \lambda} = \frac{1}{1 - \delta P(\lambda)} (\Pi' + \delta P' V_D).$$
(4.12)

Assume now that the central bank offers a blanket LLR such that failed banks are rescued with a probability β. In order to assess the incremental impact of the LLR, we keep the assumption of a full DIS. The bank's probability of survival is now given by

$$s(\lambda) = (1 - \beta)P(\lambda) + \beta,$$
(4.13)

where $s(\lambda) > P(\lambda)$ (and $0 > s'(\lambda) = (1 - \beta)P'(\lambda) > P'(\lambda)$). The bank's problem now becomes

$$V_{LLR} = \max_{\lambda} \frac{P(\lambda)[\bar{e}(\lambda)R - C(\lambda)]}{1 - \delta s(\lambda)}$$
(4.14)

and the first-order condition

$$\frac{\partial V_L}{\partial \lambda} = \frac{1}{1 - \delta s(\lambda)} (\Pi' + \delta s' V_L)$$
(4.15)

Then, it is easy to show that the presence of an LLR increases the optimal level of dollarization of a bank relative to the decentralized equilibrium, that is, $\lambda_{LLR}^* \geq \lambda_D \geq \lambda^C = 0.$[35] This should not be surprising: risk in this context is associated with dollarization. Therefore, as in section 4.2.1, by reducing the cost of risk to the banks, a blanket guarantee (in the form of an LLR) stimulates risk taking, which in the context of our model can only take the form of less costly (although riskier) dollar funding.

It should be clear to the reader that these results rely on the (quite realistic) assumption that the LLR facility is available to banks irrespective of their dollarization ratio, so the chances of preserving the insurance benefits in the event of a devaluation are enhanced, without any increase in the effective cost of dollar funding to the bank. In other words, the bank benefits from lower dollar rates, transferring the cost to the LLR.

However, the same principle that guides the optimal bailout policy in Cordella and Levy Yeyati (1999) can be extended to this case. Moreover, because the extent of individual financial dollarization is readily observable, it is easy to conceive (although possibly difficult to implement) an LLR rule contingent on the degree of dollarization of the bank, such that $\beta(\lambda)$, $\beta'(\lambda) < 0$, which can readily undo the distortion associated with the insurance policy. In this case,

$$s'(\lambda) = (1 - \beta)P' + (1 - P)\beta', \tag{4.16}$$

which can be set to the desired level by making $\beta'(\lambda)$ arbitrarily steeper so that we can obtain the first best solution.

In the setup just described, it is the currency mismatch that generates the probability of bank default, because firms are not able to hedge against currency risk. In this case, trivially, both full dollarization and the legal prohibition of dollar deposits rule out the source of distortion.

4.3.2 LLR in the Absence of Deposit Insurance

In the absence of deposit insurance, an LLR plays the role of an implicit insurance that covers deposits irrespective of their currency of denomination. This, in turn, can induce further dollarization, as dollar deposits are free from currency risk while their higher inherent risk is not punished in the case that a devaluation precipitates the bank's default. We illustrate this point with a simple example that uses the same framework as in the previous sections.

Interest rate arbitrage by depositors implies the following characterization of domestic interest rates in each currency:

$$r_p^e = [(1 - \beta)P(\lambda)\bar{e}^e + \beta e^m]r_p + [1 - P(\lambda)](1 - \beta)S_p = r_f,$$
$$r_d^e = [(1 - \beta)P(\lambda) + \beta]r_d + [1 - P(\lambda)](1 - \beta)S_p = r_f, \tag{4.17}$$

where S is the dollar value of the amount reimbursed per unit of deposit, assumed for simplicity to be the same across currencies, with $S_d = S_p = eR$. Then it follows that the peso-dollar spread

$$\frac{r_p}{r_d} = \frac{(1 - \beta)P(\lambda) + \beta}{(1 - \beta)P(\lambda)\bar{e} + \beta e^m} > \frac{1}{\bar{e}}, \tag{4.18}$$

with

$$\frac{\partial \left(\frac{r_p}{r_d} \right)}{\partial \beta} = \frac{P(\lambda^e)(\bar{e}^e - e^m)}{[(1 - \beta)P(\lambda^e)\bar{e}^e + \beta e^m]^2} > 0. \tag{4.19}$$

Thus, *for any given level of dollarization*, an increase in the probability of an LLR intervention increases the cost of peso funding vis-à-vis dollar funding to the bank. The reason for this should be clear from the 4.17 equations. In the event of a large devaluation, with certain probability the LLR indirectly subsidizes dollar deposits by paying its full dollar value, r_d, which exceeds the value of the peso deposit, er_p. Thus, dollar deposits benefit from an insurance against exchange rate risk that is funded by a pool of central bank resources. Whether these resources are obtained through regular taxes or through bank contributions (which eventually are reflected in intermediation spreads), the exchange rate insurance is always paid, at least in part, by peso deposits. This cross subsidy is the flip side of the resulting larger financial dollarization.[36]

4.4   Alternative LLR under Full Dollarization

Even though the lack of a lender of last resort function may result in a healthier system (due to less moral hazard), or reduce the distortions studied in section 3, a banking system is naturally vulnerable to exogenous liquidity shocks, which would optimally require the intervention of the central bank or some other agency to loosen the liquidity strain. Full dollarization entails the loss of the ability to print money and therefore the central bank's capacity to act as an LLR without the need to carry a stock of low-yield liquid assets.

The presence of systemic shocks—as opposed to individual bank problems—presents a challenge for alternative arrangements to the LLR. Small or idiosyncratic shocks can be diversified away domestically by a private insurer. Branch banking, for example, allows funds to be transferred from branches with surplus funds to those in need of cash. Interbank markets and commercial clearinghouses can also channel cash from high liquidity to low liquidity banks. Neither of these entities, however, can stem a nationwide demand for currency occasioned by a major aggregate shock. Private deposit insurance can prevent panics by removing the reason for the public to run to currency.[37] However, an extensive insurance scheme is needed in the event of large shocks. These encompassing schemes, in turn, give rise to doubts about the repayment capabilities of the insurance agency, doubts that can ultimately be diverted only by the presence of a monetary authority (and its power to issue notes unlimitedly) to back the schemes. Substitutes for the lack of an LLR when an economy is confronted with systemic shocks are difficult to find.

In order to fulfill the role of an LLR in a dollarized economy, the central bank should ideally have foreign exchange reserves in sufficient amounts to forestall a run on dollar deposits. Although, the reserves allow the central banker to keep a traditional function of lender of last resort even though the bank has no ability to issue dollars, this trivial solution entails significant fiscal costs that are proportional to the range of shocks the LLR expects to face. A second mechanism of the same nature is the establishment of a contingency fund specifically created to cope with exogenous liquidity crises and explicitly taken into account in the fiscal budget. In this case (such as in Hong Kong) the government can act as an LLR either by divesting the fund or by issuing debt to escape the liquidity problems.[38] Although this strategy has its advocates,[39] the differences and relative advantages of having the fund managed by the government as opposed to the central bank's accumulation of foreign reserves are not obvious. A third version of the same approach is a liquid assets requirement of the type currently in place in Argentina, where the contingency fund is raised directly by the banks by investing part of their deposit base in liquid foreign-currency-denominated assets. Again, this solution does not come without costs, which are reflected in higher intermediation margins and lower bank profits. Despite their similarities, these mechanisms differ in the ways that their costs are borne. Whereas in the first two cases, the burden is ultimately distributed among consumers, the liquidity requirement entails an implicit tax on intermediation.

The main alternative proposed in policy and academic circles to this "saving for the rainy day" approach is the simple outsourcing of the LLR function, which can take the form of an institutional (IMF-type) LLR or a private international agency. There are at least three ways in which a private lender of last resort (PLLR) can be conceived: as a contract between a consortium of international banks and the central bank, as individual contracts between (onshore and offshore) banks, or as an implicit contract between foreign subsidiaries and their parents.

An innovative version of the first type of arrangement is a repo contract that involves a swap between the central bank and a foreign consortium. In the event of a crisis, authorities are allowed to get sizable instant credit in exchange for government dollar-denominated bonds. Argentina had such contingent credit line until the demise of convertibility in early 2002.[40]

A back-of-the-envelope calculation suggests that the fiscal benefits of an agreement of this sort may be ample. Consider the fiscal costs of Argentina's contract relative to other possible alternatives. The annual fee Argentina had to pay for the option to have access to this swap was thirty-two basis points. The cost of funds implicit in the repo agreement was roughly London InterBank Offering Rate (LIBOR) plus 205 basis points.[41] The size of the agreement reached U.S.$6.7 billion or 9 percent of the deposit base. Assuming that the Argentine government had the bonds to be used in the swap operation,[42] in periods without a crisis the contract represents an annual cost of approximately U.S.$21.5 million. If the Argentine government borrowed the whole amount of the contract and hoarded it as self-insurance in the form of liquid assets (e.g., U.S. Treasury bills), it would have to pay an "annual fee," equivalent to the interest rate premium over the international risk-free rate, on the debt contracted, which in the case of Argentina would be clearly higher than the premium implicit in the repo contract. Naturally, the government can always choose not to keep a stock of reserves and come up with the funds in times of a liquidity crunch, either by issuing new debt in international markets or by tapping domestic savings. However, recent experience has shown that either source of funds dries up rapidly when the country is in financial distress. Moreover, in the event of a crisis, the costs of drawing down the funds from the repo are considerably smaller than the rate at which the treasury would have to borrow in a period of the liquidity strain, if this is at all feasible. Thus, private insurance seems to be a convenient substitute for an LLR under dollarization.

Appealing as this solution may look on paper, its practical implementation raises at least a couple of important concerns. First, the fact that the same large international players are likely to be at both sides of the contract creates a potential agency problem. More precisely, it is difficult to envisage a way for the insurance contract to credibly prevent insuring institutions from hedging the increase in perceived risk that usually anticipates episodes of financial distress, and in so doing precipitate the financial collapse. For example, if the institutions behind the PLLR are the country's regular foreign lenders, an increase in risk will raise their exposure through the insurance contract, forcing them to cut current credit lines to the country's private borrowers.[43] Note that lack of coordination is at the root of this problem: although institutions are individually aware that by their hedging they increase the probability of a collapse, their negative impact is diluted in the aggregate while the benefits from hedging accrue entirely to them. Thus, this point relies heavily on the rather realistic assumption that no bank will be willing or able to insure a middle-sized country single-handedly.

A second concern is that if this type of contract extends to several emerging markets, the scope within which the insurer may diversify risks that are highly correlated within the region narrows. Furthermore, the scheme can amplify the contagion effect of a financial collapse in the same way as a bank failure does at the domestic level, simply by impinging on the insurers liquidity and forcing them to withdraw from other markets in the region. Finally, a regional crisis may force the insurers to default on their contracts. Ultimately, the contract has never been used and its usefulness, even on this relatively minor scale, is yet to be shown.

Much along the same line as the repo contract of the Argentine Central Bank, Dornbusch and Giavazzi (1998) argue that small economies can take advantage of the international capital market to solve liquidity and emergency supervision issues, and they suggest the outright privatization of both the LLR and the supervisory function of the central bank, which according to their view, takes the form of offshore guarantees of local banks' liabilities. The foreign guarantors will at the same time have an incentive to provide the supervisory function that domestic authorities are presumably poor at implementing. In this case, given the size of the insured economy, the aforementioned coordination problems appear to be less important. However, moral hazard on the side of the creditor can still arise. Even if the government can commit to a no-bailout policy, "too big to fail" arguments can render this strategy time inconsistent. Problems related to the "who monitors the monitor" problem expressed by Diamond (1984) can also play a significant role. Although the empirical relevance of this alternative to the LLR is yet to be tested,[44] it needs to be said that apart from the outsourcing of supervision (which at any rate can always be implemented separately), it does not differ substantively from the Argentine-style insurance contract.

Irrespective of the degree of dollarization, the apparent limitations of Latin American central banks in assisting the banking sector when they are hit by a systemic shock have created a clear competitive edge for foreign-owned institutions, which has been reflected in a wave of internationalization in many cases seen with favorable eyes by local monetary authorities. International branch banking can potentially represent a solution for commercial banks to relieve their illiquidity problems without resorting to the monetary authority. If the problem indeed originates in a contraction of liquidity due to a systemic run on the system (or just if it is strategically important for the bank to have a presence in the domestic financial market), it may be in the parent's interest to bail out its own branch. Moreover, given the usual information problems that blur the distinction between illiquidity and insolvency, the parent may be in a privileged position to make a call on the situation of the subsidiary. However, the parent may be subject to the agency problems already mentioned: it may find it too costly to rescue its foreign operation, and too-big-to-fail arguments may reduce its incentives to monitor. In the end, there is still no evidence as to whether and to what extent the implicit contract with the parent will eventually pay.[45]

In the case of Panama, Moreno-Villalaz (1999) argues that when faced with unexpected shocks, international banks have reacted by increasing their exposure, using external funds to support local operations. "They have done so in 1964, 1967–9, 1973–5 and 1978–80. The home offices of international banks have functioned as lenders of last resort ... as banks did not need to balance separately their external and internal operations, they could use external funds to finance local operations. This feature has been a shock absorber, a credit reserve that substitutes for central bank reserves and reduces the risk in the economy even under conditions of strain" (p. 4). The Panamanian government has not rescued failing banks, but only a few banks have failed during the past thirty years.

An alternative, albeit indirect, way of assessing the value of bank branching as a liquidity insurance mechanism is offered by the evidence, presented in Gonsalez-Eiras (2000), that national banks reduced their excess holdings of liquid assets by more than foreign-owned banks when the repo contract was introduced in Argentina. Inverting the argument made in their paper, one could regard the holding of excess reserves, as the banks insure themselves in the absence of a credible LLR and when faced with the lack of response of foreign-owned banks, as a sign of an implicit insurance contract with the parent. More precisely, lower reserves may be viewed not as a moral-hazard-related cost but rather as a more efficient distribution of resources.[46]

A different vein of the outsourcing approach sees an international financial organization in the role of LLR for dollarized emerging markets with weak central banks. Much has been discussed lately with respect to the need and the formal implementation of an international lender of last resort (ILLR).[47] The proposal goes beyond the issue of dollarization. Fischer (1999) has argued that the International Monetary Fund (IMF) is increasingly playing this role in practice, and that changes in the international financial system now under consideration will make it possible for it to exercise that function more effectively. As crisis lender, the IMF, whose financial structure is close to that of a credit union, has access to a pool of resources that can be lent to member countries under certain conditions. It has been assigned the lead in negotiating with member countries during a crisis, and it cooperates extensively in the preparation of financing packages. Thus, it can be argued that implicitly it has already become the LLR in many emerging economies.[48] Hence, although a formal move may require international agreements, the IMF's role will not differ drastically from what it presently is. There is scant empirical work on the impact of these international agencies. Bordo and Schwartz (2000) perform a simple with-without comparison of countries receiving IMF assistance subject to similar external shocks during crises in the period 1973–1998. They find evidence that the real performance of IMF-assisted countries was possibly better than that of the unassisted ones.

The IMF as ILLR is subject to traditional moral hazard criticism. An international agency will not be tempted to protect its exposure to a country under attack, but given its international constituency it is certainly more likely to face a Samaritan's dilemma that, if anticipated by the government and international investors, may hamper its efforts to discipline domestic financial markets.[49] However, as suggested by Cordella and Levy Yeyati (1999), given that the dilemma will remain as long as the IMF is in operation, an explicit acknowledgment of its role as ILLR may be preferable to today's constructive ambiguity approach.

Finally, a central bank of a (preferably large) country has been suggested as an alternative candidate to function as an ILLR, a path recently explored by Argentina in association with its plan to fully dollarize the economy. More precisely, Argentine authorities proposed pledging the seignorage flow that Argentina enjoys under the currency board (and that would be lost once fully dollarized) as collateral to a supplementary borrowing facility, much in the way of a

premium under a regular limited insurance scheme.[50] A more ambitious proposal includes having the Fed as an LLR, which would
require a clear stand of the United States with respect to the possible
general trend toward dollarization. This consensus is far from being
reached, either in government or in academic circles. While on one
extreme Barro (1999) considers dollarization as a historic opportunity for the United States, on the other Frankel (1999) emphasizes the
potentially negative implications for the conduct of U.S. macroeconomic policy. One key issue behind this ongoing debate is that
although the impact of Argentina on U.S. policy can only be marginal, matters could change drastically if there is a general move in
Latin America toward dollarization. Moreover, even if no explicit
LLR assistance is negotiated with the U.S. government, anything but
unilateral dollarization could be interpreted as containing an implicit
guarantee by the Federal Reserve, and could ultimately force the
United States to intervene in the event of a crisis. Any steps toward
full dollarization of a country are likely to be considered by the
United States from this broader perspective.

4.5   Conclusions

In this chapter we have attempted to shed some light on two inter-
related questions: Should the loss of the central bank as an LLR be a
primary concern when deciding whether or not to fully dollarize the
economy? and How could the liquidity insurance implicit in the LLR
function be preserved under full dollarization and at what cost? Our
discussion tried to emphasize two important aspects that in our view
have not received the attention they deserve in the ongoing debate
on dollarization and the LLR.

First, we have considered the importance of initial conditions
when judging the costs and benefits of moving towards de jure dollarization. In particular, we argued that in a heavily financially dollarized economy the central bank already faces significant obstacles
to providing liquidity insurance to the banking sector, irrespective of
the exchange regime in place. We have drawn attention to two commonly overlooked issues in the current literature. On the one hand,
if financial dollarization cannot be simply regarded as dollar indexation, then the need for dollar liquidity cannot be replaced by the
capacity of the central bank to issue domestic currency, making the

move from a heavily dollarized economy to full dollarization a relatively minor one. Accordingly, the practical relevance of the loss associated with full dollarization is negatively related with the current degree of financial dollarization, a variable that draws a line between emerging economies that are potential candidates for dollarization. On the other hand, we show that the mere presence of an LLR in a bicurrency economy may in itself be a source of endogenous financial dollarization and, in turn, of currency risk. From this point of view, de jure dollarization is a superior choice to de facto dollarization, as the former removes the source of this distortion by eliminating the currency mismatch in the economy.

Second, we have examined the fact that the alternative sources of insurance regularly proposed by economists and policymakers tend to underestimate the financial costs involved as well as the implementation issues attached. Here, we have broadly grouped the different arrangements in three distinct categories. The first category is the "save it for a rainy day" approach, which we associate with self-insurance in the form of the holding of an important stock of liquid international reserves at a substantial fiscal cost. The second is the private insurance approach, which implies the purchasing of insurance from an external agency, which represents a savings compared to the previous alternative, but may face important quantitative limits as well as inverse moral hazard problems if implemented extensively. The third category is the international IMF-style lender of last resort, the most criticized but ultimately most feasible (and possibly most cost-efficient) option, which nonetheless is subject to the traditional moral hazard concerns usually associated with the LLR function. In the end, the LLR may be (at least partially) substituted only at a significant cost and countries not financially dollarized should factor in this cost when pondering the full dollarization option.

The analysis also provides some broad guidelines for future research. A more detailed examination of the efficiency of the arrangements that currently substitute for the LLR function of the central bank would provide clearer outlines for the growing body of theoretical research on the topic. The alternatives implemented by Panama, Argentina, and Hong Kong are some of the cases that should be examined by this research agenda. Indeed, they may eventually suggest new innovative contracts that reduce the problems faced by dollarized economies.

Notes

1. Henry Thornton developed some of the key ideas in 1802, but it was not until Bagehot that these ideas became respectable among theorists.

2. These are not, of course, the only means by which public intervention may contribute to the stability of the system. For example, a deposit insurance scheme can also play a preventive role in a "self-fulfilling crisis" (Diamond and Dybvig 1983), and the marketing of default-free government assets provides an instrument that fosters banks' self-insurance (Holmstrom and Tirole 1998).

3. The same, of course, applies to the issue of default-free paper or any credible liquidity insurance contract.

4. Accordingly, we use the term *dollarization* to refer to either de jure or de facto dollarization, unless otherwise noted.

5. See Calvo (1999), among others.

6. See Gianinni (1999) for a thorough discussion of these issues.

7. Alternatively, private lenders may be prevented from redistributing aggregate liquidity to illiquid but solvent firms due to the existence of information costs, as in Flannery (1996).

8. See Goodhart and Huang (2000) for a model of the related "too big to fail" argument.

9. A solvency crisis occurs when the loss on banks' assets exceeds the banks' capital and is systemic when it is generated from an aggregate shock to the economic fundamentals that affects more or less permanently the asset value of a large class of banks. If a bank's assets comprise dollar loans to producers of nontradables, the implicit currency mismatch may increase the nonperforming ratio of these loans, thus rendering the bank insolvent.

10. Bank liabilities are generally of a shorter maturity and thus more sensitive to interest rate changes than are bank assets.

11. Goodhart (1987, 1995) asserts that the clear-cut distinction between illiquidity and insolvency is a myth, because banks that require the assistance of the LLR are already suspicious of being insolvent.

12. For more examples on the bailouts of large institutions see Bordo and Schwartz (2000).

13. As noted by Friedman and Schwartz (1963), "The actions required to prevent monetary collapse did not call for a level of knowledge of the operation of the banking system ... which was developed only later and was not available for the Reserve System. On the contrary, as we have pointed out earlier, pursuit of the policies outlined by the System itself in the 1920s, or for that matter by Bagehot in 1873, would have prevented the catastrophe" 407.

14. Indeed, moral hazard concerns have been at the heart of the discussion every time a systemic crisis has induced generalized assistance to financial institutions.

15. In section 4.4 we advance an alternative interpretation of the same evidence.

16. This assumption allows us to separate the impact of bank insurance on banks' incentives from its effect on the cost of funding.

17. Note that, as usual in agency problems, observability is not always sufficient to rule out moral hazard, because ultimately the action of the agent (in this case, the bank) has to be made verifiable in a court of law to trigger any legal penalty. However, a principal who is a depositor can always punish the bank's misbehavior by walking away with his or her money to another bank.

18. In addition, to avoid corner solutions, we assume that $\partial^2 p / \partial X^2 \leq 0$, with the effect that equation 2.2 is strictly concave in the control variable X and that $X \geq \underline{X} = r_f / \mu$, with $p(\underline{X}) = 1$ and $p'(\underline{X}) > -1/\underline{X}$, with the effect that the risk-free asset is strictly dominated in expected returns by (at least) some risky portfolio.

19. In the text that follows, we assume there are no bankruptcy costs.

20. The banks maximize $V_t = \Pi_t + \delta s_t(X, \gamma)\Pi_{t+1} + \delta^2 s_{t+1}(X, \gamma)^2 \Pi_{t+1} + \ldots$, with $\Pi_t = \mu p(X)_t(X - r)$.

21. Consistent with the preceding discussion, it can be shown that a bailout's beneficial effect on effort is proportional to the degree of conservatism (represented by the discount rate δ) and the level of bank rents (alternatively, the intermediation margin).

22. Models that emphasize the banking-crisis-to-currency-crisis causality, such as Goldfajn and Valdez (1996) and Chang and Velasco (2001), typically overlook the fact that lack of confidence in the local currency may be at the origin of the banking crisis that eventually triggers the currency crisis, as appears to have been the case in Argentina in 1995.

23. A weak LLR in heavily dollarized economies may play a role in this process of internationalization, as will be discussed in more detail in section 4.

24. This, of course, is not necessarily the only consideration, because one may regard the current regime as unsustainable and hence not a viable alternative.

25. For example, the view illustrates the differences between countries such as Argentina, where the LLR is already seriously impaired, and Brazil, where the combination of a low degree of financial dollarization and a flexible exchange rate policy make these limitations relatively minor.

26. Both recourses were used by the Central Bank of Argentina at the time of the bank run that followed the Tequila Crisis in 1995.

27. The same argument is valid to a large extent for a fixed exchange rate regime, inasmuch as a significant injection of domestic currency eventually leads to unsustainable pressure on the exchange rate. One can also argue that if the available liquidity is perceived to be insufficient to forestall a currency crisis, it could actually fuel it. In addition, limited official financial rescue packages can have counterproductive effects by providing investors, who in principle would want to exit with the dollar, the liquidity to do so.

28. This is true as long as the monetary authority, loosely speaking, is able to print money faster than the currency depreciates. Thus, even disregarding the costs of inflation, monetizing dollar liabilities may not be possible, due to the collapse of the demand for real balances. This limitation is particularly important in countries

with higher de facto dollarization, where it is already easy to substitute away local currency.

29. Of course, this conclusion assumes that the implicit coverage of the LLR exceeds that of the existing deposit insurance scheme.

30. By imposing currency mismatch regulations, a central bank can trivially eliminate this problem. However, as long as the degree of financial dollarization exceeds the fraction of the real economy effectively dollarized, there is a currency mismatch somewhere in the economy. A regulation eliminating the currency mismatch in the bank's balance sheet is simply shifting the currency risk from the banks to the firms. The bank, however, has transformed its currency risk into credit risk. Whether the currency mismatch is in the balance sheet of the bank or in those of the firms is not important in this excercise; therefore, we proceed with the assumption that the banks' balance sheet is mismatched.

31. For future reference, $\underline{e}(\lambda) = (\int_0^{e_c(\lambda)} ef(e)\,de)/(1 - P(\lambda))$. Also note that $P' < 0$ because $e_c' > 0$. For the problem to be well behaved, we need $P'' > 0$.

32. Because the focus of this chapter is to study the effect of the banks' behavior on the share of dollarization, we keep the depositor's problem decision as simple as possible. All the results hold for the cases of a partial DIS. For a discussion of this portfolio decision under risk aversion, see Ize and Levy Yeyati (1998).

33. The central planner maximizes the expected return of the investment minus expected liquidation costs. We can use equation 4.10 and note 31 before computing the first-order condition of the bank, to obtain $\max_\lambda \sum_{i=0}^{\infty} \delta^i [\int eRf(e)\,de - r_f] = \max_\lambda (e^m R - r_f - [1 - P(\lambda)](1 - \theta)\underline{e}R)/(1 - \delta)$, where θ is the share of assets that the bank loses in terms of liquidation costs. From the fact that expected liquidation costs (the third term in the numerator) increase with dollarization, it follows that the optimal share of dollar deposits is $\lambda^C = 0$.

34. In turn, using $\bar{e}' = -(e_c'(\lambda)f(e_c)e_c)/P - (P'\bar{e})/P = (P'/P)(e_c - \bar{e})$, we get $\pi' = P(\bar{e}r_p - r_d) = Psr_d \geq 0$, and $\pi'' = P'r_d s \geq 0$.

35. For a given λ, $0 < s' < P'$, and $V_L > V_D$. For δ small enough, $\lambda^L = \lambda^D = 1$; for δ large enough, $\lambda^L = \lambda^D = 0$; and for the intermediate cases, $\lambda^L = 1$ and $\lambda^D = 0$.

36. We can think of several ways of financing the LLR. For the purpose of the model, the easiest alternative would be an *ex post* lump sum tax (including the issuance of public debt to distribute this tax over a longer period). Whenever the financing needs cannot be resolved through taxes (or, similarly, when projected fiscal deficits induce current inflation), there may still exist an inflation tax such that holders of pesos (consumers in general) and peso assets cross-subsidize dollar asset holders. In this case, however, the injection of peso liquidity that drives up prices may have a feedback effect on the exchange rate. In this case, dollar deposits may need to be converted at an arbitrary rate in a way similar to a confiscation. Of course, rational dollar depositors anticipate that they will be ripped off in the event of a devaluation, so the desired reduction in financing costs would not materialize whereas the peso-dollar spread would narrow, reducing dollarization.

37. In Panama, for example, a privately funded deposit insurance scheme is in the process of being established in accord with a 1998 new supervisory Superintendent of Banks office; before then, a supervisory agency existed but its powers and impact

were marginal. Foreign banks are subject to their home country's supervision and regulation.

38. It should be pointed out, however, that stabilization funds should be safely kept aside for use during a crisis. Otherwise they may be diverted to other purposes, as happened recently in Mexico and Thailand with international reserves that had been acquired through sterilization operations (for the case of Mexico, see Calvo and Mendoza 1996).

39. See Calvo (1999), for example.

40. These contingent credit lines are likely to be cheaper under full dollarization because it rules out the risk of devaluation-related bankruptcies as mentioned earlier.

41. There are many other details of the program we are ignoring here for conciseness. The maturity of the contract is three years and there is an evergreen clause such that, every three months, the life of the program is extended an additional three months. Argentine dollar-denominated bonds must be posted to a market value of 20 percent more than the actual funds delivered. If prices of the bonds delivered fall by more than 5 percent, further bonds must be delivered as margin to maintain the size of the previous condition.

42. This is true for the current level of the contract, but can be binding if bonds suffer large falls in prices or if the amount contracted increases. In the 1995 run, the amount of dollar-denominated bonds was binding when the central bank was using its capacity to act as an LLR.

43. The same can be said of insurance against a currency crisis, which can accelerate the exchange rate collapse as the insurer seeks to hedge its insurance policy-related currency risk by short-selling the domestic currency.

44. In Panama, domestic banks have established lines of credits with foreign banks and have usually been able to draw on them during liquidity crunches (though not during the 1988 crisis).

45. See Williamson (1996) and Calvo (1996) for related discussions.

46. Furthermore, inasmuch as these reserves are at least partially motivated by the probability of facing idiosyncratic liquidity shocks, the centralization of insurance in an LLR (or an LLR substitute) may benefit from risk diversification across banks.

47. See Eichengreen (1999) for a survey.

48. That includes countries that, like Argentina, have been stricken by crises in Asia, Russia, and Brazil, and currently use the IMF as a contingent facility.

49. This argument, which places the IMF in the usual dilemma faced by the typical central bank, is at the heart of the chorus of disapproval that usually follows the IMF's LLR assitance and that rapidly vanishes once critics realize that no sensible alternative is in sight.

50. In the example described in Calvo (1999), the U.S. Federal Reserve would retain U.S.$150 million in seignorage and would commit to Argentina a U.S.$600 million annual seignorage flow. The permanent flow discounted at an interest rate of, say, 5 percent could yield a stabilization fund of more than U.S.$10 billion, more than the emergency lending capacity that the BCRA now enjoys under the convertibility regime.

References

Aharony, J., and I. Swary (1983). Contagion effects of bank failures: Evidence from capital markets. *Journal of Business* 56 (3): 305–322.

Bagehot, W. (1873). Lombard Street. In Norman St. John-Stevas (ed.), *The collected works of Walter Bagehot*. London: The Economist. Vol. 9, 48–233.

Barro, R. (1999). Let the dollar reign from Seattle to Santiago. *Wall Street Journal*, March 8.

Berg, A., and E. Borenzstein (2000). The pros and cons of full dollarization. IMF Working Paper, 00/50.

Bhattacharya, S., and A. Gale (1987). Preference shocks, liquidity and central bank policy. In W. Barnett and K. Singleton (eds.), *New approaches to monetary economics*. Cambridge: Cambridge University Press.

Bordo, M. (1986). Financial crises, banking crises, stock market crashes and the money supply: Some international evidence, 1870–1933. In F. Capie and G. Wood (eds.), *Financial crisis and the world banking system*. New York: St. Martin's Press.

——— (1990). The lender of last resort: Some historical insights. NBER Working Paper, 3011.

Bordo, M., and A. Schwartz (2000). Measuring real economic effects of bailouts: Historical perspectives on how countries in financial distress have fared with and without bailouts. NBER Working Paper, 7701.

Broda, C., and E. Levy Yeyati (2000). Safety nets and endogenous financial dollarization. Mimeo, Universidad Torcuato Di Tella, Buenos Aires.

Calvo, G. (1999). On dollarization. Available at ⟨http://www.bsos.umd.edu/econ/ciecpn.htm⟩.

Calvo, G., and E. Mendoza (1996). Mexico's balance-of-payments crisis: A chronicle of a death foretold. *Journal of International Economics* 41.

Caprio, G., and D. Klingebiel (1996). Bank insolvency: Cross country experiences. World Bank Policy and Research Working Paper, 1574.

Chang, R., and A. Velasco (2001). Financial crises in emerging markets: A canonical model. *Quarterly Journal of Economics* (May): 489–518.

Cordella, T., and E. Levy Yeyati (1999). Bank bailouts: Moral hazard vs. value effect. IMF Working Paper, 99/106.

Diamond, P. (1984). Financial intermediation and delegated monitoring. *Review of Economic Studies* 51, no. 3 (July): 393–414.

Diamond, P., and D. Dybvig (1983). Bank runs, deposit insurance and liquidity. *Journal of Political Economy* 91, no. 3 (June): 401–419.

Dornbusch, R., and F. Giavazzi (1998). Hard currency and sound credit: A financial agenda for Central Europe. Available at ⟨http://www.mit.edu/~rudi/papers.html⟩.

Eichengreen, B. (1999). *Toward a new international financial architecture: A practical post-Asia agenda*. Washington DC: IIE Press.

Eichengreen, B., and A. Rose (1997). The empirics of currency and banking crises. Available at ⟨http://elsa.berkeley.edu/users/eichengr/research.htm⟩.

Fischer, S. (1999). "On the need for an International Lender of Last Resort," Available at ⟨www.imf.org/external/np/speech/1999/010399.htm⟩.

Flannery, M. (1996). "Financial crises, Payment System Problems, and Discount Window Lending." *Journal of Money, Credit and Banking* (November): 804–824.

Frankel, Jeffrey (1999). No single currency regime is right for all countries or at all times. NBER Working Paper, 7338, September.

Freixas, X., and J. Rochet (1998). *Microeconomics of banking.* Cambridge, Mass.: MIT Press.

Friedman, M., and A. Schwartz (1963). *A monetary history of the United States, 1867–1975.* New York: NBER.

Gianinni, C. (1999). Enemy of none but a common friend of all? An international perspective on the lender-of-last-resort function. IMF Working Paper, 99/10.

Goldfajn, I., and R. Valdes (1996). Capital flows and the twin crises: The role of liquidity. IMF Working Paper, 97/87.

Gonzalez-Eiras, M. (2000). The effect of contingent credit lines on bank's liquidity demand. Mimeo, Universidad de San Andrés, Buenos Aires.

Goodhart, C. (1987). Why do banks need a central bank? *Oxford Economic Papers* 39 (1): 75–89.

——— (1995). *The central bank and the financial system.* Cambridge, Mass.: MIT Press.

Goodhart, C., and H. Huang (2000). A simple model of an international lender of last resort. IMF Working Paper, 00/75.

Holmstrom, L., and J. Tirole (1998). Private and public supply of liqidity. *Journal of Political Economy* 106 (1): 1–40.

Ize, A., and E. Levy Yeyati. "Financial Dollarization."

Miron, A. (1986). Financial panics, the seasonality of the nominal interest rate, and the founding of the Fed. *American Economic Review* 76 (1): 125–140.

Moreno-Villalaz, J. L. (1999). Lessons from the monetary experience of Panama: A dollar economy with financial integration. *Cato Journal* 18 (3).

Schwartz, A. (1986). Real and pseudo-financial crises. In F. Capie and G. Wood (eds.): *Financial crisis and the world banking system.* New York: St. Martin's Press.

Williamson, J. (1995). What role for currency boards? Institute for International Economics, Washington D.C., Sept.

5 Measuring Costs and Benefits of Dollarization: An Application to Central American and Caribbean Countries

Ugo Panizza, Ernesto Stein, and Ernesto Talvi

5.1 Introduction

In recent years, the world's emerging markets have been exposed to substantial financial turbulence. One of the most noteworthy features of this period, which began with the Tequila Crisis of December 1994, is that the turbulence affected both countries with monetary and fiscal management problems and those that had followed all the orthodox formulas of macroeconomic conduct.

In this context of high financial volatility, two questions assume fundamental importance. The first relates to the debate on the new international financial architecture: What factors should be incorporated into this architecture to reduce the excessive volatility that has recently characterized the capital markets? The second question is: How can countries protect themselves from such turbulence without missing out on the opportunities provided by access to the international financial markets? Within this second topic, the debate on the optimal exchange regime has recently been gaining particular relevance.

Recent experience would seem to indicate a consensus on the problems associated with intermediate exchange rate regimes. A number of countries that attempted to defend their exchange rate parity but did not have hard pegs suffered speculative attacks on their currencies, leading to exchange rate crises and significant drops in GDP. In light of these experiences (the crises in Mexico, Asia, Russia, and Brazil), different analysts have recommended floating regimes, or "truly" fixed regimes such as a currency board or dollarization.

While a number of authors have clear preferences for either extreme in the range of exchange rate regimes, others acknowledge that countries are very diverse and therefore there is no single exchange regime appropriate for all countries at all times. Frankel (1999) provides a recent version of this last argument, but the literature on optimal currency areas (OCAs)—which began during the early 1960s with the work of Mundell (1961) and McKinnon (1963)—is based on a similar approach. This literature specifically aims to establish the conditions under which one country should form a monetary area with another. Considered from another standpoint, the question becomes: Under what conditions would it be very costly for a given country to sacrifice its monetary policy independence in order to reduce the transaction costs associated with trade and investment flows?

It is now clear that although the factors reflected in the theory of optimal currency areas—such as the degree of economic openness, the level of trade integration among the economies considering adoption of a single currency, the mobility of factors between these economies, and the symmetry of the shocks to which these economies are exposed—continue to be relevant, they overlook other important factors that should be considered in selecting the optimal exchange rate regime for a country. In this chapter, we shall expand the traditional OCA criteria, bringing into the analysis factors such as the benefits derived from establishing a credible link to a strong currency, and the level of de facto dollarization. While the benefits of credibility associated with a firm exchange rate commitment have become part of the conventional wisdom, the degree of de facto dollarization, and, in particular, the existence of debt denominated in dollars, have been overlooked in the relevant literature until quite recently (see recent studies by Calvo 1999; Hausmann et al. 1999; Hausmann 1999; Fernandez Arias and Talvi 1999; and Hausmann, Panizza and Stein 2001).

The purpose of this chapter is to develop a set of criteria that can be used to assess the benefits and costs of forming a monetary union with the United States, that incorporates the traditional criteria found in the OCA literature, and that expands the traditional criteria in directions we consider relevant to such a decision. In order to illustrate the type of analysis necessary to assess dollarization in practice, we then apply these criteria to a set of countries from Central America and the Caribbean.[1] Whenever possible, we attempt to measure the benefits and costs of dollarization in these countries, which, given their characteristics, are among the most likely in Latin America to take the first steps toward full dollarization of their economies.

Our analysis will be based primarily on two elements: (1) the structural characteristics of the countries studied, including occasional comparisons with other economies that have formed monetary unions or that have considered doing so; and (2) the comparative macroeconomic performance of these countries during the past four decades, with particular emphasis on differences in performance under different exchange rate regimes. When relevant, we shall supplement this discussion with evidence derived from other studies that encompass a larger sample of countries.

The chapter does not discuss how to resolve the practical difficulties related to the implementation of dollarization, should it be adopted. In this regard, we acknowledge that there may be important prerequisites for dollarization, such as sufficient reserves, or a relatively sound banking system. Dollarization also requires a solution to other practical issues such as loss of seignorage and the limited capacity to function as a lender of last resort.[2] Although we believe that these are important problems, they could in principle be dealt with if dollarization were to occur on the basis of a monetary association treaty with the United States.[3]

The rest of this chapter is organized as follows. In section 5.2, we provide a brief discussion of the costs and benefits of a monetary union with the United States, which will serve as a frame of reference for the analyses in the subsequent sections. In section 5.3, we briefly review the history of exchange regimes in Central America from 1960 through the present. Sections 5.4, 5.5, and 5.6 apply these assessment criteria to the Central American countries. In section 5.4, we analyze and measure the potential benefits of a monetary association treaty with the United States resulting from reduced transaction costs in trade and investment flows between the countries involved. Section 5.5 presents a simple framework that allows us to discuss the trade-off between credibility and monetary independence implicit in the decision to dollarize, and it analyzes the costs that Central American countries may incur if they decide to forgo their monetary independence. Section 5.6 discusses the benefits associated with credibility that countries stand to gain by dollarizing. Section 5.7 concludes the chapter.

5.2   The Benefits and Costs of Dollarization

It is useful to begin the discussion with a brief summary of the main benefits and costs of dollarization. In doing this, one can draw on an extensive literature discussing the relative merits of fixed versus flexible exchange rates, a very similar problem, although much less extreme and permanent. There are two important advantages associated with fixed exchange rates. First, fixed exchange rates reduce the exchange rate risk that may discourage trade and investment flows; second, fixed exchange rates provide a nominal anchor for monetary policy, reducing the economic authorities' discretion to generate inflationary "surprises." The disadvantage of fixed exchange rates is the loss of monetary independence.

The pros and cons of dollarization are essentially the same, although the permanence and credibility associated with dollarization give it special features that magnify the advantages and disadvantages alike. If fixed exchange rates reduce the exchange risk, dollarization virtually eliminates it, as the possibility of future devaluations —which is always present under fixed exchange rates—is eliminated. In addition, dollarization reduces other costs associated with trade and investment flows, derived from the need to transact in two different currencies.

Fixed exchange rates are not an automatic source of credibility. To reap the potential benefits that an exchange rate anchor may offer, first, there must be a credible commitment to fix the exchange rate, and second, the anchor currency must be a strong currency from a country with a sound reputation in monetary policy management. Fixed but adjustable exchange rates do not provide these benefits, nor does a monetary union among countries without monetary discipline. In this connection, dollarization provides the maximum benefits that one could expect, as it entails the firmest of commitments to a very strong currency.

Dollarization, however, also magnifies the costs, as it essentially represents a one-way journey entailing the loss of monetary independence. The discretion to use the exchange rate is lost, even in the event of a profound crisis. Indeed, under dollarization such crises may generate the need for costly deflationary adjustment. With less irreversibly fixed regimes, a country can always change its exchange rate regime in response to severe adverse shocks (a possibility that, for obvious reasons, has adverse effects in terms of credibility).

It should be clear from the last paragraph that the same discretion that enables the government to respond to shocks under flexible regimes also imposes costs in terms of credibility. Thus, although it makes sense to analyze the advantages associated with the reduction of transaction costs on its own, we will develop a simple framework that allows us to discuss the advantages of credibility and the disadvantages of losing monetary independence, taking into account that these dimensions are determined jointly. Before we start to analyze in more detail each of the potential benefits and costs of dollarization, it is useful to take a brief look at the recent history of exchange rate regimes in Central America, as the differences in these regimes will be used later in this chapter.

5.3   Exchange Regimes in Central America: A Historical Perspective

Although recent exchange rate regime experiences have varied substantially among the Central American countries, until the end of the 1970s, all of the countries studied in this paper had fixed exchange rates, with a reasonably high level of credibility. In Panama, this credibility stemmed from the adoption of the dollar as its currency, dating back to the 1904 monetary association treaty with the United States. In the other countries, their credibility was based on exchange rate parities that had remained perfectly stable for prolonged periods of time. In fact, most of these countries had not experienced any devaluation during the course of their history.

During the 1980s, countries gradually began to migrate toward more flexible regimes—and by the 1990s, most countries had adopted other regimes such as dirty floats, crawling pegs, and exchange rate bands. The 1980s can therefore be viewed as a transition period for these economies, during which they successively abandoned their commitment to a stable parity. These trends are clearly illustrated in figure 5.1. Whereas most countries in Central America migrated toward more flexible arrangements, Belize and Panama never abandoned their fixed regimes. Belize's currency was tied to the British pound until 1977, when it was pegged to the U.S. dollar, and the parity has remained stable throughout this period. Panama has had the utmost commitment that a country could have to a fixed exchange rate. Under the 1904 monetary association treaty with the United States, it adopted the U.S. dollar as its own currency.

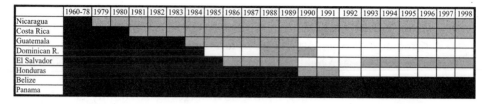

Figure 5.1
Historic trends in exchange regimes, Central America, 1960–1998. *Note:* Black indicates "truly fixed"; gray, "intermediate"; and white, "flexible."

The figure presents a stylized classification of exchange rate regimes into three categories: "truly fixed" regimes include hard pegs such as monetary unions and currency boards. It also includes fixed regimes that, even in the absence of institutional mechanisms that limit the authorities' discretionary powers to change the parity, have remained stable for a sufficiently long period of time (we consider periods of at least five years). Among the "intermediate" regimes we consider fixed exchange rates with frequent adjustments, crawling pegs, and exchange rate bands.[4] The third category is flexible regimes, which include all freely floating regimes and dirty floats. Although in the figure we make the distinction between intermediate and flexible regimes, in the comparative analysis of this chapter, we have combined these categories into one, as we are fundamentally interested in contrasting truly fixed regimes with the rest.

Figure 5.1 suggests that the exchange rate history of Central America during the last forty years can be divided into three periods. The first one, until the end of the 1970, during which all countries had truly fixed regimes. The second one, during the 1980s, represents the period of migration out of fixity for countries other than Panama and Belize. The year 1990 marks the beginning of a third period in which all countries that would abandon the fixed regime had already done so. There are several ways in which this stylized description illustrates how fruitful this region can be for the analysis of dollarization. First, one of the countries (Panama) has already adopted the dollar as its currency, and did so sufficiently long ago enough for a meaningful assessment of the results; second, migration of various countries from truly fixed to more flexible regimes makes it possible to compare the performance of these countries before and after the regime shift; and third, the variety of regimes in the latest period allows for comparisons of countries' performance across regimes.

5.4   Benefits Associated with Reduced Transaction Costs

One of the traditional criteria in defining optimal currency areas relates to the level of trade integration exhibited in economies whose monetary integration is being analyzed. As in this chapter we analyze the advantage for Central American countries' adopting the dollar as a currency for replacement of their own, we aim to determine the degree to which these economies are integrated with the United States. We are not interested, in contrast, in the share these countries represent in total U.S. trade.

Why is the level of trade integration with potential partners important? There are two reasons for this. First, a common currency reduces the uncertainty and risk involved in trade transactions and investment flows between countries. Although there are clearly ways to hedge against this risk, doing so may be costly, especially when a developing country's currency is involved. Furthermore, hedging mechanisms may not exist in some countries. Second, a common currency reduces other transaction costs in trade and investment flows, namely, those costs associated with the need to deal with multiple currencies. This is an independent effect, which may discourage trade and investment even in cases where exchange rates are perfectly stable.

Through these two channels, monetary unification may lead to expanded bilateral trade and increased investment flows between countries. Of course, it is important to question the significance of the effects of exchange rate volatility and transaction costs on trade and investment flows. Although the empirical evidence suggests that such effects exist, their significance varies considerably depending on the study in question.

5.4.1   Exchange Rate Volatility and Trade

A survey of the literature on the effects of exchange rate volatility on trade can be found in Edison and Melvin (1990). These authors survey a number of different articles published on the subject between 1984 and 1988, and they present the results in a comparative table, which is reproduced in table 5.1. The first five articles in the table are based on the effects of volatility on aggregate trade, and the latter seven articles study the effects of exchange rate volatility on bilateral trade. Of the first five, two find negative effects of volatility on trade,

Table 5.1
Exchange rate volatility's effect on trade: A survey of the literature

Author	Period	Trade flow	Variability measurement	Conclusion
Akhtar and Hilton (1984)	1974–1981	Total trade (United States and Germany)	Standard deviation of the nominal exchange rate	Negative effect
Gotur (1985)	1975–1983	Total trade (United States, Germany, France, Japan, and the United Kingdom)	Standard deviation of the effective nominal exchange rate index	Little to no effect
Kenen and Rodrik (1986)	1975–1984	Total imports of manufactured goods (eleven industrial countries)	Standard deviation of the effective exchange rate and standard error of real exchange rate equation	Negative effect
Bailey, Tavlas, and Ulan (1986)	1973–1984	Total real exports (seven largest Organization for Economic Cooperation and Development, OECD, countries)	Absolute value of the quarterly change in the effective nominal exchange rate	No effect
Bailey, Tavlas, and Ulan (1987)	1962–1985	Total real exports (OECD)	Absolute value of the quarterly change in the real and effective nominal exchange rate, standard deviation of the real and effective nominal exchange rate	Little to no effect
Thursby and Thursby (1985)	1973–1977	Real bilateral exports (twenty countries)	Standard deviation of the real and nominal exchange rate weighted to reflect trade and the absolute values of the percentage changes in the real and nominal exchange rates	Mixed results
Cushman (1986)	1965–1977 1973–1983	Real U.S. bilateral exports to six major trading partners	Standard deviation of changes in the real bilateral exchange rate combined with standard deviation and covariances with other major currencies	Negative effect

Table 5.1
(continued)

Author	Period	Trade flow	Variability measurement	Conclusion
Cushman (1988a)	1974–1983	Real U.S. bilateral exports to six major trading partners	Five alternative measurements of the standard deviation of errors in predicting the real exchange rate and future exchange rate	Negative effect on imports, inconclusive on Exports
Maskus (1986)	1974–1984	Real bilateral exports and imports by U.S. industry with other major trading partners	Unexpected change in the real exchange rate based on projected inflation and future rates	Negative effect on certain industries
DeGrauwe and De Bellefroid (1987)	1960–1969 1973–1984	Growth in real bilateral exports between the ten major industrial countries	Standard deviation of the change in the exchange rate and the absolute average change	Negative effect on growth not on level
Perl (1988)	1975–1986	U.S. real bilateral trade with four major trading partners	This component of the variability of the exchange rate not explained by relative money supply variability	Ambiguous effect
Brada and Mendez (1988)	1972–1977	Real bilateral exports (thirty countries)	Dummy variable for exchange regime	Positive effect

Source: Edison and Melvin (1990).

and the rest report negligible effects, if any. Of the seven studies focusing on bilateral trade flows, four find negative effects, two find inconclusive results, and the last one, by Brada and Mendez (1988) finds positive effects.[5] Although the results are not conclusive, table 5.1 on balance suggests that exchange rate volatility does reduce trade flows.

A more recent study on the effects of exchange volatility on trade is that of Frankel and Wei (1998). This study, based on bilateral trade flows, uses a methodology similar to Brada and Mendez (the gravity model, in which bilateral trade flows are explained as a function of the size of the countries and the distance between them) except that, rather than incorporating an exchange rate regime, it directly incorporates bilateral exchange rate volatility into the gravity model.[6]

Frankel and Wei (1998) find significant negative effects of exchange volatility on bilateral trade flows from 1965 through 1980. However, this effect disappears in more recent periods. One possible explanation is that these effects decline with the appearance of different hedging mechanisms, such as options, futures markets, and so on. However, it is important to stress that in developing countries such as the ones we are considering here, such hedging markets often do not exist or are very incomplete. If the diminishing effects of exchange rate volatility on bilateral trade result from the development of hedging mechanisms, we would expect this effect to continue to be significant for the bilateral trade flows of the countries studied here. We will analyze this issue in more detail in the text that follows.

Setting aside for now the downward trend in elasticity of bilateral trade with respect to exchange rate volatility, the average value of this elasticity during the whole period studied by Frankel and Wei (between 1965 and 1990) is −1.83.[7] It is interesting to ask, if one takes this average elasticity at face value, how dollarization would affect trade of Central American countries. To conduct this exercise, we calculate real bilateral exchange rate volatility for each of these countries with respect to the United States. We use precisely the same measurement of volatility as Frankel and Wei: the standard deviation of the logarithmic differences in the real exchange rate, based on monthly data. Exchange rate variability of each country for the period 1990–1998 is presented in the standard deviation column of table 5.2.[8]

Table 5.2
Real exchange rate volatility and effect on bilateral trade, 1990–1998

	Standard deviation	Trade effect (%)
Costa Rica	1.08	1.34
Dominican Republic	3.47	5.71
El Salvador	3.40	5.59
Guatemala	3.18	5.18
Honduras	6.57	11.39
Nicaragua	5.70	9.79
Panama	0.35	
Average	3.39	6.50

Source: International Financial Statistics (IFS), International Monetary Fund.

As we observe in the table, Panama has the lowest real exchange rate volatility. Its monthly standard deviation is 0.35 percent.[9] The volatility level in Costa Rica, which has an explicit policy of maintaining a relatively stable real exchange rate, is three times higher. In the rest of the countries, real exchange rate volatility is still higher, reaching levels of 5.7 percent and 6.6 percent in Nicaragua and Honduras, even after excluding the period of hyperinflation in Nicaragua, and the months prior to the devaluation of the lempira in early 1990, in Honduras.[10] In the trade effect column of table 5.2, we calculate the estimated increases in bilateral trade to be expected if, through the adoption of the dollar, the rest of the countries reduce their exchange rate volatility to levels similar to those observed in Panama. For example, in the case of Honduras, the calculation is $1.83 \times (6.6 - 0.35) = 11.4$ percent. In Costa Rica, the expected increase in bilateral trade is small, given its low initial volatility. In the rest of the countries, the average increase in bilateral trade is 7.5 percent.

A recent study by Rose (2000), focused primarily on the effect of common currency on trade, also examines the effects of nominal exchange rate volatility on bilateral trade, and finds them to be negative and significant.[11] In order to test our intuition that the costs of exchange rate volatility may be more important in the case of developing countries, we used the database created by Rose, which covers 186 countries for five different years between 1970 and 1990, and performed the following experiment: For each available year, we estimate the effects of nominal exchange rate volatility on (1) bilateral trade flows between pairs of Organization for Economic Cooperation and Development (OECD) countries; and (2) bilateral trade between other pairs of countries. The second group incorporates trade between developing countries, as well as trade between developing countries and industrialized countries.

The results, which are reported in table 5.3, confirm our prior results. For trade among OECD countries, the effects of exchange rate volatility on bilateral trade are usually positive, increasing over time and, for 1990, significant. In the case of other pairs of countries, the effect of exchange rate volatility is, with the exception of 1975, negative and highly significant. Furthermore, there is no clear declining trend in the effect of this variable.

Transaction costs arising from the need to operate with multiple currencies are, to a certain extent, independent of real exchange rate volatility. De Grauwe (1994), for example, presents the buying and

Table 5.3
Effect of nominal exchange rate volatility on bilateral trade

	1970	1975	1980	1985	1990
OECD countries	−0.03	0.11	0.04	0.12	0.14**
	(0.65)	(0.33)	(0.69)	(0.21)	(0.04)
Non-OECD countries	−0.06***	0.0002	−0.06***	−0.03***	−0.009***
	(0.00)	(0.98)	(0.00)	(0.00)	(0.00)

Source: Authors' calculations based on Rose (2000).
P values in parentheses. ***Statistically significant at 1 percent, **statistically significant at 5 percent.

selling spreads between the Belgian franc and various industrial country currencies. The cost of exchanging Belgian francs for guilders or deutsche marks is similar to the cost of exchanging them for French francs, pounds sterling, or U.S. dollars (approximately 0.5 percent), despite the low volatility of the Belgian franc vis-à-vis the guilder or deutsche mark. Thus, transaction costs are not eliminated when exchange rate volatility is reduced. The only way to eliminate such costs is through monetary unification.

How important are these transaction costs? The report of the EC Commission (1990) estimates transaction costs in the case of the European Union to be one-fourth to one-half of one point of product per year. We might expect significantly higher transaction costs in Central American countries, because the spreads between buying and selling prices should be greater when less liquid exchange rate markets are involved.[12]

Recent studies on the intensity of bilateral trade between the Canadian provinces and the U.S. based on the gravity model (McCallum 1995; Helliwell 1998) suggest that the combined effect of exchange volatility and transaction cost can be much greater than discussed earlier. These authors found that after controlling for distance and size of the economies, bilateral trade between two Canadian provinces on average is twenty times higher than trade between a Canadian province and a U.S. state. This result is surprising, especially considering that these countries have a large common border, share the same language and cultural values, and have a free trade agreement that minimizes trade barriers. Although there are other transaction costs associated with international trade, the need to exchange currencies might at least partially explain these surprisingly large results.

Rose (2000) provides ample support for the hypothesis that these transaction costs are in fact important for trade. He estimates the effect of currency union in a sample of 186 "countries." In fact, he includes in his sample not only countries but also all the dependencies, territories, and colonies and overseas departments for which the United Nations collects international trade data.[13] Rose finds that, other things equal—he controls for such variables as a common border, a common language, colonial links, membership in the same free trade area (FTA), and so on—two countries that share a common currency trade over three times as much as do otherwise similar countries with different currencies. Furthermore, Rose performs extensive sensitivity analysis and finds that the result is extremely robust.

Regardless of the effect of real exchange rate volatility and transaction costs of trade, these effects should have a larger impact on the economy as a whole in countries with a high degree of openness, in which trade represents a significant share of GDP. Similarly, the benefits of eliminating these transaction costs affecting trade flows between two countries should be proportional to the degree of trade integration between the countries. In the following section, we shall present information on the degree of trade integration of each of the countries studied with the United States and with the rest of Central America.

5.4.2   Trade Integration between the Countries Considered

Table 5.4 presents the share corresponding to the United States and to Central American countries as a destination for exports from each of the countries studied. On the whole, the United States and Central America are the destination for 50 to 80 percent of exports from each of the countries considered—less in the case of Belize and the Dominican Republic (approximately 50 percent in both cases) and more for El Salvador and Honduras (approximately 80 percent in both cases). As one might expect, the five countries that belong to the Central American Common Market are much more integrated among themselves than they are with the Caribbean countries and Panama.

Table 5.5 presents similar information, but with regard to imports. The share of the region comprising the United States and Central America as the origin of imports of each of the countries studied

Table 5.4
Geographic composition of exports from Central American countries (as a proportion of total exports)

	Destination										
	Belize (%)	Costa Rica (%)	D.R. (%)	El Salvador (%)	Guatemala (%)	Honduras (%)	Nicaragua (%)	Panama (%)	C.A. (%)	U.S. (%)	C.A. + U.S. (%)
Origin											
Belize		0.0	0.0	0.0	1.1	0.4	0.0	0.0	1.8	46.7	48.2
Costa Rica	0.0		0.0	2.4	1.9	0.7	3.7	1.7	10.5	52.9	63.3
Dominican Republic	0.0	0.0		0.0	0.1	0.1	0.0	0.0	0.1	53.6	53.8
El Salvador	0.1	4.5	0.0		8.9	4.7	2.5	1.9	22.7	55.5	78.0
Guatemala	0.2	3.5	0.5	9.8		5.6	2.6	1.7	24.0	45.9	69.5
Honduras	0.0	0.0	0.0	2.3	1.6		0.5	0.3	5.3	74.0	78.7
Nicaragua	0.0	2.7	0.0	7.2	0.8	0.9		0.0	12.3	56.5	68.1
Panama	0.0	6.6	0.6	0.2	2.0	4.4	1.3		16.8	51.9	66.9
Central America	0.1	1.9	0.1	3.6	2.3	2.4	2.2	1.2		56.2	69.8

Source: Directions of Trade Statistics, International Monetary Fund.

Table 5.5
Geographic composition of imports of Central American countries (as a proportion of total imports)

Destination		Origin									
	Belize (%)	Costa Rica (%)	D.R. (%)	El Salvador (%)	Guatemala (%)	Honduras (%)	Nicaragua (%)	Panama (%)	C.A. (%)	U.S. (%)	C.A. + U.S. (%)
Belize		0.2	0.0	0.6	2.6	0.2	0.0	0.4	4.4	51.8	55.8
Costa Rica	0.0		0.1	2.6	2.7	0.3	2.2	1.0	9.0	51.6	60.4
Dominican Republic	0.0	0.0		0.0	0.5	0.0	0.0	2.1	2.6	48.7	51.3
El Salvador	0.0	3.4	0.0		9.3	2.3	1.8	0.4	13.8	46.3	60.1
Guatemala	0.0	2.2	0.0	4.6		1.3	0.2	1.3	9.7	42.5	52.1
Honduras	0.0	0.9	0.3	3.1	5.1		0.2	0.8	10.4	59.4	69.7
Nicaragua	0.0	16.0	0.0	5.1	7.1	1.5		0.7	30.4	25.3	55.6
Panama	0.0	0.3	0.0	0.8	1.7	0.2	0.1		5.7	56.3	59.4
Central America	0.0	1.6	0.1	2.1	3.2	0.7	0.7	0.9		49.3	57.6

Source: Directions of Trade Statistics, International Monetary Fund.

tends to be somewhat smaller than that for exports, although it exceeds 50 percent in all cases, and is as high as 70 percent in the case of Honduras.

Of course, it is not sufficient to consider the importance of potential members of the monetary union as a proportion of total trade. A more adequate measurement of the degree of integration is bilateral trade as a share of GDP in the country considering the adoption of the other currency, calculated simply by multiplying bilateral trade over total trade by the degree of openness. Table 5.6 presents this indicator for the countries in our sample. The level of trade integration of the Central American countries with the rest of the region and the United States, measured as a share of GDP—which would be the relevant measure in the case that all the countries under study jointly decided to adopt the dollar—is on average 63 percent. That with the United States alone, more relevant for countries considering adopting the dollar unilaterally (or as the result of an agreement with the United States) is 52 percent. Although there is no obvious cutoff point above which countries become good candidates for forming a currency union it is clear that perhaps with the sole exception of Guatemala, these shares in the countries studied are quite high.[14]

It is interesting to combine these results with our estimated effects of exchange rate volatility on trade in order to assess the potential benefits of dollarization through the reduced volatility channel, in terms of increased intraregional trade as a percentage of GDP for each country. These benefits are calculated by multiplying the percentage change in trade associated with the reduction in volatility in each country to the levels found in Panama (reported in table 5.2) by intraregional trade as a proportion of GDP. The results are provided in table 5.7.

These calculations should be interpreted with caution, because the elasticity that was used (−1.83) for the calculations is not based on robust estimates. In this regard, we think it is more useful to interpret these results as an indication of the relative benefits between countries, rather than as a measurement of absolute benefits. We found in this case that Honduras and Nicaragua stand to benefit the most, with trade increases exceeding 8 and 7 percent of GDP, respectively. The Dominican Republic and El Salvador are found to be intermediate cases, with trade increases of 2–3 percentage points of GDP. The effects calculated for Costa Rica and Guatemala are small,

Table 5.6
Trade integration with the United States and Central America—Proportions between foreign trade and GDP

	Exports					Imports					Intraregional trade/GDP	
	$EXP_{US}/$ TotEXP	$EXP_{US+CA}/$ TotEXP	$EXP/$ GDP	$EXP_{US}/$ GDP	$EXP_{US+CA}/$ GDP	$IMP_{US}/$ TotEXP	$IMP_{US+CA}/$ TotEXP	$IMP/$ GDP	$IMP_{US}/$ GDP	$IMP_{US+CA}/$ GDP	$X+M$ US	$X+M$ US+CA
Belize	0.47	0.48	0.51	0.24	0.25	0.52	0.56	0.59	0.30	0.33	0.54	0.58
Costa Rica	0.53	0.63	0.46	0.24	0.29	0.52	0.60	0.48	0.25	0.29	0.49	0.58
Dominican Republic	0.54	0.54	0.47	0.25	0.25	0.49	0.51	0.52	0.25	0.26	0.5	0.51
El Salvador	0.56	0.78	0.24	0.13	0.19	0.46	0.60	0.35	0.16	0.21	0.29	0.4
Guatemala	0.46	0.70	0.18	0.08	0.12	0.43	0.52	0.24	0.10	0.12	0.18	0.24
Honduras	0.74	0.79	0.46	0.34	0.36	0.59	0.70	0.52	0.31	0.36	0.65	0.72
Nicaragua	0.57	0.68	0.43	0.24	0.29	0.25	0.56	0.80	0.20	0.44	0.44	0.73
Panama	0.52	0.67	0.99	0.52	0.66	0.56	0.59	0.99	0.56	0.59	1.06	1.25
Average	0.55	0.66	0.47	0.26	0.30	0.48	0.58	0.56	0.27	0.33	0.52	0.63

Source: Directions of Trade Statistics, International Monetary Fund.
Note: $X+M$ = exports and imports.

Table 5.7
Potential benefits of dollarization through reduction of real exchange rate volatility

	Trade integration $(X + M)/$GDP	Trade effect (in % terms) (from table 5.2)	Trade effect as a share of GDP
Costa Rica	0.58	1.34	0.78
Dominican Republic	0.51	5.71	2.91
El Salvador	0.40	5.59	2.23
Guatemala	0.21	5.18	1.11
Honduras	0.72	11.39	8.20
Nicaragua	0.73	9.79	7.15
Average	0.53	6.50	3.73

Source: Authors' calculations.
Note: $X + M$ = exports and imports.

in one case, as the result of low levels of exchange rate volatility, and in the other, owing to a low level of trade integration, at least in comparative terms.[15]

5.5 Costs and Benefits Associated with the Loss of Monetary Independence

The greatest cost of a monetary union relates to the fact that when a country replaces its own currency with that of the currency union (or that of another country), it loses the capacity to conduct independent monetary policy. However, as suggested earlier, surrendering the discretion to use monetary policy through dollarization may entail important benefits associated with gains in credibility. These benefits derive precisely from the limits imposed by the exchange rate rule on the monetary authorities. Thus, by choosing the exchange rate regime (or other monetary policy rules, for that matter) countries can in effect trade monetary independence for credibility.

We start this section by developing a simple framework in which credibility and monetary independence are both desirable objectives but can be gained only at the expense of one another (at least in the short run). A country's choice of the optimal mix between credibility and monetary independence will depend on a number of characteristics affecting the benefits it derives from monetary independence, as well as the "price" of monetary independence, that is, the rate at which it gives up credibility in order to acquire monetary independence. We should make clear from the start that the purpose of this very simple exercise is a modest one: to help think through and organize the discussion that follows. It is not intended to be a formal model of exchange rate regime choice.

After discussing this framework, we dedicate the rest of the chapter to discussing in more detail the characteristics of countries that may affect the value of monetary independence vis-à-vis credibility—such as the OCA criteria or the degree of liability dollarization—as well as those that may affect its price—such as openness or wage indexation. In addition, we will discuss how countries in Central America fare in terms of these characteristics, and we will review whether credibility and monetary independence have delivered on their promised benefits.

5.5.1   A Simple Framework

We assume that countries differ in three different respects. First, not all countries derive similar benefits from monetary independence, or from credibility. Second, countries differ regarding the "price" of monetary independence, that is, the rate at which they have to sacrifice credibility in order to obtain more monetary independence. Third, they differ in their credibility "endowment," which could be associated with the reputation of their policymakers or the institutional arrangements within which these policymakers operate.

There are several factors that can affect the relative value of monetary independence. In general, countries that comply with the criteria set forth by the OCA literature will find monetary independence to be of lesser value, other things being equal. For example, monetary independence will be of little use if the cycles in a country are perfectly synchronized with those in the United States. Liability dollarization may also affect the benefits a country derives from monetary independence, because the potential costs of depreciation in economies with significant currency mismatches may reduce the willingness of policymakers to utilize this tool. Similarly, different countries may derive different benefits from credibility. For example, countries with a history of high inflation may find credibility to be relatively more valuable.

The fact that countries derive different benefits from monetary independence and credibility suggests that they have different utility functions (at least when these are expressed in terms of these two objectives). In particular, we can describe country i's utility function as

$$U_i = (1 - \gamma^I)C_i + \gamma^I C_i M_i, \tag{5.1}$$

where M is monetary independence, C is credibility, and γ^I is a parameter that measures the relative weight of monetary independence in the utility function.[16] Utility function (5.1) assumes that credibility is a good in itself but monetary independence is useless without credibility. The idea behind this is rather simple. Although credibility is valuable even in the absence of monetary independence—which would explain why countries think about adopting the dollar as their currency but not about adopting the ruble—the extreme of zero credibility may result in hyperinflation. Hence, in the absence of credibility, monetary independence will be useless. As discussed earlier, the parameter γ^I can take different values, depending on the characteristics of the country in question. For example, countries that comply with the OCA criteria and have a high level of liabilities denominated in foreign currency will have a lower γ^I.

As discussed earlier, countries also differ with respect to their credibility endowment and the rate at which they can exchange their credibility endowment for monetary independence. A tradition of sound monetary policy, adequate institutional arrangements such as central bank independence, or the absence of political pressures for increased spending may affect both the price of monetary independence—because increased discretion should not be very costly—and the credibility endowment. Factors such as the presence of high pass-through from exchange rates to prices, or widespread price and wage indexation, may affect the cost, in terms of forgone credibility, of monetary independence. Whereas differences in the relative benefits of monetary independence affect countries' utility functions, differences in the price of monetary independence, as well as differences in the credibility endowment, will affect their budget constraint. Therefore, country i maximizes the utility function (5.1) subject to the following budget and nonnegativity constraints:

$$C^I = C_i + \alpha^I M_i,$$
$$C_i \geq 0, \quad M_i \geq 0, \tag{5.2}$$

where, C^I is the credibility endowment of country i and α^I is the relative price of monetary independence in country i. Countries that need to sacrifice a great deal of credibility in order to gain monetary independence will have a high α^I, which results in a flatter budget constraint.[17]

We start by describing the optimal mix of credibility and monetary independence for an anchor country and then we solve the problem for the other countries. We define the anchor country a as the country for which $C^A \geq C^I$, $\alpha^A \leq \alpha^I$, and $\gamma_A \geq \gamma_I$, for all is. This means that the anchor country has the highest endowment of credibility, faces the lowest price of monetary independence, and assigns the highest value to monetary independence.[18]

The anchor country maximizes its utility function (5.1) subject to the budget constraint (5.2) and sets

$$C_a^* = \frac{C^A}{2} + \frac{(1 - \gamma^A)\alpha^A}{2\gamma^A} \tag{5.3}$$

and

$$M_a^* = \frac{C^A}{2\alpha^A} - \frac{(1 - \gamma^A)}{2\gamma^A}. \tag{5.4}$$

It would be possible for the anchor country to have a corner solution, in which case it forgoes all monetary independence (for example, by adhering to the gold standard). Here, we rule out this extreme case by assuming that

$$C^A > \frac{(1 - \gamma^A)}{\gamma^A}\alpha^A,$$

which ensures an interior solution for the anchor.

By symmetry, country i's optimal levels of credibility and monetary independence will be given by

$$C_i^* = \frac{C^I}{2} + \frac{(1 - \gamma^I)\alpha^I}{2\gamma^I} \tag{5.5}$$

and

$$M_i^* = \frac{C^I}{2\alpha^I} - \frac{(1 - \gamma^I)}{2\gamma^I}. \tag{5.6}$$

Equation (5.6) implies that the optimal level of monetary independence is decreasing in α^I, and increasing in γ^I and C^I. Thus, it is easy to see that nonanchor countries will choose a level of monetary independence that is lower than that chosen by the anchor country.[19]

In the case of credibility, we do not have a clear prediction for the relative position of nonanchor countries with respect to the anchor country, because the substitution and income effects go in opposite directions.

However, a country that decides to forgo its monetary independence has the option to adopt the currency of the anchor, which, we assume, confers the country the same level of credibility achieved by the anchor country. Thus, countries that decide to forgo their monetary independence can at least achieve the level of credibility of the anchor. Notice that for high enough values of α^I and low enough values of γ^I and C^I, equation (5.6) will be negative. Because this violates the nonnegativity constraint, monetary independence will be set to zero. If the credibility endowment in country i is greater than the optimal credibility in the anchor country (i.e., if $C^I > C_a^*$) country i will forgo its monetary independence by setting a strict monetary policy rule, and will achieve credibility C^I. In contrast, if $C^I < C_a^*$, the country can do better by adopting the currency of the anchor country (i.e., dollarizing), in which case it achieves credibility C_a^*. Furthermore, if $U_i(C^A, 0) > U_i(C_i^*, M_i^*)$ a country may choose to dollarize even in the presence of an internal solution (i.e., when $C^I > ((1 - \gamma^I)/\gamma^I)\alpha^I)$. This is possible because, whenever $C^I < C_a^*$, the option to dollarize expands the budget constraint of country i.

Although the model discussed above is extremely stylized, it helps us think about the major issues that need to be considered when deciding whether to dollarize. In particular, the framework shows that dollarization will be optimal for countries endowed with low levels of credibility, and where monetary independence is not very useful or is costly to acquire. In the next sections, we will discuss in more detail the factors that affect the relative utility of monetary independence and its relative price, and, in light of these factors, we will discuss the convenience for Central American countries of adopting the dollar as their currency.

5.5.2   The Value of Monetary Independence

There are several factors that can affect the parameter γ^I in the framework introduced above, that is, the relative value of monetary independence. Several of those factors have received a lot of attention in the optimal currency area literature. This literature aims to establish the conditions under which the benefits of joining a currency union would outweigh the costs. In particular, it takes a close look at a set of criteria, such as the symmetry of cycles between the potential currency union partners, the degree of wage flexibility, and labor mobility, that would impact the cost of sacrificing monetary independence. In the first part of this section, we will review the traditional OCA criteria and discuss how these criteria may modify the benefits a country derives from having monetary independence. In addition, we will discuss how countries in Central America perform according to these criteria.

Although the OCA literature looks at the characteristics of a country that may make monetary independence less valuable, it implicitly assumes that exchange rate flexibility, and the monetary independence that comes with it, has a number of benefits. First, exchange rate flexibility should, at least in theory, enable a country to protect itself from external interest rate fluctuations. An increase in the external interest rate could be completely absorbed with an exchange rate adjustment (in this case a depreciation), without any effect on domestic interest rates. Second, exchange rate flexibility gives policymakers the option to use monetary policy as an aggregate demand management tool. The exchange rate may fluctuate to ensure external balance, while monetary policy may be used to determine output and employment levels and to dampen cyclical fluctuations. Third, regardless of the effectiveness of monetary policy as a demand management tool, it can always be used to determine domestic price levels and thus to avoid severe deflationary adjustments that may occur in extraordinary circumstances in which the country sustains a major negative external shock. We will critically examine each of these potential benefits of exchange rate flexibility and the monetary independence associated with it, drawing on evidence from the Central American countries and, in some cases, from other countries as well. Whether these potential benefits are realized in practice will have an effect on the parameter γ^I representing the relative utility derived from monetary independence.

The Traditional OCA Criteria
The theory of OCA identifies a set of criteria for determining whether it is more or less advantageous for a country to join a monetary union. One criterion, which relates to the degree of trade integration between potential members, was discussed at length in section 4. The rest generally relate to the cost of forgoing monetary

policy independence. Here we will discuss, in turn, the importance of the following factors: (1) the symmetry of economic shocks and cycles between potential members; (2) wage flexibility; (3) labor mobility between economies; (4) existence of a transfer system between potential members of the union; and (5) the degree of openness. We will also look at the characteristics of countries in Central America according to these criteria, which affect the benefits derived from monetary independence and thus the decision of whether or not to dollarize.

Degree of Asymmetry of Economic Shocks and Cycles   By adopting the dollar as a replacement for their own currencies, the Central American countries would be adopting U.S. monetary policy. This monetary policy will be more appropriate if booms and recessions in the dollarizing country tend to occur simultaneously with those in the United States. In the limit of perfect synchronicity of cycles, presumably monetary independence would have no value (i.e., the parameter γ^I in our framework would be close to zero).[20] If cycles were asymmetric, it would be possible for the United States to adopt a restrictive monetary policy precisely when the dollarized economy were going through a recession. The higher the level of asymmetry in output shocks, the more important the exchange rate becomes as a relative price adjustment mechanism.

To measure the degree of asymmetry of cycles in Central American countries with respect of the United States, we follow Bayoumi and Eichengreen (1996) in using the standard deviation of changes in the log of relative GDP between the economies. This indicator is defined formally as follows:

$$A = \sigma\left(\log\left(\frac{GDP_i^t}{GDP_{us}^t}\right) - \log\left(\frac{GDP_i^{t-1}}{GDP_{us}^{t-1}}\right)\right)$$

If the cyclical component of output is exactly equal in the two countries, this indicator will be equal to zero, even if growth trends are different across countries. The indicator increases in direct proportion with the asymmetry between the cycles. To compute the level of asymmetry, we use yearly series of GDP for the period 1966–1996. The results are presented in table 5.8. As a benchmark, we include in the second part of the table the calculation of economic cycle asymmetry of European Union countries with respect to Germany. The average asymmetry level for these countries is 0.0134.

Table 5.8
Economic cycle asymmetry with the United States or Germany, 1966–1996

Central America vs. U.S.		Europe vs. Germany	
Belize*	.0380	Austria	.0100
Costa Rica	.0120	Belgium	.0110
El Salvador	.0165	Denmark	.0120
Guatemala	.0126	Finland	.0200
Honduras	.0111	France	.0120
Nicaragua	.0340	Greece	.0140
Panama	.0247	Ireland	.0160
Dominican Republic	.0225	Italy	.0120
		Luxembourg	.0150
		Netherlands	.0100
		Portugal	.0150
		Spain	.0120
		Sweden	.0140
		England	.0150
Average	.0214		.0134

*1979–1986

Surprisingly, economic cycles are more asymmetric in Belize and Panama than in most Central American countries (only Nicaragua has economic cycles that are as asymmetric as those of Belize and Panama). According to this criterion, the rest of the countries would be better candidates to form a currency union with the United States. With the exception of Nicaragua and Belize, where the indicators are much higher, the asymmetry level of these countries is similar to the level observed in the European countries vis-à-vis Germany. In fact, Costa Rica, Guatemala, and Honduras are below the average for the European Union.

Before drawing strong implications regarding the desirability of dollarization in different countries based on these figures, it is important to consider that, as argued by Frankel and Rose (1998), the symmetry of cycles can be endogenous. Although some authors suggest that trade integration reduces the correlation between shocks, Frankel and Rose find that economic cycles tend to be more symmetrical in countries with close trade relations.[21] Accordingly, a country might meet this criterion *ex post*, even if it does not meet it *ex ante*. According to this argument, for example, if Nicaragua were to form a monetary union with the United States, trade flows between the two countries would probably increase. This increase in trade could generate changes in the correlation of cycles between the countries. A boom in the United States would increase demand for Nicaraguan products, potentially leading to a boom in Nicaragua. The fact that Nicaragua had, for political reasons, weak trade links with the United States for a substantial part of the period under consideration may therefore explain in part the low degree of symmetry reflected in the indicator used.

Wage Flexibility If the different economies forming a currency union face symmetrical shocks, the loss of exchange rate flexibility does not involve significant costs.[22] If shocks tend to be asymmetrical, exchange rate adjustment is not the only mechanism for automatically restoring economic equilibrium. Two other possible mechanisms are wage flexibility and labor mobility. In fact, if wages are perfectly flexible, restoring equilibrium through depreciation is almost equivalent to achieving this effect through a reduction in wages.[23] In contrast, when wages are downwardly inflexible, adjustment through wage reductions is much slower and much more costly, as it could lead to prolonged periods of high unemployment.[24]

We should ask, then, how flexible wages are in the countries we are considering. Although no data are available on wage flexibility, it is possible to consider other labor market factors potentially affecting the degree of flexibility. We might expect wage flexibility to decrease as the rigidity of labor legislation increases. The existence of higher dismissal costs could give workers greater negotiating power in wage disputes with companies. According to an index of labor legislation rigidity in Márquez (1997), labor regulations in Central America are generally quite rigid, with the exception of Belize, Nicaragua, and, to a lesser degree, Guatemala.

It is possible that the informal sector, which usually increases along with the rigidity of labor regulations, may partially offset the rigidity of the formal sector. Furthermore, the level of unionization, another variable that potentially affects wage flexibility, is not high in these economies, with the exception of Nicaragua and the Dominican Republic. In spite of these attenuating factors, we would expect wages in the majority of the countries considered to be fairly inflexible. This inflexibility would complicate adjustments to asymmetrical shocks, making exchange rate flexibility and monetary independence more desirable.

We suspect that wages are rigid in the downward direction, but the eight Central American countries in our sample are characterized by extremely high levels of wage indexation. In particular, Stein et al. (1999) find that each percentage point of increase in inflation is immediately translated into an increase in nominal wages of 0.8 percent. In other words, inflationary surprises are immediately and almost completely absorbed by nominal wage increases. If the benefits of monetary independence stem from the ability to adjust relative prices instead of quantities, high wage indexation would imply a higher cost in terms of inflation for a given adjustment. Within the framework developed in section 5.1.1, this means high wage indexation would be associated with a high level of α^I: in order to gain the same degree of monetary independence, a country would have to give up more in terms of inflation and hence credibility.

Degree of Labor Mobility between Economies   Mobility of factors and, in particular, of labor, plays a very important role in OCA theory. To the extent that labor mobility exists between countries that are members of a monetary union, some of the effects of asymmetric shocks can be absorbed through changes in the supply of labor in each country, without requiring relative price changes. This is particularly important when wage rigidities exist in the country that sustains a negative shock, which, in the absence of labor mobility, would lead to periods of high unemployment.

Despite its theoretical importance, this criterion, as well as the following one, is often overlooked when analyzing the advisability of forming a monetary union among different countries, as labor mobility between countries is often insignificant. This would be a major omission in the case of Central America, as many countries have substantial migration flows to the United States Figure 5.2 shows that migration levels for Central American countries are much higher than for Latin America as a whole, particularly in the case of El Salvador, Guatemala, and Nicaragua.[25] Whereas the United States is the destination of much of the migration from El Salvador, Guatemala, and the Dominican Republic, migratory flows from Nicaragua most often go to Costa Rica—a net receiver of migrants.

Migratory flows to the United States have generated a considerable population of Central American natives resident there, which serves as a center of attraction for new migrants. According to Immigration and Nationalization Service (INS) information reported by

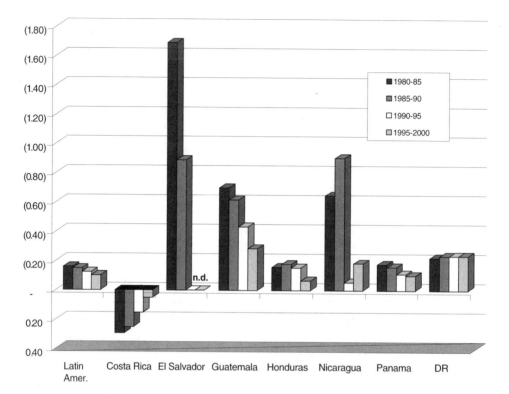

Figure 5.2
Migration rates in Central America. *Source:* Boletín Demográfico, CELADE. Note: migration rates are reported as a percentage of total population. A negative (positive) sign represents a net negative (positive) contribution to total population growth. Data refer to five-year averages for each country.

Meyers (1998) and reproduced in table 5.9, approximately 8 percent of El Salvador's population and 5 percent of the Dominican Republic's live in the United States (including legal, illegal, and temporary immigration).

These data suggest that labor mobility is a factor not to be overlooked. Further, there is a negative correlation between migratory flows and the economic growth rate in the country of origin. This is clearly observed in figure 5.3, and in table 5.10, which show the association between growth and migration for those countries with substantial migratory flows.[26] Migration is more than three times higher when GDP is declining, in comparison to migration rates during periods of strong growth.[27]

Table 5.9
Demographic impact of migrations in countries of origin

	El Salvador	Guatemala	Dominican Republic
Population in the United States	460,000	215,000	370,000
Total population	5,600,000	10,600,000	7,800,000
Percent emigrants / population	8.21	2.03	4.74

Source: Meyers (1998).

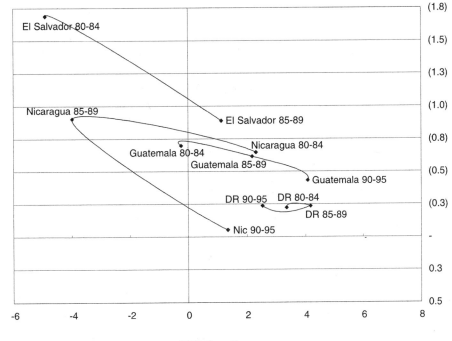

Figure 5.3
Migration and growth in Central America

Table 5.10
Migration and growth in countries of origin

Average growth rate (average growth in GDP)	Migration rate (% of total population)
Declining GDP[1]	1.10
GDP growth of 0–3%[2]	0.49
GDP growth of over 3%[3]	0.33

Source: Author's calculation based on IMF and Boletin Demografico Celade
[1] El Salvador and Guatemala 1980–1984, Nicaragua 1985–1989.
[2] Dominican Republican 1980–1984 and 1990–1995, El Salvador and Guatemala 1985–1989, Nicaragua 1980–1984 and 1990–1995.
[3] Dominican Republic 1985–1989 and Guatemala 1990–1995.

According to this criterion, the countries that seem to be the best candidates to establish a monetary union with the United States (i.e., those that would derive smaller benefits from monetary independence) are El Salvador, Guatemala, and, to a lesser extent, the Dominican Republic. Nicaragua also seems to be a good candidate, particularly if Costa Rica is also a member of the monetary area.[28] By contrast, Honduras, like Panama, has no substantial migrant flow to the United States or to other Central American countries.

Existence of a System of Transfers   When asymmetric shocks occur between regions of the same country, one region may require an expansionary monetary policy, while others may require exactly the opposite. This problem can be solved with a system of interregional (in some cases, intergovernmental) transfers, to channel resources from boom areas to those in recession. Such transfers may be discretionary or automatic, for example, in the form of a nationally financed unemployment insurance system. The existence of a system of interregional transfers therefore reduces the need for independent monetary policy.

Such transfers are normally substantial within countries but not between different countries. However, in the case of Central American countries and, in particular, those with a considerable population living in the United States, there are important transfers in the form of remittances. Such remittances in 1995 represented just under 12 percent of GDP in El Salvador, 7 percent in the Dominican Republic, and 2.5–4 percent in the rest of the countries with substantial migration rates (table 5.11).

Table 5.11
Economic significance of remittances, 1995

	El Salvador	Guatemala	Honduras	Nicaragua	Dominican Republic
Estimated remittances (millions of U.S.$)	1.061	350	120	75	795
Remittances as a percent of					
GDP	11.6	2.4	3.0	3.9	7.0
Exports, merchandise	110.2	15.9			103.9
Total exports	53.3	12.7	8.5	16.4	27.1

Source: Meyers (1998) and World Bank (1997).

Given the existence of this substantial flow of transfers, it is important to consider whether such transfers play an anticyclical role. This assumption is plausible, if we assume that Central American workers living in the United States send more money to their families when the latter are in economic difficulty. To that end, the cyclical component of remittances and the cyclical component of GDP were calculated for El Salvador and the Dominican Republic—the countries in which these transfers are most significant.[29] These variables are presented in figures 5.4a and 5.4b. The correlation between these variables is negative but insignificant for the Dominican Republic (suggesting a certain anticyclical role), and positive but insignificant for El Salvador.

Although this result seems to suggest that remittances to El Salvador do not reduce the need for independent monetary policy, this is not necessarily true. Remittances do not need to be anticyclical to play a stabilizing role. It suffices for them to be more stable than output, which is clearly evident in both El Salvador and the Dominican Republic. To illustrate this with an extreme example, if GDP were highly volatile and remittances were perfectly stable and substantial in relation to GDP, household income would be much more stable with remittances than without them.

To summarize, the characteristics of several of the countries studied conform fairly well to the criteria established in the OCA literature. Cycles in Costa Rica, Guatemala, and Honduras (and, to a lesser extent, the Dominican Republic and El Salvador) are closely correlated with those of the United States. El Salvador, Guatemala, and the Dominican Republic have a high degree of labor mobility

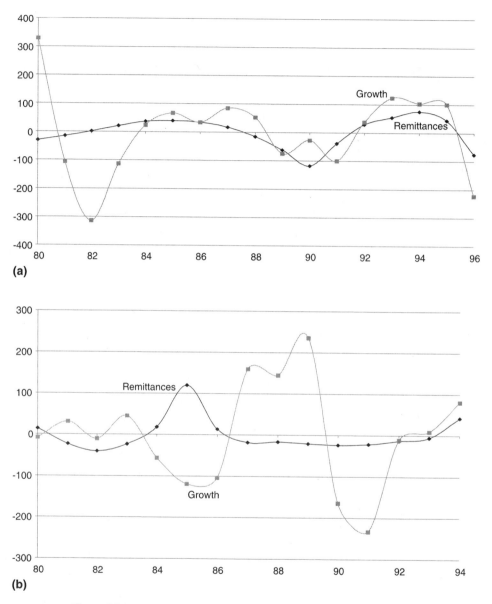

Figure 5.4
(a) Cyclical trends in remittances, El Salvador, 1980–1996. *Source:* Stein et al. (1999), based on Demographical Bulletin *Celáde*. (b) Cyclical trends in remittances, Dominican Republic, 1980–1994. *Source:* Stein et al. (1999), based on Demographical Bulletin *Celáde*.

with the United States, as does Nicaragua with Costa Rica. El Salvador and the Dominican Republic also receive remittances that that are considerable in relation to GDP and that seem to play a stabilizing role. These findings suggest that the value of monetary independence in these countries, as a general rule, should not be too large.

The Degree of Openness In section 5.4, we already discussed the high degree of openness in all of the countries in our sample. Besides being important for trade integration, openness is also one of the main factors affecting the trade-off between credibility and monetary independence. In highly open economies, in which tradables are much more important than nontradables, changes in the exchange rate are much more directly reflected in the price level, that is, the pass-through from exchange rate to prices tends to be high. In such cases, the exchange rate tends to become a central factor in contracts (including those involving labor). The consequences are similar to those we discussed in the case of high indexation. Openness, through high pass-through, increases the price of monetary independence, because any required adjustment in relative prices will come at a higher cost in terms of inflation and inflation volatility. Hausmann, Panizza, and Stein (2001) find some evidence that countries with high pass-through from exchange rates to prices are less likely to allow significant movements in their exchange rates.

The Effectiveness of Monetary Independence
The OCA literature discussed implicitly assumes that the monetary independence associated with the adoption of a flexible exchange rate has a number of benefits. The traditional literature emphasizes the ability of a country with a floating regime to use the exchange rate to protect itself from external interest rate fluctuations, and the possibility of using monetary policy as an aggregate demand management tool. In the text that follows we discuss each of these potential benefits of exchange rate flexibility.

Exchange Rate Flexibility and Protecting against External Interest Rate Fluctuations Standard textbook models indicate that with flexible exchange rates, external interest rate movements can be absorbed by changes in the exchange rate without affecting domestic interest rates. By contrast, with fixed exchange rates, the uncovered interest parity condition implies that, barring changes in devaluation expectations, domestic interest rates should respond on a one-to-one basis to external interest rate fluctuations. A more substantial response would suggest that devaluation expectations (or the risk premium) would increase in response to an increase in U.S. interest rates. In any case, conventional wisdom suggests that domestic interest rates should be more independent from external rates in countries with a floating regime than in countries with a fixed regime.

The evidence on this issue is, at best, mixed. Three recent papers that empirically explore the effects of external interest rate fluctuations on domestic rates under different exchange regimes (Frankel 1999; Hausmann et al. 1999; and Borensztein and Zettelmeyer 2000) give somewhat contrasting answers. Frankel (1999) studies the effects of nominal interest rate fluctuations in the United States on nominal interest rates in Argentina, Brazil, Hong Kong, Mexico, and Panama, and he finds that this effect is significantly larger in economies with no credible commitment to a fixed exchange rate parity (Brazil and Mexico) than in countries with "truly fixed" regimes (Argentina, Hong Kong, and Panama). Hausmann et al. (1999) use a monthly panel of eleven Latin American countries to conduct a similar exercise and find that the effect of U.S. interest rates on domestic rates is 25 percent lower for countries with fixed exchange regimes.[30] Although the difference is not statistically significant, this result suggests once again that flexible exchange regimes do not isolate domestic monetary variables from external ones.

Borensztein and Zettelmeyer (2000) study eight countries: two currency boards (Argentina and Hong Kong) and six floaters (New Zealand, South Africa, Mexico, Canada, Australia, and Singapore). After controlling for outliers, they find that U.S. monetary actions have an effect in Canada, New Zealand, Singapore, and Hong Kong and no effect in Argentina. In their Vector Auto-Regressions (VAR) analysis of the effect of the U.S. interest rate on domestic interest rates, they find a small and significant impact for the case of Australia, New Zealand, and Canada, and a large but rarely significant impact for the case of Hong Kong and Argentina. The large standard errors that characterize the estimations for Argentina and Hong Kong seem to contradict the finding in Frankel (1999) that the estimations of domestic interest rate elasticities to external shocks are lower but more precise in countries with a fixed exchange rate.

Hausmann et al. (1999) also study the relationship between daily movements in domestic short-term interest rates and dollar interest rates on the country's sovereign bonds (thirty-year terms) for Argentina, Mexico, and Venezuela between September 1997 and February 1999. This period, which encompasses the crises in Asia, Russia, and Brazil, is characterized by highly volatile conditions for access to external financing for all emerging markets and by highly correlated bond prices in the various countries. The question is the extent to which this volatility is reflected in the domestic credit markets. They find that domestic interest rates are much more sensitive to external credit conditions in Mexico, a country with a flexible regime, than in Argentina. Given the lack of daily data on the cost of long-term external financing, they do not consider the case of Panama. In what follows, we use monthly data to conduct a similar exercise but include Panama in the sample. The results are provided in table 5.12. We find that in Panama's case, unlike in the rest of the countries considered, domestic interest rates remained unchanged in response to changes in the cost of external financing.

The differences between Argentina and Panama suggest the existence of a considerable credibility gap between convertibility and dollarization. Whereas the credibility of convertibility suffers in response to increases in the cost of long-term external financing, which is reflected in higher domestic interest rates, dollarization seems to be perfectly credible. Of course, these results should be interpreted with caution, in light of the low number of observations used in the exercise. However, the fact that the coefficients for the exercise conducted with monthly data are quite similar to those reported by Hausmann et al. (1999) lends some degree of confidence to the results.[31]

We also regress domestic short-term interest rate on the spread of an index of emerging market bonds (we use the J. P. Morgan Emerging Market Bond index plus, abbreviated as EMBI+). The purpose of this exercise is to see if countries with flexible exchange rates can isolate their domestic interest rates from worldwide shocks in the international capital markets affecting emerging economies. The results of table 5.12 seem to suggest the opposite. Whereas the EMBI spread has no effect on domestic interest rates in Panama and has a small effect in domestic rates in Argentina, it has a much greater effect on the domestic rates of Venezuela and Mexico.

We think that it is fair to conclude by saying that at least in Latin America, there is no evidence that exchange flexibility insulates domestic interest rates from movements in external interest rates. If

Table 5.12
Dependent variables—Short-term domestic interest rates

	I^*	EMBI spread	R^2	Period
Regressions in levels				
Panama	0.01		0.01	March 1997–June 2000
	(0.403)			
Argentina	0.48***		0.19	September 1997–June 2000
	(2.76)			
Venezuela	1.63**		0.17	September 1997–June 2000
	(2.65)			
Mexico	6.41***		0.56	March 1997–June 2000
	(7.03)			
Panama		−0.00001	0.05	March 1997–June 2000
		(−1.4)		
Argentina		0.002***	0.39	September 1997–June 2000
		(4.97)		
Venezuela		0.01**	0.13	September 1997–June 2000
		(2.39)		
Mexico		0.10***	0.29	March 1997–June 2000
		(3.98)		
Regressions in first differences				
Panama	0.00		0.00	March 1997–June 2000
	(0.00)			
Argentina	0.69***		0.26	September 1997–June 2000
	(3.35)			
Venezuela	0.81**		0.14	September 1997–June 2000
	(2.29)			
Mexico	2.66***		0.20	March 1997–June 2000
	(3.039)			
Panama		0.00	0.00	March 1997–June 2000
		(0.00)		
Argentina		0.004***	0.43	September 1997–June 2000
		(5.38)		
Venezuela		0.005*	0.07	September 1997–June 2000
		(1.67)		
Mexico		0.016***	0.65	March 1997–June 2000
		(8.36)		

*** statistically significant at 1% confidence level
** statistically significant at 5% confidence level
* statistically significant at 10% confidence level

anything, the evidence suggests the contrary. Domestic interest rates moved more independently in truly fixed regimes, and in particular, in the case of dollarization.

Exchange Rate Flexibility and the Capacity to Use Monetary Policy as an Anticyclical Tool We now consider the extent to which independent monetary policy has been a valuable anticyclical tool in Latin American countries, and in particular, in Central America.

How can we judge the effectiveness of monetary policy as an anticyclical tool? We will conduct three different exercises. First of all, if monetary policy is a valuable aggregate demand management tool, it should be aimed at reducing cyclical fluctuations in output. We will therefore examine whether economic growth rate variability is lower in countries with flexible exchange rates.

Table 5.13 presents the volatility of GDP growth during the 1960–1996 period for the eight Central American countries. Belize is one of the least volatile countries, and Panama is slightly below average. The average coefficient of variation for Panama and Belize is 0.87, whereas it is 1.38 for the rest of the countries. This comparison may be influenced by the periods of civil war in El Salvador and Nicaragua, which explain the fact that these two countries register the most volatile growth rates. We obtain similar results if we exclude these two countries, as well as the two years corresponding to the crisis in Panama at the end of the 1980s (1987 and 1988). In this case, the coefficient of variation for Panama is reduced to 0.64 and the average for Panama and Belize to 0.68, whereas the average is 0.90 for Costa Rica, Dominican Republic, and Honduras. We obtain qualitatively similar results if we focus on the period 1980–1996, excluding the years during which all countries had "truly fixed" exchange regimes.[32]

Of course, monetary policy is only one of the factors affecting output variability. Higher volatility in countries with more flexible regimes may be due to the fact that this group of countries faces a more volatile economic environment (maybe this is why they chose to have a flexible exchange rate to start with). However, if monetary independence is effective, we would expect that with flexible regimes, term of trade shocks would be partially absorbed by exchange rate movements. To determine whether this is the case, our second exercise studies the effect of terms of trade shocks on the growth rate under different exchange rate regimes. In particular, we

Table 5.13
GDP growth and volatility, 1960–1996

	Average growth	SD of GDP growth	Coefficient of variation
1960–1979			
Belize	5.801	2.786	0.480
Costa Rica	6.152	2.560	0.416
Dominican Republic	6.600	7.095	1.075
El Salvador	4.887	3.149	0.644
Guatemala	5.691	1.891	0.332
Honduras	5.367	3.267	0.609
Nicaragua	3.963	8.924	2.252
Panama	6.308	3.045	0.483
Total	5.596	4.672	0.835
1980–1989			
Belize	5.521	6.144	1.113
Costa Rica	2.221	4.468	2.011
Dominican Republic	3.815	2.861	0.750
El Salvador	−1.950	5.425	
Guatemala	0.971	2.751	2.832
Honduras	2.511	2.584	1.029
Nicaragua	−0.789	5.114	
Panama	0.876	6.292	7.187
Total	1.647	5.013	3.043
1990–1996			
Belize	4.772	3.655	0.766
Costa Rica	3.727	2.788	0.748
Dominican Republic	3.228	4.663	1.445
El Salvador	5.448	1.912	0.351
Guatemala	3.923	0.767	0.196
Honduras	3.025	2.787	0.921
Nicaragua	1.700	2.248	1.322
Panama	5.472	3.145	0.575
Total	3.912	3.018	0.772
1960–1996			
Belize	5.52	4.02	0.73
Costa Rica	4.59	3.59	0.78
Dominican Republic	5.17	5.84	1.13
El Salvador	3.10	4.84	1.56
Guatemala	4.04	2.84	0.70
Honduras	4.12	3.22	0.78
Nicaragua	2.20	7.27	3.30

Table 5.13
(continued)

	Average growth	SD of GDP growth	Coefficient of variation
Panama	4.64	4.73	1.02
Total	4.17	4.80	1.15
Panama and Belize	5.08	4.37	0.87
Other countries	3.87	4.60	1.38
Panama and Belize*	5.50	3.74	0.68
Costa Rica, Dominican Republic, and Honduras	4.63	4.22	0.90

Source: Author's calculation based on IMF's International Financial Statistics (IFS).
*Excludes 1987 and 1988 for Panama.

ask the following question: "Do more flexible interest rates make it possible to protect economic growth from terms of trade shocks?"

To answer that question, we run a regression in which the dependent variable is annual changes in per capita GDP and the explanatory variables are terms of trade shocks (measured as the change in terms of trade multiplied by openness), a dummy (*FIX*) taking a value of one when the exchange regime is "truly fixed," and the interaction between *FIX* and terms of trade shocks.[33] Formally, we use the following specification:

$$\log(y_{i,t}) - \log(y_{i,t-1}) = \alpha + \beta \Delta TT_{i,t} + \gamma FLX_{i,t} + \theta(FIX_{i,t} * \Delta TT_{i,t}) + \varepsilon_{i,t}.$$

We run the regression for the eight countries included in our study during the 1960–1998 period. A positive and statistically significant coefficient corresponding to the interactive term (θ) would indicate that countries with flexible regimes are better positioned to protect their economies from terms of trade shocks.

The results of the regression are presented in table 5.14. As expected, changes in terms of trade are positively correlated with changes in GDP. The coefficient of the interactive term, however, is negative (but not statistically significant). This suggests that in our sample of Central American countries, more flexible regimes are no better than fixed ones in terms of the ability to protect the economy from external shocks.[34] We also check if our results are robust to the inclusion of other external shocks. To this purpose, we augment our regression with a variable that controls for the GDP growth of major trading partners (GDPTR is the growth of trading partners weighted

Table 5.14
Dependent variable: Annual changes per capita GDP, 1960–1998

	Pooled OLS		Panel, FE		Panel, RE	
	(1)	(2)	(3)	(4)	(5)	(6)
ΔTOT	0.001***	0.0001***	0.001***	0.001***	0.0001***	0.0001***
	(3.06)	(3.07)	(3.27)	(3.22)	(3.08)	(3.06)
FIX	1.93***	1.55**	1.99***	1.81*	1.93***	1.54*
	(2.94)	(1.85)	(2.87)	(1.61)	(2.94)	(1.85)
ΔTOT*FIX	−0.0005	−0.0003	−0	−0	−0.0004	−0.0003
	(−0.07)	(−0.59)	(−0.196)	(−0.732)	(−0.069)	(−0.058)
GDPTR		0.678***		0.713***		0.678***
		(3.50)		(3.69)		(3.50)
CATAS		−0.86		−1.59		−0.85
		(−1.26)		(−1.56)		(−1.257)
YEAR		0.02		0.038		0.02
		(0.51)		(0.72)		(0.51)
CONST	−0.14	−40.55	−0.18	−77.1	−0.142	−40.55
	(−0.26)	(−0.51)	(−0.324)	(−0.72)	(−0.262)	(−0.51)
R2	0.09	0.15	0.09	0.16	0.09	0.15
N	248	248	248	248	248	248

*** statistically significant at the 1 percent confidence level
** statistically significant at the 5 percent confidence level
* statistically significant at the 10 percent confidence level
ΔTOT = change in terms of trade
FIX = dummy variable that takes value 1 when the country has a fixed exchange rate
GDPTR = income of trading partners
CATAS dummy that takes value 1 if during a particular year there was a war or a natural disaster.

by trade share) and a dummy (CATAS) that takes a value of one if, in a given year, the country was at war or suffered a major natural disaster.[35] Finally, to control for the fact the 1960s were characterized by high growth and fixed exchange rates we also augment our regression with a time trend. The second, fourth, and sixth columns of table 5.14 show that controlling for these additional factors does not alter the results just discussed. To control for the fact that change of regimes may be endogenous, we drop the three years around the regime change and obtain results that are almost identical to those of table 5.14.[36]

In a larger study, of seventy-four developing countries, Broda (2000) finds somewhat different results. In particular, he finds that countries with fixed exchange rate regimes tend to face severe losses in terms of GDP growth after negative terms of trade shocks. However, he also finds that in highly dollarized economies the response to terms of trade shocks is not significantly different for pegs and floats.

A third assessment of the effectiveness of monetary policy is to look at the behavior of interest rates over the business cycle. In a country with a flexible regime, the central bank should be able to smooth the business cycle by lowering the interest rate during recessions and increasing the interest rate during expansions. We therefore conclude this section with results of our testing whether the countries in our sample used this interest rate adjustment option. In particular, we follow Hausmann et al. (1999) and study the reaction of real interest rates to the cyclical component of income measured as the difference between current industrial production and its trend component. Using panel data for Argentina, Brazil, Chile, Colombia, and Mexico, Hausmann et al. (1999) found that, during the 1960–1998 period, interest rates generally moved procyclically and that although the differences were not statistically significant, the procyclical feature was more pronounced under flexible regimes.[37]

Here, we replicate the exercise individually for Costa Rica, El Salvador, Guatemala, and Panama, using monthly data for the 1986–1999 period.[38] As shown in table 5.15, we find a significant anticyclical interest rate in Panama and El Salvador (Panama is dollarized, and El Salvador has a formally flexible but de facto fixed exchange rate), procyclical rate in Costa Rica (which has a crawling peg), and neutral rate in Guatemala (which has a flexible exchange rate).

In summary, the evidence presented in this section suggests that the monetary independence resulting from exchange rate flexibility has either not been used as an anticyclical tool or has been ineffective as such.[39] Interest rates in countries with truly fixed regimes have been less procyclical, with no disadvantage in terms of absorbing external shocks and no increase in growth rate volatility.

Liability Dollarization and the Ability to Avoid Deflationary Adjustments In the preceding discussion, it was established that monetary independence (and the exchange rate flexibility associated with it) in the Central American countries (and more generally, in the Latin American countries) does not appear to have stabilizing

Table 5.15
Dependent variable: Short-term domestic real interest rate, 1986–1999

	Constant	Gap	R2	Obs.[1]
Panama	5.89***	23.53**	0.09	48
	(69.23)	(2.17)		
El Salvador	5.10***	10.03**	0.06	61
	(15.50)	(2.03)		
Costa Rica	0.22	−89.33***	0.15	156
	(0.77)	(−5.11)		
Guatemala	−0.88***	−2.72	0.00	73
	(−3.61)	(−0.22)		

[1] Obs. = number of observations
*** statistically significant 1% confidence level
** statistically significant 5% confidence level
* statistically significant 10% confidence level

effects on domestic interest rates or on fluctuations in economic activity. However, one of the highest costs associated with the loss of monetary independence is not related to the effectiveness of monetary policy in affecting real variables but the loss of a more basic function: the capacity to print money. In losing this capacity, the central bank would not be able to avoid a severe deflationary adjustment, as it would lose the possibility of controlling the price level through monetary policy.

According to Calvo (1999), Fisher (1933) argues that debt deflation—that is, the increase in the real value of corporate debt denominated in domestic currency as a result of price deflation—is one of the most important causes of major depressions, and that although the critics of dollarization have not brought up the threat of deflation, it is probably the greatest threat for an economy that opts for dollarization.

As we show in the appendix, however, the use of monetary policy (through a depreciation or devaluation of the domestic currency) to avoid a deflationary adjustment in the wake of a substantial negative shock will be quite limited in economies in which most liabilities are dollarized. In these economies, a depreciation or devaluation loses one of its essential "advantages" in fighting deflation: the capacity to dilute the real value of domestic-currency-denominated debts.[40]

The initial degree of dollarization is, therefore, a fundamental consideration in evaluating the effectiveness of monetary indepen-

Table 5.16
Dollarization in Central America

	Bank deposits (%)	Public debt (%)	Offshore market
Belize	2.9	66.2	—
Costa Rica	41.3	45.1	Significant: 30–35 percent of total deposits
Dominican Republic	14.5	83.1	Insignificant
El Salvador	7.7	57.2	Insignificant
Guatemala	0	84.7	Significant: 25–50 percent of total deposits
Honduras	34.8	91.9	—
Nicaragua	71.3	—	Significant
Panama	100	100.0	

dence in dealing with the debt deflation problem. Put differently, the higher the initial degree of liability dollarization, the less the cost of forgoing monetary independence. This is a crucial issue for the countries of Central America because as shown in table 5.16, de facto liability dollarization is relatively high in a number of countries in the region. The IMF (see IMF 1999) classifies highly dollarized countries as those in which more than 30 percent of the financial liabilities are dollarized. In Nicaragua, Costa Rica, and Honduras, the share of bank liabilities denominated in dollars are 71 percent, 41 percent, and 35 percent, respectively. Thus, according to the IMF criterion, they are considered highly dollarized economies. The Dominican Republic and El Salvador have an intermediate degree of bank liability dollarization (15 percent and 8 percent, respectively); whereas Belize (3 percent) and Guatemala (0 percent) have low levels of dollarization.

The figures in the bank deposits column of table 5.16 are probably a lower bound for dollarization of domestic bank liabilities, as they do not reflect offshore operations. For example, in Guatemala, in which the dollarization level of the financial system is zero, offshore operations in dollars are estimated to represent 25 to 50 percent of domestic transactions.

Although the degree to which public debt is dollarized is not frequently used as an indicator of the economy's dollarization level, it is important from the standpoint of the monetary policy restrictions resulting from the existence of financial mismatches in the government balance sheet. Public debt is highly dollarized in Central American countries, varying from a maximum of 85 percent in Honduras to a minimum of 45 percent in Costa Rica.[41]

In summary, due to the high level of de facto dollarization, the advantages that exchange rate flexibility affords in terms of the ability to avoid deflationary adjustment are likely to be somewhat limited in the cases of Costa Rica, Honduras, Nicaragua, and, perhaps, Guatemala. These advantages, however, are likely to be more relevant in the cases of El Salvador and the Dominican Republic, which are dollarized to a smaller degree.

5.6   Benefits of a Credible Commitment with a Strong Currency

In addition to the reduction of transaction costs in trade and investment flows, dollarization can produce benefits associated to credibility by imposing limits on the discretion of the monetary authorities. In section 5.6.1, we discuss the expected "credibility" benefits of dollarization. In section 5.6.2, we discuss whether, in the experience of Central American and Caribbean countries, a credible commitment to a strong currency has in fact delivered on its promise.

5.6.1   Expected Benefits

The very possibility of a sharp, unexpected devaluation in the domestic currency, and the fact that such devaluations are becoming increasingly commonplace, can entail significant costs for a country. Anchoring monetary policy of a country to the U.S. dollar through dollarization—or through exchange arrangements having similar effects, such as currency boards—implies a fundamental change in the rules of the game, in which the authorities surrender their discretionary powers on monetary policy and exchange rate management and adopt U.S. monetary policy as their standard. In other words, monetary and exchange rate policy is elevated in the "hierarchy" of government policies such that it is not subject to change at the authorities' discretion, or to the activities of any pressure groups that might benefit from time to time from a devaluation.

The predictability of an exchange rate not subject to discretionary changes and anchored to a strong currency could have many benefits from a monetary and financial perspective. We group these "credibility" benefits into three categories, which we discuss in turn: those associated to inflation, to financial fragility and credit risk, and to the depth of the financial system.

Lower (and Less Volatile) Inflation Rates

Importing monetary policy from a country with a proven track record in terms of inflation may result in lower (and less volatile) rates of inflation because monetary policy would be isolated from idiosyncratic shocks (fiscal shocks, pressure by interest groups to devalue the currency to gain competitiveness, temptation to use monetary policy to dilute the real value of nominal commitments, etc.) that could undermine monetary discipline or result in erratic monetary policy behavior.

Lower Volatility in Key Relative Prices, Less Financial Fragility, and Lower Credit Risk

It is no news that countries with more flexible exchange regimes have more volatile real exchange rates. Mussa (1986) documents that real exchange rate volatility in industrial countries increased substantially when currencies began floating among themselves and the Bretton Woods fixed parity system was abandoned.[43]

From a financial perspective the volatility of the real exchange rate and real interest rates implied by the choice of the exchange rate regime may be particularly important in economies where there are substantial currency and maturity mismatches in corporate balance sheets.

Hausmann (1999) and Calvo (1999) argue that financial mismatches in emerging economies should be considered the rule rather than the exception and therefore a typical characteristic of these economies. Hausmann (1999) attributes the existence of financial mismatches in debtor balances to what he calls the "original sin" of emerging economies, that is, the combination of a weak currency (in which medium-term credit and long-term credit are nonexistent) and the need to invest to finance development (which requires medium- and long-term credit). The only long-term credit available in these cases will be expressed in strong currency.[44] Therefore, there are two options for financing medium- and long-term investment projects: short-term local currency financing, leading to maturity mismatches; or long-term foreign currency financing, leading to currency mismatches.[45]

In the presence of either currency or maturity mismatches, a higher volatility of the real exchange rate and the real interest rate will result in a higher degree of financial fragility. In the presence of currency mismatches in corporate balance sheets, a sudden depreciation of the real exchange rate will affect both the balance between the flows of peso-denominated revenues and dollar-denominated interest payments and the relative values of peso-denominated assets and dollar-denominated liabilities. In this environment, firms may face difficulties in honoring their flow of financial commitments, and they may face an increase in leverage that results from the change in the relative valuation of assets and liabilities. This may lead to a situation in which firms lose access to credit and end up in a situation of financial distress.

This connection between exchange rate changes and their impact on balance sheets is at the heart of what Calvo and Reinhart (2002) call "fear of floating." For example, Hausmann, Panizza, and Stein (2001) find evidence that countries that cannot borrow abroad in their own currency tend to allow significantly less volatility in their exchange rates. These fragilities in the case of de facto dollarized economies may also explain the finding by Broda (2000) that countries that float their currencies but are highly dollarized are not able to stabilize output in response to terms of trade shocks.

The mirror image of a more volatile real exchange rate is more volatility in real interest rates. Real interest rate parity states that

$$r = r(^*) + q + \delta,$$

where r is the real interest rate in domestic currency, $r(^*)$ is the real interest rate in foreign currency, q is the real exchange rate depreciation, and δ is a risk premium. If we assume for the sake of argument that the volatility of $r(^*)$ and δ are equal to zero, that is, $r(^*)$ and δ are constant, the volatility of the real interest rate in domestic currency should exactly mimic the volatility of the real exchange rate.

Just as in the case of currency mismatches, a more volatile real interest rate will result in higher degree of financial fragility in the presence of maturity mismatches. For example, a sudden increase in the short-term real interest rate will increase the flow of interest payments relative to the flow of revenues, making it difficult for the firm to honor its financial commitments. This, again, might result in a loss of access to credit and to financial distress.

Finally, because a higher volatility in the real exchange rate and real interest rates implies a higher degree of financial fragility, it will also lead to a higher credit risk than in an otherwise identical economy with a lower volatility in relative prices.

A Deepening of the Financial System

In an economy with a higher volatility of relative prices and therefore a higher volatility of expected returns on firms' equity, optimal investment in risky assets will be smaller than in an otherwise identical economy with a lower volatility in relative prices and firms' equity.[46] Higher volatility may thus lead to a reduction in risky investments and, as a result, a reduction of the size of the financial system—as measured by the level of credit in the economy.

Hausmann et al. (1999) use a standard risk diversification argument to explain the fact that emerging countries with a floating exchange rate tend to have smaller financial systems. The argument goes as follows: Consider the investment decisions of residents of a country that is subject to large terms of trade shocks and that adopts a flexible exchange rate. If the government uses the exchange rate to smooth terms of trade shocks, we will observe depreciations in presence of negative terms of trade shock and appreciations in presence of positive terms of trade shocks. Consider now a negative terms of trade shock. If investors hold their savings in domestic currency, they will be hit twice by the negative terms of trade shock because both their income and the real value of their savings in local currency will decline. Investors will therefore have an incentive not to invest in the local currency but in a currency whose value is negatively correlated (or, at least, not positively correlated) with their income process.

In the following sections we shall provide a comparative analysis of the performance of the different exchange regimes in Central America in terms of the three groups of factors just discussed: inflation; volatility of relative prices, financial fragility, and credit risk; and the size of the financial system. The variety of regimes that have existed in the region in the long term (from 1960 to the present) and the variety of regimes across countries during the 1990s makes this comparative analysis particularly relevant.

5.6.2   Has Credibility Delivered?

**Countries with Credible Exchange Arrangements Have
Experienced a Lower and Less Volatile Inflation Rate**
Countries in Central America with more flexible exchange rate
regimes have generally experienced higher and more volatile inflation rates than those that have opted for truly fixed exchange rate
regimes. This is observed when we compare countries with more
flexible regimes during the 1990s (Costa Rica, the Dominican Republic, El Salvador, Guatemala, Honduras, and Nicaragua) with those
having truly fixed exchange regimes (Panama and Belize) and when
we compare the 1990s with the 1960s and 1970s, when all countries
in the region had fixed exchange rates vis-à-vis the dollar.

Convergence in the level and volatility of the inflation rate to the
levels prevailing in the country of the adoptive currency when the
exchange regimes are credible and nondiscretionary is clearly exem-
plified in the region in the cases of Panama and Belize. As we observe in table 5.17, Panama and Belize had average inflation rates
and inflation rate variability quite similar to the United States between 1960 and 1998, and during each of the subperiods considered.

The story is quite different in the remaining six Central American
countries. During the 1960s and 1970s, when exchange rates were
fixed vis-à-vis the dollar, average inflation in the six countries was
quite similar to levels in the United States, although inflation variability nearly doubled the U.S. level. This average performance is
also representative of each of the countries considered individually.
During the 1980s, a period of transition to more flexible regimes,
inflation and inflation variability increased significantly, reaching
three times the U.S. level. During the third period, with more flexible
exchange rates, average inflation and inflation variability continued
to increase to five times and ten times the levels in the United States,
respectively. Even El Salvador, which has maintained a de facto
fixed exchange rate since 1993—though with no explicit commitment
to defend the parity—had inflation variability four times greater
than that of the United States during the 1990s.

The evidence therefore suggests that the adoption of exchange rate
arrangements credibly linking the currencies of Central America to
the dollar would result in lower, more stable inflation rates for the
countries of the region, possibly similar to those of the United States.
For many Central American countries, this would entail a consider-

Table 5.17
Inflation in Central America, 1960–1998 (values relative to U.S. inflation)

		1960–1979	1980–1989	1990–1998
Belize	Inflation	—	0.78	0.89
	standard deviation	—	0.94	1.48
Costa Rica	Inflation	1.26	4.88	5.69
	standard deviation	2.29	6.56	5.55
Dominican Republic	Inflation	1.17	3.76	5.72
	standard deviation	1.79	4.48	17.39
El Salvador	Inflation	1.05	3.34	3.79
	standard deviation	2.07	1.79	5.92
Guatemala	Inflation	1.02	2.17	5.13
	standard deviation	1.86	2.83	11.08
Honduras	Inflation	0.93	1.33	6.67
	standard deviation	1.09	1.28	7.52
Nicaragua	Inflation	—	305.13	4.75
	standard deviation	—	921.77	6.01
Panama	Inflation	0.75	0.57	0.35
	standard deviation	1.19	1.21	0.37
Central America	Inflation	1.03	2.40	4.03
(excluding Nicaragua)	standard deviation	1.71	2.73	7.05
Belize and Panama	Inflation	0.75	0.67	0.62
	standard deviation	1.19	1.08	0.92
Rest of Countries	Inflation	1.09	3.10	5.40
(excluding Nicaragua)	standard deviation	1.82	3.39	9.49

Note: For Nicaragua, inflation during the period 1992–1997 was considered for the 1990s, to eliminate the hyperinflationary years.

able improvement in relation to their present situation. This evidence is consistent with that in Ghosh et al. (1997), who find that pegging the nominal exchange rate is associated with lower inflation.

Countries with Credible Exchange Rate Arrangements Have Experienced Lower Real Exchange Rate and Real Interest Rate Volatility and Lower Credit Risk

In general, the Central American countries with more flexible regimes experienced greater real exchange rate and real interest rate volatility.

Table 5.18 clearly shows the close association between more flexible exchange regimes and real bilateral exchange rate volatility with

Table 5.18
Real bilateral exchange rate volatility with the United States

	1960–1979	1980–1989	1990–1998*	1990–1998/ 1960–1979
Costa Rica	1.10	8.21	1.08	0.98
Dominican Republic	1.97	10.95	3.47	1.76
El Salvador	1.04	6.41	3.40	3.27
Guatemala	2.17	8.52	3.17	1.46
Honduras	1.11	0.59	6.57	5.92
Nicaragua	6.62	46.75	5.70	0.86
Panama	0.54	0.48	0.34	0.63
Belize			1.64	
Central America	2.08	11.70	3.39	2.13
Panama	0.54	0.48	0.34	0.63
Rest of Countries	2.34	13.57	3.90	2.38
Rest of countries in relation to Panama	4.32	28.27	11.47	3.77

Note: Real exchange rate volatility is calculated as the standard deviation of the logarithmic differences between real exchange rates.
*Nicaragua, April 1991–May 1998.

the United States.[47] Between 1960 and 1979, when the exchange regimes of all Central American countries were fixed, average real exchange rate volatility (excluding Panama)—measured with the standard deviation of the logarithmic differences—amounted to 2.34 percent per month, varying between a maximum of 6.62 percent for Nicaragua and a minimum of 1.04 percent for El Salvador. We note that the real bilateral exchange rate volatility between Panama—the only dollarized country in the region—and the United States was 0.54 percent per month, the lowest in the region, during that period.

As the countries converged to more flexible exchange regimes, volatility increased significantly in all Central American countries, in relation to the period during which the exchange rates were fixed and in relation to Panama. During the period 1990–1998, for all Central American countries excluding Panama, average volatility of the real bilateral exchange rate with the United States, practically doubled as compared with the period 1960–1979, when exchange rates were fixed. For example, volatility increased sixfold in Honduras, threefold in El Salvador, and almost twofold in the Dominican

Table 5.19
Real domestic interest rate volatility, 1992–1998 (Central America and United States)

	Borrowing			Lending			
	Average	SD	CV	Average	SD	CV	Period
Costa Rica	1.09	3.98	3.64	11.21	4.98	0.44	1/92–12/98
Dominican Republic	6.06	3.55	0.59	16.13	3.70	0.23	1/95–7/98
Honduras	−2.59	6.98		7.50	6.39	0.85	1/92–12/98
Nicaragua	2.22	1.47	0.66	7.36	1.88	0.26	1/95–1/97
Guatemala	−0.90	1.99		9.71	1.79	0.18	1/92–12/98
El Salvador	3.13	4.23	1.35	7.51	4.46	0.59	1/92–12/98
Panama	5.92	0.60	0.10	9.74	0.89	0.09	1/95–12/98

CV = coefficient of variation

Republic. Only in Costa Rica, which had an explicit policy to maintain a stable real exchange rate during the 1990s, did volatility remained at levels similar to those observed during the first period.

This performance is in stark contrast with that of Panama, where real exchange rate volatility remained fairly stable and declined gradually throughout the period under study. As a result, volatility levels in Central American countries were, on average, 4.3 times higher than in Panama during the period 1960–1979, when exchange regimes were fixed, but 11 times higher in 1990–1998, when the exchange regimes were more flexible.

During the 1990s, real interest rates in domestic currency performed similarly to real exchange rate volatility—with extraordinary volatility levels in all countries except Panama.[48]

Table 5.19 shows the volatility of real interest rates during the period 1992–1998. Real interest rate volatility was very low in Panama (even by U.S. standards) and much higher in the rest of the countries. On average, real interest rates were six times more volatile in countries with flexible regimes than they were in Panama, ranging from a maximum of 11 times more volatile in Honduras to a minimum of 2.5 times in Guatemala.

Regardless of the source of financial mismatches in debtor balances—relative price volatility itself, original sin according to Hausmann (1999), or regulatory or information issues as presented by Calvo (1999)—we should expect that in the presence of these mismatches and high interest and real exchange rate volatility, credit

Table 5.20
Banking spreads in Central America and the United States, 1990–1998

Country	Spread (%)
Panama	3.65
El Salvador	3.88
Belize	6.03
Nicaragua	8.05
Dominican Republic	8.45
Costa Rica	9.85
Honduras	9.99
Guatemala	10.24
United States	2.76
Central America	7.52
Belize and Panama	4.84
Rest of Countries	8.41

risk would be greater than would be observed in the absence of such mismatches in a context of more stable relative prices.

Table 5.20 presents data on banking spreads, as a proxy for credit risk.[49] Panama has the lowest spreads between borrowing and lending rates, with an average markup of 3.7 percent for the entire period 1990–1998. The average markup between borrowing and lending rates for all the rest of the Central American countries (excluding Belize) is 8.4 percent, that is, more than twice the level observed in Panama. For Central American countries with more flexible exchange rate regimes, the spread varied between a maximum of 10.2 percent for Guatemala and a minimum of 3.9 percent for El Salvador, the country with the greatest nominal exchange rate stability. Therefore, the presumption that credit risk would be greater under flexible regimes in the presence of currency and maturity mismatches seems to be supported by the facts.

Countries with Credible Exchange Arrangements Have Experienced More Vigorous Growth in Their Financial Systems

The more stable context in the Central American countries with less discretionary powers and more rigid exchange arrangements has promoted more vigorous development in the financial system.

Table 5.21 and figure 5.5 show trends in the development of the financial system during the period 1975–1980, when most Central

Table 5.21
Size of the financial system in Central America (M2 as a percentage of GDP)

	1975–1980	1992–1998
Belize	34.0	44.3
Costa Rica	31.4	35.9
Dominican Republic	19.6	22.3
El Salvador	26.0	35.3
Guatemala	21.0	23.5
Honduras	21.6	26.2
Nicaragua	19.2	28.7
Panama	29.9	59.8
Central America	27.3	40.4
Belize and Panama	31.6	52.1
Rest of countries	23.1	28.6

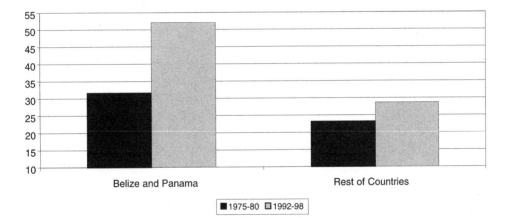

Figure 5.5
Size of the financial system in Central America (M2 as a percentage of GDP). *Source:* Authors' calculation based on IMF's International Financial Statistics.

American countries still had not abandoned their fixed parities with the dollar, and 1992–1998, when these countries moved toward more flexible exchange regimes. During the period 1975–1980, the size of the financial system—measured as the ratio of M2 to GDP—averaged 34 percent of GDP in Belize and 30 percent of GDP in Panama, while averaging 23 percent of GDP in the rest of the Central American countries—and varied between a maximum of 31 percent of GDP in Costa Rica and a minimum of 19 percent of GDP in Nicaragua.

During the period 1992–1998, the average size of Belize's financial system increased to 44.3 percent of GDP, and Panama's increased to 60 percent of GDP, while the average for the Central American countries increased to 29 percent of GDP. Accordingly, the differences between these two groups of countries—those with truly fixed exchange regimes as compared with those having more flexible regimes—were sharply accentuated. Costa Rica, the only country in Central America whose financial system was comparable in size to that of Belize and Panama during the period 1975–1980, experienced very low levels of growth in the financial system, to reach only 36 percent of GDP during the period 1992–1998.

This evidence is consistent with the results reported by Hausmann et al. (1999), who found, for a sample of the twenty-six Latin American member countries of the Inter-American Development Bank studied during the period 1960–1994, that countries with more flexible exchange regimes have substantially less developed financial systems than those with fixed regimes. Their results, as well as ours, suggests that the effect of the exchange system on the size of financial system are not only significant from the statistical standpoint but also quantitatively important from the economic standpoint.

However it is not only a question of size. Countries with credible exchange rate arrangements appear to be the only ones where access to long-term credit at fixed rates is available.[50] Evidence on mortgage credit in the countries studied here seems to indicate that where long-term credit exists, the rates are variable and the terms are relatively short, as compared with mortgage credit standards in industrial countries (see table 5.22). Specific exceptions are Belize and Panama, where fixed-rate mortgage credit is available for terms of up to twenty years at 12 percent per annum (Belize) and for terms of up to twenty-five years at 8.5 percent per annum (Panama). Interestingly, conditions for accessing the mortgage credit market in

Table 5.22
Mortgage credit in Central America (most liquid mortgage market)

	Rates	Local currency component	Term (years)
Belize	Fixed (12% per annum)	All	10–20
Costa Rica	Variable	Almost all	10–15
Dominican Republic	The mortgage market is virtually nonexistent.		
El Salvador	Variable	All	15
Guatemala	Variable	Almost all	15–20
Honduras	Variable	Almost all	15–20
Nicaragua	Variable		
Panama	Fixed (8.5% per annum)		15–25

Panama are for all intents and purposes similar to those in the United States.

In summary, the evidence presented in this section suggests that the adoption of exchange arrangements credibly linking Central American currencies to the dollar, through dollarization or the adoption of exchange arrangements having similar effects, may lead to lower and less volatile rates of inflation, lower real exchange rate and real interest rate volatility, lower financial fragility, lower credit risk (i.e., smaller spreads between borrowing and lending rates), and larger and more diverse financial systems.

5.7   Conclusions

As discussed in the introduction, the aim of this chapter has been to develop a methodology to assess the cost and benefits of dollarization and apply it to a set of Central American countries. Wherever possible, efforts were made to provide measurement of the potential effects of dollarization. Although there are many important factors involved in making such a fundamental and permanent decision, including political and cultural factors, in this chapter we have concentrated on those factors that depend on the structural characteristics of the potential dollarizing countries, as well as the strength of their links to the United States.

In our view, based on the set of criteria discussed in this chapter, several of the countries under study should give dollarization serious consideration. The benefits in terms of transaction cost reduction in trade and investment are potentially large. The evidence on the importance of reducing exchange rate volatility is mixed, but our results suggest that it is more important for the case of developing countries, in which adequate mechanisms to reduce risk are less developed or nonexistent. Furthermore, other costs associated with the need to transact in two currencies appear to be quite large.

Benefits from credibility appear to be potentially important as well. Our analysis suggests that beyond the reduction in inflation, dollarization may reduce financial fragility by reducing the volatility of key relative prices in the economy, as well as contribute to the development of the financial system. Although higher inflation and more volatile relative prices are clearly undesirable outcomes under flexible exchange rate regimes, within the framework developed in section 5.5.1, they may just be the result of a rational choice, in which the government decides to trade some credibility for more monetary independence and output stabilization. The analysis of section 5.5.2, however, seems to indicate that this is not the case. The Central American countries with flexible exchange rate regimes appear to be worse off than their counterparts with credibly fixed regimes in terms of the volatility of nominal variables, without any noticeable gain in terms of the volatility of real variables. We therefore conclude that although Central American countries with flexible regimes paid large cost in terms of credibility, they did not appear to gain very much in terms of the benefits of monetary independence.

Appendix

In this appendix,[51] we will go through a set of examples that will serve to illustrate the concept of debt deflation, and to illustrate (1) why losing the capacity to avoid a deflationary adjustment can be quite costly in some circumstances; and (2) why the benefits of preventing a deflationary adjustment will significantly diminish if the economy has a high degree of liability dollarization, that is, if corporate liabilities are de facto denominated in dollars.

Let us imagine for a moment that the economy it is hit by an external shock (e.g., a drastic decline in the terms of trade, a real devaluation in a neighboring country with which a considerable volume of trade exists, or a sudden decrease in the availability of external capital) that requires a considerable real exchange rate depreciation.

If we presume that purchasing power parity applies to tradables, the real exchange rate, defined as the relative price of tradables in terms of nontradables, will be expressed with the equation

$$q = P(T)/P(NT) = eP(^{*}, T)/P(NT),$$

where $P(T)$ is the domestic price of tradables, $P(NT)$ is the domestic price of nontradables, e is the nominal exchange rate, and $P(^{*}, T)$ is the price of tradables expressed in dollars.

This equation clearly shows that a depreciation in the real exchange rate—that is, an increase in q—may occur, all other things being equal, either through a devaluation of the domestic currency—that is, an increase in e—or through a decline in the price of nontradables—that is, a decline in $P(NT)$. We shall refer to the adjustment in the former case as a devaluation adjustment and to the latter as a deflationary adjustment.[52]

The conventional reason for which it is normally argued that a central bank will prefer a devaluation adjustment to a deflationary one is that prices of nontradables are downwardly rigid. In such a case, all other things being equal, the central bank would prefer a devaluation adjustment—which would immediately restore real exchange rate equilibrium—rather than a deflationary adjustment—which would require an economic recession phase during which nontradable prices gradually decline and real exchange rate equilibrium is restored.

However, let us assume that nontradable prices are perfectly flexible. Why, then, would the central bank prefer a devaluation adjustment to a deflationary one? The answer relates to the asymmetric effects of a devaluation and deflation on corporate balance sheets.[53]

Let us consider a firm that sells nontradables and that the value of its assets (the present discounted value of future income from the sale of nontradables) is equal to 100 units of tradables (that is, U.S.$100). Let us also assume that the firm is fully financed with equity, so its equity is also equivalent to 100. Let us now assume that the nominal exchange rate is one peso per dollar. The company's initial balance sheet denominated in dollars would appear as follows:

Initial Balance Sheet
(in units of tradables)

100 Assets	100 Equity

If a real exchange shock resulted in a 100 percent depreciation, and the central bank opted for a devaluation adjustment, the exchange rate would rise from one to two pesos to restore equilibrium. The price of tradables would double, and the price of nontradables would remain constant. In this case, the value of the firm's assets in dollars would be cut in half, in terms of tradables, and the same would occur for its equity. The firm's balance sheet denominated in dollars after the nominal and real devaluation would be as follows:

Balance Sheet Following Devaluation Adjustment
(in units of tradables)

50 Assets	50 Equity

If, on the other hand, the central bank decided on a deflationary adjustment, the price of nontradables would be cut in half, but the nominal exchange rate, and therefore the price of tradables, would remain constant. Again, the value of the firm's assets and equity would be cut in half in terms of dollars. With flexible prices and assets financed entirely by equity, the central bank would be indifferent to a devaluation adjustment or a deflationary one.

Let us now assume that half of the assets are financed with debt in domestic currency. In other words, the firm's initial balance sheet, denominated in dollars, would read as follows:

Initial Balance Sheet
(in units of tradables)

100 Assets	50 Liabilities in domestic currency
	50 Equity

In such a case, as in the previous situation, a devaluation adjustment would cut the value of the firm's assets in terms of dollars in half. However. as debts are denominated in pesos, they would also be cut in half expressed in dollars. As in the case of the firm that was fully financed by equity, a devaluation adjustment would cut the firm's equity in dollar terms to half of the initial value:

Balance Sheet Following Devaluation Adjustment
(in units of tradables)

| 50 Assets | 25 Liabilities in domestic currency |
| | 25 Equity |

The effects of a deflationary adjustment on the firm's balance sheet would differ substantially from a devaluation adjustment. In this case, nontradable prices would be cut in half, as would the value of the firm's assets in dollar terms. However, as the nominal exchange rate remains constant, the value of the debts in pesos expressed in dollars also remains constant. The firm's situation after a deflationary adjustment would be as follows:

Balance Sheet Following Deflationary Adjustment
(in units of tradables)

| 50 Assets | 50 Liabilities in domestic currency |
| | 0 Equity |

In other words, in a deflationary adjustment, the firm would lose all of its equity, and would enter bankruptcy. To the extent that bankruptcy, that is, the transfer of ownership, is costly (as is the rule, especially when such processes have systemic features) the central bank would prefer a devaluation adjustment of the real exchange rate over a deflationary adjustment, as a devaluation adjustment could restore the same equilibrium level that would be obtained in an economy in which all assets are financed by equity. In other words, a nominal devaluation would have the effect of transforming an *ex ante* fixed nominal contract into an *ex post* contingent contract.

This asymmetry between the effects of a devaluation adjustment and a deflationary adjustment on the corporate balance sheets, when some assets are financed with liabilities in domestic currency, is an important consideration when assessing the cost of relinquishing monetary independence. If the economy is required to process a major relative price adjustment, and in particular a real exchange rate depreciation, a deflationary adjustment may place numerous firms in financial difficulty or bankrupt them straightaway—with tremendous costs in terms of economic activity. Conversely, if the devaluation mechanism is available to the authorities, a devaluation adjustment could save numerous firms from bankruptcy by diluting the value of their debts as well. Surrendering this instrument in this context can be quite costly.

The conclusions of the analysis change radically if we assume that the corporate liabilities are initially denominated in dollars rather than in pesos. The initial balance sheet of the firm in this case reads as follows:

Initial Balance Sheet
(in units of tradables)

| 100 Assets | 50 Liabilities in foreign currency |
| | 50 Equity |

When corporate liabilities are dollarized, a devaluation adjustment cuts the value of the firm's assets in half in dollar terms but does not reduce the value of its debt, as it is denominated in dollars. Therefore, there is a difference with respect to what would happen to a firm that had debts denominated in pesos. The adjustment would immediately place the firm in our example in bankruptcy:

Balance Sheet Following Devaluation Adjustment
(in units of tradables)

| 50 Assets | 50 Liabilities in foreign currency |
| | 0 Equity |

With liabilities in dollars, a deflationary adjustment would have the same balance sheet effect as a devaluation adjustment. In this case, cutting the price of nontradables in half also cuts the value of the firm's assets in dollar terms in half, while the value of its debt remains unchanged. The deflationary adjustment would therefore also place the firm in this example in a bankruptcy situation:

Balance Sheet Following Deflationary Adjustment
(in units of tradables)

| 50 Assets | 50 Liabilities in foreign currency |
| | 0 Equity |

When the assets in an economy are highly dollarized the advantage of the devaluation mechanism, originating from its capacity to dilute the dollar value of debts, is eliminated. In dollarized economies, devaluations cannot prevent the financial distress and bankruptcies arising from a deflationary adjustment. The cost of forgoing this instrument is therefore much lower in economies where liabilities are partially dollarized. Furthermore, whereas a devaluation adjustment leads to a rapid change in the real exchange rate, a deflationary adjustment may lead to a slower, more gradual change in the real exchange rate, as nontradable prices also decline slowly. The difference in the speed at which the real exchange rate adjusts in an economy with dollar-denominated liabilities may lead the central bank to prefer a deflationary adjustment (which would have less immediate effects on corporate balance sheets) over a devaluation adjustment (which would have an immediate effect on corporate balance sheets), which may have an even more contractionary effect.[54]

To conclude, the cost of forgoing the use of monetary independence to avoid deflationary adjustments will be different for each Central American country and will depend substantially on two factors: the degree of initial liability dollarization in the economy, and the probability that a shock severe enough would occur and require a drastic change in relative prices. Economies that have a large degree of liability dollarization, and that are exposed to smaller shocks (and therefore have less need for major relative price changes), face a lower cost of surrendering their monetary independence.

Notes

Panizza and Stein are economists in the Research Department of the Inter-American Development Bank, 1300, New York Ave. NW, Washington, D.C., 20577; e-mail: ⟨ugop@iadb.org⟩, and ⟨ernestos@iadb.org⟩. Talvi is the director of CERES (Centro de Estudios de la Realidad Economica y Social), Antonio Costa 3476, C.P. 11300, Montevideo, Uruguay; e-mail: ⟨etalvi@ceres-uy.org⟩. The authors wish to thank Michele Cavallo, Laura Dos Reis, and Akinori Tomohara for their excellent work as research assistants. We gratefully acknowledge the contributions of Gustavo Márquez on all aspects related to labor market and migration. We thank Fernando Aportela, Ilan Goldfajn, Ricardo Hausmann, Eduardo Levi Yeyati, Federico Sturzenegger, and seminar participants at the Universidad Torcuato Di Tella, Buenos Aires, for their comments and suggestions. The ideas expressed in this paper are those of the authors, and do not necessarily reflect those of the Inter-American Development Bank.

1. These countries are Belize, the Dominican Republic, Costa Rica, El Salvador, Guatemala, Honduras, and Nicaragua. In addition to these countries, the experience of

Panama as a fully dollarized economy is used throughout the paper as a constant point of reference.

2. See Hausmann and Powell (1999) for a discussion of implementation issues associated with dollarization in the same set of countries.

3. A bill sponsored by Senator Mack in the U.S. Congress proposed a system through which the United States could share up to 85 percent of seignorage with countries that decide to adopt the dollar as their currency.

4. We include El Salvador's regime since 1993 in this category. Although the country maintained the same parity for more than five years, it is formally a dirty float with no formal agreement to maintain the exchange rate parity.

5. This last study uses a gravity model of bilateral trade augmented by a dummy variable for the exchange rate regime. It does not include a variable directly measuring exchange rate volatility. Thus, these results could be attributable to countries with fixed but adjustable exchange rates, with a high level of real exchange rate volatility.

6. In addition, it uses a much larger sample, encompassing sixty-three countries rather than the thirty used by Brada and Mendez, and it analyzes data between 1965 and 1990.

7. Frankel and Wei report regressions using instrumental variables to resolve potential endogeneity problems: countries may attempt to reduce exchange rate volatility with their major trading partners. The average elasticity value that we use corresponds to Ordinary Least Squares (OLS) regressions. Instrumental variable estimations yield an average elasticity that is four times higher, although the difference is explained entirely by the coefficient corresponding to 1965.

8. Belize was excluded due to insufficient data. The real exchange rate series used to calculate variability reported in the table use the U.S. consumer price index as the measure of external inflation. The results are quite similar when we use the wholesale price index in its place.

9. As a benchmark, Frankel and Wei (1998) report that the average volatility in the countries of the European Economic Community was 1.2 percent in 1990 and was slightly more than 2 percent before the European Monetary System (EMS) was established.

10. Real exchange rate volatility in Nicaragua and Honduras was much higher before these periods were excluded.

11. The effect of exchange rate volatility is an order of magnitude smaller than Rose's estimated common currency effect. We will discuss the common currency results in the next subsection.

12. López (1994) estimates that a person who begins a journey in Panama; travels through Costa Rica, El Salvador, Guatemala, Honduras, and Nicaragua; and returns to Panama, and who exchanges money in the banking sector in each country will have, at the end of the journey, eighty-eight cents for each dollar he or she had when the journey began. This suggests that the transaction cost may be approximately 2 percent for each stopover.

13. Within this sample, there are more than 300 observations in which two countries trade and share a common currency, which allows for the estimation of the currency union effect.

14. In fact, in proportion to GDP, the United States and the rest of Central America are more important as trading partners for the countries under study than the European Union is for its own members, even for the case of the smaller countries such as Portugal and Greece. The importance of other Mercosur countries for the members of the block is much smaller still (see Stein, Talvi, Panizza, and Márquez 1999).

15. For these calculations we used the figures that represent trade integration with the United States and the rest of the countries under study. Effects would be a little smaller in the case of a currency union with the United States alone.

It is also possible to estimate the impact of dollarization on trade through the currency union effect measured by Rose (2000). If one took the results of Rose at face value, the impact would simply be enormous (implying increases in intraregional trade from 50 percent of GDP in Guatemala, to numbers well in excess of 100 percent of GDP in Honduras and Nicaragua). These numbers are too large to be taken seriously. One would expect the currency union effect to be smaller for countries that already are highly integrated, such as the ones we are considering here. Yet, the simple message of this exercise is that the impact of dollarization on trade among members of the currency union can be expected to be quite large.

16. Our use of credibility and independence as arguments of the utility function is somewhat unsatisfying. We recognize that a better model specification would have as arguments of the utility function outcomes such as inflation and output variability. In such a framework, monetary independence and credibility would be intermediate objectives to achieve the ultimate goals. The current framework, however, is simpler and is enough to help us build our intuition regarding the trade-offs involved in the decision to dollarize.

17. An interesting extension of this model would be, in a dynamic setting, to allow for credibility building, that is, for outward shifts in the budget constraint. In this regard, Checchetti and Ehrmann (1999) find that there is a clear trade-off between inflation and output variability but that the adoption of a credible institutional agreement (they study the case of inflation targeting) can improve the efficiency of the system and reduce the trade-off between these two policy goals. Such extension, however, is beyond the scope of the present chapter.

18. We abstract from the fact that in the real world there is more than one anchor country.

19. The fact that anchor countries have a higher credibility endowment and face a lower price of monetary independence implies that both the income and the substitution effects work, in the case of monetary independence, in the same direction. This is reinforced by the fact that the anchor country values monetary independence relatively more than the nonanchor country does.

20. Even if cycles were perfectly synchronized, monetary independence could still retain some value if preferences (for example, the disutility of inflation) differed across countries.

21. The theoretical argument that goes in the opposite direction is that an increase in trade relations raises the degree to which countries specialize in different goods, which makes them more likely to be subject to asymmetric idiosyncratic shocks.

22. This section, as well as those on labor mobility and transfers that follow, draw heavily on background material prepared by Gustavo Márquez, previously included in Stein et al. (1999).

23. As we will note later, the existence of noncontingent debt contracts introduces differences between these two types of adjustment, even in the case of price flexibility.

24. As we argue later, the relative virtue of a deflationary or devaluation adjustment can depend on the degree of de facto dollarization in the economy.

25. No data were available for Belize.

26. The only exception is the Dominican Republic, where changes in growth have been much smaller than in the rest of the countries included in the figure.

27. Of course, the civil war in Nicaragua and El Salvador during the periods of contraction may have played an even greater role than economic stagnation.

28. In fact, even if Costa Rica were not included in the group, the fact that labor mobility exists between Nicaragua and Costa Rica would enable part of the adjustment in Nicaragua to a negative asymmetrical shock with the United States to be absorbed through a reduction in the labor supply.

29. Cyclical components were calculated as residuals in a regression of GDP and remittances against linear and quadratic trends.

30. Whereas Frankel (1999) uses nominal interest rates, Hausmann et al. (1999) use real rates.

31. Using daily data, and working in levels, Hausmann et al. (1999) estimates the following coefficients: 1.45 for Argentina, 2.77 for Venezuela, and 5.93 for Mexico. If we restrict our estimations to the mid-1997–mid-1999 period (i.e., the same as the one studied by Hausmann et al.), we find a coefficient of 0.99 for Argentina, 2.40 for Venezuela, and 6.56 for Mexico.

32. Preliminary exercises suggest that unemployment variability was also not particularly high in the case of Panama, although the unemployment rate was higher than in the rest of the countries, with the exception of the Dominican Republic. This is probably attributable to the fact that Panama has the most rigid labor legislation of all countries considered.

33. The results are robust to the use of total GDP growth instead of per capita growth.

34. We use a pooled OLS regression and fixed and random effects panel estimations. We find that the results are robust to different model specifications.

35. Data on wars and natural disasters come from *The World Alamanac and Book of Facts* (2000).

36. If anything, we find that the evidence against the stabilizing power of flexible exchange regimes is even stronger than in the case of table 5.14. The results are available upon request.

37. It should be stressed that an increase in the interest rate is not necessarily indicative of contractionary monetary policy. For example, in Argentina, in the wake of the Tequila Crisis, interest rates increased, while the Argentine Central Bank made every effort to increase the liquidity in the financial system. However, it is interesting to note that monetary outcomes are more procyclical in flexible exchange rate regimes.

38. The data are not available for a uniform period. We look at only four countries because no monthly data were available on industrial production in the rest of the countries.

39. Hausmann et al. (1999) argue that in many cases, countries choose not to use the exchange rate flexibility formally available to them, even in response to severe terms of trade shocks. For example, in Chile, only minimal changes in the exchange rate were allowed despite the collapse in copper prices in early 1998. In this case, one of the reasons for this revealed preference for exchange stability is precisely the existence of considerable dollar-denominated liabilities in the private sector.

40. In the appendix we go through a set of examples that serve to illustrate the concept of debt deflation and to illustrate (1) why losing the capacity to avoid a deflationary adjustment can be quite costly in some circumstances; and (2) why the benefits of preventing a deflationary adjustment will significantly diminish if the economy has a high degree of liability dollarization, that is, if corporate liabilities are de facto denominated in dollars.

41. Although 92 percent of Nicaragua's public debt is denominated in foreign currency, some of this debt is denominated in Eastern European currencies.

42. The benefits of having a credible commitment to a strong currency can also be thought of as the costs of retaining monetary independence.

43. The evidence found by Mussa (1986) was confirmed in subsequent studies, for example, Baxter and Stockman (1989) and Flood and Rose (1995).

44. It is interesting that 95 percent of cross-border financing in the world is done in only ten currencies.

45. Calvo (1999) argues that emerging economies have depended and probably will continue to depend on external saving, specifically bank credit, to finance investment. Financial mismatches are created as external bank loans are normally denominated in foreign currency. This is so either for institutional reasons—regulations normally prohibit major mismatches in the denomination of assets and liabilities—or as the result of asymmetric information problems. In the latter case, if borrowers in pesos—normally domestic firms—are in a better position than international banks to know when a devaluation will occur—or perhaps to precipitate one—international loans in domestic currency offered by international banks will be quite limited and quite expensive.

46. This is a standard result in the portfolio choice literature.

47. Real bilateral exchange rates were calculated as the quotient between the price level in U.S. dollars and the price level in dollars in each Central American country.

48. Belize was not included in the real exchange rate and real interest rate analysis presented in this section, as no monthly price indices were available.

49. It must be borne in mind that banking spreads may reflect factors related to the structure of the banking market other than differences in debtor credit risk.

50. This means that for any given volatility of relative prices—which has been substantially lower in countries with credible exchange rate arrangements—financial fragility will diminish because a richer menu of financial assets allows for a better match between assets and liabilities.

51. For a formal treatment of the issues in this appendix, see Fernández-Arias and Talvi (1999).

52. A vivid example of severe deflationary adjustment is the situation Argentina endured as the result of the devaluation of the real in Brazil. Argentina had a

convertibility regime under which a one-to-one ratio is established by law between the peso and the dollar.

53. Calvo (1998) and Krugman (1999) recently argued that the effects of changes in relative prices on the corporate balance sheets play a fundamental role in explaining the economic collapses observed in some emerging economies in Asia and Latin America.

54. Although the economic authorities deem Argentina's devaluation adjustment following Brazil's devaluation to be severe, a devaluation adjustment, given the country's highly dollarized economy, would be even more contractionary. There was a similar situation in Uruguay: even though its exchange rate regime is more flexible than Argentina's (the exchange rate is allowed to float within a band of 3.5 percent width), it also opted for a severe deflationary adjustment. Highly dollarized debts and the potential impact of a devaluation on corporate balance sheets is the reason Uruguay did not choose a devaluation adjustment in response to Brazil's devaluation of the real.

References

Baxter, M., and Stockman, A. (1989). "Business Cycles and the Exchange Rate Regime: Some International Evidence." *Journal of Monetary Economics* 23 (May): 377–400.

Bayoumi, T., and Eichengreen, B. (1996). "Ever Closer to Heaven? An Optimum-Currency Area Index for European Countries." CIDER WP C96-078, August 1996.

Borensztein, E., and Zettelmeyer, J. (2000). "Does The Exchange Rate Regime Make a Difference?" Mimeo, IMF.

Brada, J., and Mendez, J. (1988). "Exchange Rate Risk, Exchange Rate Regimes, and the Level of International Trade." *Kyklos* 41 (2): 198.

Broda, C. (2000). "Terms of Trade and Exchange Rate Regimes in Developing Countries." Mimeo, MIT.

Calvo, G. (1999). "On Dollarization." Mimeo, University of Maryland, College Park.

———. (1998). "Capital Flows and Capital Market Crises: The Simple Economics of Sudden Stops." *Journal of Applied Economics* (CEMA) 1, no. 1 (November): 35–54.

Calvo, G., and Reinhart, C. (2002). "Fear of Floating." *Quarterly Journal of Economics*, forthcoming.

Chechetti, S., and Ehrmann, M. (1999). "Does Inflation Targeting Increase Output Volatility? An Interantional Comparison of Policymakers' Preferences." NBER Working Paper, no. 7426.

De Grauwe, P. (1994). *The Economics of Monetary Integration.* Oxford, United Kingdom: Oxford University Press.

European Commission (1990). "One Market, One Money." *European Economy* 44.

Edison, H., and Melvin, M. (1990). "The Determinants and Implications of the Choice of an Exchange Rate System." In W. Haraf and T. Willet, eds., *Monetary Policy for a Volatile Global Economy.* Washington, D.C.: AEI Press.

Fernández-Arias, E., and Talvi, E. (1999). "Devaluation or Deflation: Adjustment Under Liability Dollarization." Working Paper, Research Department, Inter-American Development Bank and CERES, Montevideo, Uruguay.

Fisher, I. (1933). "The Debt-Deflation Theory of Great Depressions." *Econometrica* 1, no. 4 (October): 337–357.

Flood, R., and Rose, A. (1995). "Fixing Exchange Rates: A Virtual Quest for Fundamentals." *Journal of Monetary Economics* 36 (August): 3–37.

Frankel, J. (1999). "No Single Currency Regime Is Right for All Countries or at All Times." Paper presented at the Grahm Lecture, Princeton University, Princeton, N.J.

Frankel, J., and Rose, A. (1998). "The Endogeneity of the Optimum Currency Area Criteria." *Economic Journal* 108: 1009–1025.

Frankel, J., and Wei, S.-J. (1998). "Regionalization of World Trade and Currencies: Economics and Politics." In J. Frankel, ed., *The Regionalization of the World Economy.* Chicago: University of Chicago Press.

Ghosh, A., Gulde, A., Ostry, J., and Wolf, H. (1997). "Does the Nominal Exchange Rate Regime Matter?" NBER Working Paper, no. 5874, January.

Hausmann, R. (1999). "Currencies: Should There be Five or One Hundred and Five?" Mimeo, Washington, D.C.

Hausmann, R., Gavin, M., Pages-Serra, C., and Stein, E. (1999). "Financial Turmoil and the Choice of Exchange Rate Regime." Paper presented at New Initiatives to Tackle International Financial Turmoil Seminar, Inter-American Development Bank's Annual Meetings of the Board of Governors, Paris.

Hausmann, R., Panizza, U., and Stein, E. (2001). "Why Do Countries Float the Way They Float?." *Journal of Development Economics* 66: 387–414.

Hausmann, R., and Powell, A. (1999). "Dollarization: Issues of Implementation." Mimeo, Inter-American Development Bank.

Helliwell, J. (1998). *How Much Do National Borders Matter?* Brookings Institution, Washington, D.C.

International Monetary Fund (IMF) (1999). "Monetary Policy in Dollarized Economies." Occasional Paper, no. 171, Washington, D.C.

Krugman, P. (1999). "Balance Sheets, The Transfer Problem, and Financial Crises." Mimeo, MIT, Cambridge, Mass.

López, J. R. (1994). "La transición hacia la unión monetaria de Centroamérica." Consejo Monetario Centroamericano, San José, Costa Rica.

Márquez, G. (1997). "Protección al empleo y funcionamiento del mercado de trabajo: Una aproximación comparativa." In *Empleo, flexibilidad laboral y protección social*, proceedings of the second Reunión Técnica Círculo de Montevideo, Montevideo, December 1 and 2.

McCallum, J. (1995). "National Borders Matter: Canada-U.S. Regional Trade Patterns." *American Economic Review* 85 (3): 615–623.

McKinnon, R. (1963). "Optimum Currency Areas." *American Economic Review* 53: 717–725.

Meyers, D. W. (1998). "Migrant Remittances to Latin America: Reviewing the Literature." Tomás Rivera Policy Institute and Inter-American Dialogue Working Paper, Washington, D.C., May.

Mundell, R. (1961). "A Theory of Optimal Currency Areas." *American Economic Review* 51: 657–665.

Mussa, M. (1986). "Nominal Exchange Rate Regimes and the Behavior of Real Exchange Rates: Evidence and Implications." *Carnegie Rochester Series on Public Policy* 25 (Autumn): 117–124.

Rose, Andrew (2000). "One Money, One Market: Estimating The Effect of Common Currencies on Trade." *Economic Policy* 15: 7–46.

Stein, Ernesto, Ernesto Talvi, Ugo Panizza, and Gustavo Márquez (1999). "Evaluando la Dolarización: Una Aplicación a Países de América Central y del Caribe." Mimeo, Inter-American Development Bank.

The World Almanac and Book of Facts (2000). Press Publishing Company (The New York World), New York.

World Bank (1997). *World Development Report: The State in a Changing World*. Oxford University Press, Cambridge.

6 Dollarization: The Link between Devaluation and Default Risk

Andrew Powell and Federico Sturzenegger

6.1 Introduction

Recent exchange rate crises have led many to conclude that countries should either adopt floating rates or a fixed rate with strong institutional backing (see, for example, Eichengreen 1994; Mussa et al. 2000).[1] The advice stemming from the Washington institutions has tended to be toward the floating end of the spectrum, but the recent launch of the euro has brought the other extreme (fixed for good) to the forefront of monetary policy discussion.[2] In this corner solution debate, strong institutional backing for the fixed end of the spectrum has been interpreted as either a currency board rule, "dollarization," or even full monetary union.

We refer to *dollarization* as either the unilateral adoption of the dollar or other internationally used currency (the euro might be a good candidate for several Eastern European countries) or as the adoption of such a currency through the means of a monetary agreement that might fall short of full monetary union (we would advocate that full monetary union implies institutions to jointly determine monetary policy). The advantages of such a dramatic policy shift are normally couched in terms of the benefits of the elimination of currency risk and the effect of that elimination on interest rates and the potential for greater integration (in terms of trade and investment) with the adopted currency country (see, for example, Guidotti and Powell forthcoming). Greater integration, though supported by recent papers (see Frankel and Rose 2000; Rose 1999), appears as a somewhat intangible benefit. In contrast, the elimination of devaluation risk appears as extremely direct. However, less clear is the link between eliminating devaluation risk and the reduction in interest rates in the adopted currency. In our view, then, eliminating devaluation risk is potentially the most important benefit from dollarizing, and yet the mechanism by which that benefit feeds through to lower interest rates, higher investment, and growth remains poorly understood and largely untested. This is then the focus of this chapter.

The question we address is, What would happen to interest rates in the economy in the event of dollarization? There are a wide set of issues relevant here including potential gains in credibility and discipline, the effects of dollarization on the budget constraint of the government, the possibility of bank runs, and so on. The primary purpose of this chapter is to attempt to measure how all these forces impact local interest rates.

On the one hand, it is obviously true that local currency rates will disappear together with the local currency. On the other, this apparent interest rate reduction may even have a negative welfare effect, as the economy loses instruments for financial diversification.[3] However, the more relevant question is: What would be the effect on interest rates at large once all debt, public and private, became foreign currency denominated? Because public sector spreads generally provide a lower bound for private sector financing costs, the answer to this question can be obtained by estimating what would happen to country risk in the aftermath of dollarization. We believe, then, that measuring how dollarization affects country risk becomes an essential (if not the most important) issue in the dollarization debate. Therefore, this chapter concentrates on evaluating, empirically, whether there is any relation between the elimination of local currency risk and country risk.

The relevance of this question can easily be illustrated by a simple calculation. If the capital output ratio equals 4 and the rate of return of this capital equals 10 percent, the impact of a 1 percent reduction in the interest rate is equivalent to an increase in the value of the domestic capital stock of about 10 percent of GDP. As long as intertemporal consumption is related to initial wealth levels, the impact on feasible consumption may be significant and overshadows any potential welfare loss associated to seignorage or lender of last resort considerations. It is surprising that although these wealth effects seem to overshadow whatever cost dollarization may have on other dimensions, it is usually not stressed enough in the literature.

This chapter proceeds as follows: section 6.2 outlines briefly the theoretical reasons why country risk could be associated with currency risk. Section 6.3 discuss our empirical methodology, which is based on event studies. Section 6.4 applies the event study methodology to European data. Here we look at events associated with the risks, consolidation, or both, in the process of monetary unification, and we evaluate the events' impact on sovereign spreads. In section 6.5 we undertake a similar exercise for Latin American economies. Section 6.6 discusses the results.

6.2   The Theoretical Relation of Currency and Country Risk

Several issues have been identified in the literature as being relevant when assessing the impact of the elimination of the domestic currency risk on country risk. However, there is as yet no consensus on the quantitative impact nor even the direction. Some arguments actually suggest that country risk can increase as a result of dollarization, whereas others suggest that it could decline. In this section we review the arguments in both directions.

6.2.1   Arguments for an Increase in Country Risk

In what follows we present several arguments for why there may be an increase in country risk as result of the elimination of devaluation risk.

First, a country that has both local currency and foreign currency instruments outstanding may treat foreign currency instruments as senior.[4] If, however, that country fully dollarizes, outstanding debt may become more homogenous in terms of seniority, diluting the predollarization status of foreign currency instruments. Eliminating devaluation risk through dollarization will then tend to increase the country risk premium. This argument relies on a set of assumptions including the view that there are states in the world where a government may opt for defaulting on the domestic-currency-denominated debt instruments but not on those in foreign currency. Indeed, although it might be argued that foreign versus domestic debt might correlate to some extent with seniority, currency denomination is not always the right definition of domestic versus foreign debt.[5] If foreign debt is senior with respect to domestic but domestic debt is as dollarized as foreign debt, then eliminating devaluation risk may have no impact on seniorities and hence no impact on currency risk.

Second, dollarization implies eliminating access to the inflation tax as a way of financing government spending.[6] As a result, the intertemporal budget constraint of the government, and thus its ability to pay back its foreign-denominated bonds, may be weakened. This may, all things being equal, increase default risk and increase country risk.

A third channel is the weakening of the government's budget constraint as a result of the loss of seignorage revenues. Once again, the reduction in government resources increases the default risk on the government's debt instruments.

A fourth channel is that in a world with imperfect substitutability of assets, investors may want to hold a diversified portfolio of domestic- and foreign-currency-denominated bonds. Forcing the investor to shift the entire portfolio to foreign currency liabilities may induce a higher equilibrium risk premium on those instruments. This argument, however, assumes that by tilting toward domestic currency instruments a portfolio of foreign currency instruments will reduce risk, which is debatable in practice.

A final channel we list here is that dollarization may imply greater rigidities (e.g., wages and, more controversially, prices cannot adjust to a negative shock through changes in the exchange rate but must adjust through nominal reductions). These rigidities might produce greater output volatility, therefore inducing larger risk premiums on that country's assets.

6.2.2   Arguments for a Decrease in Country Risk

Similarly, several arguments, discussed in the following subsections, suggest that a reduction in currency risk should induce a reduction in country risk.

The Balance Sheet Effect

A first argument relates to balance sheets. Suppose a country exhibits a substantial currency mismatch between assets and liabilities. For example, when liabilities are denominated largely in foreign currency and assets in domestic currency, a sharp exchange rate depreciation may lead to insolvency. Under these circumstances there is, then, the potential for a direct link between the risk of a change in the level of the currency (currency risk) and default risk.

Table 6.1
Balance sheet effects for Argentina (in Billions of U.S.$, November 1999)

	Assets	Liabilities	Net position
Central government	2.7	111.0	−108.3
Central bank	25.8	8.9	16.9
Nonfinancial private sector	191.9	144.2	47.7
Financial sector	119.1	98.9	20.2
Total	339.5	363.0	−23.5

Source: Ministry of Economics and Central Bank and authors' calculations.
Note: Here we include only the central government, although we note that Argentine provinces and other decentralized agencies may also have dollar mismatches. Assets are reserves held in foreign currency, and liabilities include all foreign-currency-denominated debt (issued domestically or abroad). For the case of the central bank, assets include international reserves plus Argentine U.S.-dollar-denominated government bonds held in the Central Bank. Liabilities include dollar liabilities with the domestic financial system—liquidity requirements held in the central bank. Nonfinancial private sector assets include external assets, plus dollar-denominated deposits in the financial sector, plus dollar-denominated assets held in Argentine pension funds, plus holdings of U.S. dollars in cash employing an official (Ministry) estimate. Liabilities include external liabilities, plus dollar-denominated loans in the financial sector. Financial sector assets include dollar loans, plus reserves held in dollars abroad (liquidity requirements held offshore), and financial sector liabilities include dollar-denominated deposits and other foreign currency liabilities.

Table 6.1 exhibits a simplified computation of the balance sheet mismatch for Argentina. On the one hand as can be seen the central government is seriously exposed to a dollar devaluation, as more than 90 percent of liabilities are in dollars. In the case of Argentina, central bank reserves back the monetary base due to the currency board rule, so it is unclear whether central bank reserves should be consolidated with the central government. On the other hand, in the event of a devaluation the current level of reserves would exceed the value of the monetary base, assuming no change in the quantities. However, even if the central bank's dollar assets and liabilities are consolidated with those of the central government, there remains a significant currency mismatch in the public sector.

In the private sector, the table shows that the nonfinancial private sector has a positive mismatch of about $50 billion and the financial sector (excluding the central bank) also has a positive mismatch, albeit smaller (about $20 billion). However, it is likely that within the private sector there are sectors that have very significant negative mismatches. In other words, it is likely that private sector dollar wealth is highly concentrated. This implies that a devaluation would not only harm sectors of the nonfinancial private sector but would also then affect the financial sector in the form of increased credit risk and higher nonperforming loans. In summary, mismatches are such that a devaluation would provoke a serious deterioration of the government's financial position, increasing the likelihood of default, and also would create severe problems for areas of the private sector. It follows, therefore, that an increased perceived risk of devaluation may lead to higher credit spreads.[7]

Other Arguments

A second argument that explains a positive relation between country and currency risk relates to the fact that while a country maintains its own currency it may be subject to speculative attacks. The European experience during the early 1990s, and that of emerging economies since 1995 are witness to the potential for these speculative attacks. These attacks may force the central bank to raise interest rates in order to defend the peg, inducing a domestic recession and interest rate hikes that will most likely weaken the budget constraint of the government or, alternatively, increase its contingent liabilities. Eliminating the risk of currency collapses may reduce this instability, which is the cause of a higher risk premium. The potential for these speculative attacks increases in a world with substantial contagion.

A third argument is that the elimination of the local currency accelerates financial integration, allowing for a reduction in interest rates through increased efficiency of local financial intermediaries. This process has been an important factor during the path leading to the launch of the euro in Europe. In a similar vein, the use of a common currency has been suggested as potentially increasing significantly the amount of trade among the geographical regions using the same currency. This increased economic efficiency is likely to reduce risk across the board and thus reduce sovereign risk.[8]

Finally, dollarization may decrease interest rates through an increase in the credibility of policymakers, as it imposes a straightjacket for monetary and fiscal policy with high reversion costs. For a country such as Ecuador, for example, this appears to have been an essential part of the motivation for pursuing dollarization.

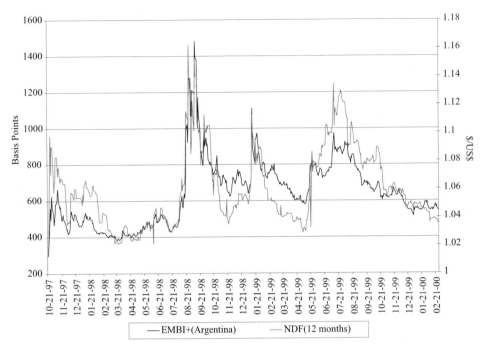

Figure 6.1
Country risk and the forward discount for Argentina. *Source:* J. P. Morgan.

6.3 The Event Study Methodology

Figures 6.1 and 6.2 show the evolution of country risk and currency risk for Argentina and Mexico, respectively. As can easily be seen, there is a strong positive correlation between the two.

However, it is well known that such a correlation (.82 in the case of Argentina and .93 in the case of Mexico) does not necessarily imply any particular causal relationship. Currency risk could cause country risk or vice versa; causality could exist in both directions; or there may be no causal relationship, as the correlation might be produced by a third common factor. Thus, by looking at this graph we can in no way conclude that the elimination of currency risk will entail a reduction in country risk.

This is nothing but a standard identification problem. One potential route to solving this problem is through time series analyses (Vector Auto-Regressions, and so on). Given the nature of the measures of country risk and currency risk available, however, it is in

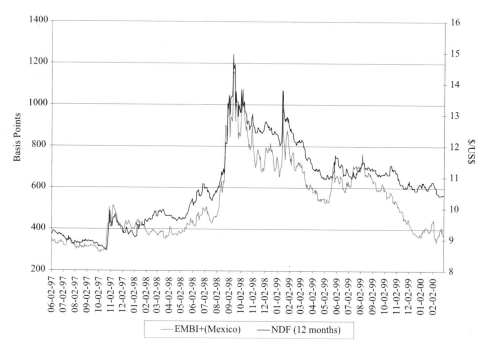

Figure 6.2
Country risk and the forward discount for Mexico. *Source:* J. P. Morgan.

our view problematic to use conventional time series methods to test for causality. The measures available stem from market prices, and hence if markets operate efficiently both series will adjust instantaneously to news. In practice, we hypothesize that local currency asset markets are less liquid for many emerging countries than for their foreign currency counterparts, and this implies that country risk spreads may react more rapidly than currency risk spreads, biasing the results, when using conventional time series methods, toward a finding that country risk causes currency risk and not vice versa.

In order to solve this identification problem, we chose to undertake an event study of the phenomena. Our methodology is to look at "events" that we can associate with changes in currency risk. We then study the evolution of sovereign risk in response to these currency events. The use of the event study ensures, on the one hand, that the currency shock is exogenous, thus allowing us to solve the endogeneity problem present. On the other hand, it allows us to keep all other variables constant, providing a natural experiment for the analysis and allowing us to isolate the impact of currency shocks on country risk.

Following Campbell, Lo, and MacKinley (1997) once the events are identified, we have to establish an estimation, event, and postevent window, all of which will allow for the test. As with any event study the excercise consists of computing a model for the returns using the data of the estimation window and checking if there are significant deviations from this model in the postevent window. In this chapter the object of study is the sovereign spread, and we test whether it changes in a statistically significant way after a currency shock. We present next two models for the estimation of the normal returns: the constant mean model and the market model.

6.3.1 The Constant Mean Model

In the constant mean model we assume that the expected return is a constant value; thus an abnormal return in the postevent window will correspond to deviations from the average prior to the event. The event window is chosen as the date in which the event occurs together with the three previous dates.[9] The estimation window comprises the ten days immediately prior to the beginning of the event window, and the postevent window includes the five days immediately following the event window.[10] The setup is described graphically in figure 6.3.

After the events have been identified and the time frame for the experiment determined, it is necessary to define how to compute the abnormal returns after the event. Following Campbell, Lo, and Mac-Kinlay (1997) we start with the simplest model, which assumes that the normal return is constant. Call X_t the sovereign spread of any country at moment t. We assume the model that describes this spread is

$$X_t = \mu + \varepsilon_t,$$

where μ indicates the normal return and ε indicates the "abnormal" return. We assume that

$$\varepsilon_t = N(0, \sigma^2).$$

The estimated abnormal return is:

$$\hat{\varepsilon} = X_t - \hat{\mu},$$

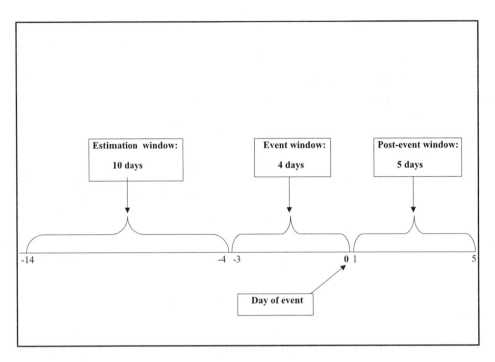

Figure 6.3
The setup for the constant mean model

where the hat indicates an estimated value. Our estimator will be
then

$$\overline{\varepsilon^*} = \frac{\sum_t \hat{\varepsilon}_t^*}{N} = \frac{\sum_t (X_t^* - \hat{\mu})}{N},$$

which defines the average estimated abnormal return in the postevent window (the * indicates belonging to the postestimation window). Our null hypothesis is

$$H_0 : \overline{\varepsilon^*} = 0.$$

If the null hypothesis holds, it will indicate that there is an impact of
currency risk on country risk, that is, we would conclude that there
is no evidence that currency risk affects country risk.

In order to construct the test we need to estimate the variance
covariance matrix of $\overline{\varepsilon}^*$. Notice that $\hat{\varepsilon}_t^*$ can be considered a forecast
error of the return, and thus its covariance matrix will have two
parts. The first is the variance of the disturbances, and the second

is the additional variance due to sampling error in the estimation of the normal return. This sampling error, which is common for all the abnormal returns estimated in the postevent window, will lead to serial correlation despite the fact that the true disturbances are independent through time. This serial correlation will imply a nondiagonal variance covariance matrix, which has to be taken into account when estimating the variance of average estimated abnormal returns. To start, we need to estimate the variance of the estimated abnormal return in the postevent window. More precisely,

$$V(\hat{\varepsilon}^*) = E[\hat{\varepsilon}^* \hat{\varepsilon}^{*'} \,|\, X^*]$$

$$= E[(\varepsilon^* - \iota(\hat{\mu} - \mu))(\varepsilon^* - \iota(\hat{\mu} - \mu))' \,|\, X^*]$$

$$= E[\varepsilon^* \varepsilon^{*'} + \iota(\hat{\mu} - \mu)(\hat{\mu} - \mu)' \iota' \,|\, X^*]$$

$$= E\varepsilon^* \varepsilon^{*'} \,|\, X^*] + \iota \sigma \varepsilon^2 (\iota' \iota)^{-1} \iota'$$

$$= \begin{pmatrix} \sigma \varepsilon^2 \left(1 + \dfrac{1}{n}\right) & \dfrac{\sigma \varepsilon^2}{n} & \cdots & \cdots & \dfrac{\sigma \varepsilon^2}{n} \\ \dfrac{\sigma \varepsilon^2}{n} & \sigma \varepsilon^2 \left(1 + \dfrac{1}{n}\right) & & & \vdots \\ \vdots & & \ddots & & \vdots \\ \vdots & & & \ddots & \vdots \\ \dfrac{\sigma \varepsilon^2}{n} & & \cdots & \cdots & \sigma \varepsilon^2 \left(1 + \dfrac{1}{n}\right) \end{pmatrix},$$

where ι indicates a vector of ones. Having estimated the variance covariance matrix of each individual forecast error, we compute the variance of our statistic:[11]

$$V(\overline{\varepsilon^*}) = V\left(\frac{\sum_i \varepsilon_i^*}{N}\right) = \frac{1}{N^2}\left[N\left(1 + \frac{1}{N}\right)\sigma \varepsilon^2 + N(N-1)\frac{\sigma \varepsilon^2}{N}\right] = \frac{2\sigma \varepsilon^2}{N}.$$

Substituting the estimate for the variance by its unbiased sample estimate, we can construct the statistic:

$$t_{N-1} = \frac{\overline{\varepsilon^*}}{\sqrt{\dfrac{2s_\varepsilon^2}{N}}},$$

which is the statistic we use to estimate if currency risk has any impact on country risk.

This test however, corresponds to a test of abnormal returns only for the case of one event. In order to gain more degrees of freedom, and assuming independence across events for each country, the tests can easily be aggregated to

$$t_{n*(N-1)} = \frac{\sum_n \overline{\varepsilon_n^*}}{\sqrt{\sum_n \dfrac{2s_{\varepsilon_n}^2}{N}}},$$

where n indicates the number of events considered for each country. In the following specification we distinguish between positive and negative shocks, which are tested separately.

6.3.2   The Market Model

In the market model the event window is chosen as the date in which the event occurs together with the three previous dates. The estimation window comprises the twenty days immediately prior to the beginning of the event window, and the postevent window includes the five days immediately following the event window.[12] The setup is described graphically in figure 6.4.

In the specification we assume that the sovereign spread is related to an average market return (in the following empirical specification we will compare, for example, the sovereign spread of a specific Latin American country with the overall spread for Latin American). In short

$$R_t = \alpha + \beta R_{mt} + \varepsilon_t.$$

This can be expressed as a regression system:

$$\mathbf{R} = \mathbf{X}\boldsymbol{\theta} + \boldsymbol{\varepsilon}.$$

As in any model, we will have that the estimate of the market model obtained from the data in the estimation window will be

$$\hat{\theta} = (\mathbf{X}'\mathbf{X})^{-1}\mathbf{X}'\mathbf{R},$$

with

$$\hat{\sigma}_\varepsilon^2 = \frac{1}{L-2}\hat{\varepsilon}\hat{\varepsilon},$$

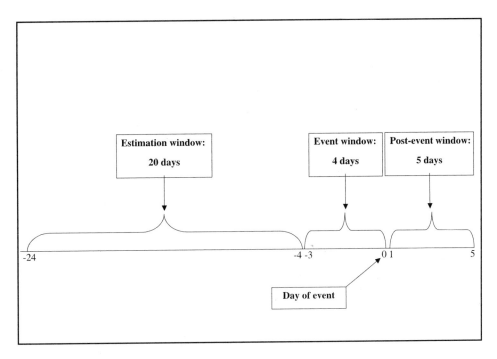

Figure 6.4
The setup for the market model

where L is the length of the estimation window. The estimation error is

$$\hat{\varepsilon} = \mathbf{R} - \mathbf{X}\hat{\theta}.$$

As before, the estimated abnormal return in the postevent window will equal

$$\hat{\varepsilon}^* = \mathbf{R}^* - \mathbf{X}^*\hat{\theta},$$

and its variance-covariance matrix will equal

$$
\begin{aligned}
V(\hat{\varepsilon}^*) &= E[\hat{\varepsilon}^* \hat{\varepsilon}^{*'} \mid \mathbf{X}^*] \\
&= E[(\varepsilon^* - \mathbf{X}^*(\hat{\theta} - \theta))(\varepsilon^* - \mathbf{X}^*(\hat{\theta} - \theta))' \mid X^*] \\
&= E[\varepsilon^* \varepsilon^{*'} - \varepsilon^*(\hat{\theta} - \theta)'\mathbf{X}' - \mathbf{X}^*(\hat{\theta} - \theta)\varepsilon^{*'} + \mathbf{X}^*(\hat{\theta} - \theta)(\hat{\theta} - \theta)'\mathbf{X}' \mid \mathbf{X}^*] \\
&= \mathbf{I}\sigma_{\varepsilon}^2 + \mathbf{X}^*(\mathbf{X}'\mathbf{X})^{-1}\mathbf{X}'\sigma_{\varepsilon}^2,
\end{aligned}
$$

where I is $M \times M$, where M is the length of the postevent window.

Again our estimate is

$$\overline{\varepsilon^*} = \frac{\sum_t \hat{\varepsilon}_t^*}{N},$$

and its variance is

$$V(\overline{\varepsilon^*}) = \frac{1}{N^2} \iota' V(\hat{\varepsilon}^*) \iota.$$

Similar to the aggregation in 6.3.1, the aggregate test can be computed in this case, as

$$t_{n*(N-2)} = \frac{\sum_n \overline{\varepsilon_n^*}}{\sqrt{\sum_n \hat{V}(\overline{\varepsilon^*})}},$$

where the estimated variance uses the unbiased sample moments.

6.4   The European Experience

In order to assess the relationship between country and currency risk we start by looking at the European experience during the 1990s. We believe Europe is an excellent testing ground for the relationship between these two spreads, as during that decade the continent was subject to several shocks exclusively related to the consolidation or weakening of the monetary integration process. Changes in the prospects for monetary unification affect directly the currency risk of the countries involved, thus allowing for an almost perfect natural experiment for testing the impact of currency risk on country risk. For example, the result of a referendum on monetary union in one country of the continent is a shock that affects directly the degree of currency risk in all other countries in the sample. These types of largely institutional shocks then provide a set of observations of exogenous shocks to currency risk. We can then test whether these shocks have a significant effect on country risk.

In order to apply our event study methodology to the European experience, we proceed as follows. We first compute the sovereign risk for some selected European countries: Austria, Belgium, Denmark, Finland, Ireland, Spain, and Sweden. The reason for choosing these countries is that they had outstanding deutsche-mark-denominated debt throughout most of the period, which allows,

Table 6.2
Sovereign spread characteristics

	Austria	Belgium	Denmark	Finland	Ireland	Portugal	Spain	Sweden
Average (1992–2000)	14.95	19.76	19.29	27.58	24.14	19.04	20.21	13.99
Standard deviation	8.57	9.63	11.20	12.72	9.30	11.10	6.55	9.08

Source: Datastream, note 13.

when comparing their yield with that of German bonds, to obtain an estimate of sovereign spreads. Table A.6.1 in the appendix gives the characteristics of the deutsche mark bonds used for each country.

The yield of these bonds was compared to a daily estimate of Germany's yield curve at the same maturity.[13] The matching of maturities is essential, as many of the bonds were approaching maturity toward the end of the sample. Table 6.2 summarizes the characteristics of these spreads. As can be seen, the spreads are positive, are low, and have a fairly small standard deviation.

Table 6.3 shows the currency events identified for Europe. Our events are taken from two sources. The first source is the comprehensive compilation in Zettelmeyer (1996). Zettelmeyer discusses institutional shocks, establishing their potential impact on currency risk (whether they were good news or bad news for EMU). Also, by checking whether the events made it to the financial reports written at the time he identifies those that were important from those that were not. Our second source is Ungerer (1997), who also provides a classification of the most important events in the process toward monetary unification. In table 6.3 shocks labeled with a Z were taken from Zettelmeyer (1996), and those labeled with a *U* were taken from Ungerer (1997). Those labeled with an * correspond to noninstitutional events (mostly devaluations) we believe had an impact on currency risk. It is somewhat more debatable whether these noninstitutional shocks are not correlated with a general deterioration of economic conditions. If they are, then it is possible that country risk is affected directly rather than through the channel of currency risk. Although we believe that it is likely that a devaluation carries new information regarding currency risk and hence still represents a valid event for our purposes, we compute our event studies with and without these events.

Table 6.3
Events for Europe

Date	Event
4/6/92	Portugal joins the EU's Exchange Rate Mechanism (ERM). (U)(−)
6/2/92	Danish voters reject the Maastricht Treaty. (U/Z)(+)
6/18/92	Irish referendum on Maastricht is approved by a wide margin. (Z)(−)
9/21/92	French referendum on Maastricht on September 20 is approved by a slight margin. (U/Z)(−)
12/12/92	European Community (EC) Edinburgh Summit: success for EMU. (Z)(−)
1/29/93	Ten percent devaluation of the Irish pound on January 30. (U*)(+)
5/18/93	Second referendum in Denmark. This time Maastricht is approved. (U/Z)(−)
7/23/93	Maastricht Treaty ratified by members of the European Community. (Z)(−)
8/2/93	After sustained unrest in financial markets, ERM fluctuation margins widened temporarily to +/−15%. (U*)(+)
10/12/93	German constitutional court rejects challenge to Maastricht. (Z)(−)
11/1/93	Maastricht Treaty goes into effect. (U)(−)
6/12/94	European elections: victory for anti-Maastricht forces. (Z)(+)
12/30/94	January 1, Austria, Finland, and Sweden become members of the EU. Norway rejects joining in a referendum and stays out. (U)(−)
1/9/95	Austria joins the ERM. (U)(−)
3/6/95	Devaluation of the Spanish peseta and the Portuguese escudo. (U*)(+)
5/31/95	European Committee releases "Green Paper" on EMU. (Z)(−)
6/22/95	First Alain Juppé minibudget. (Z)(−)
8/25/95	Alain Madelin resigns over proposed spending cuts. (Z)(+)
10/10/95	First French public sector strike (24 hours). (Z)(+)
10/26/95	Jacques Chirac commits to deficit cutting as first priority. (Z)(−)
11/7/95	Composition of new French cabinet announced: fiscally conservative. (Z)(−)
11/15/95	Juppé unveils welfare reform package. (Z)(−)
11/29/95	Bundestag hearing on EMU: Germans tough on criteria for membership together with 12/3/95, French unions vow to intensify strike. (Z)(+)
12/15/95	By a vote of 15 to 16 the European Council in Madrid adopts changeover scenario, based on EMI (European Monetary Institute) scenario, the common currency will be called the "euro". (U/Z)(−)
11/25/96	Italy rejoins the EMS (European Monetary System). (U)(−)
12/13/96	The EC agrees in Dublin on the EMS II and the pact for stability and growth. (U)(−)

EMI = European Monetary Institute; was forerunner of European Central Bank (ECB)
EMS = European Monetary System; incorporated the ERM (Exchange Rate Mechanism) and predecessor of EMU as well as other agreements.
Source: Zettelmeyer (1996) and Ungerer (1997).

Table 6.3
(continued)

Note: We divide the events into *good news* (−) events and *bad news* (+) events. *Good news* events are associated with a reduction in currency risk, whereas *bad news* events are associated to an increase in currency risk. The devaluation of the Irish pound, for example, was considered to increase the currency risk for all other countries, whereas the approval of the Maastricht treaty in France was assumed to reduce currency risk.

Tables 6.4 and 6.5 show the results for Europe, by indicating the *T*-statistics corresponding to the test for the null hypothesis that there are no abnormal returns after the currency events. Table 6.4 considers favorable shocks to EMU whereas table 6.5 considers negative shocks. In the case of positive shocks, we find that these decrease country risk for Austria, Belgium, and Ireland with *T*-statistics indicating a significant effect, whereas we find significant results in the opposite direction for Denmark, Sweden, and Portugal. Finally, results for Finland and Spain are not significant at the 10% level.[14]

We divide the events into *good news* (−) events and *bad news* (+) events. Good news events are associated with a reduction in currency risk, whereas bad news events are associated with an increase in currency risk. The devaluation of the Irish pound, for example, was considered to increase the currency risk for all other countries, whereas the approval of the Maastricht Treaty in France was assumed to reduce currency risk.

Tables 6.4 and 6.5 show the results for Europe, by indicating the *t*-statistics corresponding to the test for the null hypothesis that there are no abnormal returns after the currency events. Table 6.4 considers favorable shocks to the European Monetary Union (EMU), whereas table 6.5 considers negative shocks. In the case of positive shocks we find that these decrease country risk for Austria, Belgium, and Ireland, with *t*-statistics indicating a significant effect, whereas we find significant results in the opposite direction for Denmark, Sweden, and Portugal. Finally, results for Finland and Spain are not significant at the 10 percent level.[14]

Our results are therefore quite mixed, with some countries appearing to have a positive relationship between currency and country risk and others going in the opposite direction. Our theoretical discussion highlighted the fact that the relationship could go either way, so perhaps these results are not very surprising. On closer inspection, in the case of negative institutional shocks there is clearly less evidence of an association between currency and sovereign spreads (in this case we have fewer events to work with). However, in the case of positive institutional shocks we see there is stronger

Table 6.4
Effect of a favorable institutional shock to EMU on sovereign spreads (five-day window)

	Austria	Belgium	Denmark	Finland	Ireland	Portugal	Spain	Sweden
T-statistic	−2.65	−4.52	3.01	−1.55	−3.01	5.39	0.62	3.08
P-value	0.00	0.00	0.00	0.12	0.00	0.00	0.53	0.00
Degrees of freedom	153	162	54	153	135	108	126	54

Table 6.5
Effect of a negative institutional shock to EMU on sovereign spreads (five-day window)

	Austria	Belgium	Denmark	Finland	Ireland	Portugal	Spain	Sweden
T-statistic	−0.18	1.64	−2.32	−1.18	2.01	0.79	−0.24	−1.19
P-value	0.85	0.10	0.03	0.24	0.05	0.42	0.81	0.24
Degrees of freedom	36	45	18	36	36	54	54	18

evidence, and, interestingly, the country pattern appears roughly consistent between both positive and negative events.

One interpretation is that positive (negative) news about EMU reduced (increased) country risk in those countries that were sure to enter but actually increased (decreased) country risk in those countries where entry was far from certain. This interpretation appears consistent with our country pattern, because in the case of Denmark, Sweden, and Portugal, we find that good news about EMU increases country risk—Denmark and Sweden did not enter and it was unclear for some time whether Portugal would meet the convergence criteria. In contrast, we find that for Austria, Belgium, and Ireland, where EMU entry was more certain, good news about EMU decreased country risk.[15] In summary, our results on Europe do not provide evidence for a clear one-way relationship between currency and country risk and show that although a significant relationship might exist, it may go either way depending on country characteristics.

6.5   Emerging Economies

The experience of European economies supports our theoretical discussion that the effect of currency risk on country risk may go either way, depending on individual country characteristics. In the case of emerging economies in Latin American countries (LACs hereafter), however, the results may be quite different. Unfortunately for LACs, there is no set of institutional events comparable to those considered for Europe. Thus, most of the currency shocks will carry the risk of being endogenous to a general deterioration in economic conditions, or "contagion." Our events, rather than being general events that affect several countries, will apply largely to the countries where the event occured. In those cases (essentially Argentina) where we also include certain events that take place outside of the country, we choose events we think are primarily currency-related in nature. We want to emphasize that we were interested not so much in having as many events as possible but rather in having good events, that is, events that could be clearly be identified as those whose impact primarily changed exchange rate risk.

Thus, we have attempted to isolate events related to actual changes in exchange rate policy or (in the case of Argentina) events that led to a perception of a higher probability of exchange rate policy change. Although the market usually discounts changes in exchange rate policy, it is undeniable that when the event (a devaluation or a change in exchange rate bands, etc.) occurs, there is new information about future exchange rate behavior and as a result an impact on currency risk. What we test is the impact of this new information on country risk. Even if the shock is not purely exogenous, the endogeneity problem should be, to a great extent, muted by the fact that our data are very high frequency and that we test for changes between a short span of just a few days, which implies that our benchmark for comparison includes most of the information relevant until prior to the disclosure of the news of the change in exchange rate policy.[16]

Tables 6.6 through 6.11 indicate the events that have been considered for Argentina, Brazil, Mexico, Ecuador, Colombia, and Chile. As can be seen, most changes correspond to explicit changes of exchange rate policy or statements made by top officials or candidates on exchange rate policy. The case of Argentina is an exception. There, due to the existence of the currency board since April 1991, we consider exogenous shocks that we believe primarily affected the perception of risk about the currency board system.

Again, shocks are identified as good news ($-$) and bad news ($+$) according to whether they decrease or increase currency risk. Tables

Table 6.6
Events for Argentina

Date	Event
12/20/94	The Mexican peso is devalued. (+)
1/12/95	Banks' deposits in the Argentine Central Bank are dollarized. (−)
10/23/97	Speculative attack against the Hong Kong currency board. (+)
5/19/99	Domingo Cavallo's *Financial Times* interview. (+)

Source: Authors.

Note: In this footnote we discuss the events for Argentina. (1) Although the devaluation of the Mexican peso heralded a sharp fall in Argentine asset prices, dollar deposits in the banking system initially rose, suggesting that this was first and foremost a currency event. (2) Dollarizing commercial banks' deposits in the Central Bank was seen as a policy strongly reinforcing the currency board during a difficult period. (3) The attack against the Hong Kong currency board suggested that even currency boards might be subjected to attack. Argentina and Hong Kong shared virtually nothing else in common except the exchange rate system. A commonly held view in the market at the time was that if the Hong Kong currency board was changed, there was little chance the Argentine one would survive. (4) Domingo Cavallo (presidential candidate and former economy minister) appeared to suggest in an interview in the *Financial Times* that Argentina could abandon the currency board—at least that was the title that the *Times* used, even if the arguments in the article itself were more subtle in nature.

Table 6.7
Events for Brazil

Date	Event
6/30/94	The Real Plan is launched. (−)
3/6/95	The fixed exchange rate band is changed to a crawling peg band. (+)
1/15/99	The real is devalued. (+)
11/12/99	The IMF frees 2 billion of Brazil's reserves at the fund for use in stabilizing the exchange rate. (−)

Source: Ilan Goldfajn suggested these events. The exact dates were provided by Luis Sampaio Malan.

Table 6.8
Events for Mexico

Date	Event
12/20/94	Devaluation of the Mexican peso. (+)
11/30/98	*Ampliación del corto* (contractive monetary policy). (−)
1/18/00	Ampliación del corto. (−)

Source: The dates for the ampliación del corto were provided by Juan Seade. Alejandro Werner also advised about events and dates.

Table 6.9
Events for Ecuador

Date	Event
3/3/97	Devaluation. $(+)$
3/31/98	Devaluation. $(+)$
1/9/00	President Jamil Mahuad announces the dollarization of the economy. $(-)$
3/1/00	Congress approves dollarization. $(-)$

Source: Goldman Sachs' Emerging Market Weekly (various issues) and local media newspapers.

Table 6.10
Events for Colombia

Date	Event
12/12/94	Downward movement in the exchange rate band. $(-)$
3/15/96	Relaxation of restrictions to capital inflows. $(-)$
10/11/96	Resolution limits the demand for dollars by intermediaries of the exchange market. $(-)$
1/13/97	Tax on foreign exchange borrowing is established. $(+)$
3/12/97	More restrictions on capital inflows. $(+)$
4/23/98	Mauricio Cárdenas (from Colombian private sector think-tank, Fedesarollo unexpectedly proposed an increase in the width of the exchange rate band. $(+)$
6/28/99	Upward movement in the exchange rate band. $(+)$
9/27/99	Elimination of the exchange rate band. $(+)$
4/28/00	Deposit for borrowing abroad is eliminated. $(-)$

Source: Events and dates were provided by Alberto Carrasquilla and Roberto Steiner. Events and dates were obtained also from Alesina, Carrasquilla, and Steiner (2000).

Table 6.11
Events for Chile

Date	Event
2/3/98	Interest rate is increased to 8.5%. Return to active interest rate management. $(-)$
9/16/98	Policy interest rate is increased from 8.5 to 14%. Return to active interest rate management. Market interest rate starts reducing to a 14% level. The exchange rate band gradually starts to widen. $(-)$
9/2/99	The exchange rate band is eliminated. $(+)$

Source: Events and dates were provided by Felipe Morandé.

Table 6.12
The impact of currency risk on country risk: The constant mean model

	Argentina	Brazil	Mexico	Ecuador	Colombia	Chile
Bad news						
T-statistic	56.83	16.25	67.11	7.99	−2.73	−9.66
Degrees of freedom	12	8	4	8	20	4
P-value	0.00	0.00	0.00	0.00	0.01	0.00
Good news						
T-statistic	1.13	−0.20	1.39	−6.71	9.41	0.24
Degrees of freedom	4	8	8	8	16	4
P-value	0.32	0.85	0.20	0.00	0.00	0.83

Table 6.13
The impact of currency risk on country risk: The market model

	Argentina	Brazil	Mexico	Ecuador	Colombia	Chile
Bad news						
T-statistic	3.61	1.97	14.08	4.28	−0.43	0.33
Degrees of freedom	12	8	4	8	20	4
P-value	0.00	0.08	0.00	0.00	0.67	0.76
Good news						
T-statistic	−4.57	−2.55	−1.30	−4.51	9.68	4.31
Degrees of freedom	4	8	8	8	16	4
P-value	0.01	0.03	0.23	0.00	0.00	0.01

6.12 and 6.13 present the results for the five-day postevent window for the constant mean and market model.[17]

The tables show a similar pattern, with a strong impact of currency on country risk in Argentina, Brazil, Mexico, and Ecuador but a different pattern for Colombia and Chile. We prefer to test using the market model, as here we control for other aspects affecting country risk over the event window, and hence we use table 6.14 to guide the discussion. As can be seen, the impact of an increase in currency risk is very significant in the first four countries, and, similarly, the reduction in country risk as a result of a reduction in currency risk is equally significant. The opposite pattern is evident for Chile and Colombia. There, an increase in currency risk seems to have no effect (it does decrease country risk significantly in the constant mean model), whereas reductions in currency risk seem to increase country risk significantly.

Table 6.14
Response of country risk to bad news about currency for Chile

Country	Date	Event Description	T-stat/ currency risk	T-stat/ sovereign risk
Argentina	5/19/99	Cavallo's *Financial Times* interview	46.97 (0.00)	30.15 (0.00)
Brazil	1/15/99	Devaluation of real	406.94 (0.00)	8.35 (0.00)
	11/12/99	IMF's release	−1.73 (0.12)	−4.45 (0.00)
Mexico	11/30/98	Tighter money	4.86 (0.00)	2.06 (0.00)
	1/18/00	Tighter money	−5.70 (0.00)	1.92 (0.00)
Ecuador	1/9/00	Announcement of dollarization	6.18 (0.00)	27.01 (0.00)
Colombia	4/23/98	Proposal of widening band	0.42 (0.68)	4.70 (0.00)
	6/28/99	Band adjusted upward	20.51 (0.00)	1.69 (0.13)
	9/25/00	Removal of the band	4.96 (0.00)	−3.72 (0.00)
Chile	2/3/98	Increase in interest rates	−2.45 (0.04)	−9.05 (0.00)
	9/16/98	Increase in interest rates	−2.35 (0.04)	2.51 (0.03)
	9/2/99	Band abandoned	13.62 (0.00)	−18.54 (0.00)

We conjecture that these results are roughly consistent with the extent of dollarization. Chile and Colombia are arguably the least dollarized countries in our sample, and hence balance sheet effects may be less relevant. Argentina and Ecuador are probably the most dollarized countries, and here we find very significant effects. Dollarization is also important in Mexico and to a lesser extent in Brazil. Our results then broadly support the view that countries with higher indexes of dollarization may also experience a greater impact of currency risk on country risk.

Figures 6.5 through 6.16 show the impulse responses for the events in table 6.13.

Finally, in this section, we address the question of whether events depicted in tables 6.6 through 6.11 represent true events for which currency risk actually increased. In order to check this, we replicate our analysis (using the constant mean specification) in order to verify that as a result of the events considered currency risk moved in the direction suggested. The data correspond to forward contracts. Although our database does not allow testing of this hypothesis in the case of all events, the table is persuasive enough in showing that the events considered had a significant effect on currency risk, which in all but two cases moved in the expected direction.

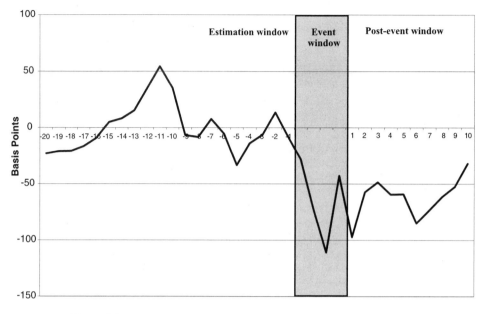

Figure 6.5
Response of country risk to good news on currency for Argentina

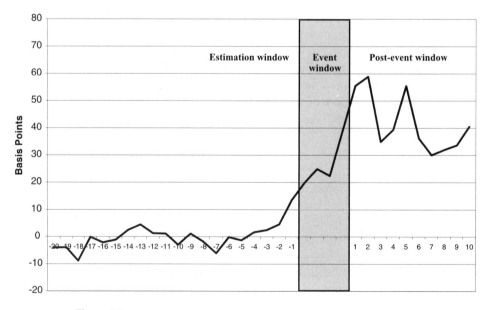

Figure 6.6
Response of country risk to bad news on currency for Argentina

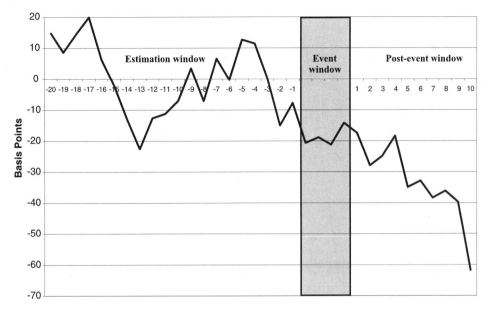

Figure 6.7
Response of country risk to good news on currency for Brazil

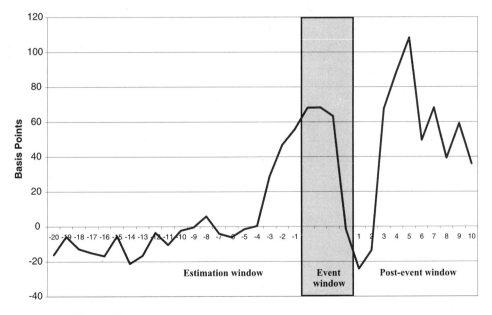

Figure 6.8
Response of country risk to bad news on currency for Brazil

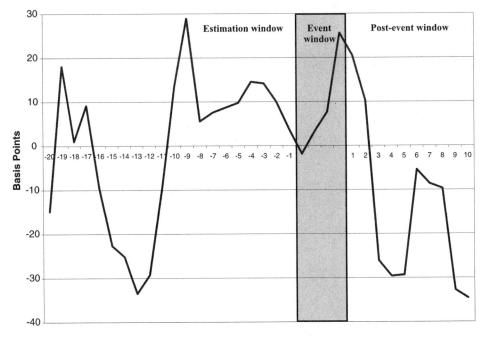

Figure 6.9
Response of country risk to good news on currency for Mexico

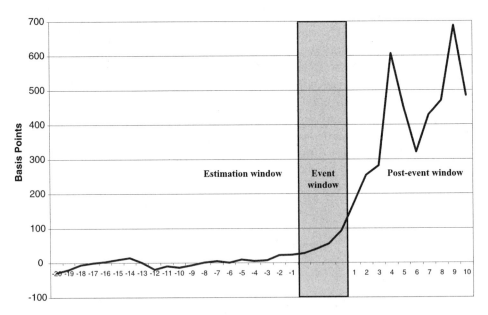

Figure 6.10
Response of country risk to bad news on currency for Mexico

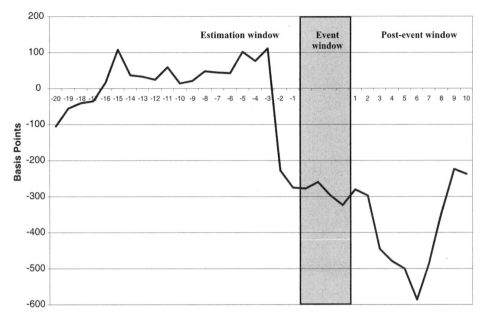

Figure 6.11
Response of country risk to good news on currency for Ecuador

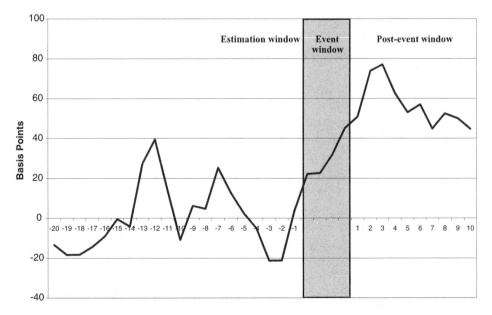

Figure 6.12
Response of country risk to bad news on currency for Ecuador

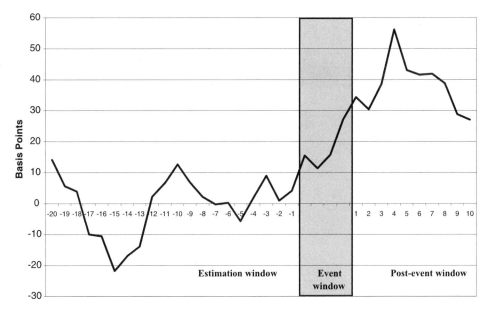

Figure 6.13
Response of country risk to good news on currency for Columbia

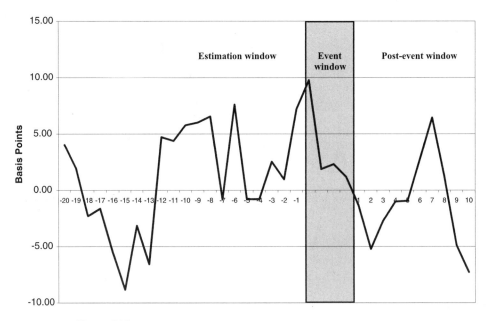

Figure 6.14
Response of country risk to bad news on currency for Columbia

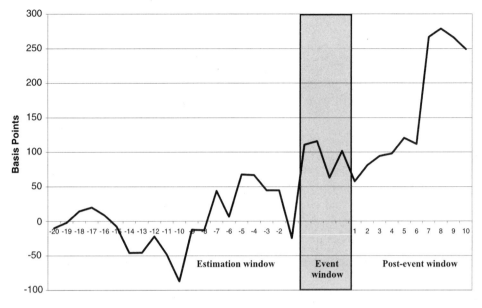

Figure 6.15
Response of country risk to good news on currency for Chile

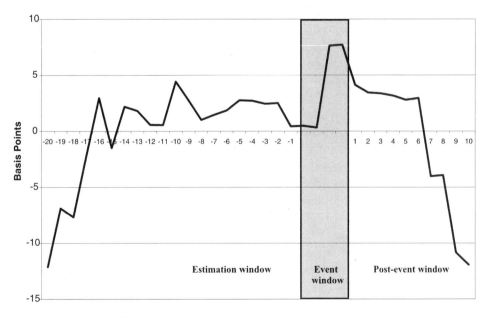

Figure 6.16
Response of country risk to bad news on currency for Chile

As can be seen, except in the first *ampliación del corto* (contractionary monetary policy) in Mexico and in the announcement of the dollarization in Ecuador, the movement in the forward market indicates a change in the expected exchange rate in the direction assumed in our test. This gives us some comfort that the events selected were indeed significant in altering currency risk.

6.6   Conclusions

In this chapter we have attempted to investigate the relationship between currency risk and country risk. Casual empiricism reveals that for several emerging countries, measures of these two risks are highly correlated, and several authors have hypothesized that the elimination of currency risk through dollarization may then lead to a significant reduction in country risk. However, a correlation does not imply causality in a particular direction and, as discussed in the first section of this chapter, there are theoretical arguments that suggest a causal relationship in both directions. Given the nature of the measures of country risk and currency risk available, it is extremely difficult using conventional time series methods to test for causality, that is, to establish exogeneity. The measures available stem from market prices, and hence if markets operate efficiently both series will adjust instantaneously to news. In practice, we hypothesize that local currency asset markets are less liquid for many emerging countries than their foreign currency counterparts. This hypothesis implies that country risk spreads may react more rapidly than currency risk spreads, biasing the results toward a finding, using conventional time series methods, that country risk causes currency risk and not vice versa.

In this chapter, we therefore have adopted a different approach. We have developed an event study methodology in which we choose particular events we believe are primarily currency events and, within a defined event window, analyze how country risk reacts to them. We considered first a set of European countries and second a set of emerging countries in Latin America. The case of Europe is particularly interesting. Here, a set of institutional events pertaining to the changing likelihood of successful monetary integration provide a natural set of exogenous currency risk shocks. Our results are mixed in that in some countries we found a positive effect of currency risk on country risk, in other countries we found the opposite relationship, and in another group we found no significant relationship. These results reflect our theoretical discussion that the relationship could go either way. A fascinating interpretation of our results, however, divides countries into those where EMU entry was essentially guaranteed and those countries where EMU entry was uncertain or unlikely. In the first group we found a positive relation between currency risk and country risk (i.e., good news for EMU, implying reduced currency risk and leading to reduced country risk), whereas in the second group the opposite result held.

In the case of emerging countries in Latin America our results are quite different. Unfortunately, we do not have such a natural set of exogenous, institutional events for this analysis as we used for Europe. However, we have attempted to define events that represented actual changes in exchange rate policy or (as in the case of Argentina), events that changed the perception of the probability of future changes. We also attempted to limit ourselves to events we felt comfortable deeming exogenous and primarily currency related. Finally, the short event window employed gives comfort against the charge that the currency events employed are endogenous to, say, a general decline in economic conditions.

Given these safeguards, our results for Latin American emerging countries are strong and in broad terms support those that argue that the elimination of currency risk will have a significant impact on country risk spreads. However, there is also variation in our results for our sample of countries. We found that for Colombia and Chile there is less evidence that currency risk affects country risk and indeed even found that good news about the currency increases country risk. It is interesting to note that these are the least dollarized countries in our sample. In contrast, we find significant impacts of country risk on country risk for the more highly dollarized Argentina, Brazil, Mexico, and Ecuador such that good news about the currency reduces country risk, and bad news about the currency increases country risk. Our results then also broadly support the view that the effect of currency risk on country risk may depend on the degree of de facto dollarization.

Appendix 6.1

In the following table, we provide salient characteristics of the bonds used to obtain the relevant spreads for the European event study.

Table A.6.1
Characteristics of bonds used for the European event study

Country	Issue date	Expiring date	Coupon %	Amortiza-tion	Currency	Available since
Austria	5/19/92	6/17/02	Fixed: 8	Bullet	DM	6/5/92
Belgium	1/22/92	2/25/02	Fixed: $7\frac{3}{4}$	Bullet	DM	2/7/92
Denmark	6/13/95	7/6/00	Fixed: $6\frac{1}{8}$	Bullet	DM	9/18/95
Finland	5/18/92	6/25/02	Fixed: $8\frac{1}{4}$	Bullet	DM	5/29/92
Ireland	10/1/92	10/22/02	Fixed: $7\frac{3}{4}$	Bullet	DM	10/9/92
Portugal	6/3/93	7/2/03	Fixed: $7\frac{1}{8}$	Bullet	DM	6/18/93
Spain	2/4/93	3/4/03	Fixed: $7\frac{1}{4}$	Bullet	DM	2/12/93
Sweden	8/23/95	9/12/00	Fixed: 6	Bullet	DM	9/12/95
Colombia	2/19/94	2/23/04	Fixed: $7\frac{1}{4}$	Bullet	U.S.$	11/17/94
Chile	4/22/99	4/28/09	Fixed: $6\frac{7}{8}$	Bulles	U.S.$	4/22/99

Source: Datastream.

Table A.6.2
Ten-day postevent window: Good news (institutional shocks only)

	Austria	Belgium	Denmark	Finland	Ireland	Portugal	Spain	Sweden
T-statistic	1.22	−0.59	4.94	.39	−2.75	4.46	1.05	2.51
P-value	0.23	0.55	0.00	0.70	0.01	0.00	0.30	0.02
Degrees of freedom	126	135	45	126	108	90	99	45

Table A.6.3
Ten-day postevent window: Bad news (institutional shocks only)

	Austria	Belgium	Denmark	Finland	Ireland	Portugal	Spain	Sweden
T-statistic	0.13	1.58	−2.52	−1.47	1.70	2.99	−0.44	−1.64
P-value	0.89	0.12	0.03	0.15	0.10	0.01	0.67	0.14
Degrees of freedom	27	36	9	27	27	27	27	9

Table A.6.4
Constant mean model with ten-day postevent window

	Argentina	Brazil	Mexico	Ecuador	Colombia	Chile
Bad news						
T-statistic	81.98	15.54	79.24	7.05	−2.36	−18.54
Degrees of freedom	27	18	9	18	45	9
P-value	0.00	0.00	0.00	0.00	0.02	0.00
Good news						
T-statistic	2.04	−1.62	2.50	−6.46	21.70	1.61
Degrees of freedom	9	18	18	18	36	9
P-value	0.07	0.12	0.02	0.00	0.00	0.14

Table A.6.5
Market model with ten-day postevent window

	Argentina	Brazil	Mexico	Ecuador	Colombia	Chile
Bad news						
T-statistic	2.98	2.14	15.15	4.35	−0.60	−0.82
Degrees of freedom	12	18	9	18	45	9
P-value	0.01	0.05	0.00	0.00	0.55	0.44
Good news						
T-statistic	−5.02	−4.04	−2.09	−4.57	9.45	10.06
Degrees of freedom	4	18	18	18	36	9
P-value	0.01	0.00	0.05	0.00	0.00	0.00

Appendix 6.2

In this appendix we include, in tables A.6.2 through A.6.5, the results of the tests presented for Europe and Latin American countries for a ten-day event window, rather than the five-day event window included earlier in the chapter. Note that the pattern of the results is similar indeed to those presented for the five-day event window.

Notes

We thank Klaus Schmidt Hebbel, Hildegart Ahumada, Ernesto Talvi, John Driffil, Tim Kehoe, and participants at the closed meeting on dollarization held at Universidad Torcuato Di Tella, Buenos Aires, May 2000, for very useful comments. We also thank all those who helped use gather the information on our events: Alberto Carrasquilla, Willie Fuchs, Ilan Goldfajn, Luis Sampaio Malan, Felipe Morandé, Sergio Schmukler,

Luis Seade, Roberto Steiner, and Alejandro Werner. Matías Gutiérrez Girault contributed with excellent research assistance.

1. However, Levy Yeyati and Sturzenegger (2000a), employing a de facto classification of exchange rate regimes, do not find a trend toward the extremes. See also Powell (2002) for related comments.

2. See Bayoumi and Eichengreen (1994), Eichengreen (1998), Frankel (1999), Martirena Mantel (1997), and Levy Yeyati and Sturzenegger (2000c). Carrera and Sturzenegger (2000) provide a collection of papers which analyze the convenience of launching a monetary union, European style, among Mercosur economies. In that volume, Cohen (2000) discusses other comparable historical experiences of monetary union. For experiences during the nineteenth century, he mentions the Latin Monetary Union undertaken by France with some of its neighbors and the Scandinavian Monetary Union between Denmark, Norway, and Sweden. For experiences during the twentieth century, he mentions the economic union between Belgium and Luxembourg, the Caribbean dollar area, the franc zone in Africa, and the monetary union of South Africa with three of its neighbors.

3. See Neumeyer (1998) for an application to the European Monetary Union.

4. Chapter 3 in this volume argues the opposite, that domestic-denominated debt may have a lower default risk as it can always be inflated away rather than defaulted on. The authors discuss the conditions under which this is a valid assumption.

5. Powell (2002) suggests three different definitions for foreign versus domestic debt, depending on the question under discussion: currency of issue, if the question is related to curency mismatches; residence of purchaser, if the question is current account sustainability; or location of issue, if the question is how debt might be restructured in default scenarios.

6. The recent Argentine experience with subnational quasi currencies suggests dollarizing may not entirely remove the possibility of capturing some seignorage.

7. Sturzenegger (2000) challenges this view by suggesting that the balance sheet of the government is not properly measured when looking at current assets and liabilities. He claims that a present value appraoch is needed taking into account the true intertemporal assets of the government (expected future tax income) and liabilities (expected expenditure). Once this is done, one finds that mismatches are less severe as most government spending is on nontradables, whereas a sizable fraction of tax revenue arises from the tradable sector.

8. There is an extensive literature on this issue. Panizza, Stein, and Talvi (2000) provide a good survey. See also Rose (1999) and Levy Yeyati and Sturzenegger (2000b).

9. This is done in order to avoid any possible spillover of news regarding the impending event.

10. In all cases, we refer to working days. In appendix 6.2, we show the results for a ten-day postevent window excercise.

11. Our test is based on the change in the average abnormal return. It would be identical if we were to compute it on the cumulative abnormal return, as is more standard in the literature.

12. In all cases we refer to working days. In appendix 2 we show the results for a ten-day postevent window excercise.

13. All data on European bond prices was obtained form Datastream and Thomson Financial, ⟨www.datastream.com⟩. Germany's yield curve was approximated by a third-order polynomial.

14. In appendix 2 we show similar results with a ten-day postevent window and also including institutional shocks in the group. The results are similar under these alternative specifications to those presented in the body of the paper.

15. We are indebted to John Driffill for suggesting this interpretation of our results.

16. We selected events both from newspapers and by asking experts in each country. The latter method has the drawback that people will remember only relevant events, thus increasing dramatically the significance of the events analyzed. We are grateful to Tim Kehoe for pointing this out to us. However, this tendency should not bias the results in either direction (positive or negative), and therefore though the t-statistics should be considered with care we believe the exercise remains correct and highly relevant.

17. The appendix shows the same tables for the ten-day postevent window. As can be seen, the results remain unchanged.

References

Alesina, Alberto, Alberto Carrasquilla, and Roberto Steiner (2000). "Monetary Institutions in Colombia," mimeo, Universidad de los Ardes, Bógotre, Colombia.

Bayoumi, T., and Barry Eichengreen (1994). "One Money or Many? Analyzing the Prospects for Monetary Unification in Various Parts of the World," *Princeton Studies in International Finance*, no. 76, September.

Campbell John, Andrew Lo, and Craig MacKinley (1997). *The Econometrics of Financial Markets*, Princeton University Press, Princeton, NJ.

Carrera, Jorge, and Federico Sturzenegger, eds. (2000). *"Coordinación de políticas macroeconómicas en el Mercosur"* ("Coordination of Macroeconomic Policies in Mercosur"), Fondo de Cultura Económica, Buenos Aires.

Cohen, Benjamin (2000). "La política de las uniones monetarias: Reflexiones para el Mercosur" ("The Policy of Monetary Unions: Reflections on Mercosur"), in Jorge Carrera and Federico Sturzenegger, eds., *Coordinación de políticas macroeconómicas en el Mercosur*, Fondo de Cultura Económica, Buenos Aires.

Eichengreen, Barry (1994). *International Monetary Arrangements for the 21st Century*, Brookings Institution, Washington, DC.

——— (1998). "Does Mercosur Need a Single Currency?" NBER working paper, no. 6821.

Frankel, Jeffrey (1999). "No Single Currency Regime Is Right for All Countries or at All Times," NBER working paper, no. 7338, available at ⟨http://www.nber.org/papers/w7338⟩.

Frankel, Jeffrey, and Andrew Rose (2000). "Estimating the Effect of Currency Unions on Trade and Output," NBER working paper, no. 7857.

Guidotti, Pablo, and Andrew Powell, (forthcoming). "The Dollarization Debate in Argentina and Latin America," in Leonardo Auernheimer, ed., *International Financial Markets*, University of Chicago Press, Chicago.

Levy Yeyati, Eduardo, and Federico Sturzenegger (2000a). "Classifying Exchange Rate Regimes: Deeds vs. Words," mimeo, Business School, Universidad Torcuato Di Tella, Buenos Aires.

——— (2000b). "Implications of the Euro for Latin America's Financial and Banking Systems," *Emerging Markets Review*, vol. 1, no. 1, pp. 53–81.

——— (2000c). Is EMU a Blueprint for Mercosur? *Cuadernos de Economía*, vol. 37, no. 110, pp. 63–99.

Martirena Mantel, Ana Maria (1997). "Reflexiones sobre uniones monetarias: Pensando el Mercosur desde el caso Europeo" ("Reflections on Monetary Unions: Thoughts on Mercosur from the European case/experience"), *Anales de la Academia Nacional de Ciencias Económicas*.

Mussa, M., P. Mason, A. Swoboda, E. Jadresic, P. Mauro, and A. Berg (2000). "Exchange Rate Regimes in an Increasingly Integrated World," mimeo, IMF.

Neumeyer, Andrés (1998). "The Welfare Effects of Optimum Currency Areas," *American Economic Review*, vol. 98, no. 6.

Nicolini, Juan Pablo, and Andrés Neumeyer (2000). "Using Balance Sheet Data to Identify Sovereign Default and Devaluation Risk," mimeo, Universidad Torcuato Di Tella, Buenos Aires.

Panizza Ugo, Ernesto Stein, and Ernesto Talvi (2000). "Assessing Dollarization: An Application to Central American and Caribbean Countries," mimeo, Inter-American Development Bank.

Powell, A. (2002). "Safety First Monetary and Financial Policies for Emerging Economies," in Omotunde E. G. Johnson, ed., *Financial Risks, Stability and Globalization*, International Monetary Fund, Washington D.C.

Rose, Andrew (1999). "One Money, One Market: Estimating the Effect of Common Currencies on Trade," working paper 7432. National Bureau of Economic Research.

Sturzenegger, Federico (2000). "Measuring Balance Sheet Effects," mimeo, Business School, Universidad Torcuato Di Tella, Buenos Aires.

Ungerer, Horst (1997). *A Concise History of European Monetary Integration*, Quorum, London.

Zettelmeyer, Jeromin (1996). "EMU and Long Interest Rates in Germany," IMF working paper.

7 Implementation Guidelines for Dollarization and Monetary Unions

William C. Gruben, Mark A. Wynne, and Carlos E. J. M. Zarazaga

7.1 Introduction

The purpose of this chapter is to discuss the main aspects of the implementation of a dollarization plan or of a monetary union, once the appropriate authorities have decided either course of action. Thus, the chapter stays away from any normative issues. It is devoted to answering the question of *how* to dollarize or form a monetary union rather than the question of whether any given country *should* adopt any particular monetary regime.

It is important to emphasize also that the chapter does not attempt to address all of the implementation issues that will emerge before, during, and after a dollarization plan or the creation of a monetary union. Rather, the chapter tries to complement the material on dollarization covered by previous work on the topic, paramount among them Hausmann and Powell (1999) and the prolific literature on dollarization prepared by the Joint Economic Committee of the U.S. Senate. A thorough understanding and anticipation of all the important implementation issues that are likely to emerge in the course of a dollarization program would be incomplete without a careful reading of those studies, which have influenced the organization and choice of thematic units in this chapter. Likewise, the voluminous literature on Europe's Economic and Monetary Union (EMU hereafter) is an essential starting point for any discussion about the creation of a monetary union in Latin America.[1]

Many of the issues that would arise in the process of dollarization would also need to be addressed to form a monetary union, and vice versa. The essential distinction between dollarization and monetary union in the sense generally understood revolves around the issues

Table 7.1
Seignorage revenues and currency sovereignty under different monetary regimes

		Retain monetary sovereignty?	
		Yes	No
Share in seignorage?	Yes	New common currency	Currency board
	No	Not applicable	Dollarization

of seignorage and monetary sovereignty. Table 7.1 presents a simple schema of the different regimes.

Monetary unions in the general sense can be differentiated according to the extent that participating countries obtain a share of the seignorage revenue generated by the shared currency, the extent to which they have a say in the management of the shared currency, and the extent to which they retain a degree of sovereignty in monetary affairs.

In the simplest type of monetary union one country adopts another country's currency without obtaining any say in how that currency will be managed or even a share of the seignorage revenues. This type of asymmetric monetary union is what we will refer to as "dollarization."[2] A second type of asymmetric monetary union comes about when a country adopts a currency board and backs its currency with a foreign currency. The degree of asymmetry involved in this type of monetary union is less than under dollarization, as the country adopting the currency board at least retains the seignorage revenue generated by the domestic money stock. An even more symmetric monetary union involves one country's adoption of another country's currency but in an arrangement whereby the adopting country also obtains some say in the management of the currency. That would be the case, for example, if Canada and Mexico adopted the U.S. dollar as their currency and obtained voting seats on the Federal Open Market Committee (FOMC hereafter.)[3] This type of monetary union was created when East Germany adopted the deutsche mark in 1990. A more ambitious form of symmetric monetary union occurs when two or more countries agree to abolish their national currencies and replace them with a new currency that will be jointly managed by representatives from all of the countries involved. This type of "symmetric" monetary union is what the European Union (EU) has recently adopted, abolishing the national currencies of the twelve participating nations and replacing them with a new currency, the euro.

Symmetric monetary unions can themselves take different forms. The shared currency could be a completely new, unbacked fiat currency, such as the euro. Alternatively, the currency could be backed (in the sense of a currency board) by one or more other currencies (such as the dollar, euro, or yen).[4] In the text that follows we will use the term *monetary union* to refer to symmetric monetary unions of the former, unbacked, type. It is also important to mention that although the issues of implementing monetary unions discussed in this chapter will be frequently framed with Latin America in mind, they are general enough to be readily applicable to other regions.

7.2 Dollarization

7.2.1 Conditions for Dollarization

A theme that will appear consistently throughout the chapter is that dollarization or the creation of a monetary union should be considered part of an integral process of institutional, political, and economic reforms with the ultimate goal of full financial and commercial integration of a country with the rest of the world, and not just as a mere monetary reform capable of magically solving all of a country's economic maladies when implemented in isolation. In fact, there is the danger, frequently perceived in private or public statements by the advocates of dollarization or monetary unions, that these regimes will be enthusiastically embraced with the secret hope of their providing a painless substitute for other much needed but perhaps painful economic reforms. Such a motivation to dollarize or adopt a monetary union would certainly be detrimental to the success of either regime.

Therefore, a first step in the process of dollarizing an economy or adopting a monetary union is to make the countries and policymakers considering any of those regimes aware that choosing either of them will inevitably entail the explicit or implicit commitment to implementing all of the complementary reforms crucial for the final stability and success of the regime.

For that reason, dollarization or monetary unions are likely to bring about lively discussions about the correct order in which those complementary reforms should be introduced. Those discussions conjure up the "correct order of liberalization" problem that dominated policymaking forums until not long ago, when several countries all over the world, from Latin America to the former Soviet Union, were considering or had engaged already in sweeping structural reforms of their economies.

Should fiscal reform predate, follow, or be simultaneous with dollarization? Should a sound financial system precede dollarization, or will dollarization help to make the financial system sounder? The issue of whether financial, fiscal, and labor reform should precede dollarization has been addressed in a recent paper that Barry Eichengreen, from the University of Berkeley at California, presented in a conference on dollarization organized by the Federal Reserve Bank of Dallas in March 2000.[5] The paper shows economists divided in the two predictable camps: the "just do it" approach and the "dollarize last," or "coronation," approach.

The "just do it" camp argues that dollarization will act as a catalyst for all the other necessary reforms, because it will induce fiscal discipline, it will weed weak institutions out of the financial system, and it will give societies the right incentives to revise legislation and regulations responsible for labor market rigidities. The "dollarization last" camp insists instead that dollarization must be the "coronation" of a concerted effort to bring about fiscal discipline, a solid financial system, and flexible labor markets. This is the approach effectively followed by the EU in creating EMU.

Eichengreen provides some evidence suggesting that the coronation approach is the ideal one. However, it can take a long time to crown the required reforms with dollarization, as was the case with the common currency that crowned the Maastricht Treaty and the long sequence of intermediate steps that preceded the emergence of the European Monetary Union.

Unfortunately, dollarization is most likely to be proposed first for those countries whose currencies are under heavy pressure, as was the case of Argentina after the devaluation of the Brazilian real in January 1999, or are experiencing out-of-control inflation, as happened in Ecuador at the time of launching its dollarization program in April 2000. Policymakers of countries facing those circumstances will most likely be pressed to act without much time to discuss which reforms should take place first. Dollarization may appear to them as an experimental "drug" that, because they lack others of proven success, may offer the only chance for survival, at least for the time required to plan and implement all the other necessary complementary reforms that in ideal conditions should have preceded the ingestion of the experimental dollarization "drug."

The theoretical debate and practice of dollarization could take, therefore, a course reminiscent of the one followed by the discussions and events accompanying the liberalization programs of the last two decades mentioned earlier. The needed reforms continued moving ahead while the experts continued debating what their "correct" order was, until the object of their speculations became a moot point: most liberalization processes had concluded, in all shapes and forms, without providing any definite conclusion on which of them had been implemented in the right order.

The same fate may be awaiting the debate prompted by different dollarization proposals. Perhaps several years from now, the conclusion from the dollarization experiences that may have taken place by then will be something like "it is ... in the credibility sphere where the most important lesson on the sequencing of [dollarization] lies. In a sense, the implementation of a consistent and credible policy package is more important than determining 'the correct' order of [dollarization]," the statement Edwards and Cox Edwards (1987, 193) used to summarize the lesson from the liberalization programs of the 1980s and 1990s, except that the word *dollarization* appears here in lieu of the original text's *liberalization*.

Institutional Requirements

The sort of "order of reforms irrelevance" proposition just presented suggests that the credibility of dollarization as a process of several inextricably intertwined reforms is more crucial for its success than any considerations regarding the sequence in which those reforms will be implemented. Broad, solid political support can go a long way toward building credibility for the ultimate sustainability of the difficult dollarization effort. Only with the support of a substantial fraction of the population will the government be able to push forward not only the perhaps psychologically traumatic, albeit mechanically simple, operation of replacing the domestic currency with the dollar but also the other more challenging reforms that must necessarily be part of the process as well. As vigorously stated in the related contribution by Hausmann and Powell mentioned in the introduction, "It is critical that the countries considering dollarization carry out a serious, open and broad discussion of the subject and go forward only on the basis of strong political consensus" (3).

In this spirit, the citizens of a dollarizing country ought to be able to fully evaluate the goals of the dollarization process, its advantages and disadvantages, its short- as well as long-term consequences. After all, replacing the national currency with a foreign one is not a minor historical event. In this regard, it is critical that societies do not interpret the substitution of the domestic currency with a foreign one as surrendering national sovereignty or the loss of dignity and identity of the country in the community of nations.[6]

These considerations immediately suggest that the first step on the road to dollarization should be a national referendum whose results will be binding for the government. A simple majority approval should be enough to get the dollarization process going.

The subject of the referendum should be the simple one of whether or not the national currency should be replaced with the dollar. The appropriate institutional channels should deal later with more complex details, such as the timetable of the dollarization process and other technical aspects of it.

The practice of direct consultation with citizens on the matter of a major monetary reform is not new and has a recent important precedent in the institutional steps that preceded the launch of the euro on January 1, 1999. The Maastricht Treaty, which governs EMU, was ratified by the national parliaments of all the countries in the EU, and in some countries it was put before the electorate in national referenda.[7] Both the United Kingdom and Denmark negotiated protocols of the Maastricht Treaty that allowed them to abstain from participation in EMU. Both countries subsequently announced that the decision to join EMU would only be taken after national referenda (and in the case of Denmark, a referendum in September 2000 ruled out Danish participation for the foreseeable future). In fact, when EMU was launched Sweden also abstained, although technically it met the conditions for membership.

The referendum may appear as a nuisance in countries that, under the pressure of adverse economic circumstances, might prefer to skip it and dollarize right away. However, bypassing the referendum stage has the serious drawback of the lack of an explicit and clear mandate to the government. Without it, the dollarization process may get stuck in factious political infighting and noisy minorities who oppose it might be able to derail it, even if a majority of the population were in favor of it.

Timetable for Dollarization   As the recent experience of Ecuador indicates, dollarization can be implemented relatively fast, perhaps in just six months. It is hard to think, however, that any feasible timetable could make the process faster than that, once the national referendum has approved the decision to dollarize.

For reasons given later, when discussing the treatment of existing contracts, the timetable for dollarization will likely be different for countries experiencing high inflation rates from those experiencing low ones. In the latter, existing contracts will tend to have longer maturities, and the parties to them may therefore need more time to adjust to the new dollarized environment.

Timetables will depend not only on the prevailing inflation rate but also on the institutional features of the financial system. Countries that already allow contracts and financial transactions to be denominated in dollars at the time of the national referendum will have a much easier time adapting to the new conditions than countries in which that is not the case. For the latter group of countries, the timetable for dollarization should prescribe a transition period of at least a year during which contracts in dollars and the domestic currency will be allowed to coexist.

These idiosyncratic considerations aside, a reasonable timetable should specify the following sequence of events:

1. The date of the national referendum.

2. If the referendum approves dollarization, the date at which the relevant legislation will be submitted to congress. Typically, not all the necessary legislation will require a constitutional amendment, and therefore the congress can consider it while the process leading to the constitutional reform, if needed, is set in motion. A strong mandate from the referendum should help speed up the passage of the legislation, perhaps within one or two months of its submission to congress. Simultaneously, the constitutional reform process should be initiated in countries where the dollarization requires a constitutional amendment.

3. Length of the transition period. Countries with low inflation rates or where contracts denominated in dollars have been forbidden

should contemplate a transition period of at least a year during which the domestic currency will be allowed to coexist with the dollar as legal tender. However, all the parties to contracts entered during this transition period should be made aware that outstanding obligations and contractual agreements in the domestic currency, including wages, will be transformed into dollars at a specified date and at the exchange rate that will be established by the procedure described in section 7.2.2. They should also recognize that except for the issue of the denomination, all the other terms and conditions of the corresponding contractual agreements, *including the nominal interest rate*, will remain in effect (this procedure is thoroughly justified in the next section).

4. The date at which the central bank will start to replace the domestic currency in circulation with dollars and at which this latter currency will be recognized as legal tender. Care must be taken that this date will not predate the eventually required constitutional reform.

5. The date at which the domestic currency, except for small change in coins, will be definitely phased out from circulation.

The Complementary Economic Reforms

Once the approval of dollarization by a national referendum has cleared the way to start the process, the more technical aspects of the dollarization program come into play. Besides the measures indicated in the timetable just presented, the dollarization program would have to consider the timing for implementation of other associated reforms.

For the reasons given earlier, and lacking any insights from economic theory, this chapter stays away from recommending any order of reform measures in the process of dollarization. It is possible to agree with the "just-doers" that a long list of prerequisites is the best way to make sure that dollarization will never happen.

However, although dollarization can act as a catalyst in setting in motion the necessary complementary reforms, it will not just make them happen as if a magic automatic pilot were turned on to guide the process. As it was argued at the beginning of this chapter, dollarization should not be implemented *instead of* but *along with* all other complementary reforms. In particular, a deliberate, conscious effort will be required to introduce, sooner or later, fiscal reforms to allay any fears of default on the sovereign debt, financial system reforms to allay fears of recurrent banking crises, and labor market reforms to allay fears that nominal wage rigidities will result in high unemployment rates. Each of these reforms is discussed in some detail in the text that follows.

Fiscal Reform   Without any doubt, fiscal reform must be part of any dollarization process because one of the much proclaimed goals of dollarization is to bring about a substantial reduction of the country risk premium and, therefore, in the borrowing costs dollarizing countries face in international capital markets. Needless to say, fiscal profligacy would raise the specter of default and upset whatever interest rate reductions the dollarization program may have otherwise induced.

As mentioned earlier, whether fiscal reform should precede or follow the dollarization of the currency is a matter of controversy, and theoretical arguments can be found on both sides of the debate. On the one hand, a modest attempt to rationalize the claim that dollarization will contribute to create better conditions for fiscal discipline can be found in Zarazaga (1999), in the context of a game-theoretic, political economy model of endogenous fiscal profligacy where the level of government spending is not invariant to the monetary regime in place.

On the other hand, Sims (2001) has argued in a recent paper especially prepared for a dollarization conference organized by the Federal Reserve Bank of Cleveland that dollarization may eventually increase, rather than decrease, the probability that a country will default on its sovereign debt. The basic argument is that while the domestic currency is still circulating, the reduction of the real value of the outstanding fiat money debt through a higher inflation rate can absorb unanticipated shocks to the government budget constraint. Because dollarization forces a country to relinquish the ability to default on the real value of nominal commitments, it may end up increasing the likelihood that governments will suspend payments on dollar-denominated sovereign debt more often than they would if they could inflate away at least their liabilities in the form of non-interest-bearing domestic currency.[8]

Financial Reform   A country considering dollarization either must strengthen its banking system or run the risk of significant real sector consequences from financial crises. The reason, of course, is that countries that dollarize cannot print money to bail out the banking system—as they can when they have their own currencies.

Dollarization advocates' response to this alleged shortcoming of dollarization is that financial systems are typically exposed to currency and maturity mismatches. These mismatches are easily recognized by foreign investors, who will pull their funds from a country at the hint of an exchange rate crisis. That is, leaving open the options for currency depreciation can pave the way to recurrent banking crises—even when a nation can print money so as to serve as a lender of last resort (LLR) for the financial system. One reason is that devaluations induce a reduction in the prices of nontradable goods (office buildings, for example) relative to tradable goods. Whether the government uses the printing press or not, an associated real estate crash can mean a banking crisis with long-lasting real effects— as certainly Thailand, Indonesia, and even Mexico have found out within the last decade.

In a study of the relation between banking crises and exchange rate regimes over the period 1975–1992, however, Eichengreen and Rose (1997) find that it is not true that more stable exchange rates are associated with fewer banking crises. Moreover, in an update of this result, Eichengreen (2000) shows that hard pegs (including currency boards and dollarized economies) are more fully associated with banking crises than soft pegs (other fixed rate arrangements). Although it may be true that the removal of some of the LLR function discourages risky bank behavior, the results obtained by Eichengreen suggest that this "moral hazard reduction" effect may be not enough to offset the increase in bank difficulties originated in the lack of an LLR function.

It is important to point out that much of the discussion in the existing literature fails to evaluate the welfare implications of the alternative policies. It may be true that countries with access to a discount window will experience fewer financial crises than those without that facility. But that doesn't mean that a society with fewer crises is necessarily better off than one in which those crises are more frequent. The recent experience with several financial crises (Mexico 1994, Southeast Asia 1997, Russia 1998, Turkey 2001) suggests that assistance to ailing financial institutions does not end up solving just a liquidity problem but also a solvency problem. As a result, discount window operations become the instrument of massive bailouts that increase the public debt (as much as 15 percent of GDP in some cases, as Mexico or South Korea) and, therefore, the burden of future taxation. It is fair to conclude then that a heavier tax burden seems to be the price to pay for reducing the frequency of financial crises. Given the distorted nature of most taxes in practice, it may be that a society will be better off by simply doing away with LLR functions and the higher taxation eventually associated with them, even if doing so implies more frequent financial crises. An additional benefit from severely restricting or eliminating altogether LLR facilities is the more efficient allocation of risk by financial institutions now subject to the discipline of the market and, therefore, the elimination of the moral hazard distortions that those facilities typically induce in the portfolio choices of financial institutions.

It should be clear, then, that the issue of whether or not an LLR function improves welfare is empirical in nature. Unfortunately, as already mentioned, economic models capable of evaluating the welfare implications of the relevant trade-offs just stated are still in their infancy.

Labor Markets   The presence of nominal wage rigidities would certainly be problematic for labor market adjustment in a country that has forfeited the ability to choose the inflation rate necessary to eventually bring real wages in line with labor market equilibrium conditions. Herein perhaps lies the Achilles' heel of the "just-do-it" approach, because the empirical and theoretical evidence that hard currency regimes motivate labor market flexibility is certainly weak to nonexistent.

Argentina's currency board system was in place for more than a decade, but only very minor relaxations of labor market regulations accompanied the double-digit unemployment rates observed there during that period. Therefore, the notion that a "drastic monetary reform" will by itself induce a relaxation of labor market regulations seems suspect when we consider that the implementation of even moderate labor market reforms typically faces fierce opposition in many countries, with different monetary regimes.

It may be that dollarization will induce labor market reforms that otherwise would have never happened, but experience suggests that the pace of progress may be extremely slow and, therefore, that dollarizing countries may eventually experience a long spell of unemployment in the initial stages of the dollarization program. Rather than being in denial, and as a way of mitigating the social consequences of this problem, countries about to dollarize should consider some form of unemployment insurance in their budgetary provisions, a requirement that without doubt will make fiscal reform all the more urgent.

7.2.2   The Mechanics of Dollarization

The Choice of the Exchange Rate: Does It Matter?
An obvious step in the dollarization process is determining the exchange rate at which the domestic currency will be converted into dollars. It seems sensible that the selection of an exchange rate should be consistent with dollarization's stated purpose of giving back to the public the reserves accumulated over time by the central bank, in exchange for the domestic currency. This naturally suggests that dollarization should take place at the exchange rate at which *exactly all* the relevant liabilities of the central bank are exchanged by *exactly all* the international reserves of the central bank *at the moment of dollarization.*

In other words, the laws enacting the dollarization do not need to establish a specific exchange rate in advance of the effective date of enactment of the dollarization but, rather, the procedure by which such exchange rate should be determined at that date.

Accordingly, rather than picking a specific exchange rate, the legislation would establish an official date for dollarization and mandate that starting then, each unit of local currency will be exchanged for the amount of dollars that resulted from application of the formula

Exchange rate at which conversion will take place =
Stock of international reserves/(Money base + interest-bearing securities denominated in domestic currency issued by the central bank)

in which the amounts in both the numerator and denominator are determined as of the specific date at which the domestic currency will start to be exchanged for dollars.

Four remarks about this procedure are in order: First, this formula guarantees that the central bank will have enough reserves to buy back not only the entire money base in circulation but also all the liabilities in domestic currency that it issued for the purpose of open market operations in the past.

Second, as long as the international reserves position of the central bank is positive, there is not such a thing as an "insufficient level of reserves" with which to start the dollarization process.[9]

Third, this is a simple, market-based procedure that guarantees that the government of the dollarizing country will not manipulate the process to take advantage of its last opportunity to extract seignorage revenues through the inflation tax. That would be the case, for example, if the central bank decided to set aside part of its reserves with the purpose of acting as an LLR later on and, in determining the exchange rate, applied instead the following formula:

Stock international reserves at the central bank/(Money base + interest-bearing securities denominated in domestic currency issued by the central bank + desired level of lender of last resort funds)

Use of this alternative formula would result, of course, in fewer dollars per unit of the domestic currency than with the previous one and should be considered part, therefore, of a "devaluation-followed-by-dollarization" strategy that could seriously undermine the credibility buildup the dollarization process is meant to accomplish.

Fourth, use of the first formula has no consequences for the real economy under the assumption of perfectly flexible prices. Under such an assumption, the simple procedure summarized by the formula would not result in anything like "a wrong exchange rate" because all prices would adjust to restore equilibrium conditions in all markets. After all, what matters for real allocations are the relative prices, not their absolute levels. If markets are flexible enough, individual prices will adjust downward or upward in whichever unit of account, to reflect the relative scarcity and social value of the goods and services involved.

Thus, the issue of the choice of the "appropriate" exchange rate is only relevant in the presence of significant frictions, such as in the labor market. In that case, the choice of an initial nominal exchange rate would be equivalent to the selection of a real wage in dollars. The "wrong" exchange rate choice might impair the proper functioning of the labor market for a long time and create social frictions that would conspire against the success of the dollarization program.

It follows, as emphasized in the previous section, that an important condition for a successful dollarization plan is price flexibility in all markets, and in particular labor reforms that guarantee that nominal wages and any other forms of labor compensation can freely adjust downward or upward, depending on the economic conditions prevailing at each point in time. Indeed, one could argue that economies where nominal rigidities are pervasive and long lasting should never dollarize. Thus, the alternative procedures to select the initial exchange rate suggested by some dollarization advocates do not seem fully consistent with their underlying belief in the efficiency of markets. For example, the proposals prepared by the staff of the Joint Economic Committee of the U.S. Senate, discussed in more detail later, maintain that the domestic currency ought to be allowed to float cleanly for a brief preestablished period but not longer than thirty days before the exchange rate at which dollarization will take place is definitely fixed. It is unclear why a transition period is needed at all. The only possible answer is that some market frictions prevent the immediate adjustment of prices. But in that case, the recommendation of the thirty-day transition period must be inspired by the belief that such a period is long enough to remove those frictions, a presumption whose empirical underpinnings need to be better justified.

Substitution of the Domestic Currency (Money Base) with Dollars
The dollarization process requires specifying the procedures by which different monetary aggregates, financial assets, and contracts in general, will be converted into dollars.

There is an important difference between the money base and all the other components of different monetary aggregates: the former represents a government liability, in particular, a non-interest-bearing one, whereas all other monetary aggregates involve typically private sector liabilities. This difference may suggest that dollarizing the monetary base will involve different steps from dollarizing, for example, the less liquid components of M2.

Indeed, dollarization will require that the public *physically* hand over its domestic currency holdings to the central bank in exchange for dollars. By contrast, as we demonstrate in the next subsection, the conversion of the components of the monetary aggregates other than the money base, financial obligations, and contracts in general is a fairly straightforward process that involves only simple accounting entries.

The rest of this section discusses the procedures for dollarizing the money base. The procedures to dollarize all other monetary aggregates, financial obligations, contracts, and so on, are discussed in the next subsection.

How is the conversion of the money base, a non-interest-earning government liability, accomplished? A first step is to make sure that there will be enough dollar notes to redeem the domestic ones at the set exchange rate. To that end, the central bank will have accumulated a considerable stock of dollar notes by selling, over a prudential period of time previous to the day scheduled for the initiation of the dollarization process, securities and other financial instruments in its reserves portfolio.

At the closing of business on the day prior to the one the dollarization process has been scheduled to start, the central bank will distribute cash payments to financial institutions, as it normally does as part of the daily settlement of accounts with the private sector, except that such payments will be made in dollars notes—and not in local currency as was previously the case—applying to that effect the exchange rate determined by any of the procedures discussed in the previous section.

In that way, some financial institutions in the system will open the following day, the day officially set for the initiation of the dollarization process, with part of the cash in their vaults in dollar notes. The dollarization process can then be initiated by instructing all financial institutions to change the denomination of all existing deposits and obligations from domestic currency to dollars, applying the "dollarization" exchange rate previously announced. Likewise, from that day on financial institutions will be instructed to honor deposit withdrawals in dollar notes. The use of the domestic currency to that end will be allowed only after the daily stock of dollar notes in each financial institution's vaults has been depleted.

Simultaneously, the appropriate authority will have mandated already that from the day scheduled for the initiation of the dollarization process, all wages and salaries will be paid in dollars. This regulation will considerably speed up the dollarization process by forcing all businesses in the country to turn in a considerable fraction of their domestic currency holdings to their banks, which in turn will proceed to convert them to dollar notes at the central bank. In the meantime, the central bank constantly replenishes its stock of dollar notes by selling securities and financial instruments in its reserves portfolio. As financial institutions receive domestic currency notes for payments and deposits, turn them into the central bank, and receive dollars notes in the daily settlements of their accounts with that institution, the domestic currency notes will be progressively replaced by their dollar value in dollar notes.

After enough time has elapsed, this process will have eventually allowed the central bank to buy back all the domestic money base with dollar notes through the financial intermediaries, without any need of a direct interaction with nonfinancial entities or the public. The more financially integrated and developed a country, the faster the replacement of the domestic currency with dollar notes will be accomplished. In Ecuador, for example, the dollarization process was completed in six months.

In any case, it is only fair to admit that if the process is left to function on its own, a small fraction of the domestic currency may continue circulating for a long time after the dollarization process has started. That could be the case, for example, in small and fairly isolated communities in which almost all transactions are typically carried out in cash. A complete dollarization of the economy, therefore, is unlikely to occur unless the legislation specifies a date after which the central bank no longer will exchange the domestic currency for dollars. However, that "expiration date" clause has the inconvenience that individuals in isolated communities without proper financial services could end up stuck with piles of worthless domestic currency, which they could not exchange on time simply because the value of the notes would be lower than the cost of traveling to the nearest central bank agency, possibly several thousands of miles from their homes, where the transaction could be conducted. To avoid this kind of situation, the central bank should reduce the transaction costs of exchanging domestic currency notes for dollar notes by opening, two or three months before the scheduled domestic currency phaseout, temporary agencies in the locations where the problem has been identified to be particularly severe. Of course, this task also could be delegated to properly monitored and supervised private contractors for a fee.

Treatment of Existing Contracts

The dollarization of the money base described in the previous section is a fairly simple process and should not be the subject of much controversy once the exchange rate for the conversion has been determined. This simplicity reflects, of course, that of the underlying financial instrument: although currency is a government liability, it does not commit the government contractually to anything. The government does not have to redeem the notes at any time, it does not pay interest on them, and it does not have to keep their value in real terms at any agreed target level. The lack of explicit contractual arrangements between currency holders and its issuer, the government, makes it possible to avoid the lengthy considerations otherwise required in deciding how to proceed to dollarize the more complex components of the monetary aggregates or other financial instruments.

Explicit contractual arrangements between two parties (one of which could be a government agency) for which the dimension of time is of the essence may pose great challenges for designing the appropriate dollarization procedure of the underlying financial instrument.

Even the treatment of contracts already denominated in dollars may raise some thorny issues. In principle, the parties to those contracts should be indifferent to the dollarization process because the corresponding contractual obligations were in dollars to start with. However, the debate on dollarization often maintains (see chapter 6, by Powell and Sturzenegger, this volume) that even the risk-free devaluation interest rate of those contracts may contain a country-risk premium that is not invariant to the monetary regime in general and, in particular, to the act of dollarization.

The problem may come from the claim that the dollarization of a country will bring about a decline in the country-risk premium component of the interest rate in dollar-denominated contracts. Materialization of such a reduction in postdollarization contracts may create among some of the parties to existing contracts the perception that, as written in their original terms, those contracts are unfair because the conditions (such as the nominal interest rate) agreed upon at some point in the past did not contemplate that the economy might be dollarized in the foreseeable future. The government might receive pressures, under such circumstances, to coerce a renegotiation of the original contract to grant borrowers, for example, access to the new, more favorable interest rate environment.

Even more questions are likely to emerge regarding the treatment of existing contracts denominated in the domestic currency. For example, should time deposits (a contract between a financial institution and a deposit holder) denominated in the domestic currency be converted into dollars as of their expiration date or as of their initiation date? Should the conversion of the principal and accrued interest take place at the same point in time, or could they be converted at different dates? In either case, should the conversion of the nominal denomination of the contract be accompanied by any other modifications, such as a change in the nominal interest rate established in the original contractual arrangement?

The purpose of the following sections is to demonstrate that despite appearances to the contrary, the dollarization of *all* financial instruments and existing contracts is a fairly straightforward process that involves only simple accounting entries. This simplicity does not emerge as obvious without a thorough discussion of the theory of contracts and the revision of a relevant historical experience discussed in the text that follows.

A Digression on the Theory of Contracts and the Time-Inconsistency Problem   Contracts were born to overcome what is known in economics jargon as the *time-inconsistency problem*. This term refers to the tendency of economic agents to renege on past commitments. For example, not mediating a written policy enforceable in a court of law, an insurance company will have every incentive to renege on its commitment to pay for damages once a casualty has occurred, because by that time it will have pocketed anyway the premiums that the customer may have been paying perhaps for many years.

Therefore, after-the-fact modifications of contracts not freely agreed upon the contracts' parties should not be allowed, because such alterations will tend to reintroduce the time-inconsistency problem that contracts were meant to solve. Unfortunately, well-meaning governments are often not aware of the bad side effects associated with mandatory alterations of contracts and proceed with them anyway with the perception that the new terms will reflect better what the parties to them originally meant and intended. Such a perception is rather questionable.

In the first place, it is unclear how an outsider, such as the government, can interfere with a contract on the grounds that under current circumstances, the terms of the contract no longer reflect the intentions or expectations the parties had when they entered into it. Because intentions and expectations are not observable, such a justification implies formidable mind-reading capabilities denied to most regular citizens.

That is not to say that expectations and intentions do not influence the terms of contractual arrangements. Good or bad intentions, wishful thinking, wrong or right perceptions about the likely turn of events, foolish or wise attitudes toward risk, lack of information or excess thereof, and even brilliant insights or outright incompetence are all elements that influence how a contract is written, but unfortunately they are not observable. That is precisely why contracts exist: to avoid the frustrating attempt of second-guessing what each party to a deal meant or intended.

True, some or all of the parties to a contract may have entered into it out of miscalculation. But it is not the government's role to protect parties to a contract from their own mistakes. Such intervention would only introduce serious moral hazard elements and lead economic agents to consider the terms of contracts with greater carelessness, in the conviction that the government would step in to protect them from whatever mistakes they made in assessing the implications the contractual obligations had for them.[10]

The prestigious Argentine jurist Dalmacio Vélez Sarsfield understood all too well the dire consequences of *ex post* modifications of contracts when he refused to incorporate into the Argentine Civil Code he was commissioned to draft the doctrine of *lesión enorme* present in other legal traditions. He explained his rejection of the doctrine in the following terms: "We should cease to be responsible for our acts if the law should permit us to make amends for all errors or all our acts of imprudence. Free consent given without fraud, error or duress, and with the solemnities required by law, should make contracts irrevocable" (as cited by Berensztein and Spector, forthcoming). Nor did the code, enacted in 1869, accept the theory of imprevision, which authorizes the judicial termination or modification of the contract terms when the payment owed by one of the parties has become excessively onerous because of extraordinary or allegedly unforeseeable events.

In summary, it is important to keep in mind when examining modifications of contracts in past experiences that contracts are based on *ex ante* considerations of different contingencies, some of which will materialize and some of which will not. But that observation doesn't mean the nonmaterializing contingencies have influenced the terms and conditions of the contract and that the materializing contingencies did not exert any influence. In particular, it is not necessarily true that the contingencies that do materialize (such as a dollarization plan) were not fully taken into account, in some way or the other, in the decision process that led to a past contractual agreement. And in any case, letting some of the parties to a contract introduce after-the-fact changes to it on the grounds that they would have not agreed to its terms and conditions had they known the events were not going to turn out in their favor defeats the purpose of contracts, which is to overcome the time-inconsistency temptation to renege *ex post* on commitments acquired *ex ante*.[11]

However, it should be recognized that policymakers have often shrugged off the concerns about government-mandated alterations of contracts raised by the time-inconsistency literature. That is a fortunate development for our purposes, because the analysis of the treatment that outstanding contracts have received in past experiences involving fairly drastic changes of economic policy can help in developing some guidelines for the conversion of existing contracts under dollarization.

Some Insights from Past Experiences   An interesting case study for the purpose of deciding the treatment of existing contracts under dollarization is the anti-inflation plan implemented in Argentina in June 1985. The plan has come to be known in history as the Austral Plan, in reference to the fact that it included, among other things, a monetary reform that replaced the existing domestic currency, the peso, with a new one, the austral.

At the time the plan was implemented, on June 15, 1985, inflation in Argentina was running high. It had been at an average of 8 percent a month in the preceding decade and at about 30 percent a month, or roughly 1 percent *a day*, immediately before the Austral Plan. Understandably, nominal interest rates were running high as well, reflecting investors' attempts to preserve the real value of their investments in domestic currency. Thus, in the first two weeks of June, time deposits of thirty days' maturity carried *on average* a 30 percent monthly nominal interest rate. From an *ex ante* perspective, this nominal interest rate would have been barely enough to make up for inflation if prices continued to rise at the 30 percent rate of the immediately preceding month. But of course, this same interest rate would be associated with hefty real returns if, by contrast, inflation came abruptly to an end.

The authorities behind the Austral Plan were worried about the consequences of the second contingency. In particular, they were concerned that the combination of the high nominal interest rates prevailing before the plan, and the very low inflation rates they were convinced the plan would bring about,[12] would result in transfers of wealth that none of the parties to many existing contracts had originally intended.

This preoccupation is clearly described in an Economic Commission for Latin America and the Caribbean report of the time, when it asserts that the plan's intellectual architects were concerned that "an abrupt decline in the inflation rate would cause in and by itself an equally sudden change in the real conditions of existing obligations."[13] Therefore, the program "included a system of conversion of contractual obligations, whose purpose was to neutralize the transfers of wealth that could have otherwise taken place as a result of the disinflation, without at the same time modifying the terms of the contracts."[14]

Restoration of the real terms in which the contracts were meant to be settled—according to the interpretation of the administrators of the Austral Plan, rather than that of the parties involved—required, therefore, the implementation of a mechanism that would preserve "justice." To that end, the plan included the novelty of an unusual conversion mechanism between the old currency, the peso, and the new one, the austral, that in practice was equivalent to a government-mandated modification of the original terms of almost all existing contracts denominated in pesos.

The mechanism essentially established that at maturity all contracts in pesos should be converted to australes according to a sliding scale that implied that the amounts of australes received for each peso declined at a rate of 0.85 percent per day. In other words, contractual obligations denominated in pesos were converted to australes at an exchange rate that devalued the peso (with respect to the austral) at a daily rate of 0.85 percent, which reflected the daily inflation rate corresponding to a 29 percent monthly inflation rate.

The guiding principle behind this mechanism was that under the previous regime, "nominal amounts committed to be paid at a future date depreciated, in real terms, at a daily rate of approximately 1%. In other words, the purchasing power of the sums involved declined with the maturity of the obligation.... Therefore, the nominal amounts [of existing contracts in pesos] had to be corrected according to the erosion that the purchasing power of that currency [the peso] would have experienced [should the change in regime not have occurred]."[15] Another underlying principle was that "in the assumption of a perfectly anticipated and uniform inflation rate, this system would have exactly validated (in real terms) the expectations implicit in the existing contracts."[16]

From the operational point of view, this mechanism was equivalent to changing the interest rate on existing contracts. An example will help to clarify this implication. Consider a thirty-day time deposit for an amount of 100 pesos at a 30 percent monthly nominal interest rate, made the day before the Austral Plan was implemented. For the sake of simplicity, assume also that the price level that day was one, so the value of the deposit in real terms was 100 units of some basket of representative consumption goods. The deposit slip (a contract with the financial institution), therefore, established that the deposit holder should receive 130 pesos at maturity. If the inflation rate were going to be also 30 percent in the intervening month, the price level by the time the deposit were due would be 1.3 and the transaction would have preserved intact the real value of the deposit at 100 "consumption baskets."

If, however, the same inflation rate turned out to be zero, the price level would still be one at maturity and the real value of the deposit would be 130 consumption baskets. The intellectual architects of the Austral Plan thought that the latter outcome was unfair and needed to be corrected by essentially taking away all the nominal interest accumulated during the period, on the grounds that that nominal interest was meant to "exactly" compensate for the loss of purchasing power of the principal and not to entitle the deposit holder to a 30 percent return in real terms.

More metaphorically, the conversion mechanism worked as a time travel machine that put the deposit holders back at the window of the financial institutions at the date they had made their deposits, and forced them to make the deposit again, but this time denominated in the new currency and at a 0 percent nominal interest rate.

It is interesting to note that in the view of the policymakers of the time, that metaphorical travel to the past did nothing but validate in real terms "the expectations implicit in the existing contracts." This claim is really intriguing because, as was pointed out earlier, expectations are not observable. How can a policymaker know why a depositor accepted one interest rate and not any other? How can the policymaker be certain that the deposit holder did not attach, at the time he or she made the deposit, a positive probability to the implementation of an anti-inflation program and that, therefore, that the deposit holder accepted what he or she regarded as a low (given the inflation rate) 30 percent monthly nominal interest rate precisely and only because of the possibility of a large reward in real terms if the change in regime did occur?

That was precisely the argument of those angered investors for whom the application of the conversion mechanism in the Austral Plan turned out to be equivalent to a *negative* nominal interest rate on the original contract. This situation was not uncommon and emerged for those contracts whose original nominal interest rate was below the inflation rate at the time the Austral Plan was launched. The government responded that the unusual situation appeared because at the inflation rate prevailing before the plan, the real value of those contractual obligations would have been lower at maturity anyway; the recontracted negative nominal interest rate just reflected the same reduction in purchasing power that those contractual obligations would have experienced at a real, rather than a nominal, negative interest rate.

But this defense of government interference with existing contracts ignores, once more, that contracts reflect *ex ante* considerations that are impossible to elucidate on the basis of *ex post* outcomes. The problem is that a nominal interest rate below the current inflation rate did not necessarily imply that investors were knowingly and freely accepting a negative interest rate in real terms. It might have been that they were anticipating the change of regime and, therefore, that the *ex ante* expectations of their reward in real terms were positive. Such anticipation of a change of regime is not completely unreasonable in light of the findings of Cagan (1956) and Flood and Garber (1980). These authors claimed to have detected signs that right at the peak of the intense inflationary experiences they studied, economic agents were behaving as if an anti-inflation program were going to be implemented (as it indeed was) in the near future.

In the case of the Austral Plan experience, some holders of thirty-day time deposits could have been demanding an expected real return of 2 percent a month on their investments.[17] This would have translated into a nominal interest rate of 17 percent if the investor had assessed that there was a 50 percent chance that the current 30 percent inflation rate regime would continue and a 50 percent chance that a stabilization plan like the Austral Plan would bring the inflation rate down to zero. The investor would indeed obtain a −13 percent return on the investment, in real terms, if the first event had materialized thirty days later but a hefty positive return of 17 percent if the anti-inflation program materialized instead. The expected (average) return from those two outcomes was, however, the desired 2 percent in real terms.[18]

Notice that in its attempt to restore "justice," the conversion mechanism introduced by the Austral Plan may have ended up unfairly penalizing the most optimistic investors, the ones who accepted the more moderate nominal returns in their contracts on the expectations that something would be done, and sooner rather than later, about the high inflation rate prevailing at the time. In other words, modification of contracts with conversion schemes such as those the Austral Plan used may have the perverse effect of discouraging "optimistic" views about the future and of inducing investors to take their capital out of the country on the anticipation that positive (*ex post*) real returns on their investment will be taken away from them if the returns turn out to be "too big" for some government agency eager to "make things even."

There is another interesting feature of the Austral Plan that is particularly relevant for the issue of the treatment that existing contracts should be given under dollarization: although the plan devalued the domestic currency by 18 percent, it did not contain any provisions for compensating the resulting transfers of wealth in dollar terms. In making that decision, the architects of the plan must have decided that all that mattered to investors was the real returns in the domestic currency. That may not have been true, however, at a time when deposits in a foreign currency were not an option.[19]

Perhaps a more important reason the Austral Plan may have decided not to compensate losses (or gains) in dollar terms was because the event of a devaluation was not alien to investors at the time. That could be hardly the case in a country that had seen devaluations by the dozens in the immediately preceding past.

The idea that economic agents can anticipate changes in regime with respect to the returns on their investments in terms of a foreign currency, but lose that ability when it comes to returns in the domestic currency, is intriguing, if not logically inconsistent.[20] In any case, for the purposes of this chapter it is not necessary to uncover the reasons for that asymmetric treatment, because both the practice in relevant experiences, such as the Austral Plan, and the theory of contracts examined in the previous section seem to suggest that devaluations are somehow expected and incorporated in all contracts that predate an important change of regime such as dollarization. This coincidence of the treatment actually given to existing contracts in the past with normative prescriptions from the theory of contracts is fortunate, because it will lead to little disagreement over the guidelines for converting existing contractual agreements under a dollarization program presented in the next section.

Guidelines for the Treatment of Existing Contracts under a Dollarization Plan   The analysis of the previous section suggests that governments considering different alternatives for dealing with existing contracts under a dollarization program should heed the warning that altering a contract on the grounds that its terms have implicitly attached *ex ante* zero probability to an event that did in the end occur is a policy that would set a precedent with potentially serious moral hazard implications. In fact, it could erode confidence in the enforceability of future contracts to the point of completely undoing the reductions in the country-risk premium the dollarization was supposed to accomplish. To preserve such a hard-earned reduction in the risk premium, the legal and operational framework within which dollarization occurs should affect existing contractual arrangements as little as possible.

In particular, a dollarization plan should not be concerned with the transfers of wealth it can bring about if the conversion of the domestic currency into dollars takes place at an exchange rate significantly different from the one that prevailed before the dollarization, or even its announcement.

On theoretical grounds, this principle applies because economic agents tend to be forward looking when they enter into contracts and make them, therefore, contingent on circumstances that will unavoidably result, as they know in advance, in after-the-fact redistributions of risk and wealth among the parties involved. This principle pertains also on more pragmatic grounds because the preoccupation with compensating transfers of wealth in terms of foreign currencies eventually brought about by changes of monetary regime (such as the Austral Plan's initial devaluation) does not seem to have been overwhelmingly present in past experiences.

Consistent with the theoretical and pragmatic considerations just presented, the guiding principle for the treatment of existing contracts under a dollarization plan is that all their original terms and conditions should be preserved and that when a conversion of the domestic currency into dollars is required, the contracts should receive the same treatment they would receive had the domestic currency not been retired from circulation but just suffered a change of its parity with respect to the dollar.

Application of this principle suggests that the government should abstain from any mandatory renegotiation of *dollar-denominated* contracts. In fact, to avoid any confusion and prevent political pressures to the contrary, the legislation implementing dollarization should explicitly instruct the courts that such contracts should be considered fully enforceable in their original terms and conditions, including maturities and the nominal interest rate (in dollars).

Preservation of the same principle is not as straightforward for contracts in the domestic currency, however, because dollarization, by definition, will modify at least one of the terms of the contract: the currency in which the contractual obligations should be settled. The least disruptive way to dollarize those contracts is to preserve their original terms, including the interest rate, and establish that assets, liabilities, installments, or any obligations originated in existing contracts denominated in the domestic currency should be valued in dollars at the expiration of the relevant contractual clauses, using the exchange rate established by the dollarization plan for the conversion. This is basically the same procedure followed in the introduction of the euro. The creation of the new currency posed the problem of how to convert outstanding contracts denominated in the currencies of the member countries to the newly adopted common currency. The conversion mechanism simply established that starting on January 1, 1999, all contracts, equities, securities, corporate and government bonds, and financial assets and obligations in general, would be expressed in euros using the December 31, 1998, exchange rates between the ecu and the European currencies in which those contracts and securities were originally denominated.[21] Because, as discussed earlier, not all the domestic currency notes will be replaced by dollar notes immediately on the date the dollarization process starts, the conversion scheme associated with that process should specify, in addition, that any cash payments originated in outstanding contracts should be settled in dollar notes after that date.

The conversion mechanism just outlined will avoid *ex ante* unforeseen transfers of wealth. For example, take the case of a thirty-day loan in 100 units of the domestic currency signed just a day before the announcement of dollarization. Because the contract was signed before the announcement, the monthly nominal interest rate on the loan, say 20 percent, contains most likely an inflation or devaluation risk premium. In other words, the interest rate already contemplates the possibility of exchange rate modifications. Therefore, at the time of the loan's expiration, the amount due of 120 units of domestic currency should be converted to dollars at the set exchange rate. Obviously, the resulting amount may or may not be *ex post* the same *ex ante* amount it was at the prevailing exchange rate at the beginning of the contract, but this contingency is precisely what the interest rate meant to capture through its inflation/devaluation risk premium.

The alternative of converting the loan into dollars before maturity is certainly possible, but it would raise a host of questions about the conditions (the interest rate, among them) that the parties to the contract would have accepted had they perfectly anticipated the dollarization regime at the time of entering into the contract. This kind of "second guessing" is subject to all the complications and time inconsistency issues described in the previous section when analyzing the mechanism for the conversion of contracts implemented by Argentina's failed Austral Plan experiment in 1985. Therefore, it is better to stay away from those complexities by following the principles established in the preceding paragraph, that is, by converting all financial obligations emerging from existing contracts into dollars at the expiration date originally stipulated in those contracts.

Two factors will contribute to minimizing undesired consequences from the preservation of the original terms and conditions of existing contracts, especially the nominal interest rate.

First, the timetable for the dollarization plan outlined in the previous section includes a transition period whose main purpose is, precisely, to give all parties to existing contracts time to adjust to the new conditions that are likely to prevail once the dollarization is effectively implemented. Contracts will be typically short term, perhaps one year long at the most, in high-inflation environments.

A transition period of similar length for those countries will ensure that most contracts that predated the formal announcement of dollarization will have expired by the time the economy is effectively dollarized.

Of course, that does not mean that existing contracts will be protected from contingencies of the transition period and, in particular, of the fluctuations in the exchange rate that can be attributed to the announcement of the plan and that arguably would not have occurred absent that announcement. But as stated earlier, the attempt to protect contracts from the vagaries of economic policy regimes leads to an endless sequence of side effects and attempts to correct them that end up restoring the damaging time-inconsistent inefficiencies that contracts were supposed to eliminate.

The second mitigating factor of the effects of dollarization on existing contracts is the possibility of voluntary renegotiation. To the extent that the renegotiation of contracts involves some fixed costs, this option is more likely to emerge in countries where long-term contracts are a standard practice at the time dollarization is implemented. In such an environment, many financial institutions will find it profitable to attract customers from competitors by offering refinancing packages at more favorable interest rates than in the original contract. Competition among financial intermediaries will guarantee that eventually every individual or business can benefit from the lower interest rate environment that dollarization will eventually bring about.

A successful dollarization process will typically be accompanied, therefore, by a wave of refinancing not very different from that observed in many countries that have experienced substantial reductions in their long-term interest rates in the recent past. The United States, for example, witnessed a wave of voluntary mortgage loan refinancing in the early 1990s, when the long-term interest rates experienced a large decline prompted by the expectations of fiscal surpluses that did indeed materialize a few years later.

There is no need, therefore, for the government to step in to the renegotiation of existing contracts, except indirectly, by guaranteeing free entry into the financial intermediation industry and by making sure that banks and financial institutions will not have enough market power to keep their customers captive with existing contractual arrangements.

Governments prone to exercise more direct forms of intervention in existing contracts on the eve of dollarization programs should pay heed to the Austral Plan experience related earlier. For the reasons already given, it is possible to make the argument that the government intervention in contracts implied by the plan's prescribed conversion mechanisms was, in the end, more distorting than intended.[22]

7.2.3   The Loss of Seignorage Problem

The literature on dollarization has repeatedly pointed out that a dollarizing country will necessarily give up the seignorage revenues it used to earn on its domestic currency. The loss of income arises because, as already explained in section 7.2.2, the dollarization process requires that the central bank of the dollarizing country buy back the entire outstanding money base with dollars. To accumulate the necessary amount of dollars in cash, the central bank of the dollarizing country must sell first the typically very liquid securities in its international reserves portfolio in exchange for the U.S. currency. In practice, this operation is a simple swap of U.S. securities for U.S. dollars, because a substantial fraction of the central banks' portfolios all over the world is composed of U.S. securities deposited with the U.S. Federal Reserve System.

When any central bank liquidates its position in U.S. securities, the Federal Reserve "swaps" those securities for dollars through a simple sequence of entries in its books. After the required record-keeping steps have been completed, the central bank of the dollarizing country withdraws the cash from its account with the Federal Reserve System and proceeds to exchange the domestic currency for the U.S. dollars.

Notice that in the process, the central bank of the dollarizing country has swapped an interest-bearing U.S. security for a non-interest-bearing one. This implies that the central bank of the dollarizing country will lose the interest payments it used to earn on the U.S. securities, that is, the seignorage revenues. The opposite is true for the United States: the swap implies that the U.S. Treasury no longer will have to pay interest on the U.S. securities that it has been able to buy back in exchange for non-interest-bearing ones. In other words, the United States will get to keep the seignorage (the interest payments) that before was captured by the dollarizing country.

The loss of seignorage revenues may discourage many countries from adopting the dollar as their currency and has motivated numerous proposals for "seignorage-sharing" agreements. The basic logic behind those proposals is that they are merely compensating mechanism schemes aimed at restoring the fiscal situation of both the United States and the dollarizing country to the same conditions that prevailed before the dollarization took place.

Although that basic proposition is true, it ignores an important aspect of the economics of seignorage: governments keep the monopoly of paper note issue precisely because they want to keep all the seignorage "rents" from lucrative money-printing activities. Thus, it is not clear why the government of any country will willingly give up any seignorage that it collects from foreigners.

From the perspective of the "seignior" issuing the notes, holders of those notes abroad are happy customers who must pay for the satisfaction they surely get from willingly holding the sovereign's notes in their portfolios. Nothing of value is given away or obtained for free, and, therefore, holders of the notes must pay for whatever service the notes provide them, in the form of the forgone interest on the alternative interest-bearing security they could have bought instead.

In fact, the whole point of producing a very stable currency is to increase the market share of that currency in the currency markets. The dollarization of foreign economies must be interpreted, therefore, as confirming the success of the marketing strategy behind producing a widely recognized and respected currency. It may not appear sensible, therefore, to expect that the producer of such high-quality notes will give back the additional earnings that motivated and justified the pursuit of a high-quality product strategy. Chances are, therefore, that the citizens of a country whose currency is being adopted by other nations will receive seignorage-sharing proposals with the same enthusiasm that a producer of high-quality tires would welcome the idea of sharing with a competitor the additional revenues it may obtain from successfully displacing from the market the low-quality, blowout-prone tires of that competitor.

Likewise, most seignorage-sharing agreements circulated in policy forums ignore the potential trade-off between seignorage-sharing arrangements and the quality, that is, the stability, of the dollar. The lower the seignorage revenues captured by the U.S. government, the lower the "option value" of the stability of the currency it issues and, therefore, the higher the risk that once many economies have dollarized, the United States will not resist the temptation to switch gears to a higher inflation rate. In other words, the lower the seignorage the United States receives from keeping a low inflation policy, the fewer the incentives it will have to continue producing "high-quality" money in the future. To continue with the previous analogy, the producer of high-quality tires would have no incentives to keep manufacturing them if it were not rewarded with higher profits than those of a low-quality-tire producer.[23]

Thus, there is the risk that seignorage-sharing agreements may become another one of those instances in which good intentions pave the road to hell. Graciously shared seignorage revenue may not be as generous a gesture as it appears. Shrewd customers may be right to be suspicious of the "free" offer, because this one may come with a higher inflation rate popping out of the box as soon as the package is opened. It might be wiser, in fact, to return the present unopened with a polite "thank you, but it is against our policies" note attached to it.

This normative implication no doubt goes against the conventional wisdom behind many seignorage-sharing proposals and might be received with skepticism and even uproar, but it follows naturally not only from the analogy with "brand name" products just suggested but also more formally from the analytical framework developed to address the optimality of "zero nominal interest rate" monetary policies (the celebrated "Friedman rule").

It is somewhat unfortunate, therefore, that the exclusive emphasis on the positive aspects of seignorage-sharing agreements has led to consideration of the issue as solely a matter of "goodwill" of the United States toward the countries adopting its currency. When normative considerations and economic incentives are introduced into the equation, however, the convenience of a commendable goodwill foreign policy approach may not be not as clear cut, because it may well cause the United States to abandon its predisposition for keeping its inflation low, that is, the very reason that made the adoption of the U.S. currency desirable in the first place.

Under the reinterpretation suggested by this more normative line of inquiry, dollarizing countries are not really "giving up" seignorage for nothing. Rather, they are buying price stability with it. And because that is the whole point of dollarizing an economy, it is a price well paid.[24] Therefore, the lack of seignorage-sharing agreements should not prevent countries from giving dollarization serious consideration.

In any case, it is fair to recognize that the normative considerations just presented are based exclusively on the issue of seignorage revenues from dollarization. But, as discussed at the introduction of this chapter, dollarization should be viewed only as one step in a more comprehensive, ambitious, and deliberate plan of financial and commercial integration into the global economy. To the extent that the United States will benefit from a closer integration with other economies, as the recent experience with the North American Free Trade Agreement (NAFTA) seems to demonstrate, seignorage-sharing agreements may act as the catalytic "goodwill" element necessary to encourage perhaps otherwise reluctant economies to embrace an effort whose gains can potentially overwhelm, for all the countries involved, including the United States, any mean-spirited seignorage revenue "bean counting."

To that end, it is important to present and evaluate in the next section some proposals for seignorage-sharing agreements that are being circulated or considered in different dollarization forums and in political institutions, such as the U.S. Congress.

7.2.4 Proposals to Alleviate the Loss of Seignorage Problem

Proposal of the U.S. Senate Joint Economic Committee
An important proposal has been prepared by the staff of the Economic Policy Subcommittee of the U.S. Senate Committee on Banking, Housing, and Urban Affairs and presented to the U.S. Congress by the Joint Economic Committee of that U.S. legislative body. It would take up more space than is available in this chapter to account for all the details of this carefully crafted proposal. This section will therefore present and discuss its fundamental features and direct the interested reader to the source for a complete version of the proposal.[25]

The guiding principle behind the Joint Economic Committee proposal (JEC proposal hereafter) is that seignorage sharing is a gesture of goodwill from the United States and not an entitlement for the countries that benefit from it. This implies that the proposal does not contemplate any international treaty involving complex multilateral negotiations but rather a bill that will be subject to the exclusive consideration of the U.S. Congress.

It is important to emphasize in that regard that the JEC proposal leaves open the possibility of a unilateral suspension of seignorage-sharing revenues by the U.S. government. However, the proposal does contain provisions for a "certification process" by which a country would gain access to its share of the U.S. seignorage revenues. The proposal considers qualification criteria in three areas: economic, legal, and political. A summary of the three criteria follows.

Economic: at least 75 percent of the country's local currency must have been exchanged for dollars, and all commercial and financial transactions must be quoted and carried out predominantly in dollars.

Legal: The dollar must have legal tender status, in the sense that it should be regarded as an acceptable means of payments for settling all contractual obligations and taxes in a court of law.

Political: A country should act in good faith and refrain from exploiting the seignorage-sharing agreement in any way that is detrimental to U.S. national interest. However, the United States should, in turn, abstain from withholding seignorage payments as a political weapon to interfere in the domestic affairs of the dollarizing country. Only under carefully specified circumstances, such as war against the United States or its allies or a military conflict, should a country be decertified.

According to the JEC, only Japan and a few countries in Europe (mostly those west of the Ukraine) and in Africa (those that being formerly in the franc zone belong now to the euro zone) will not be able to meet the criteria for qualification.

The JEC proposes to distribute the seignorage revenues to the dollarizing countries on a quarterly basis, according to the following formula:

Dollar amount of seignorage rebated to a dollarized country =
Net seignorage ×
Dollarized country's share of the U.S. dollar monetary base ×
Proportion of the seignorage revenue that the United States has agreed to distribute to the dollarized country,

where

Net seignorage =
Total average monetary base of the U.S. over the quarter ×
Average interest rate on 90-day Treasury bills during the period −
Net cost of operating the Federal Reserve System.

Discussion of each of the components of this formula follows.

Net Seignorage   The U.S. central bank, that is, the Federal Reserve, introduces money into circulation basically through open market operations. These operations swap government bonds for currency: the Federal Reserve buys high-rated securities, such as U.S. Treasury bills, from the public with notes and coins. The end result of an open market operation is that the Federal Reserve has issued non-interest-bearing liabilities, such as notes and coins, in exchange for interest-bearing ones.

The Federal Reserve profits from these open market operations because it gets to keep the interest that the U.S. Treasury pays on the stock of government bonds that end up in the Federal Reserve's portfolio as a result of those operations. These interest earnings are, precisely, the gross seignorage revenues the Federal Reserve obtains from successfully placing its notes among the public.

However, parts of those earnings must cover the costs of printing notes, minting coins, and operating the Federal Reserve System.[26] It seems only fair, then, that it is the seignorage net of those costs that is distributed back to the dollarized countries.

Average Interest on 90-day Treasury Bills during the Period   The JEC proposal suggests that the distribution of seignorage to the dollarizing countries should take place quarterly. The interest rate on the ninety-day Treasury bills seems a logical choice with which to calculate the seignorage revenues for the purpose of its distribution among the dollarized economies.

Dollarized Country's Share of the U.S. Dollar Monetary Base   Strictly speaking, the correct computation of the amount of seignorage that should be transferred to a given country depends on the amount of U.S. currency in circulation in that country. However, keeping track of the amount of U.S. currency in use in any country at any given point in time is an impossible task. Therefore, the JEC suggests that a country's share of seignorage revenues should be determined by dividing the relevant component of that country's money base by the U.S. monetary base at the time of dollarizing the economy.

The "relevant component" part of the formula for computing the country's share in seignorage refers to the fact that the money base of a country is typically divided between notes and coins in circulation and commercial banks' reserves at the central bank. Central banks typically keep the latter in the form of highly liquid interest-bearing securities such as U.S. Treasury bills. If all of the money base were used for the purpose of computing the country's seignorage share, the United States might eventually pay seignorage twice: once in the form of the interest payments on the U.S. securities acquired with the money base set aside as reserve requirements and a second time in the form of the seignorage rebates on such a portion of the money base. In other words, dollarizing countries would find a way to artificially increase their seignorage share with the simple expedient of increasing the reserve requirements of the banking system well above the technical ratio.[27] To avoid this "double-dipping" in seignorage revenues, the JEC proposal suggests calculating the seignorage share using only the currency part of the dollarizing country's monetary base.

For example, suppose that the money base of a dollarizing country about to dollarize is $24 billion, of which $16 billion correspond to currency in circulation, that is, notes and coins outside banks. That is the amount of the country's monetary base that should be used in computing that country's share in seignorage revenue. If the U.S. monetary base increased from $600 billion to $616 billion as a consequence of that country's dollarization, then that country's seignorage share would be 2.6 percent, as obtained from the calculation $16/\$616 = 0.0259$.

It is important to emphasize, however, that dollarizing countries could easily get around this double-dipping seignorage-prevention mechanism. For example, they could reduce reserve requirements to zero right before the dollarization were to take place, so the whole money base would be in currency in circulation and the seignorage share would be as large as possible. Once this action guaranteed that this share would be as high as it can get (3.9 percent in the example just presented) the dollarizing country could increase the reserve requirements again. Although there are ways to counteract such actions, they would certainly complicate the administration of the seignorage-sharing agreement, almost to the point of forcing the office in charge of managing and monitoring the system to keep track of changes in the financial intermediation regulatory body of each participating country.

Another complication of the JEC seignorage share determination mechanism is that incorporation of new countries into the system will reduce the share of already participating ones, although the dollar amount of the seignorage rebate received by each country will not fall and in fact will increase over time, with the growth of the U.S. monetary base.

Continuing with the preceding example, suppose that a year later another country dollarizes and joins the system and that its currency in circulation at that time is also \$16 billion. The seignorage shares for each country will be determined therefore by the calculation \$16/ \$632 = 0.0253. That is, the share of the country that was already dollarized will fall from approximately 2.6 percent to 2.5 percent. The dollar amount of the seignorage rebate will remain unchanged, however. The reason is that the decline in the seignorage share of the already dollarized countries will be exactly offset by the increase that the U.S. money base will experience as a result of a new country's dollarization.

It should be clear, therefore, that a constant inflow and outflow of participating countries or frequent changes in the reserve requirements imposed by their central banks would undermine the transparency, and therefore, feasibility of the system. This suggests that at the very least the seignorage-sharing mechanism should include provisions for excluding those countries that exit from the system from participating in it again, at least not until after a long "penance" period.

Proportion of the Seignorage Revenue That the United States Has Agreed to Distribute to the Dollarized Country   The JEC does not give any particular recommendation about which fraction of the seignorage revenues the United States should consider rebating to the dollarized countries. However, it is unlikely that 100 percent of the seignorage earned on currency circulating outside of the United States will be transferred to the beneficiary countries. This is because the net seignorage as set forth in the proposal does not include the expenses of administering the seignorage-sharing agreement, not necessarily negligible if the system requires, among other things, monitoring of the reserve requirement policies of the countries included in it. Besides, as explained earlier, distributing all the seignorage back to dollarizing countries may not be such a great idea, because it may not give the United States the right incentives to not inflate away the expanded monetary base that will eventually result from a worldwide spread dollarization process.

To help fix ideas, suppose that this proportion were established at 85 percent. Further, assume that the average interest rate on ninety-day Treasury bills were 5 percent over the period. Continuing with the previous example, the countries in the seignorage-sharing agreement would receive the following amount of seignorage revenue:

Dollar amount of seignorage rebated to a dollarized country =
($632 billion × 0.05 − $1.5 billion) × 0.0253 × 0.85 = $647 million.

Escape Clauses   Aware that dollarization is not necessarily an irreversible process, the JEC proposal contains provisions that require a periodic review of the dollarization status of the countries receiving the seignorage rebates, to make sure they still meet the criteria to participate in the system. Failure to recertify would result in automatic suspension of the seignorage payments to that country. The purpose of this recertification process should be only technical and mainly to determine that the dollar continues being the main currency in use and that a country has not switched in the interim period to a different currency zone, such as the euro or the yen.

Furthermore, the JEC proposal specifically contains provisions clearly stating that the voluntary sharing of seignorage does not imply the intention of the Federal Reserve System to provide LLR assistance to any of the beneficiary countries or perform any multinational central bank functions, such as those the European Central Bank offers the European Monetary Union.

The Lump Sum Payment Proposal

The seignorage-sharing system proposed by the JEC involves a constant stream of seignorage payments to the dollarized countries over time. Barro (1999) has recently proposed instead that the net present value of that stream of payments be given to the dollarized country up front in the form of a once and for all lump sum payment.

The advantage of this system is that it will front load the seignorage payments and provide the dollarizing country with the additional cash necessary to buy back the money base without the need of a large devaluation if international reserves are too low for that purpose at the predollarization exchange rate.

Another advantage of the lump-sum payment proposal is that the part of the payment not used up in the process of retiring the domestic currency from circulation could be applied to perform LLR functions, if required. In addition, this system will certainly eliminate the complications of administering a seignorage-sharing mechanism. The big and perhaps insurmountable drawback of this mechanism, however, is that it will deprive the United States from the threat of suspending seignorage payments to countries that decide to reintroduce the domestic currency after they have cashed the seignorage rebate.

The Monetary Association Treaty Proposal

A way to circumvent the shortcoming of the previous proposal is that the dollarizing country guarantees its dollarized status with a dollar-denominated, non-interest-bearing bond, redeemable upon demand only in the contingency that the country fails to pass the recertification process outlined by the JEC proposal. By virtue of a bilateral monetary association treaty, this bond would be swapped with the Federal Reserve for dollar notes.

One potentially serious drawback of this proposal is that the bond that the dollarizing country will issue as a guarantee will result in an increase of its outstanding external debt obligations, which may have the undesirable side effect of inducing an increase in the international interest rate the country will face. This problematic side effect will be addressed again in the next section, when discussing the LLR functions under dollarization.

It is not clear, anyway, what aspects of this monetary association proposal would be the subject of negotiations under an international (bilateral or multilateral) treaty. International agreements make sense when the parties involved can make mutual concessions. What a dollarizing country has to offer to the United States, within the strict boundaries of a monetary regime, is precisely the seignorage revenues that the United States would be asked, paradoxically, to rebate in exchange for perhaps lower-than-investment grade bonds. It is unlikely that U.S. citizens will find this proposition enticing, unless they see it associated with substantial benefits to the United

States from the more integrated world markets that a dollarization process will eventually help to bring about.

Finally, it is appropriate to close this section with the observation that an alleged advantage of all the seignorage-sharing proposals considered here is that the dollarizing countries participating in the scheme could apply the seignorage rebates from the United States to collateralize international credit lines with which to complement whatever funds those countries may have available to perform LLR functions. However, there are reasons to suspect that this theoretical possibility will encounter substantial obstacles in practice, as explained in the next section, devoted precisely to discuss the challenges that a dollarization regime poses for the LLR functions traditionally regarded as an inalienable attribute of effective, full-fledged central banks.

7.2.5   The Lender of Last Resort Problem and How to Solve It

It is often argued that a dollarizing country relinquishes to a foreign monetary authority the power to provide liquidity to its banking system. However, this is not strictly true. A country under a currency board or dollarization regime can still obtain currency with which to assist its banking sector. What it cannot do is print currency not backed by foreign reserves, and, dollarization advocates would quickly argue, it is not clear why that is a bad feature of the regime. Quite to the contrary, it may be a blessing in disguise. After all, bank bailouts may be an extremely expensive proposition, at least judging by the costs involved in the Mexican crisis of 1994 and the Asian crisis of 1997.

The perception that liquidity assistance through the central bank does not have costs is just an illusion, as has been repeatedly observed in the literature (see, for example, Hausmann and Powell 1999). History has proved that massive bailouts are in the end financed with increases in the public debt hidden in the central bank books. And in disguise or in the open, as discussed in section 7.2.1, such bailout packages involve potentially huge government transfers that must be paid for with taxes, as it would be the case, except in a more transparent fashion, in a dollarized country.

If the citizens of a country are ready to pay taxes to save their financial institutions from dreadful "systemic risks," they will surely prefer a transparent mechanism with which to do so to one in which they are kept in the dark about the actual monies the bailouts, however "patriotic," end up taking away from their pockets.

In fact, a dollarizing country wishing to be in conditions of providing assistance to solvent but troubled (allegedly only in the short-term) financial institutions could set up an LLR agency to that end. The fiscal authority will provide the necessary funds with the proceeds from current taxes or increases in the public debt. The exact amount of funds that the fiscal authority should make available to the LLR agency will depend on a number of factors, such as the frequency of financial crises, their impact on the real economy, and the government's taxation powers.

It is important to emphasize that however financed, such government agency will still play the role of an LLR and introduce into the economy, therefore, the moral hazard inherent to its trade. In particular, as discussed in section 7.2.1, financial institutions will have incentives to take on riskier investment projects than they would in the absence of such an agency, thus increasing the chances of a "systemic risk" crisis. For that reason, a "banking panic prevention fund" should not be too generous anyway.

In any case, the fact that currency boards have the same implication as dollarization for the LLR issue should be of some assistance in evaluating the options open to a dollarizing country in the contingency of a banking crisis. Countries considering dollarization could model the relevant institutional arrangements after those of the countries that operated or operate under currency board regimes, such as Argentina and Bulgaria, to mention a few.

Contingent Liquidity Facility

Argentina, for example, before its Convertibility Law was abandoned on January 6, 2002, had arranged "contingent liquidity" lines of credit with fourteen private banks that provided, in total, access to about $7 billion in cash that the Central Bank of Argentina could use to quench an incipient bank run. The contracts with the private banks had, on average, a maturity of three years and contained an "evergreen clause" by virtue of which they could be extended every three months for another three-month period. The cost of the premium for this "liquidity insurance" policy was roughly 250 basis points over London Inter Bank Offered Rate (LIBOR) at the end of 1999.

The lines of credit were collateralized, basically, with Argentina's bonds denominated in dollars whose market value had to meet a 20 percent "margin call" requirement. This meant that in the event that it decided to exercise the option to tap those credit lines, Argentina obtained $1 of cash for every $1.2 of the market value of those bonds. The contingent liquidity agreements contained provisions that ensured that this implicit 20 percent margin was maintained at all times. Thus, when the market price of the bonds offered as collateral declined by more than 5 percent, Argentina had to deliver additional bonds in the amount necessary to make sure that the market value of all the bonds placed as collateral exceeded by at least 20 percent the amount of the credit lines used. If the price of the bonds fell by more than 20 percent, the necessary additional collateral had to be make up in cash, rather than with additional bonds.[28]

The fact that the credit lines were collateralized with sovereign debt should make apparent that this contingent liquidity facility was, in reality, a fiscal instrument because, in the end, the public debt must be paid for with taxes. Therefore, nothing prevents the fiscal authority, rather than the central banks of dollarizing countries, from reaching similar agreements.

In fact, an argument can be made that in the interest of transparency, the fiscal authority of the dollarizing country, rather than its central bank, should be responsible for these kind of agreements. After all, the collateral that guarantees those credit lines will increase the public debt, an issue that falls clearly in the jurisdiction of the fiscal authority. This is even more so because the public debt issued to collateralize credit lines supporting LLR functions will, in the presence of borrowing constraints (which dollarizing countries almost surely will face) "crowd out" other credit lines that the fiscal authority could have obtained otherwise.[29]

In any case, contingent lines such as the one just described can provide a dollarizing country with some mechanism with which to confront potential liquidity squeezes in the financial sector. Thus, the amounts that Argentina could obtain under its contingent liquidity program represented about 9 percent of the total deposits in the financial system at the end of 1999. It is only fair to admit, however, that although such an amount is by no means negligible, it would be insufficient to stop a full-fledged bank run.[30]

For that reason, some proposals have suggested that arrangements like the one set up by Argentina can be complemented with additional credit lines collateralized with the seignorage rebates contemplated in the seignorage-sharing agreements described in the previous section. However, as was also mentioned there, those schemes come unavoidably associated with escape clauses that impinge on the seignorage rebates a conditionality that will surely impair their value as a collateral. There are reasons, therefore, to be skeptical that countries that dollarize will be able to perform LLR activities to the same extent as they allegedly could before the dollarization program.

On the other hand, it is unclear, as suggested earlier, that central banks should not face strict limits to their LLR functions, lest the citizens of the country involved don't mind their monetary authority taking on taxation powers typically reserved to the fiscal authority. Limits to LLR assistance should be regarded as a strength of a dollarization regime in those countries where past experience indicates that the monetary authority has used that function not just to confront a short-lived liquidity squeeze in the financial system, as it was supposed to, but rather to implement large-scale bailouts that more often than not result in corresponding increases of the public debt (and, therefore, of future taxes) without the explicit approval of institutions such as the parliament or congress, for which such decisions are typically reserved.

In any case, it is perhaps the perception of the clear limits dollarization imposes to the LLR functions that makes such a regime unattractive to policymakers and politicians who favor unlimited provision of liquidity to financial systems under the stress of "self-fulfilling" panics, that is, bank runs allegedly not supported by fundamentals. In that sense, a monetary union, the regime discussed in the next section, seems to offer a more attractive alternative.

7.3   Monetary Union

The main alternative to dollarization (apart from maintaining the status quo) is a formal monetary union and the creation of a new common currency. This is perhaps the most radical alternative to existing arrangements. It would take a lot longer to put in place than either a currency board or dollarization, but with the right institutional framework and sufficient popular support, it might stand a better chance of delivering long-term monetary stability, while avoiding some of the potentially thorny issues related to sovereignty that would accompany dollarization.

Monetary unions between sovereign nations are rare. The best example is the recently launched Economic and Monetary Union (EMU) between twelve of the fifteen members of the European Union (EU). Prior to the launch of EMU the most significant move to monetary union in recent years was the monetary unification (before political unification) of the former West and East Germany in 1990. In the case of EMU the monetary union was overlaid, so to speak, on an existing free trade area.[31] The literature on optimum currency areas suggests that two nations contemplating a monetary union ought to have strong trade ties with one another.[32] However, there is no reason in principle why, for example, a Latin American Monetary Union (LAMU) could not also include countries that are not currently members of existing free trade areas such as Mercosur.[33] Some recent authors have argued that the optimum currency area criteria are endogenous and increased trade flows will follow the creation of a monetary union.[34]

A monetary union could take one of two forms. The first is a sort of super currency board, where the participating countries would share a common currency that would be jointly managed by a central supranational institution but would be pegged to and fully backed by one or more of the world's major currencies (the dollar, the euro, or the yen). This is the essential nature of the monetary union proposed by Edwards (1998). The benefit of such an arrangement as opposed to, say, separate currency boards is that it would require an international treaty between the participating states, which would presumably make the commitment to the new arrangement all the more credible. Furthermore, insofar as there is not an obvious "anchor institution" in potential members of a potential LAMU (comparable to the role played by the Bundesbank in EMU) on which a new supranational institution could be modeled, a super currency board might be the only viable option. The second alternative is a monetary union along the lines of EMU. We are going to focus on this type for the rest of this section. We should note that most, if not all, of the preparatory work for an EMU-like arrangement would also need to be done for a super currency board, and vice versa. The essential difference would be the scope for independent action that the new common central bank would enjoy.

Europe's experience with launching and managing EMU provides a useful blueprint for what it would take to create a LAMU and what the end product might look like. The criteria typically used to evaluate the economics of EMU are the optimal currency area criteria first advanced by Robert Mundell (1961) and subsequently elaborated upon by McKinnon (1963) and Kenen (1969). We will not go into the question of whether the candidate countries satisfy the traditional criteria for an optimal currency area. It is interesting to note, however, that the fact that Europe does not seem to satisfy the traditional criteria for an optimum currency area has not prevented Mundell from becoming one of the most prominent supporters of EMU. Mundell's later writings on common currencies have tended to emphasize the gains in terms of monetary stability that monetary unions can bring about.[35]

It is well known that there is an important political dimension to EMU, the desire to create a European identity separate from that of the individual nation-states in the EU, to tie the countries of Europe so closely together as to preclude the possibility of conflicts of the sort that marred the first half of the twentieth century.[36] There does not appear to be a similar drive to create a new Latin American superstate to avoid future conflicts. However, arguably the desire to preclude a replay of the hyperinflations that plagued the region for much of the late twentieth century could provide the impetus to create and sustain a monetary union among the countries of Latin America.

What would such a monetary union entail? The creation of a monetary union would require that a myriad of constitutional and technical issues be addressed. At the constitutional level, a monetary union would require that the participating countries negotiate a treaty that would govern the terms of the union, create the institutions that would manage the common currency, and address the issue of how these institutions would be held accountable. At the technical level, a monetary union would require that the institutions charged with the management of the common currency have at their disposal the requisite tools for the job. This would require that the necessary statistical information be available to the new monetary authority and that the payments systems of the countries participating in the monetary union be integrated to allow funds to be transferred as easily across borders as within countries.

In what follows we will discuss some of these constitutional and technical issues in some detail. Because monetary unions are rare, we will refer regularly to the precedent set by the EU in setting up EMU. However, it should be noted that the Maastricht model is not the only route to a monetary union. An alternative route (and one proposed in the European context by Basevi et al. 1975 in the so-called All Saints' Day Manifesto) would be to create a parallel currency that could be freely used in all of the countries interested in forming a monetary union. This currency would circulate alongside the existing national currencies and would enjoy the same legal tender status. The currency would be governed by international treaty and would be managed by a supranational institution according to some rule. The idea behind the proposal of Basevi et al. is that if this parallel currency preserved its purchasing power better than any of the existing national currencies, then it would inevitably drive the other currencies out of circulation. The main argument in favor of the All Saints' Day approach is that the adoption of the new currency is a matter of choice for individual consumers and is not imposed. The mere existence of the alternative currency may suffice to achieve most of the stability gains of a formal monetary union. Note that the All Saints' Day approach would still entail addressing the sort of constitutional and technical issues that arose in the creation of EMU by the Maastricht route. Whether it would succeed is open to question. As noted earlier, there is a significant collective-good aspect to currency. Money is useful because others are willing to take it. Currency users will only be willing to switch to an alternative currency if they are reasonably confident that many others will switch also. Experience with hyperinflations suggests that even when a currency is losing its value rapidly, consumers are reluctant to switch to alternatives.

7.3.1 Constitutional Issues

The first step toward creating a monetary union would be to negotiate an international treaty creating the common currency and the institutions that would manage it. Such a treaty would need to have four key components. First, it would set down the timetable for the launch of the monetary union. Second, it would elaborate criteria for determining whether countries that wished to participate would be allowed to do so. Third, it would create the institutions that would manage the currency of the new monetary union. At a minimum a monetary union would need a supranational central bank to conduct monetary policy. Fourth, the treaty would have to specify the objectives of this new institution and various other institutional matters such as appointment procedures, voting rights, and capital subscription standards.

Negotiating and Ratifying a Treaty

The first step toward the creation of a monetary union would be the negotiation and ratification of an international treaty between the interested parties. Senior civil servants and central bankers from the different countries would work out the details of the treaty and would then present it to the heads of state or government of the various countries for approval. Depending on the national constitutions of the countries involved, the treaty would have to be ratified by one or both houses of the national parliaments and possibly put to the electorate in a referendum. It would seem that for a step so dramatic as abolition of national currencies and creation of a monetary union a referendum is essential even if not required by the national constitutions in order to ensure full public support for the new monetary regime.

The Maastricht Treaty, which forms the constitutional basis for EMU, was the outcome of negotiations between the (then twelve) governments of the EU and lasted about a year.[37] Before the negotiations, the heads of government had appointed a committee (the Delors Committee) to examine the ways in which the monetary union might come into existence. The treaty was agreed upon by the heads of state and government of the EU at a summit meeting in Maastricht, Netherlands, in December 1991 and subsequently ratified by national parliaments (albeit not without some difficulty) and electorates. It is important to note that the proposal for monetary union was not put to a referendum in all of the EU member states. In particular, in Germany the decision to proceed with EMU was made by the government and approved by parliament but was never brought before the electorate. Furthermore, support for the greater integration that monetary union implies is significantly greater among the business and political elites in the different countries than it is among the general electorate. When the Maastricht Treaty was first put to a referendum in Denmark in 1992, it was rejected by the slimmest of margins (50.7 percent of the electorate). It was only after the treaty was amended to address Danish concerns that it was approved, and it finally entered into force on November 1, 1993.

Timetable for Monetary Union

The creation of a monetary union is not something that could be easily accomplished overnight. Rather, it would need to follow a timetable to allow the necessary preparatory work to be done. The preparations would be along two dimensions: First, some degree of "convergence" will be needed if two or more countries are to adopt a common currency. The exact form this convergence should take is a matter for debate, and we will return to this issue later. Second, at a more mundane level, time will be needed to take care of the various technical issues to address prior to the creation of a monetary union.

At the level of economic policy and performance, it is essential that countries considering a monetary union begin coordinating their economic policies long before the formal launch of the monetary union. This would start with sharing information on proposed spending and taxation plans, but more importantly would involve beginning to think of policy as a matter of common concern. There is some debate over just how much harmonization of fiscal policies is needed for a monetary union to work, but clearly if a group of countries are going to share a currency and jointly manage it, they might not want to spring policy surprises on each other. A treaty creating a Latin American Monetary Union would need to specify when the formal union would be launched. One option would be to make the launch date conditional on achieving some degree of convergence (however defined) by all the countries involved. A risk associated with this approach is that the decision to launch the monetary union might be postponed indefinitely. A second option would be that the treaty could specify a set date for the beginning of the monetary union and for the replacement of the national currencies with the new currency.

Again, looking to the precedent set by EMU is instructive. The Maastricht Treaty specified a three-stage transition to full monetary union. Stage 1 was deemed to have begun on July 1, 1990, with the abolition of all restrictions on movements of capital within the EU. Stage 2 of EMU began on January 1, 1994 after the Maastricht Treaty had been ratified by all of its signatories. Stage 2 of EMU was to be a period of enhanced monetary cooperation between the state members of the EU with the objective of facilitating the transition to full monetary union at some specified future date. Article 109j of the Maastricht Treaty stipulates: "If by the end of 1997 the date for the beginning of the third stage has not been set, the third stage shall start on 1 January 1999" EU (1995). In fulfillment of this clause, Stage 3 began on the latter date, with the irrevocable locking of the exchange rates of eleven EU members, joined later by Greece on January 1, 2001. The governments of the EU agreed to a three-year transition period before the circulating stocks of national currencies were replaced by euro notes and coins, and the transition to EMU was completed by February 2002, when the legacy currencies of the participating currencies had been completely replaced by the euro. There is some debate as to whether the three-year transition period between the formal start of EMU and the introduction of the euro notes and coins was really necessary. In retrospect it appears that a shorter transition period might have been preferable, although at the time the Maastricht Treaty was being written it was probably not obvious that the launch of EMU would go as well as it did.

From initiation (with the appointment of the Delors Committee in 1988) to completion (with the introduction of euro notes and coins in 2002), the launch of EMU will have taken nearly fifteen years. Arguably this is the *minimum* amount of time needed to launch a monetary union between sovereign states. It is worth noting that the countries of the EU had considered monetary union proposals before (most notably in the Werner Report of 1970). It was only in the late 1980s and early 1990s that the confluence of economic and (importantly) political factors was just right for the launch of the EMU process. We should also bear in mind that the process leading to EMU was nearly derailed by the currency crisis of 1992–1993, and up until launch there were concerns that the project could collapse because of constitutional challenges in individual members states (the project was not and is not uniformly popular across the EU) or speculative attacks on candidate countries.[38] Table 7.2 sketches a hypothetical timeline for the creation of a monetary union by the Maastricht route.

Convergence Criteria

Any treaty creating a monetary union will also have to specify the criteria (if any) to be used in assessing the suitability of individual

Table 7.2
Timetable for creation of a Latin American Monetary Union by the Maastricht route

Steps	Time
Decision made to create a Latin American Monetary Union between two or more members of Mercosur	T
Negotiate treaty	$T + 1$–2 years
Creation of Latin American Monetary Institute	$T + 2$–3 years
Convergence period	$T + 3$–5 years?
Creation of Latin American Central Bank	$T + 6$ years
Formal launch of LAMU and introduction of notes and coins	$T + 5$–7 years

countries for participation in the union. The traditional literature on optimum currency areas suggests a number of criteria that countries should satisfy if they are to share a common currency. In Mundell's original contribution (1961) the emphasis was on factor mobility, in particular, labor mobility. If a group of countries are to share a common currency it is important that factors of production be mobile between them to ease adjustment following shocks. The subsequent literature has emphasized additional factors such as a high degree of trade integration, the degree of diversification of production, and the extent to which national business cycles are synchronized.

The Maastricht Treaty laid down four convergence criteria that were used to assess the candidacies of EU countries for EMU.[39] Interestingly none of these convergence criteria dealt with the sort of real factors emphasized by the academic literature as making for successful monetary unions. The Maastricht criteria were (and remain for countries contemplating entry to EMU at some point in the future):

· An annual rate of inflation that is no more than 1.5 percentage points above the average of the three best-performing countries.

· A sustainable fiscal position, as reflected in a government budget deficit of no more than 3 percent of GDP and a government debt–GDP ratio of no more than 60 percent of (GDP).

· Observance of the normal fluctuation bands of the Exchange Rate Mechanism (ERM) without devaluation against the currency of any other member state during the previous two years.

· An average nominal long-term interest rate that is no more than two percentage points above that of the three best-performing countries in terms of price stability.

Some observations about these criteria are warranted. The inflation criterion was specified in relative rather than absolute terms—inflation performance was to be judged relative to the three best-performing countries. Likewise, the sustainability of convergence (as reflected in the level of long-term interest rates) was assessed in relative terms. The requirement that candidates observe the normal fluctuation bands of the ERM for at least two years essentially means that inflation rates and interest rates had to converge to German levels prior to the start of EMU. Finally, the public finance criteria were arrived at somewhat arbitrarily. The chosen target value for the debt to GDP ratio of 60 percent happened to be about the average ratio in the EU at the time (see Bini-Smaghi, Padoa-Schioppa, and Papadia 1994) and was not chosen because it was in some sense felt to be the optimal level. Likewise, the choice of a 3 percent deficit to GDP ratio was arrived at somewhat arbitrarily, although as a matter of arithmetic a 3 percent value is consistent with a long-run debt-to-GDP ratio of 60 percent if long-run nominal GDP growth is 5 percent a year.[40] Furthermore, these criteria were to be applied with some flexibility. Article 104c of the Maastricht Treaty allows that countries could be judged to have met the deficit criterion if "the ratio has declined substantially and continuously and reached a level that comes close to the [3 percent] reference value" or if "the excess over the reference value is only exceptional and temporary and the ratio remains close to the reference value." The same article also allows for the possibility that the debt-to-GDP criterion could be deemed to have been met if "the ratio is sufficiently diminishing and approaching the [60 percent] reference value at a satisfactory pace." When the time came to make the decision about which countries would enter EMU in the first wave, both Italy and Belgium were deemed to have satisfied the criteria for participation despite having debt-to-GDP ratios in excess of 100 percent.

Institutions

The treaty governing a potential LAMU will also have to create the institutions needed to manage the monetary union. At a minimum, the treaty would need to create a central bank to manage the common currency. Would national central banks be abolished and replaced by a single supranational institution charged with management of the new common currency? Or would the national central banks continue to exist and play a role like the regional Federal Reserve Banks in the U.S. Federal Reserve System or the National Central Banks in the European System of Central Banks? If the option of a federal system of central banks were chosen, with a Latin American Central Bank at the center, how would power be distributed between the existing national central banks and the new institution? Would the central policymaking committee be dominated by the center (as in the U.S. Federal Reserve System) or by the national central banks (as in the European System of Central Banks)? It is worth noting that the present highly centralized structure of the Federal Reserve System was not how the system was originally set up. When the Federal Reserve System was first set up, the regional banks were more powerful than the Board of Governors, with the Federal Reserve Bank of New York playing a particularly important role. It was only with the passage of the Banking Acts of 1933 and 1935 that the institutional structure that we know today was created (with a Federal Open Market Committee for making monetary policy decisions dominated by the Board of Governors). Some have argued that the more diffuse distribution of power in the European System of Central Banks poses an important threat to the viability of EMU.[41] Would the new central bank or system of central banks operate as a central bank in the traditional sense or as a super currency board? This question gets to the very heart of the issue of just how much monetary sovereignty the countries would be willing to give up for the sake of monetary stability.

Again, looking to the experience of Europe with EMU is instructive. The Maastricht Treaty specifies the institutions that would manage EMU. It contains provisions for the creation of the European Central Bank (ECB), which manages the euro, and the European Monetary Institute, which managed the transition from stage 2 to stage 3.[42] It also lays down the primary objective of the ECB ("price stability"), the terms of office for members of the Executive Board of the ECB, and the myriad of other details needing to be addressed to allow the ECB to take over the conduct for monetary policy for the euro area. The Treaty also specifies the nature of the relationship between the ECB and other EU institutions. Here the EU is at a distinct advantage relative to other groups of countries contemplating monetary union. The process of integration that began with the creation of the European Coal and Steel Community in 1952 has lead over the years to the development of an array of supranational institutions, such as the European Commission, the European Parliament, and the European Court of Justice, that play a key role in managing the EU. For example, the European Commission plays a crucial role in harmonizing statistical practices across the EU, something essential if the ECB is to have the statistical information necessary to allow it to conduct monetary policy for the euro area. The ECB must address an annual report to and testify before the European Parliament on a regular basis, thereby meeting the democratic accountability requirements of an independent central bank.[43] The European Court of Justice ensures that the various treaties governing the EU and European law are interpreted correctly and applied uniformly across the EU.

Is a Lengthy Transition Needed?

We have been using EMU as a model for how a Latin American Monetary Union might be created. One of the key features of EMU was the lengthy transition period and the requirement that candidate countries satisfy the convergence criteria laid down in the Maastricht Treaty. It is important to note that the approach to monetary union laid out in the Maastricht Treaty is not without critics. Some have argued that the convergence criteria unnecessarily subjected most of Europe to a decade of slow growth and high unemployment.[44] The critics point to the fact that German monetary unification was accomplished in a little more than six months: the decision to create a monetary union between the former West and East Germany was made in late 1989, and by July 1, 1990, German monetary union was a reality.

However, even if it is *feasible* to implement a monetary union quickly, there remains the question of whether it is in all circumstances *desirable* to do so. There are important differences between, on the one hand, German monetary union, and, on the other, monetary union between the countries of the EU or a potential Latin American Monetary Union. German monetary unification amounted to the adoption of an existing currency by a political entity that was to be merged with an existing state. No new institutions needed to be created to manage the currency of the unified entity: the Bundesbank was simply reorganized to include representatives from the former East German states. German monetary unification is similar to a hypothetical symmetric monetary union between the countries of NAFTA, where Canada and Mexico would adopt the U.S. dollar and obtain the right to vote on the setting of interest rates.[45] It is true that asymmetric monetary unions can be implemented relatively quickly (as the recent example of Ecuador shows), but symmetric monetary unions based on a new currency by their nature take time to put in place.

Although some transition period thus seems warranted, arguably the transition in EMU was longer than was necessary to accomplish all of the technical tasks (discussed in the following section) that need to be carried out to create a viable and credible single currency area. As noted, it will be almost fifteen years from when the Maastricht Treaty was signed to when euro notes and coins fully replace existing national currencies. It has been argued that the final three years of this transition period, when the euro came into being as the de facto currency of the participating nations but did not yet exist in the form of notes and coins, is essentially redundant and the notes and coins should have been introduced as soon as the decision had been made to proceed with EMU. Arguably, by introducing the notes and coins at the same time the new currency is introduced makes the monetary reform associated with monetary union all the more real for the "man in the street." By allowing a final transition period between the creation of the monetary union and the introduction of the notes and coins, participating nations seem to be given one last chance to opt out.

7.3.2   Technical Issues

Creating a monetary union entails addressing a myriad a technical questions that typically do not appear in the academic literature on optimum currency areas or monetary unions. These issues are all relatively straightforward, and they range from the mundane issue of what denominations the new currency will be issued in and where the "coin-note" boundary will be, to harmonization of statistics (either for the purposes of assessing compliance with convergence criteria or for the purpose of putting the statistical infrastructure in place for the new central-banking institutions), to linking national payment systems together to create a single money market.

Statistical Infrastructure

Consistent application of convergence criteria for participation in a monetary union (assuming that the Maastricht route is followed) requires that government accounts be kept on a consistent basis across all countries; that GDP be measured on a consistent basis across all countries; that inflation be measured on a consistent basis across all countries; and that there be a long-term bond with common liquidity characteristics issued by all countries.[46] Within the EU, national accounts are constructed using the ESA95 version of the European System of Accounts under the aegis of Eurostat, the statistical office of the EU. Inflation measurement is based on the Harmonised Index of Consumer Prices (HICP). The HICP program uses a common price concept for all fifteen EU countries (household final monetary consumption) and differs in significant respects from the national consumer price indexes (CPIs). However, even after almost a decade of harmonization there are important differences in how the different countries that participate in EMU go about measuring inflation at the consumer level.

Statistical harmonization prior to the creation of a LAMU would greatly facilitate the job of the Latin American Central Bank (LACB) after monetary union starts. Monetary policy for the LAMU area would require an areawide perspective, which (assuming that statistics continue to be collected primarily at the national level) will require measures of real activity, inflation, and the financial sector for different countries that can easily be aggregated. Measurement of broad monetary aggregates (such as M1, M2, and M3) will need to be done on a consistent basis to allow the construction of areawide aggregates.[47]

Again looking at the experience of Europe in establishing EMU gives one a sense of the magnitude of the task involved. Before EMU there were significant differences in measures of the money stock across the EU. Although this might to some extent be expected when looking at broad aggregates, even the narrow aggregate (money base) was not defined the same way in all countries. These differences are discussed at some length in European Central Bank (1999).

Payment System

Another major technical challenge to a LAMU would be the creation of an integrated infrastructure for the payment system. A single monetary policy will require that individuals be able to move funds as freely within the single currency area as they now do within national borders. One of the key challenges facing the architects of EMU was to create an EU-wide payment system that linked together the payment systems of the fifteen countries. The result was the TARGET system (Trans-European Automated Real-time Gross settlement Express Transfer), which consists of the fifteen national settlement systems and the ECB payment mechanism. This system began operation on January 4, 1999, and handles the bulk of the high-value transfers within the euro area. The success of the system is apparent in the rapid elimination of money market spreads shortly after the start of EMU.

Currency

An additional technical issue that will need to be addressed is the design of the new currency. What will the common currency be called, what will it look like, and what symbol will be used to denote it? Prior to the decision to name the new European currency the euro, there were proposals to name the currency the ecu, the Euro-dollar, the eurofranc, the euromark or the Europa.

What denominations will be issued? In creating EMU, the EU agreed that euro banknotes will not carry any national symbols but will instead be representative of Europe as a whole.[48] Note issuance is the exclusive domain of the ECB. Euro coins will be issued by national treasuries, subject to ECB approval, and will carry national symbols. The denominational structure settled on by the EU follows the so-called binary-decimal (1-2-5) pattern. Coins will be issued at 1, 2, 5, 10, 20, and 50 euro cent denominations and at 1 and 2 euro denominations. Notes will be issued at denominations of 5, 10, 20, 50, 100, 200, and 500 euro.

The current denominational structure of the Argentine peso and the Uruguayan peso approximately follow the binary-decimal pattern, whereas the denomination structure of the Brazilian real and the Paraguayan guarani follow the fractional decimal (1-5) system. A common currency with a denominational structure that followed the binary-decimal system would probably offer the most flexibility to currency users.

Finally, the nations will need to agree on the coin-note boundary: What will be the highest denominated coin and the lowest denominated note? At the time of writing, the purchasing power in dollars of the lowest denominated circulating note in Argentina (the Argentine one peso note) was almost twice the purchasing power of the lowest denominated circulating note in Brazil (the one real note), although Brazil also issues a coin at this denomination. The highest denominated circulating note in Brazil is the 100-real note, whose purchasing power in dollars is (currently) about half that of the highest denominated circulating Argentine note.

Once the design of the currency is agreed on, it will need to be decided when to introduce the notes and coins. As noted earlier, the EU took a rather conservative approach in this regard, allowing for a three-year transition period following the start of EMU before the euro notes and coins were introduced. At the time, it was argued that a long transition period was needed to allow all the needed coins to be minted and the notes to be printed. Plus, the private sector operators of the physical payment infrastructure (vending machines, etc.) needed time to recalibrate their equipment. In retrospect, it now seems that the three-year transition is longer than necessary. For Latin American countries contemplating a monetary union, the costs of adjusting the physical payment infrastructure to handle a new currency are probably smaller than the costs faced by Europeans, due to the recent experience of most Latin American countries with high inflation. Also, it might be possible to introduce the notes before the coins: it is with the latter that the largest costs of adopting the payments infrastructure would be incurred. Experience with monetary reforms in Latin America over the past two decades suggests that it should be possible to completely replace the existing stocks of national notes with a new common currency relatively quickly.

Finally, recall that the three-year transition between the creation of the euro and the introduction of euro notes and coins was interpreted by some as giving countries that are less than enthusiastic about EMU one last chance of opting out: the costs of doing so will be a lot greater once the national currencies have been completely eliminated. If one of the objectives of monetary union is to shift to a new, more stable, monetary regime, and the move has popular support, delaying it any longer than is absolutely necessary makes little sense.

Allocation of Seignorage

Under monetary union, seignorage income will accrue to the new central bank or system of central banks rather than to the national central banks. It will need to be decided how this revenue should be used. Will this revenue be retained by the new central bank, used to finance expenses of other institutions created to manage the monetary union, or rebated to national governments? Will the seignorage be booked by the national central banks (if the federal model is adopted), with the central institution obtaining a share only after submitting a budget? One option would be to use seignorage revenue to finance the operations of other common institutions created to manage the monetary union and make the new central-banking institutions accountable to the electorate. Alternatively, the revenue could be returned to national treasuries to finance national government expenditures. This is the option chosen by the EU. Article 32 of the Statute of the ECB provides for the allocation of the ECB's seignorage income to the national central banks on the basis of a weighting scheme in which each country's weight is equal to the sum of 50 percent of the country's share of EU population and 50 percent of its share of EU GDP.

Institutional Setting, Financial Stability, and Other Issues

What other institutions, if any, would be needed for a Latin American Monetary Union to succeed? A common assembly along the lines of the European Parliament to which the LACB would be accountable for its actions? A court for adjudicating disputes? Restrictions on fiscal policy at the national level? An economic government to balance the new monetary institutions? A new financial regulator? Let us consider each of these issues in turn.

In recent years there has emerged a consensus among students of monetary policy that independent central banks typically do a better job at delivering long-term price stability than do banks that are subject to a lot of direct political control. Politicians' growing appreciation of this fact has led to significant reforms of central bank legislation in a number of countries, granting central banks the sort of independence that for much of the postwar period was enjoyed only by Germany's Bundesbank. In May 1997 the just-elected Labor government in the United Kingdom granted the Bank of England full operational independence, whereas article 107 of the Maastricht Treaty stipulates that "neither the ECB, nor a national central bank, nor any member of their decision-making bodies shall seek or take instructions from Community institutions or bodies, from any government of a Member State or from any other body." However, the quid pro quo for independence of this sort is that the central bank should be accountable for its actions and decisions. The Bank of England is accountable to the chancellor of the Exchequer in Britain, and through him to the United Kingdom's parliament. The ECB is accountable to the European Parliament, although some have argued that the European Parliament lacks the stature needed to fulfill the needs of accountability. Critics claim that EMU (and the EU in general) suffers from a "democratic deficit" that threatens to undermine the enterprise in the long run. The long-term viability of EMU, they argue, requires strengthening the European Parliament and eventually a move toward political union.

To whom would an independent Latin American Central Bank be accountable for its actions? Making the LACB accountable to each of the national parliaments is not really feasible. It would hamper the development of a monetary-union-wide perspective on policy. Furthermore, even in a well-functioning monetary union, regional conflicts of interest will develop, as different regions will occasionally find themselves at different stages in the business cycle. Absent a directly elected common deliberative body, a committee of representatives from each of the national parliaments might serve the needs of accountability in the short run. However, in the long term the question of political integration of some sort would have to be addressed.

In addition to an elected body to which the LACB would be accountable, there would also be a need for an institution to adjudicate disputes between participants in the monetary union. Even with the best of intentions, disputes will arise over the interpretation of the treaty that creates the monetary union and about the decisions of the LACB. Clearly, it will not be feasible to leave the adjudication of these issues to national courts: some form of supranational or international court will be needed and the decisions of this court will need to be binding on all participants in the monetary union.

Is there a need for an "economic government" to act as a counterweight to the central bank in LAMU? A source of ongoing tension in EMU is the issue of whether the ECB's power needs in some sense to be balanced on the fiscal side by an economic government for the euro area. Does the existence of a single monetary policy for the euro area mean that a single fiscal policy is needed also? Creation of a monetary union will make tax differences within the monetary union all the more transparent and will promote the flow of mobile factors to low-tax regions. This will put pressure on the high-tax states to either cut taxes or seek to have tax rates harmonized (up) across the monetary union. A more controversial line of argument for fiscal rules in a monetary union can be made from the perspective of the fiscal theory of the price level. Sims (1998) argues that the rigid delinking of the fiscal and monetary authorities in EMU (through treaty prohibitions on ECB financing of national government deficits) will create problems. Arguing from the perspective of the fiscal theory of the price level, Sims argues that the fiscal policy provisions of the Maastricht Treaty call for a passive fiscal policy. When combined with an active monetary policy (one that stabilizes a monetary aggregate or increases interest rates when inflation rises), the possibility emerges of a self-sustaining inflation that drives the value of the money stock to zero. This possibility can only be ruled out by a commitment on the part of the fiscal authorities to put a floor under the value of the currency. However, with fiscal policy decentralized to the national governments, such a commitment might be difficult to make and certainly difficult to make credible.

Finally, we come to the issue of financial sector supervision and regulation. Assuming that the creation of a Latin American Monetary Union is accompanied by free trade in financial services, it seems reasonable to expect that financial institutions will begin to operate on a monetary-union-wide scale. The question then arises of how these institutions will be supervised and regulated and who will act as lender of last resort in the event of a financial crisis. One option would be to leave these responsibilities with the institutions that currently have them but to promote closer ties between national regulators. This would be in keeping with the narrow concept of central banking found in the Maastricht Treaty, in which the ECB focuses on price stability and financial sector supervision and regulation is left in the hands of national authorities.[49] The risk of this approach is that when a crisis hits, the central bank does not have at its disposal information for assessing the need for it to provide LLR services. A superior arrangement would appear to be to consolidate the supervision and regulation functions in parallel with the central-banking function when creating the monetary union and to ensure that the new central bank has full and regular access to information on the health of financial institutions based in the monetary union.

7.4 Conclusions

In this chapter we have attempted to give a basic description of what either dollarization or the creation of a monetary union would entail for the countries adopting either regime. As noted in the introduction, we have not addressed the question of whether adoption of either regime would be welfare enhancing in an economic sense. Rather, we have attempted to explain what the move to such a regime would entail given that it were decided that such a move would be in the best interest of a nation.

In our discussion of dollarization we have addressed a number of technical issues that would arise in the process of replacing a national currency with the dollar. Foremost among these issues is what other reforms would be needed to make dollarization a success. We have also examined the question of seignorage losses that would accompany dollarization and the various proposals that have been put forward to offset these losses.

Many of the theoretical issues that arise in contemplating dollarization are relevant to monetary union proposals. However, as our discussion of monetary unions should have made clear, the creation of a Latin American Monetary Union (along EMU lines) would be a massive undertaking. We noted that the Maastricht Route to EMU was probably excessively cautious, leaving plenty of time for less-than-fully-committed countries to back out. However, the massive amount of technical work that would need to be done prior to the creation of a Latin American Monetary Union means that it would be unrealistic to expect that such an arrangement could come about in less than 7 years. As mentioned in the introduction, all these guidelines and issues are general enough to be valid for prospect monetary unions in any region of the world.

Notes

All three authors are economists at the Research Department of the Federal Reserve Bank of Dallas. William C. Gruben is vice president and director of the Center for Latin American Economies, Mark A. Wynne is assistant vice president, and Carlos E. J. M. Zarazaga is senior economist and executive director of the Center for Latin American Economies. The corresponding author is Carlos Zarazaga: FRB Dallas, 2200 N. Pearl St., Dallas, TX 75201; e-mail: ⟨clae@dal.frb.org⟩. The views expressed in this chapter are those of the authors and do not necessarily reflect the positions of the Federal Reserve Bank of Dallas or the Federal Reserve System.

1. Essential references include Kenen (1995), Eichengreen (1997), Ungerer (1997), De Grauwe (1999), and Gros and Thygesen (1998).

2. There have been proposals to set up some sort of seignorage sharing arrangements with countries that dollarize. This hybrid form of dollarization would be similar in many respects to a currency board arrangement.

3. Say, in the form of one member from each country in the FOMC Board of Governors and the appointment of the governors of the Bank of Canada and the Bank of Mexico as permanent voting members of the FOMC.

4. As proposed in Edwards (1998).

5. "When to Dollarize." This paper, along with the proceedings of the conference, can be found on the Dallas Fed Website: ⟨www.dallasfed.org⟩.

6. Drazen (1999) shows how a monetary regime such as dollarization is consistent with the democratic principle of popular control. The loss of exclusive domestic sovereignty over monetary policy that such a regime entails is in keeping with constitutionalism, as long as the electorate supports the decision. The difference between dollarization or monetary union and simply granting a central bank independence to pursue sound monetary policy is one of degree, not substance. A society may well decide that the putative gains from dollarization or monetary union outweigh the costs in terms of loss of domestic sovereignty over monetary policy.

7. It is significant that the Maastricht Treaty was not put to a referendum in all EU countries, and in particular Germany. It is well documented that support for EMU among the German electorate has always been at best lukewarm. Some have argued that the failure to solidify popular support before moving to EMU may doom the monetary union in the long run.

8. It is important to mention, however, that Sims's results hinge critically on the standard assumption that government spending is invariant to the monetary regime in place. This assumption is the one likely to be targeted for criticism by those who maintain that monetary and fiscal institutions do affect the ability of societies to choose fiscal policies that exclude default in the sovereign debt along the equilibrium path.

9. The only source of concern is that the exchange rate resulting from the application of the preceding formula gave rise to a serious currency denomination divisibility problem. For example, that would be the case if the exchange rate determined by the above procedure turned out to be a penny, the smallest denomination in the U.S. currency system. However, this is a theoretical possibility that may emerge only in extreme hyperinflationary conditions that have driven the real value of the money base virtually to zero. In such economies the dollar will be typically widely used as currency and the dollarization process will do nothing but to formalize what it is already standard practice.

10. In this sense, government intervention in private contracts will have the same effect as an LLR has on risk management. It is well known that the prospect of financial bailouts induces financial institutions to take more risks than they would otherwise.

11. Unfortunately, Argentine courts seem to have missed Vélez Sarsfield's insights when in the 1960s they made several rulings validating the doctrine of *lesión enorme* and the theory of imprevision, paving the way to the formal incorporation of these principles in the civil code in 1968.

12. Despite this declaration of faith, the policymakers of the time sought reassurance in a sophisticated array of price controls throughout the economy.

13. Economic Commission for Latin America and the Caribbean (1985, 96).

14. Economic Commission for Latin America and the Caribbean (1986).

15. Economic Commission for Latin America and the Caribbean (1985, 96).

16. Economic Commission for Latin America and the Caribbean (1986).

17. Such a high real rate would not have been unreasonable at a time when Argentina was in default on its sovereign debt and the country-risk premium was extremely high, as reflected in the implicit yearly return of 10 percent or more on dollar-denominated government securities (the so-called BONEX.)

18. It is not necessarily true, therefore, that those investors suffered from "monetary illusion" (see CEPAL, ECLAC, 1986, p. 164). The only illusion investors may have suffered is that the government would not tamper with their contracts.

19. The payment of existing deposits in dollars had been suspended for 120 days and new deposits in that currency forbidden on May 20, 1985, about a month before the Austral Plan was launched.

20. Perhaps this apparent inconsistency in expectation gives away the true reason for the Austral Plan's prescribed mechanism for conversion of existing contractual arrangements: the motivation may not have been so much preventing "undesired" (however defined) transfers of wealth but, rather, sustaining the stability of the financial system, in very precarious shape since the liquidation of an important private bank (Banco de Italia) the immediately preceding April. The financial institutions would have had trouble honoring the hefty real returns most depositors would have obtained after the deceleration of the inflation rate, unless those institutions were able to recall loans in their portfolio and extract from borrowers an equivalent amount of real resources, a transfer that might have been difficult to implement in the recessionary conditions prevailing at the time.

21. Because the euro did not exist yet, the currency of reference was the ecu, the unit of account created in the late 1970s in the context of the European Monetary System and whose exchange rate with the euro was set at one as of December 31, 1998. The legal consequences of this procedure and its ability to withstand scrutiny by courts of law were thoroughly evaluated by Lenihan (1997).

22. In fact, it would not be unwarranted to assert that the very high returns investors seem to have been demanding from Argentina during the 1990s and the beginning of the twenty-first century are related to the abuses with existing contractual arrangements they experienced during the past. The investors' fears were specially reinforced in the 1980s when, after a sequence of devaluations in 1981, Argentine courts made several rulings that implied the modification of contracts, mostly in favor of borrowers, invoking the so-called imprevision theory that had been introduced in the civil code in 1968. "Paranoid" investors' behavior is understandable in a country where not only contractual arrangements have been overridden but also deposits have been frozen or overtly or covertly confiscated on numerous occasions in the past.

23. The basic intuition for this result is that a government will resist the temptation to inflate away an expanded monetary base only if it is rewarded with the future seignorage payments it will obtain from keeping the currency it produces widely

accepted. The government will struggle not to succumb to that temptation the minute a seignorage-sharing scheme takes away the reward of future seignorage revenues.

24. Of course, this reasoning will lead the citizens of a country considering dollarization to wonder what prevents their own country from producing an equally high-quality note. Dollarization advocates usually conjure up the "original sin" problem, to which dollarization critics wittily respond that the faithful also believe in redemption.

25. A more complete version of the proposal can be found in the April 1999 Joint Economic Committee Staff Report "Encouraging Official Dollarization in Emerging Markets," posted on the Website of the U.S. Congress Joint Economic Committee, ⟨www.senate.gov/~jec⟩, under the JEC reports section. The site also contains other background material of great relevance for the dollarization debate.

26. In recent years, those costs have represented an amount of about $1.5 billion.

27. This recourse will be of limited use under dollarization, however, because it is equivalent to a tax on banking activities, which will be hard to maintain in the environment of more financial integration in global markets that the dollarization should bring about. As pointed out by Hausmann and Powell (1999), too high a reserve requirement will simply put domestic banks out of business at the hands of offshore financial intermediaries.

28. For a more detailed description of the terms of this liquidity facility, see Gavin and Powell (1998.)

29. In the case of Argentina, for example, its central bank may have obtained the credit lines negotiated under the contingent liquidity facility at the expense of reducing or making more expensive the amounts that the treasury of that country can borrow in domestic and international capital markets.

30. In fact, this facility proved to be insufficient to stop the bank run that Argentina started to experience in the second quarter of 2001 and ended up in the suspension of payments of all bank deposits on December 1, 2001 (the so-called corralito). See Levy Yeyati and Sturzenegger (2000) and Broda and Levy Yeyati in chapter 4 of this volume for other significant limitations of this kind of LLR facilities.

31. Kohler (1998) elucidates the advantages of having monetary unions coincide with customs unions or free trade areas.

32. This criterion was emphasized by McKinnon (1963).

33. As mentioned in the introduction, we focus here on the example of Latin American countries, but the conclusions drawn here can be easily extended to other cases.

34. See, for example, Frankel and Rose (1998).

35. See, for example, Mundell (1973, 1998a, 1998b).

36. The political dimension to monetary union was present in spades when the decision was made to create a monetary union between West and East Germany. For a recent discussion see, for example, Lindsey (1999), especially pages 97–114.

37. For details on the negotiations leading up to the Maastricht Treaty, see Italianer (1993), Sandholtz (1993), Bini-Smaghi, Padoa-Schioppa and Papadia (1994), and Dyson and Featherstone (1999).

38. It turned out that the certainty of membership in EMU helped insulate some European countries (in particular Italy, Spain, Portugal, and Finland) from the spillover effects of the Russian default in late 1998.

39. See Buiter, Corsetti, and Roubini (1993) for a skeptical discussion of the Maastricht convergence criteria.

40. The underlying arithmetic is $d(DEBT/GDP)/dt = ((dDEBT/dt) - (DEBT/GDP) \cdot (dGDP/dt))/GDP$.

41. See, for example, Begg et al. (1998).

42. The European Monetary Institute was essentially an embryonic European Central Bank. The last president of the European Monetary Institute became the first president of the European Central Bank, and almost all of the staff of the European Monetary Institute (which no longer exists) transferred to the European Central Bank when the latter was formally established in 1998.

43. However, it is argued (with some justification) that the European Parliament lacks the power to make the European Central Bank fully accountable to the citizens of Europe.

44. See, for example, De Grauwe (1999).

45. Of course, German monetary unification was followed quickly by the creation of a single political entity, something that no one has proposed for possible monetary unions in the Americas.

46. On the statistical requirements for EMU, see European Monetary Institute (1996). For an example of some of the difficulties that arise in creating harmonized statistics, see European Commission (1998).

47. Note that at the December 1999 summit meeting of the four Mercosur presidents in Montevideo, the leaders agreed on three measures that could begin to pave the path toward a Maastricht-type agreement. First, it was agreed that the four countries would begin to harmonize their statistics to facilitate comparisons between them. It was also agreed that the four countries would work toward establishing common standards for fiscal responsibility that would constrain public spending. Finally, it was agreed that at future summits the countries would report progress in their efforts to achieve stability.

48. It is interesting to note that one of the arguments advanced by "euroskeptics" in Britain is that the Queen of England's head will no longer be depicted on the paper currency should Britain adopt the euro (although Britain will be free to put the Queen's head on euro coins).

49. For a detailed analysis of the arrangements for financial stability under EMU, see Prati and Schinasi (1999).

References

Barro, Robert J. (1999). "Let the Dollar Reign from Seattle to Santiago." *Wall Street Journal*, March 8, p. A18.

Basevi, Giorgio, Michele Fratianni, Herbert Giersch, Pieter Korteweg, David O'Mahony, Michael Parkin, Theo Peeters, Pascal Salin, and Niels Thygesen (1975).

"The All Saints' Day Manifesto for European Monetary Union." *The Economist* (November 1): 33–34.

Begg, David, Paul De Grauwe, Francesco Giavazzi, Harald Uhlig, and Charles Wyplosz (1998). "The ECB: Safe at Any Speed?" in *Monitoring the European Central Bank*, vol. 1. London: Center for Economic Policy Research.

Berensztein, Sergio, and Horacio Spector (n.d.). "Business, Government, and Law." In Gerardo della Paolera and Alan M. Taylor (eds.), *Argentina: Essays in the New Economics History*. Cambridge: Cambridge University Press, forthcoming.

Bini-Smaghi, Lorenzo, Tommaso Padoa-Schioppa, and Francesco Papadia (1994). "The Transition to EMU in the Maastricht Treaty." Essays in International Finance, no. 194, Department of Economics, Princeton University, Princeton, N.J., November.

Buiter, Willem, Giancarlo Corsetti, and Nouriel Roubini (1993). "Excessive Deficits: Sense and Nonsense in the Treaty of Maastricht." *Economic Policy* 16: 57–100.

Cagan, Phillip (1956). "The Monetary Dynamics of Hyperinflation." in M. Friedman (ed.), *Studies in the Quantity Theory of Money*. Chicago: University of Chicago Press.

De Grauwe, Paul (1999). *The Economics of Monetary Integration* (third ed.). Oxford: Oxford University Press.

Drazen, Allan (1999). "Central Bank Independence, Democracy, and Dollarization." Paper prepared for Conference on Argentine Political Economy, August 19, sponsored by Banco Central de la República Argentina and the Universidad Torcuato di Tella.

Dyson, Kenneth, and Kevin Featherstone (1999). *The Road to Maastricht: Negotiating Economic and Monetary Union*. Oxford: Oxford University Press.

ECLAC. Economic Commission for Latin America and the Caribbean (1985). "Estudio económico de América Latina yel Caribe" (Economic Survey of Latin America and the Caribbean). Buenos Aires.

——— (1986): "El Plan Austral. Una experiencia de estabilización de shock" pp. 156–157 in "Tres ensayos sobre inflación y políticas de estabilización." ("The Austral Plan: An experience with shock stabilization" pp. 156–157 in "Three essays on inflation and stabilization policies") Working document, no. 18, Buenos Aires, February.

Edwards, Sebastian (1998). "How about a Single Currency for Mercosur?" *Wall Street Journal*, August 28, A11.

Edwards, Sebastian, and Alejandra Cox Edwards (1987). *Monetarism and Liberalization: The Chilean Experiment*. N.p.: Ballinger.

Eichengreen, Barry (1997). *European Monetary Integration: Theory, Practice and Analysis*. Cambridge, MA: MIT Press.

——— (2000). "When to Dollarize." Paper presented at the conference "Dollarization: A Common Currency for the Americas?" organized by the Federal Reserve Bank Dallas, March, published by Department of Economics, University of California, Berkeley, available at ⟨www.dallasfed.org⟩.

Eichengreen, Barry, and Andrew K. Rose (1997). "Staying Afloat When the Wind Shifts: External Factors and Emerging Market Banking Crises." NBER Working Paper, no. 6370.

European Central Bank (1999). *Euro Area Monetary Aggregates: Conceptual Reconciliation Exercise*. Frankfurt am Main: European Central Bank.

European Commission (1998). *Report from the Commission to the Council: On the Harmonization of Consumer Price Indices in the European Union*. Brussels: Commission of the European Communities.

European Monetary Institute (1996). "The Statistical Requirements for Monetary Union." Frankfurt am Main: European Monetary Institute.

European Union (1995). *Selected Instruments Taken from the Treaties*, Book 1, Vol. 1, Luxemburg: Office of Official Publications of the European Communities.

Flood, Robert P., and Peter M. Garber (1980). "An Economic Theory of Monetary Reform." *Journal of Political Economy* 11: 24–58.

Frankel, Jeffrey A., and Andrew K. Rose (1998). "The Endogeneity of the Optimum Currency Area Criteria." *Economic Journal* 108: 1009–1025.

Gavin, Michael, and Andrew Powell (1998). "Public versus Private Provision of International Lender of Last Resort Assistance." Mimeo.

Gros, Daniel, and Niels Thygesen (1998). *European Monetary Integration: From the European Monetary System to Economic and Monetary Union* (second ed.). New York: Addison Wesley Longman.

Hausmann, Ricardo, and Andrew Powell (1999). "Dollarization: Issues of Implementation." Mimeo.

Italianer, Alexander (1993). "Mastering Maastricht: EMU Issues and How They Were Settled." In Klaus Gretschmann (ed.), *Economic and Monetary Union: Implications for National Policy-Makers*. Dordrecht, Netherlands: Martinus Nijhoff.

Joint Economic Committee Staff Report (1999). "Encouraging Official Dollarization in Emerging Markets," posted on the U.S. Senate Website: ⟨www.senate.gov/~jec⟩.

Kenen, Peter B. (1969). "The Theory of Optimum Currency Areas: An Eclectic View." In Robert A. Mundell and Alexander K. Swoboda (eds.), *Monetary Problems of the International Economy*. Chicago: University of Chicago Press.

——— (1995). *Economic and Monetary Union in Europe: Moving Beyond Maastricht*. Cambridge: Cambridge University Press.

Kohler, Marion (1998). "Optimal Currency Areas and Customs Unions: Are They Related?" Bank of England, Working Paper, no. 89.

Lenihan, Niall (1997). "The Legal Implications of the European Monetary Union Under U.S. and New York Law." European Central Bank.

Levy Yeyati, Eduardo, and Federico Sturzenegger (2000). "Is EMU a Blueprint for Mercosur?" *Cuadernos de Economía* 37, no. 110 (April): 63–99.

Lindsey, Lawrence (1999). *Economic Puppetmasters: Lessons from the Halls of Power*. Washington, DC: AEI Press.

McKinnon, Ronald I. (1963). "Optimum Currency Areas." *American Economic Review* 53: 717–725.

Mundell, Robert A. (1961). "A Theory of Optimum Currency Areas." *American Economic Review* 51: 657–665.

—— (1973). "Uncommon Arguments for Common Currencies." In Harry G. Johnson and Alexander K. Swoboda (eds.), *The Economics of Common Currencies*. London: George Allen and Unwin.

—— (1998a). "The Case for the Euro—I." *Wall Street Journal*, March 24, p. A22.

—— (1998b). "The Case for the Euro—II." *Wall Street Journal*, March 25, p. A22.

Prati, Alessandro, and Gary Schinasi (1999). "Financial Stability in European Economic and Monetary Union." Princeton Studies in International Finance, no. 86, Department of Economics, Princeton University, Princeton, N.J., August.

Sandholtz, Wayne (1993). "Monetary Bargains: The Treaty on EMU." In Alan W. Cafruny and Glenda G. Rosenthal (eds.), *The State of the European Community: The Maastricht Debates and Beyond*. London: Lynne Rienner/Longman.

Sims, Christopher A. (1998). "The Precarious Fiscal Foundations of EMU." Mimeo, Princeton University, Princeton, N.J.

—— (2001). "Fiscal Consequences for Mexico of Adopting the Dollar." Proceedings of the conference on "Global Monetary Integration" organized by the Federal Reserve Bank of Cleveland. Published in the *Journal of Money, Credit, and Banking* 33, no. 2 (May): 597–616.

Ungerer Horst (1997). *A Concise History of European Monetary Integration: From EPU to EMU*. Westport, CT: Quorum Books.

Zarazaga, Carlos E. J. M. (1999). "Building a Case for Currency Boards." *Pacific Economic Review* 4:2 (June): 139–164.

8 The Political Economy of Dollarization: Domestic and International Factors

Jeffry A. Frieden

Decisions about whether to dollarize Latin American currencies will be made by politicians and depend on domestic and international political constraints. The trade-offs politicians confront vary across countries, and their valuation varies among individuals and groups. Those who would try to analyze the decision to dollarize need to understand the politics of the trade-offs, and of their weighting in the political process.

Most discussions of the issue are, however, of little use in analyzing the likelihood of dollarization. They typically focus on whether dollarization is a good or bad idea, in general or for a particular country. These normative economic arguments about the welfare effects of dollarization are in and of themselves almost certainly irrelevant to explaining actual policy choices—the social welfare implications of economic policies are notoriously poor predictors of the probability of their adoption. Also, most of the literature evaluates the welfare implications (hence desirability) of dollarization on the basis of its impact on the anti-inflationary credibility of the authorities. This focus on macroeconomic credibility may resonate with some strains of the scholarly literature—especially that which rejects any lasting real effects of nominal variables. However, it is of little relevance to the majority of exchange rate policy choices, which are typically driven by concerns about the impact of currency policy on the relative price of foreign and domestic products, and on cross-border trade, investment, and financial flows.

In this chapter, I focus on these two, generally neglected, dimensions of dollarization. My first purpose is to help *explain* potential policy choice, rather than comment on its wisdom. I do so largely by drawing on the small existing literature on the political economy of exchange rate regime choice, under the assumption that the reasons for dollarizing are related to the reasons for adopting a fixed exchange rate. My second purpose is to emphasize the importance of concern for real factors—especially policy preferences with regard to relative prices and to international trade and investment—for exchange rate regime choice. I draw upon the experience of Latin America, with a few references to monetary integration in Europe, but the implications of the analysis are of relevance in other settings.

Within their national political economies, there are typically two powerful countervailing pressures on politicians in the making of currency policy. The first is the desire for monetary stability, especially reduced exchange rate volatility. The second is the desire for flexibility to allow policymakers to affect the competitiveness of locally produced tradables. The empirical evidence is, for example, that governments in very open economies with powerful private interests in cross-border economic activity are likely to face stronger pressures to fix, hence dollarize; whereas for policymakers in relatively more closed economies with powerful import-competing interests, such pressures are likely to be weaker.

Analysis of international constraints on dollarization is more difficult, due especially to the lack of pertinent comparisons. One experience that may have some relevance is that of European monetary integration. This, and general principles, suggest the importance of two sets of relationships of the dollarizing country. The first is with other nations in the region, especially if it is part of a preferential trade or other integration agreement. In this context, movement toward dollarization may be linked to broader integration initiatives, so the likelihood of dollarization will be tied to developments in regional integration. The second is with the United States. Although there is no explicit connection between adoption of the U.S. dollar and other policy initiatives, it is possible that dollarization could benefit the United States and that the United States could offer concessions on other dimensions to dollarizing countries. In addition, dollarizing countries are likely to come under pressure to harmonize their financial regulations with those of the United States. This might be a barrier to dollarization, and at a minimum it implies that consultations with the United States will be important.

I start by defining terms and evincing a few first principles. Then I summarize the state of our theoretical and empirical knowledge about the domestic political economy of fixing exchange rates. Although the choice of a fixed exchange rate is not identical to the choice of dollarization, it is the closest empirical and theoretical referent we have and provides some insights into the constraints and opportunities associated with dollarization. I also consider the difference between dollarization in a country that has a floating currency, and dollarization in a country that has a long-standing and credible peg already in place. I then consider the international political economy factors that might be important.

8.1   Definitions and First Principles

I consider dollarization the endpoint of a continuum of exchange rate policies that runs from a free float, through various forms of managed floating, to different sorts of fixed exchange rates. Dollarization may well be the most binding commitment to a fixed rate, for it is probably more difficult to unwind dollarization than to leave a peg or currency board, but leaving any of these arrangements is conceivable, at some political price. The value of regarding dollarization as one form of peg is that it allows us to analyze pressures for and against dollarization on the basis, more generally, of the theoretical and empirical literature on the political economy of exchange rate regime choice, and, specifically, on the basis of the choice of fixing exchange rates or of forming a monetary union. To be sure, there are differences among all these regimes, but the similarities are great—and considering them together allows us to draw lessons from a variety of previous experiences.

The assertion that dollarization is functionally equivalent to a particularly credible peg is reasonable for countries that are contemplating dollarizing from a starting point at which the currency is formally or informally, fully or partially, flexible. Where, however, the starting point is a long-standing fixed exchange rate, one that has acquired substantial credibility, then the comparison is far less relevant. I return to this special case later, but here focus on the more common instances in which dollarization is considered for a country with a flexible currency.

Another preliminary issue is worth mentioning. Most economic analyses of exchange rate regime choice focus on the steady state, comparing the welfare or distributional effects of one regime (such as dollarization) against another. This is important, but to understand the *politics* of this policy, a shorter time horizon is appropriate. Policymakers have to worry about the impact of the *transition* to a new exchange rate regime as well as its longer-term effects. This is likely to be as true of dollarization as it was, for example, with Europe's Economic and Monetary Union (EMU), in which many of the reservations about the process had to do not with its goal but with the transitional difficulties of achieving monetary convergence. Analyzing the political economy of dollarization requires taking into account both the transition and the steady state.[1]

With these preliminaries out of the way, we can turn to our central question: given the general and historical importance of the exchange rate in Latin America, what circumstances will affect the propensity of economic policymakers to give up such a powerful weapon of economic policy? Both the expected costs and the expected benefits of dollarization have important domestic and international aspects, to which the discussion now turns.

8.2   The Domestic Political Economy of Dollarization

National policymakers are responsive first and foremost to national political constituents. Decisions on dollarization, as on all national economic policies, are thus a function of real or potential support for and opposition to the proposed policy and of the institutional environment within which policy evolves. I do not attempt a complete survey of the political economy factors that affect dollarization but rather emphasize those expected to be central. The principal supporters of dollarization are likely to be found in those segments of the population most strongly involved in international trade and payments, for whom currency stability is especially important. Dollarization's principal opponents are likely to be among those especially concerned about the potential loss of an active exchange rate policy that has served to improve their ability to compete with foreign products at home or abroad.

Most discussions of dollarization, and of fixed rates generally, emphasize the value of a fixed rate for anti-inflationary credibility, and the countervailing value of a flexible rate in allowing monetary policy to respond to exogenous shocks.[2] Both considerations are reasonable and almost certainly operate at some level. But evidence of their empirical importance is very spotty and in the case of the latter—and other factors associated with the literature on optimal currency areas—almost nonexistent. This is not surprising. Responsiveness to exogenous shocks is a very diffuse concern, and it is hard to see by what channel it would have politically relevant effects. Inflation is of more immediate political relevance, but its impact on exchange rate choice is ambiguous. On the one hand, a relatively high inflation rate increases the desirability of reducing it, but on the other hand, fixing the exchange rate with a high initial rate of inflation is almost certain to lead to a substantial real appreciation with disastrous effects for local producers of tradables. Hyperinflation increases the likelihood of fixing, but there are no hyperinflationary countries left in Latin America.

In fact, the available empirical evidence implies that the trade-off between exchange rate stability and currency flexibility is of relevance primarily because of its expected impact on the cost of cross-border trade and investment and on the "competitiveness" of local producers. By definition, dollarization effectively eliminates exchange rate volatility, stabilizing the currency risk inherent in most cross-border transactions. However, the loss of the exchange rate as a policy instrument makes it impossible for governments to use currency movements to affect the competitive position of national tradables producers. It is this dilemma that is at the core of the *political economy* of dollarization, for it implicates different *distributional* interests and pressures. Issues related to credibility and monetary autonomy may be relevant for evaluating the aggregate social welfare effects of different exchange rate policies but have little direct impact on their politics—or, by extension, on the likelihood of their being adopted by policymakers.[3]

So I expect the principal determinant of the propensity to dollarize to be the relative socioeconomic and political importance of those interested in stabilizing currency values to facilititate cross-border economic activity, on the one hand, and those anxious about the impact of the currency's value on the relative price of their products. This determinant implies that the more open a national economy is to flows of goods and capital (especially to and from the United States, in the case of dollarization), the stronger the political incentives to act to reduce currency fluctuations.[4] To the extent that substantial segments of the population have extensive cross-border commitments, this relationship is especially the case.[5] Groups with important cross-border interests tend to want stable exchange rates and typically are more sympathetic to fixing.

Although economists tend to see few major direct effects from the elimination of currency volatility, there is strong evidence that elements of the private sector have powerful interests in reducing exchange rate fluctuations.[6] This is especially true of those with nominal foreign currency contractual or quasi-contractual obligations. This category might include cross-border investors and debtors, and exporters (or consumers) of differentiated manufactured products. For example, there is substantial anecdotal evidence that for more than twenty years, concerns about exchange rate movements on the part of private agents with large dollar debts have played a major part in the politics of exchange rates in Latin America. For all these groups, currency fluctuations can have a powerful impact on profitability. These sectors of the economy can be expected to support the stabilization of nominal currency values, including dollarization. And in fact some of the more prominent private sector supporters of fixing exchange rates in Latin America have been multinational corporations, international banks, local firms tied to international financial markets, and those with large outstanding foreign currency liabilities.[7] In some instances, financial institutions may be torn, as dollarization takes away most of their foreign exchange trading profits and may expose them to additional competition from foreign banks; but (as in Europe) the general expectation is that the large increase in the volume of financal intermediation will substantially outweigh the negative impact of increased competition.

On the other hand, producers of tradables tend to want a relatively weak (depreciated) exchange rate and typically are more sympathetic to floating. For them, there is bound to be concern about a fixed rate's elimination of the ability to use the exchange rate to affect the competitiveness of local products in domestic and foreign markets. Exporters may be conflicted about this, inasmuch as fixing might increase the level of trade but risk a real appreciation; which effect dominates presumably depends on the industry and the macroeconomic context. Import-competing firms and sectors have little to gain, and much to lose, from a policy that removes depreciation from the government's arsenal of policy instruments.

A more general, related, point is that inasmuch as dollarization increases the level of international trade and investment, firms and industries that anticipate gaining from this greater integration of markets will support dollarization. Andrew Rose (2000) estimates that sharing a currency roughly triples the level of trade between two countries; in this context, dollarization should be supported by those who expect to do well as their market is more tightly integrated with that of the United States and opposed by those worried about greater competition from abroad. This point simply reinforces the previous ones. The conclusion from all this is that more internationally oriented firms and sectors are likely to support dollarization, whereas those competing with imports are likely to oppose it.

Other factors have an impact on the political economy of exchange rate regime choice. As mentioned earlier, the effect of inflation is unlikely to be simple. If the political benefits of fighting inflation rise with inflation, governments will be more likely to fix currencies in conditions of very high or hyperinflation. A related point is that where a large proportion of private contracts have come to be written in or indexed to dollars—typically in countries with a long history of high and variable inflation—the costs of moving to full legal dollarization are lower than otherwise. It may also be the case that in conditions of hyperinflation the difficulties of adjusting to a new monetary regime are less severe, as universal indexation and great nominal wage and price flexibility allow for a rapid change to a low-inflation regime. But countries with moderate levels of inflation are less likely to fix their exchange rates—the benefits of inflation reduction are low, and the costs of the anticipated real appreciation are high. For countries with very low inflation, monetary conditions are probably neutral: fixing the currency does not risk real appreciation, but it also does not improve macroeconomic performance. The result is the expectation that the probability of fixing might follow a U in relationship to inflation: it declines as inflation rises to moderate levels, then rises as it reaches hyperinflationary levels.[8]

Features of national political systems may also affect decisions about exchange rates, inasmuch as they are made by incumbent politicians and are subject to the incentives faced by these politicians. Probably the most important electoral consideration is the impact of government weakness on the willingness and ability to implement a policy of fixing the exchange rate. A strong government will be better able to sustain the policies necessary to maintain the fixed rate. It is possible to imagine this going in the opposite direction, for a weak government may be more desperately in need of the "imported" credibility the peg brings. However, as a currency peg is no magic potion, the former effect is likely to dominate: politically strong governments will be more capable of sustaining a commitment to a fixed exchange rate or dollarization.[9]

In summary, I anticipate that the probability of dollarization will rise with the relative influence of groups with cross-border economic interests and decline with the influence of tradables producers concerned about the impact of currency values on "competitiveness." I also anticipate the dollarization will be more likely in conditions of hyperinflation, and with relatively strong governments.

8.2.1   The Exception: Dollarization from a Credible Peg

The discussion so far has assumed that the government's starting point is a more or less flexible exchange rate and that movement toward dollarization is analogous to fixing the currency in a particularly visible and credible way. But for some of the countries considering dollarization, the starting point is instead a currency peg of long standing, with a high degree of credibility. Many of the small island nations of the Caribbean share this sort of starting point. In these circumstances, the issues are quite different.

Where the initial policy condition is a moderately to highly credible fixed rate, the issue is whether the costs of dollarizing are worth the increment in the credibility of the currency peg. This means that movement to dollarization is likely to involve much more marginal calculations than movement from a float, where the question is not whether to make the peg more credible but whether a peg is in and of itself desirable. In these conditions, the benefits of dollarizing are much smaller, as inflation is already low and the exchange rate is stable. And the costs of dollarizing are also smaller, as most of the monetary adjustment has already been accomplished. I expect pressure for and against dollarization to come from roughly similar quarters to the ones discussed earlier but at a much lower level of intensity. It would normally take some significant shock to lead to much open acrimony over the issue, such as a serious recession or severe trade difficulties (as, to some extent, Brazil's 1999 devaluation led to pressures on the Argentine currency board).

Many of the tools desribed here are relevant to debates over dollarization in countries that already have a credibly fixed currency. But the analogy to the choice between floating and fixing is flawed, or at least vastly overdrawn, and attention will focus primariliy on the costs and benefits of increased credibility for the existing fixed rate. This in itself is an important issue, but it is much less likely to respond to the factors discussed here in so striking a way.

8.2.2 Empirical Findings and Implications

We can assess this array of factors on the basis of the small but growing empirical literature that attempts to explain exchange rate policy choice.[10] In what follows, for consistency, I rely primarily upon work done by myself and coauthors, along with a bit of other empirical work of relevance. The following summary is an undoubtedly biased and incomplete one but may help fix ideas. The empirical work is typically cast in terms of fixing or floating the currency; I recast it in terms of dollarization for current purposes.

The results used are based on the analysis of data about virtually all Latin American countries from 1960 to 1994 (Frieden, Ghezzi, and Stein 2001). The data include a finely differentiated definition of the currency regime in place and a wide array of socioeconomic and political variables. Rather than present full results and an explanation of them, for which the interested reader can consult the original study, I use them to illustrate the likelihood of dollarization.

Table 8.1 presents estimates of the impact of the significant explanatory variables on the probability that a government will fix its currency. As the original empirical work is an ordered logistic regression, these estimates are only illustrative: they demonstrate the impact of each variable, holding all others constant at their means. Some of the variables are dummies, for which table 8.1 shows the difference between 0 and 1; for others, the table shows the impact of moving one standard deviation away from the variable's mean. From the table, it can be seen that inflation has no appreciable impact on exchange rate regime choice (in fact, it is not statistically significant), whereas hyperinflation increases the likelihood of fixing by over 20 percent. As indicated, openness has a powerful impact: a one standard deviation increase in trade as a share of GDP increases the likelihood of a peg by 25 percent. The impact of tradable producers can also be seen: a one standard deviation increase in the size of the manufacturing sector is associated with an 11 percent decline in the probability of fixing. These are the aforementioned interest-group-based considerations.

Table 8.1
Change in the probability of a fixed exchange rate regime in response to changes in explanatory variables

	Log inflation	Hyper-inflation	Openness (X + M)/GDP	Mfg./GDP	Political instability	Govt. seat share	Effective no. of parties
Mean of variable	0.3363	0.0254	0.6650	0.1857	0.1503	0.595	2.4429
Change in variable[1]	0.6299	1	0.3968	0.0553	1	0.2009	1.3122
Δp (fixed)	0.0012	0.2076**	0.2503***	−0.1129***	0.1928**	0.0695*	0.0632*

Source: Adapted from Frieden, Ghezzi, and Stein (2001).

[1] The magnitude of the change in the explanatory variable is one standard deviation around the mean, in the case of the nondummy variables, and one in the case of dummy variables.

Estimates are derived from regression coefficients whose significance (see Frieden, Ghezzi, and Stein 2001) is as follows:

* = significant at .05 level.
** = significant at .01 level.
***significant at .001 level.

Purely political factors also appear to matter. Political instability is a dummy that takes a value of one if a country has gone through three or more government changes in the previous five years, or if it has gone through two or more government changes in the previous three years. It also takes a value of one in years in which there were successful coups and in the first year following a successful coup. It appears to increase the likelihood of a peg substantially, by 19 percent. The last two columns measure the government's strength: the higher the government's seat share, the more likely a fixed rate, and similarly the more fragmented the opposition, the more likely a peg.[11] Both effects are relatively small.

As another exercise, I use these results and more recent data to predict the likelihood that Latin American countries will have fixed rates as of the year 2000. Table 8.2 presents 1995–1999 country averages for all the variables just discussed, apart from the electoral variables, whose impact is relatively small. It can be seen that no country has recently experienced hyperinflation, and political instability is currently rare (only Ecuador, Guyana, and Paraguay have experienced it recently); recall that the estimated impact of inflation is very small. That leaves openness and the size of the manufacturing sector as major determinants of the propensity to fix, hence dollarize.

Table 8.3 presents estimates of the predicted probabilities that each Latin American country will fix its exchange rate, given the actual values of the explanatory variables between 1995 and 1999. The official exchange rate regime column presents the actual exchange rate regime in place at the beginning of the year 2000, as reported by the IMF in its *Exchange Arrangements and Exchange Restrictions*. The next two columns present numerical codings of regimes. The de facto exchange rate regime column uses a three-point de facto definition of the exchange rate regime constructed by Levy Yeyati and Sturzenegger (2000), where a higher number is a more fixed rate; the regime reported is the average for 1997–1999. The fix/float column presents the IMF coding, where a 0 is a fixed rate and a 1 is floating. The final column reports the actual movements of nominal exchange rates between 1995 and 1999, expressed as the standard deviation of monthly currency changes. It can be seen that there are differences among regime measures.

The point of this exercise is not to evaluate the out-of-sample predictions of earlier work, for there is no necessary expectation that the

Table 8.2
Country averages, Latin America, 1995–1999

Country	Inflation	Log inflation	Hyper-inflation	Openness [(X + M)/GDP]	Manufacturing (% GDP)	Political instability	Dictator-ship
Argentina	0.76	−0.12	0.00	22.24	16.58	0.00	0.00
Bahamas	1.32	0.12	0.00	110.95	2.72	0.00	0.00
Barbados	2.45	0.39	0.00	130.45	6.28	0.00	0.00
Belize	1.65	0.22	0.00	102.52	13.50	0.00	0.00
Bolivia	7.43	0.87	0.00	48.77	17.74	0.00	0.00
Brazil	19.35	1.29	0.00	17.26	22.39	0.00	0.00
Chile	6.04	0.78	0.00	57.33	21.24	0.00	0.00
Colombia	18.33	1.26	0.00	33.84	13.31	0.00	0.00
Costa Rica	15.13	1.18	0.00	94.36	22.08	0.00	0.00
Dominican Republic	7.44	0.87	0.00	67.86	21.87	0.00	0.00
Ecuador	33.25	1.52	0.00	59.13	21.48	0.00	0.00
El Salvador	5.47	0.74	0.00	58.89	21.46	0.00	0.00
Guatemala	8.11	0.91	0.00	43.72	5.73	0.00	0.00
Guyana	7.00	0.84	0.00	207.71	11.10	0.00	0.00
Haiti	17.61	1.25	0.00	37.48	6.72	0.00	0.00
Honduras	19.77	1.30	0.00	97.23	18.40	0.00	0.00
Jamaica	14.11	1.15	0.00	118.97	14.70	0.00	0.00
Mexico	24.50	1.39	0.00	62.02	21.08	0.00	0.00
Nicaragua	11.21	1.05	0.00	108.55	15.38	0.00	0.00
Panama	1.09	0.04	0.00	78.32	8.56	0.00	0.00
Paraguay	9.70	0.99	0.00	98.96	15.34	0.00	0.00
Peru	8.39	0.92	0.00	28.58	14.98	0.00	0.00
Suriname	71.98	1.86	0.00	149.02	12.06	0.00	0.00
Trinidad and Tobago	4.25	0.63	0.00	98.68	15.06	0.00	0.00
Uruguay	21.38	1.33	0.00	43.47	18.70	0.00	0.00
Venezuela	21.38	1.33	0.00	47.07	15.72	0.00	0.00
All Countries	13.81	0.93	0.00	77.82	15.16	0.12	0.00

Table 8.3
Predicted, official, and de facto exchange rate regimes in Latin America, 1995–1999

Country	Predicted probability of fixing	Official exchange rate regime*	De facto exchange rate regime**	Fix/float (0 = fix)*	Exchange rate variability***
Bahamas	1.000	Peg to dollar	3.00	0	0.000
Barbados	1.000	Peg to dollar	3.00	0	0.000
Guyana	1.000	Float	2.00	1	0.050
Suriname	1.000	Managed float		1	0.118
Panama	.998	Dollarization		0	0.000
Guatemala	.997	Managed float	1.33	1	0.012
Jamaica	.997	Managed float	2.00	1	0.018
Belize	.996	Peg to dollar		0	0.000
Nicaragua	.994	Crawling peg	2.67	1	0.001
Trinidad and Tobago	.992	Peg to dollar		0	0.010
Paraguay	.991	Managed float	1.33	1	0.018
Haiti	.975	Float	1.00	1	0.028
Honduras	.956	Crawling band	2.33	1	0.010
Costa Rica	.861	Crawling band	2.00	1	0.002
Dominican Republic	.532	Managed float	1.33	1	0.019
Venezuela	.506	Crawling band	2.67	1	0.119
Mexico	.478	Float	1.00	1	0.043
Ecuador	.411	Float	1.67	1	0.068
Bolivia	.407	Crawling peg	2.00	1	0.003
El Salvador	.400	Peg to dollar		0	0.000
Chile	.386	Float	1.00	1	0.018
Colombia	.354	Float	1.00	1	0.028
Uruguay	.277	Crawling band	1.00	1	0.008
Peru	.156	Float	1.33	1	0.013
Argentina	.038	Dollarization	3.00	0	0.000
Brazil	.005	Float	2.33	1	0.088

*As reported in IMF *Exchange Arrangements and Exchange Restrictions*, various years.
**1 = float; 2 = intermediate; 3 = fix—data taken from Levy Yeyati and Sturzenegger 2000.
***Standard deviation of monthly percent changes in nominal exchange rate, 1995–1999.

expected regime choice will be immediately implemented.[12] Rather, it is to indicate the general implications of existing empirical work for the choice of exchange rate regime—and, most centrally, the near irrelevance of credibility-related factors and the overwhelming importance of trade. Table 8.3 demonstrates the centrality of openness to these results: all the very small, very open economies in and around the Caribbean basin have probabilities of fixing over .85, as does Paraguay. Of the thirteen countries on the top half of the table, predicted to be more likely to fix, seven have done so or are on this path: five are on fixed rates or dollarized (Bahamas, Barbados, Belize, Panama, and Trinidad and Tobago), and two (Guatemala and Haiti) are "semiofficially dollarized," meaning that the U.S. dollar circulates freely and legally as an alternative to the local currency. Of the thirteen countries on the bottom half of the table, predicted to be less likely to fix, only three have done so or are doing so: Argentina, Ecuador, and El Salvador. The remaining countries expected to tend to fix are Nicaragua, Honduras, and Costa Rica; Jamaica, Guyana, and Suriname; and Paraguay. If economic openness is, as these results indicate, the single most powerful predictor of dollarization, this seems a reasonable candidate list (although Paraguay's membership in Mercosur is a complicating factor, to be discussed further). Ecuador and El Salvador, both recently dollarized or on this path, were predicted to have about .4 probability of doing so.[13]

The most obvious error in prediction is Argentina, with .04 probability of fixing despite more than ten years of a currency board. This reinforces the earlier point made that the Argentine experience is very unusual and unlikely to have many lessons for other potential dollarizers in the region. Argentina fixed in the context of a roaring hyperinflation, a problem no longer relevant to the region; severe political instability, now unusual; and after a raft of unsuccessful stabilization programs. Although the Argentine experience holds substantial scholarly and general interest for a whole host of reasons, it has virtually no relevance to the future of fixed exchange rates, or dollarization, in Latin America. Not surprisingly, Argentina abandoned its fixed exchange rate commitment in early 2002 after the writing of the first draft of this chapter.

A complementary approach is that of Jeffrey Frankel and Andrew Rose (2001). They use previous work by Rose to argue that dollarization will increase trade with the United States threefold, and they assume also that a percentage point increase in trade as a share

Table 8.4
Frankel-Rose estimated effects of dollarization on trade and output

	Actual data		Estimated effects	
	Openness (% GDP)	Trade with dollar zone (%)	Estimated openness after dollarization (% GDP)	Estimated impact of dollarization on GDP (% GDP)
Belize	103	44	194	30
Brazil	15	23	22	2
Chile	55	21	78	8
Colombia	36	38	63	9
Costa Rica	86	53	177	30
Dominican Republic	63	76	159	32
Ecuador	58	45	110	17
El Salvador	59	50	118	19
Guatemala	45	44	85	13
Guyana	211	28	329	39
Haiti	36	67	84	16
Honduras	91	52	186	31
Jamaica	136	53	280	48
Mexico	59	79	152	31
Nicaragua	91	38	160	23
Paraguay	48	19	66	6
Peru	28	24	41	4
Trinidad and Tobago	97	42	178	27
Uruguay	38	9	45	2
Venezuela	48	50	96	16

Source: Frankel and Rose (2001).
Note: Based on 1995 trade data. Assumptions: currency union triples trade; .33 effect of openness on GDP.

of GDP increases GDP by 0.33. The results for the Latin American countries for which they have data are reported in table 8.4 (note that the countries already on very fixed rates are excluded, because their goal is to *predict* effects from adoption of a regime not in existence). It can be seen that the countries that they expect to have the largest gain in output are similar to those predicted to be most likely to dollarize in the preceding discussion. This correspondence is due to the fact that their emphasis is on the effects of dollarization on cross-border trade, as opposed to the more common presumption that its impact will primarily be on credibility.

A final illustration of the argument made here is the parallel with the process of monetary integration in the European Union. Again, I rely on previous work of my own to demonstrate the powerful impact of cross-border trade interests on the propensity to peg currencies or, at the limit, join a currency union. Table 8.5 presents some simple data to this effect, for all current EU member states plus Norway and except Luxembourg (more systematic empirical work is available in Frieden 1996 and Frieden 2001). The table shows the relationship between a country's trade patterns and its propensity to fix its exchange rate to the deutsche mark (DM). The first four columns (starting with EU exports, 1970–1973) show how important manufactured exports were to each country's GDP in the early 1970s; first with a share of GDP, then by ranking them. The EU exports column and the one following it refer to exports to all current EU members; the DM-zone exports column and the following one refer to exports to Germany plus Benelux—Belgium, the Netherlands, and Luxemburg (the "DM zone"). Agricultural exports are excluded, as they are almost entirely covered by the EU's Common Agricultural Program, which does not use market exchange rates. The idea is that inasmuch as those heavily involved in cross-border trade prefer to stabilize nominal exchange rates, countries with more trade with the EU or with its DM core are more likely to fix their currencies against the DM, so countries trading more have more stable exchange rates. The last four columns, then, provide some measures of exchange rate variability from 1973 to 1993. The average annual depreciation and following country rank columns refer simply to the average annual depreciation rate against the DM, and relevant rankings; the last two columns refer to the coefficient of variation (standard deviation divided by the mean, in this case multiplied by 100 for ease of presentation), and relevant rankings. The use of pre-1973 trade data and 1973–1993 exchange rate data should eliminate most concerns about simultaneity.

The measures used in table 8.5 are crude but expressive. The relationship between a country's trade in the early 1970s and its exchange rate policies over the subsequent *twenty years* is extremely strong; the correlation among the various measures is about .4, depending on the measures used, while the correlation among the rankings is about .6. It may also be noted that this association holds at a more disaggregated level: trade in 1970–1973 is a strong predictor of exchange rate movements in 1973–1978, trade in 1979–1982

is a strong predictor of exchange rate movements in 1979–1989, and trade in 1987–1989 is a strong predictor of exchange rate movements in 1990–1993. The relationship is confirmed in more systematic empirical work (especially Frieden 2001), which uses annual data, a wide range of economic and political controls, and more reliable statistical methods. None of the variables associated with monetary policy credibility has any statistically significant effects. The single best predictor of a nation's currency policy in Western Europe over the course of the 1970s, 1980s, and 1990s was the importance of its trade with the EU, especially with the DM zone.

Although parallels between European monetary integration and dollarization should not be overdrawn, again the very strong indication is that national policy choices were largely a function of national patterns of cross-border trade (and investment, for which data are much harder to obtain). Various interpretations of this fact are possible, especially in light of some recent work that does in fact find welfare effects of exchange rate regimes by way of the regime's impact on trade and investment (Rose 2000; Engel forthcoming and 2000). The interpretation I find most convincing, and for which there is the largest extant literature, is one that associates patterns of trade and investment with the policy preferences of special interest groups. The evidence presented here calls into question much of the scholarly attention to monetary policy credibility as a principal reason for the choice of a currency peg (or currency union, in Europe). This is not to say that credibility considerations have never mattered—they almost certainly did for some European countries, some of the time—but that, especially in current conditions, they are unlikely to dominate the choice problems associated with the political economy of dollarization in the foreseeable future.

This discussion of the domestic political economy of dollarization highlights the distributional, rather than aggregate welfare, effects of adopting the U.S. dollar. It suggests that the issue will be joined largely as a battle between those with strong interests in stabilizing currency volatility that can impede cross-border economic activity, on the one hand, and those concerned about losing the "competitive edge" that currency depreciations can bring, on the other hand. It also suggests that dollarization is most likely in the small, very open nations in and around the Caribbean. Of course, dollarization of all of Central America and the Caribbean could in turn affect the attractiveness of choices open to such neighboring countries as Mexico and Colombia. More generally, there are substantial international political dimensions to dollarization. It is to this set of considerations that I now turn.

8.3   The International Political Economy of Dollarization

There are two international dimensions, broadly understood, to dollarization. The first has to do with relations *among* Latin American countries considering dollarization, the second with relations with the United States. I take these up in turn. In both instances, I use the European experience as something of a guide to discussion of the Latin American prospects, for EMU is close to the only relevant parallel available to us.

8.3.1   Relations among Latin American Nations

One powerful lesson of European monetary integration is that its success depended upon the degree to which it was linked to European integration more broadly.[14] Countries that would not otherwise have been particularly interested in fixing their currencies against the deutsche mark, or in creating a single currency, ended up doing so once it became clear that being out of the eventual EMU might mean relegation to second-class citizenship within the EU more generally. The idea that participation in monetary integration was a prerequisite of "a seat at the table" for other important European decisions was almost certainly essential to the breadth and depth of the success of EMU.[15]

The most direct effect of European regional integration on European monetary integration was between trade and exchange rates, often expressed by participants and observers with the idea that the single European market made the single European currency inevitable. The logic here is based not on economics but on political economy. With no trade barriers among member states of the European Union, exchange rate fluctuations gave rise to protectionist pressures and to charges that devaluing countries were not playing by the rules of the game. Giving up an active trade policy was meaningless, the argument went, if countries simply replaced it with an active exchange rate policy—and the latter might even drive the EU into a spiral of "competitive devaluations." These political pressures were particularly strong after the devaluations of 1992–1994, as producers in Northern Europe insisted that Southern European nations be locked into EMU. The single European market was not politically sustainable without a single European currency, for competitive depreciations brought forth demands to reinstate trade barriers.

Although trade integration efforts in Latin America are far from European levels, these sorts of arguments are still relevant, and indeed there is mounting evidence for a political economy connection between trade agreements and currency conflicts. Mercosur, NAFTA, the Andean Pact, the Central American Common Market, and other such ventures have had increasing success of late. They do not involve the sort of thorough-going integration we associate with the EU, as they are limited primarily to trade. The Eastern Caribbean Currency Area, linked as it is to the Caricom (Caribbean Community and Common Market) trading area and to other forms of cooperation among the small island nations that make up the currency union, is similar to the EU on these dimensions, but it is quite a special case in the Latin American context.[16] Nonetheless, the regional preferential trade agreements (PTAs) that have been developing in the region may in fact have an impact on the incentives to dollarize, in ways analogous to the European exemplar.

Latin American countries that have agreed to reduce or eliminate trade barriers among themselves are no less favorable about devaluation by other members than were Europeans. Even if the weakening of the currency is argued to be "necessary," other members of the PTA may feel that this gives the devaluing country's producers an unfair competitive advantage.[17] So devaluation, or chronic currency weakness, on the part of one member of a PTA may in fact threaten the PTA more generally. The recent experience of Brazil within Mercosur is illustrative of this fact, as the depreciation of the real led many Argentine producers who compete with Brazilian firms to cry "foul" and even question the trend toward Mercosur liberalization. It is in fact notable that American concern about Mexican competition within NAFTA heated up substantially after the 1994–1995 devaluation of the peso.

In this way, regional trade integration creates pressures on governments to forgo the devaluation option, thus making a floating rate less attractive. In addition, to the extent that PTAs increase intraregional trade and investment, they will (per our previous discussion) increase pressures to stabilize exchange rates. And in a PTA there may be resistance to using any one member nation's currency as the regional anchor, as in fact there was in the EU. In this context, dollarization by some or all of the members of the PTA might appear to be a reasonable alternative.

This scenario implies that there may be formal or informal pressures for members of a regional trade agreement to dollarize together. This could, of course, work both ways: just as PTA members that would not otherwise dollarize might do so as part of a concerted effort, so might a member of a PTA that would otherwise be a likely candidate for dollarization be less likely to dollarize on its own if fellow PTA members did not concur—thus Argentine dollarization is to some extent encumbered by its membership in Mercosur. To the extent that these considerations operate, we would expect to see phased dollarization by members of regional trade agreements.[18] It is not implausible, for example, that current movement toward dollarization by El Salvador and, less definitively, by Guatemala, might lead to a common initiative by other Central American Common Market members to dollarize. And the existence of a formal PTA is not essential to this dynamic; it might just as well be the result of analogous pressures flowing from trade relations such that countries are reluctant to lose advantage if one among their number gains what may amount to privileged access to American goods or capital markets. There may well be a tendency for the course and pace of dollarization to track existing or embryonic regional trade and integration assocations.

8.3.2 Relations with the United States

Another, related, lesson of the European experience with monetary integration was the importance of links between currency policy and other political relations.[19] The most common such instance of "linkage politics" invoked by participants and observers was a geopolitical one between France and Germany. It was often argued that Germany had no inherent desire for EMU but was willing to go along with French demands for currency union in return for French support for German unification. Although the argument is not universally accepted (Moravcsik 1998 is a strong dissent), certainly there is the logical possibility that currency ties could be traded off for noneconomic policy goals. The most obvious parallel with dollarization would be if the United States felt that dollarization was in its interest and encouraged other countries to pursue it in return for consideration of unrelated political concerns of theirs (say, for foreign aid or diplomatic support).

There may in fact be mild American pressure on countries in Latin America to dollarize, although this seems far less important than in Europe. The European linkage stories relied on France's having a very strong desire for a single currency, and this is hardly the case in the Western Hemisphere. It is nonetheless plausible that the United States will not be completely uninterested, as there has been mild American interest in dollarization in other countries. This support has come primarily from American financial institutions and transnational corporations. Their views reflect their expectation that American firms are likely to realize competitive advantages over third-country investors in dollarized markets. Financial institutions, for example, anticipate receiving greater "denomination rents" as the use of the U.S. dollar expands.[20] The idea behind these rents is that widespread use of a currency increases demand for financial services from firms whose home base is the country of issue, given the deeper financial markets and greater security of the home market. Related denomination rents might accrue to investors, multinational corporations, exporters, and traders. All this is to say that there could be private pressure on the United States government to facilitate dollarization and that this pressure might lead to the sorts of diplomatic horse-trading that characterized some of European monetary integration.

However, the more likely scenario is one in which Latin American countries decide to dollarize, and this decision has follow-on effects for the United States that make its involvement desirable or even necessary.[21] The principal issue associated with dollarization for the United States is the implication of a large dollar currency area not coterminous with the jurisdiction of the American government. This raises, most directly, the question of how to deal with the functions of central banking typically associated with currency issue—such as lender of last resort facilities, prudential control and regulation. Although the dollarization of such small countries as Panama and El Salvador does not raise major issues, if a substantial portion of Latin America were part of a dollar zone, this would almost certainly require consideration of the possible links across countries within the same currency area. The most important such links would be financial, as it would be difficult or impossible to insulate the United

States completely from financial problems in one large part of the dollar zone.

One possibility would be to have the United States extend its financial management to the broader currency area, becoming the de facto financial regulator for the entire dollar zone. The United States might resist taking on substantial responsibility for financial conditions in countries that have chosen to dollarize, and Latin American countries might likewise resist handing over financial regulation to the U.S. government. In addition, asking the U.S. government to implicitly or explicitly regulate and supervise the financial systems of dollarized countries could encourage opportunistic behavior on the part of the relevant Latin American authorities, who might have an incentive to pawn problems off on the United States.

The other possibility would be to keep these functions restricted to one small part of the currency area, the United States. This would require the relevant dollarizing authorities to maintain their own independent financial supervision and regulation. There are two problems here. First, it seems impractical to ask Latin American countries to take full responsibility for their financial systems without giving them any influence over monetary and currency policy. Indeed, this too could be seen as encouraging opportunistic behavior, in this case on the part of the U.S. authorities, who have an incentive to pursue monetary policies without regard to their impact on other countries using the dollar. Second, it is not clear that an American commitment not to "bail out" dollarized financial systems in trouble would be credible, for financial crises in large dollar-based countries would almost certainly have important implications for the United States. It is easy to imagine the U.S. Federal Reserve and Treasury coming under domestic and international pressure to respond to a financial crisis in a dollarized Mexico, either by loosening monetary policy or by bankrolling a financial rescue package.

Europe claimed to have resolved this problem by adopting a new currency for which no national government is responsible and continuing to vest financial regulation and prudential control in national governments. But this has proven not to be stable, for the moral hazard and credibility reasons discussed earlier. The Europeans are clearly moving toward some shared form of EMU LLR facilities, and some harmonized EMU-wide financial supervision and regulation. The problem is that much more immediate in the case of the adoption of a national currency by other countries, especially when they are as geographically and economically closely linked as much of Latin America is with the United States.

So at the international level, dollarization is likely to raise major questions for the United States. It is conceivable that the questions could be ignored were dollarization confined to a few very small countries (as it is now). Were the number to grow, policymakers would have to confront the issues directly. The most obvious resolution would be for dollarizing countries to adopt regulatory and supervisory institutions consistent with American standards and to cooperate with the American authorities so as to guard against the realization of moral hazard problems. This would be politically complex, especially for countries whose financial systems are very different from that of the United States. However, it has the advantage of requiring little in the way of American policy change.

In a way, then, the international aspects of dollarization are likely to have their principal impact on the domestic cost-benefit calculations of potential dollarizers in Latin America. A country that wants to dollarize is likely to find itself under concurrent pressure to undertake substantial financial regulatory changes, and so the decision to dollarize might come to implicate a broader suite of financial decisions. Making these decisions would presumably slow down the process, but it would also tend to make policy more thoroughgoing for those countries that decided on pushing forward with dollarization. The result would be a nearly Europe-like tendency for currency integration to be associated with integration of trade in goods and capital (for the reasons already mentioned) and with financial regulatory harmonization.

Both of these international dimensions make it likely that a substantial trend toward dollarization on the part of the region's larger countries would require explicit political agreements among them and with the United States. This consideration says little about the probability of dollarization, for international agreements sometimes make national policies more likely and sometimes less so. It does imply that current regional economic agreements, especially such preferential trade agreements as Mercosur and the Central American Common Market, are more likely to move together than separately. It also implies that explicit negotiations with the United States, especially over the relationship between currency and financial policies, will be required.

8.4 Conclusions

There is no need to repeat what has come before. What should be emphasized is the general point: like all economic policies, dollarization is a political decision. It is useful to analyze the welfare effects of dollarization and its expected impact on regional trade and investment. But the eventual decisions about whether countries will dollarize can only be understood in the light of a systematic analysis of the domestic and international political economy of the policy.

The principal domestic factors in dollarization are the economic and political importance of special interests both for and against locking currencies. Those with strong cross-border financial, investment, or commercial interests are likely to be the principal supporters. Local producers of tradable goods will, on the contrary, be opposed to dollarization because it eliminates the ability to devalue to improve their competitive position. Internationally, the European experience indicates that countries joined together in regional trade agreements are likely to make joint dollarization (or nondollarization) decisions. It is also likely that the realities of dollarization will require direct consultation and coordination with the United States before it goes much farther.

Whether these specific conclusions are right or not, certainly it is true that an accurate forecast of exchange rate policies requires much more than the usual normative treatment of dollarization. Expectations of policy outcomes can only be formed accurately by considering both economic, political, and political economy considerations.

Notes

The author acknowledges helpful comments and suggestions from Sergio Berensztein, Miguel Kiguel, Eduardo Levy Yeyati, Ernesto Stein, and Federico Sturzenegger; and excellent research assistance by Mark Copelovitch.

1. Here, too, the analogy breaks down for countries contemplating a move from a credible fix to dollarization, for the transitional problems are likely to be much less severe.

2. One exception, in which effects on trade are central, is discussed in Alesina and Barro (2000).

3. The one exception is the occasional use of dollarization (or hard currency pegs) in times of serious crisis, in which the government typically attempts to use the currency as a signal of credibility on a series of dimensions, often not directly related to

monetary policy. Ecuador's recent dollarization is an example. These cases are relatively rare and are not addressed here.

4. The advantages of eliminating currency risk are a function of the size of the country and the depth of its currency's forward market, but for most of Latin America it is safe to assume that forward markets are not well developed.

5. It is also the case that more open economies are less likely to be able to affect the real exchange rate, as a depreciation will be translated quickly into higher prices for imports. Where imports are a very substantial share of consumption, exchange rate movements have less real effect. This runs in the same direction as the interest group factor.

6. It may be that economists focus on welfare effects but that the private sector concerns are simply one side of this—the cost of one firm's hedging is the income of another's. I believe that in fact the standard economic view is only partial and that exchange rate volatility does have a substantial dampening effect on trade and investment. This effect holds true especially in countries with thin currency markets—such as virtually all of Latin America—and in sectors for which longer-term cross-border contracts are most relevant.

7. It is probably not coincidental that some of the most prominent private sector supporters of monetary unification in Europe were very similar to the most prominent private sectors supporters of dollarization, especially among large multinational banks and corporations. See Hefeker (1996) for one argument to this effect.

8. Again, I focus here on circumstances in which policymakers make a considered decision to dollarize, rather than conditions of extreme crisis in which dollarization may be a last-ditch measure.

9. Bernhard and Leblang (1999) argue that fragmented political systems (especially coalition governments) will be *more* likely to opt for a peg, focusing on the inability of politicians in multiparty governments to take party-specific credit for effective policy. This should, they argue, reduce the desire to maintain the policy options associated with floating. While plausible, I find the counterargument more compelling, and the evidence with which I am familiar from Latin America is more consistent with the latter.

10. Among the works surveyed are Blomberg, Frieden, and Stein (2000); Clark and Reichert (1998); Collins (1996); Edison and Melvin (1990); Edwards (1994, 1996); Eichengreen (1995); Frieden (1994, 2001); Frieden, Ghezzi, and Stein (2001); and Klein and Marion (1997). I also have in mind the country studies in Frieden and Stein (2001).

11. The two variables are significant only together, indicating that party fragmentation in itself is not important—a multiparty coalition with many seats is strong.

12. For the record, the correlation coefficients between the estimated probabilities of fixing, on the one hand, and the Levy Yeyati–Sturzenegger and actual variability measures, on the other, are .17 and .3.

13. Ecuador is one of the few countries that have used dollarization or other exchange rate measures in the midst of a serious crisis. As for El Salvador, it is possible that the great importance of emigrants' remittances into the country's economy may have increased the attractiveness of dollarization.

14. Eichengreen and Frieden (2001) surveys the experience.

15. This is not to deny that the linkage arguments might be overblown, only that this is a common view.

16. Cohen (2001) summarizes the Eastern Caribbean Currency Area case and several other analogous examples.

17. This is, again, a political economy argument, not an economic one; from a welfare standpoint, of course, the devaluing country is simply reducing its terms of trade and generously providing its trading partners with cheaper goods. The political realities of the response to increased import competition are otherwise.

18. This is in fact largely already the case with Caricom, whose members have both integrated their trade relations and stabilized currencies, typically against the dollar.

19. For examples of some of the many arguments to this effect, see Garrett (2001) and Martin (2001).

20. For example, see Swodboda (1968, 105–106).

21. This scenario contrasts with the routine official American insistence that dollarization has no implications for the United States. This view is either naive or disingenuous. The obvious point that the United States would realize increased seignorage revenues (at the expense of the dollarizing countries) is of trivial importance on both sides. The amounts involved are small, and it is likely that a simple formula for dividing the revenues could easily be found (although some congressional objections to giving any of the money back to Latin Americans might arise).

References

Alesina, Alberto, and Robert Barro. 2000. Currency Unions. Unpublished paper. Harvard University.

Bernhard, William, and David Leblang. 1999. Democratic Institutions and Exchange-rate Commitments. *International Organization* 53, No. 1 (Winter), pages 71–97.

Blomberg, Brock, Jeffry Frieden, and Ernesto Stein. 2000. Latin American Exchange Rate Regimes: Duration and Sustainability 1960–1994. Unpublished paper. Harvard University.

Clark, William, and Usha Reichert. 1998. International and Domestic Constraints on Political Business Cycles in OECD Economies. *International Organization* 52, No. 1 (Winter), pages 87–120.

Cohen, Benjamin J. 2001. Beyond EMU: The Problem of Sustainability. In *The Political Economy of European Monetary Unification*, second edition. Ed. Barry Eichengreen and Jeffry Frieden. Boulder, Colo.: Westview Press.

Collins, Susan. 1996. On Becoming More Flexible: Exchange Rate Regimes in Latin America and the Caribbean. *Journal of Development Economics* 51, pages 117–138.

Edison, Hali, and Michael Melvin. 1990. The Determinants and Implications of the Choice of an Exchange Rate System. In *Monetary Policy for a Volatile Global Economy*. Ed. William Haraf and Thomas Willett. Washington: American Enterprise Institute, pages 1–44.

Edwards, Sebastian. 1994. The Political Economy of Inflation and Stabilization in Developing Countries. *Economic Development and Cultural Change* 42, no. 2 (January), pages 235–267.

———. 1996. "The Determinants of the Choice between Fixed and Flexible Exchange Rate Regimes." NBER working paper, no. 5576.

Eichengreen, Barry. 1995. The Endogeneity of Exchange Rate Regimes. In *Understanding Interdependence: The Macroeconomics of the Open Economy*. Ed. Peter Kenen. Princeton, N.J.: Princeton University Press.

Eichengreen, Barry, and Jeffry Frieden. 2001. The Political Economy of European Monetary Unification: An Analytical Introduction. In *The Political Economy of European Monetary Unification*, second edition. Ed. Barry Eichengreen and Jeffry Frieden. Boulder, Colo.: Westview Press.

Engel, Charles. 2001a. A Retrial in the Case against the EMU: Local-Currency Pricing and the Choice of Exchange-Rate Regime. In *The Political Economy of European Monetary Unification*. Ed. Barry Eichengreen and Jeffry Frieden. Boulder, Colo.: Westview Press.

———. 2001b. Optimal Exchange Rate Policy: The Influence of Price-Setting and Asset Markets. *Journal of Money, Credit and Banking* 33, (May), pages 518–541.

Frankel, Jeffrey, and Andrew Rose. 2001. An Estimate of the Effect of Currency Unions on Trade and Growth. Unpublished paper. Harvard University.

Frieden, Jeffry. 1994. Exchange Rate Politics: Contemporary Lessons from American History. *Review of International Political Economy* 1, No. 1 (Spring), pages 81–103.

———. 1996. The Impact of Goods and Capital Market Integration on European Monetary Politics. *Comparative Political Studies* 29, no. 2 (April), pages 193–222.

———. 2001. The Political Economy of European Exchange Rates: An Empirical Assessment. Unpublished paper. Harvard University.

Frieden, Jeffry, Piero Ghezzi, and Ernesto Stein. 2001. The Political Economy of Exchange Rate Policy in Latin America. In *The Currency Game: Exchange Rate Politics in Latin America*. Ed. Jeffry Frieden and Ernesto Stein. Washington: Interamerican Development Bank.

Frieden, Jeffry, and Ernesto Stein, editors. 2001. *The Currency Game: Exchange Rate Politics in Latin America*. Washington: Interamerican Development Bank.

Garrett, Geoffrey. 2001. The Politics of Maastricht. In *The Political Economy of European Monetary Unification*, second edition. Ed. Barry Eichengreen and Jeffry Frieden. Boulder, Colo.: Westview Press.

Hefeker, Carsten. 1996. The Political Choice and Collapse of Fixed Exchange Rates. *Journal of Institutional and Theoretical Economics* 152, pages 360–379.

International Monetary Fund (IMF). *Exchange Arrangements and Exchange Restrictions*. Washington: IMF, various dates.

Klein, Michael, and Nancy Marion. 1997. Explaining the Duration of Exchange-Rate Pegs. *Journal of Development Economics* 54, pages 387–404.

Levy Yeyati, Eduardo, and Federico Sturzenegger. 2000. Classifying Exchange Rate Regimes: Deeds versus Words. Unpublished paper. Universidad di Tella.

Martin, Lisa. 2001. International and Domestic Institutions in the EMU Process and Beyond. In *The Political Economy of European Monetary Unification*, second edition. Ed. Barry Eichengreen and Jeffry Frieden. Boulder: Westview Press.

Moravcsik, Andrew. 1998. *The Choice for Europe*. Ithaca: Cornell University Press.

Rose, Andrew. 2000. One Money, One Market: Estimating The Effect of Common Currencies on Trade. *Economic Policy* 15, No. 30, pages 9–45.

Swoboda, Alexander. 1968. *The Euro-Dollar Market: An Interpretation*. Essays in International Finance, No. 64. Princeton, N.J.: Department of Economics, International Finance Section.

Index